Philosophy and the
Mirror of Nature

Philosophy and the Mirror of Nature

RICHARD RORTY

Princeton University Press
Princeton, New Jersey

Library of Congress Cataloging-in-Publication Data

Rorty, Richard.
  Philosophy and the mirror of nature.

  Includes index.
  1. Philosophy. 2. Philosophy, Modern. 3. Mind
and body. 4. Representation (Philosophy) 5. Analysis
(Philosophy) 6. Civilization—Philosophy. I. Title.
B53.R68   190   79-84013
ISBN 0-691-07236-1
ISBN 0-691-02016-7 pbk.

Publication of this book has been aided by a grant from
The National Endowment for the Humanities

This book has been composed in Linotype Baskerville

Princeton University Press books are printed on acid-free paper and
meet the guidelines for permanence and durability of the Committee on
Production Guidelines for Book Longevity of the Council on Library
Resources

Printed in the United States of America

Second printing, with corrections, 1980

First Princeton Paperback printing, 1980

20   19   18   17   16   15   14   13   12

When we think about the future of the world, we always have in mind its being at the place where it would be if it continued to move as we see it moving now. We do not realize that it moves not in a straight line, but in a curve, and that its direction constantly changes.

Philosophy has made no progress? If somebody scratches where it itches, does that count as progress? If not, does that mean it wasn't an authentic scratch? Not an authentic itch? Couldn't this response to the stimulus go on for quite a long time until a remedy for itching is found?

Wenn wir an die Zukunft der Welt denken, so meinen wir immer den Ort, wo sie sein wird, wenn sie so weiter läuft, wie wir sie jetzt laufen sehen, und denken nicht, dass sie nicht gerade läuft, sondern in einer Kurve, und ihre Richtung sich konstant ändert. (Ludwig Wittgenstein, *Vermischte Bemerkungen*, Frankfurt, 1977, p. 14.)

Die Philosophie hat keinen Fortschritt gemacht? Wenn Einer kratzt, wo es ihn juckt, muss ein Fortschritt zu sehen sein? Ist es sonst kein echtes Kratzen, oder kein echtes Jucken? Und kann nicht diese Reaktion auf die Reizung lange Zeit so weitergehen, ehe ein Mittel gegen das Jucken gefunden wird? (Ibid., pp. 163-164.)

Contents

CONTENTS

CONTENTS

Preface

ALMOST as soon as I began to study philosophy, I was impressed by the way in which philosophical problems appeared, disappeared, or changed shape, as a result of new assumptions or vocabularies. From Richard McKeon and Robert Brumbaugh I learned to view the history of philosophy as a series, not of alternative solutions to the same problems, but of quite different sets of problems. From Rudolph Carnap and Carl Hempel I learned how pseudo-problems could be revealed as such by restating them in the formal mode of speech. From Charles Hartshorne and Paul Weiss I learned how they could be so revealed by being translated into Whiteheadian or Hegelian terms. I was very fortunate in having these men as my teachers, but, for better or worse, I treated them all as saying the same thing: that a "philosophical problem" was a product of the unconscious adoption of assumptions built into the vocabulary in which the problem was stated—assumptions which were to be questioned before the problem itself was taken seriously.

Somewhat later on, I began to read the work of Wilfrid Sellars. Sellars's attack on the Myth of the Given seemed to me to render doubtful the assumptions behind most of modern philosophy. Still later, I began to take Quine's skeptical approach to the language-fact distinction seriously, and to try to combine Quine's point of view with Sellars's. Since then, I have been trying to isolate more of the assumptions behind the problematic of modern philosophy, in the hope of generalizing and extending Sellars's and Quine's criticisms of traditional empiricism. Getting back to these assumptions, and making clear that they are optional, I believed, would be "therapeutic" in the way in which Carnap's original dissolution of standard textbook problems was "therapeutic." This book is the result of that attempt.

The book has been long in the making. Princeton University is remarkably generous with research time and sabbaticals, so it is embarrassing to confess that without the further assistance of the American Council of Learned Societies and the John Simon Guggenheim Memorial Foundation I should probably never have written it. I began thinking out its plot while holding an ACLS Fellowship in 1969-1970, and wrote the bulk of the first draft while holding a Guggenheim Fellowship in 1973-1974. I am most grateful to all three institutions for their assistance.

Many people—students at Princeton and elsewhere, audiences at papers given at various conferences, colleagues and friends—have read or listened to various drafts of various sections of this book. I made many changes of both substance and style in response to their objections, and am very grateful. I regret that my memory is too poor to list even the most important instances of such help, but I hope that here and there readers may recognize the beneficial results of their own comments. I do wish, however, to thank two people—Michael Williams and Richard Bernstein—who made very helpful comments on the penultimate version of the entire book, as did an anonymous reader for the Princeton University Press. I am also grateful to Raymond Geuss, David Hoy, and Jeffrey Stout, who took time out to help me resolve last-minute doubts about the final chapter.

Finally, I should like to thank Laura Bell, Pearl Cavanaugh, Lee Ritins, Carol Roan, Sanford Thatcher, Jean Toll, and David Velleman for patient help in transforming what I wrote from rough copy into a printed volume.

* * * * *

Portions of Chapter IV appeared in *Neue Hefte für Philosophie* 14 (1978). Portions of Chapter V appeared in *Body, Mind and Method: Essays in Honor of Virgil C.*

Aldrich, ed. Donald F. Gustafson and Bangs L. Tapscott (Dordrecht, 1979). Other portions of that chapter appeared in *Philosophical Studies* 31 (1977). Portions of Chapter VII appeared in *Acta Philosophica Fennica,* 1979. I am grateful to the editors and publishers concerned for permission to reprint this material.

Philosophy and the
Mirror of Nature

Introduction

PHILOSOPHERS usually think of their discipline as one which discusses perennial, eternal problems—problems which arise as soon as one reflects. Some of these concern the difference between human beings and other beings, and are crystallized in questions concerning the relation between the mind and the body. Other problems concern the legitimation of claims to know, and are crystallized in questions concerning the "foundations" of knowledge. To discover these foundations is to discover something about the mind, and conversely. Philosophy as a discipline thus sees itself as the attempt to underwrite or debunk claims to knowledge made by science, morality, art, or religion. It purports to do this on the basis of its special understanding of the nature of knowledge and of mind. Philosophy can be foundational in respect to the rest of culture because culture is the assemblage of claims to knowledge, and philosophy adjudicates such claims. It can do so because it understands the foundations of knowledge, and it finds these foundations in a study of man-as-knower, of the "mental processes" or the "activity of representation" which make knowledge possible. To know is to represent accurately what is outside the mind; so to understand the possibility and nature of knowledge is to understand the way in which the mind is able to construct such representations. Philosophy's central concern is to be a general theory of representation, a theory which will divide culture up into the areas which represent reality well, those which represent it less well, and those which do not represent it at all (despite their pretense of doing so).

We owe the notion of a "theory of knowledge" based on an understanding of "mental processes" to the seventeenth century, and especially to Locke. We owe the notion of "the mind" as a separate entity in which "processes" occur to the same period, and especially to Descartes. We owe the notion of philosophy as a tribunal of pure reason, upholding or denying the claims of the rest of culture, to the eighteenth century and especially to Kant, but this Kantian notion presupposed general assent to Lockean notions of mental processes and Cartesian notions of mental substance. In the nineteenth century, the notion of philosophy as a foundational discipline which "grounds" knowledge-claims was consolidated in the writings of the neo-Kantians. Occasional protests against this conception of culture as in need of "grounding" and against the pretensions of a theory of knowledge to perform this task (in, for example, Nietzsche and William James) went largely unheard. "Philosophy" became, for the intellectuals, a substitute for religion. It was the area of culture where one touched bottom, where one found the vocabulary and the convictions which permitted one to explain and justify one's activity *as* an intellectual, and thus to discover the significance of one's life.

At the beginning of our century, this claim was reaffirmed by philosophers (notably Russell and Husserl) who were concerned to keep philosophy "rigorous" and "scientific." But there was a note of desperation in their voices, for by this time the triumph of the secular over the claims of religion was almost complete. Thus the philosopher could no longer see himself as in the intellectual avant-garde, or as protecting men against the forces of superstition.[1] Further, in the course of the nineteenth century, a new form of culture had arisen—the culture of the man of letters, the intellectual who wrote poems and novels and political treatises, and criticisms of other people's poems and novels and treatises. Descartes, Locke, and Kant had written in a

---

[1] Terms such as "himself" and "men" should, throughout this book, be taken as abbreviations for "himself or herself," "men and women," and so on.

period in which the secularization of culture was being made possible by the success of natural science. But by the early twentieth century the scientists had become as remote from most intellectuals as had the theologians. Poets and novelists had taken the place of both preachers and philosophers as the moral teachers of the youth. The result was that the more "scientific" and "rigorous" philosophy became, the less it had to do with the rest of culture and the more absurd its traditional pretensions seemed. The attempts of both analytic philosophers and phenomenologists to "ground" this and "criticize" that were shrugged off by those whose activities were purportedly being grounded or criticized. Philosophy as a whole was shrugged off by those who wanted an ideology or a self-image.

It is against this background that we should see the work of the three most important philosophers of our century—Wittgenstein, Heidegger, and Dewey. Each tried, in his early years, to find a new way of making philosophy "foundational"—a new way of formulating an ultimate context for thought. Wittgenstein tried to construct a new theory of representation which would have nothing to do with mentalism, Heidegger to construct a new set of philosophical categories which would have nothing to do with science, epistemology, or the Cartesian quest for certainty, and Dewey to construct a naturalized version of Hegel's vision of history. Each of the three came to see his earlier effort as self-deceptive, as an attempt to retain a certain conception of philosophy after the notions needed to flesh out that conception (the seventeenth-century notions of knowledge and mind) had been discarded. Each of the three, in his later work, broke free of the Kantian conception of philosophy as foundational, and spent his time warning us against those very temptations to which he himself had once succumbed. Thus their later work is therapeutic rather than constructive, edifying rather than systematic, designed to make the reader question his own motives for philosophizing rather than to supply him with a new philosophical program.

Wittgenstein, Heidegger, and Dewey are in agreement that the notion of knowledge as accurate representation, made possible by special mental processes, and intelligible through a general theory of representation, needs to be abandoned. For all three, the notions of "foundations of knowledge" and of philosophy as revolving around the Cartesian attempt to answer the epistemological skeptic are set aside. Further, they set aside the notion of "the mind" common to Descartes, Locke, and Kant—as a special subject of study, located in inner space, containing elements or processes which make knowledge possible. This is not to say that they have *alternative* "theories of knowledge" or "philosophies of mind." They set aside epistemology and metaphysics as possible disciplines. I say "set aside" rather than "argue against" because their attitude toward the traditional problematic is like the attitude of seventeenth-century philosophers toward the scholastic problematic. They do not devote themselves to discovering false propositions or bad arguments in the works of their predecessors (though they occasionally do that too). Rather, they glimpse the possibility of a form of intellectual life in which the vocabulary of philosophical reflection inherited from the seventeenth century would seem as pointless as the thirteenth-century philosophical vocabulary had seemed to the Enlightenment. To assert the possibility of a post-Kantian culture, one in which there is no all-encompassing discipline which legitimizes or grounds the others, is not necessarily to argue against any particular Kantian doctrine, any more than to glimpse the possibility of a culture in which religion either did not exist, or had no connection with science or politics, was necessarily to argue against Aquinas's claim that God's existence can be proved by natural reason. Wittgenstein, Heidegger, and Dewey have brought us into a period of "revolutionary" philosophy (in the sense of Kuhn's "revolutionary" science) by introducing new maps of the terrain (viz., of the whole panorama of human activities) which simply do not include those features which previously seemed to dominate.

This book is a survey of some recent developments in philosophy, especially analytic philosophy, from the point of view of the anti-Cartesian and anti-Kantian revolution which I have just described. The aim of the book is to undermine the reader's confidence in "the mind" as something about which one should have a "philosophical" view, in "knowledge" as something about which there ought to be a "theory" and which has "foundations," and in "philosophy" as it has been conceived since Kant. Thus the reader in search of a new theory on any of the subjects discussed will be disappointed. Although I discuss "solutions to the mind-body problem" this is not in order to propose one but to illustrate why I do not think there is a problem. Again, although I discuss "theories of reference" I do not offer one, but offer only suggestions about why the search for such a theory is misguided. The book, like the writings of the philosophers I most admire, is therapeutic rather than constructive. The therapy offered is, nevertheless, parasitic upon the constructive efforts of the very analytic philosophers whose frame of reference I am trying to put in question. Thus most of the particular criticisms of the tradition which I offer are borrowed from such systematic philosophers as Sellars, Quine, Davidson, Ryle, Malcolm, Kuhn, and Putnam.

I am as much indebted to these philosophers for the means I employ as I am to Wittgenstein, Heidegger, and Dewey for the ends to which these means are put. I hope to convince the reader that the dialectic within analytic philosophy, which has carried philosophy of mind from Broad to Smart, philosophy of language from Frege to Davidson, epistemology from Russell to Sellars, and philosophy of science from Carnap to Kuhn, needs to be carried a few steps further. These additional steps will, I think, put us in a position to criticize the very notion of "analytic philosophy," and indeed of "philosophy" itself as it has been understood since the time of Kant.

From the standpoint I am adopting, indeed, the difference between "analytic" and other sorts of philosophy is relatively unimportant—a matter of style and tradition rather than a difference of "method" or of first principles. The reason why the book is largely written in the vocabulary of contemporary analytic philosophers, and with reference to problems discussed in the analytic literature, is merely autobiographical. They are the vocabulary and the literature with which I am most familiar, and to which I owe what grasp I have of philosophical issues. Had I been equally familiar with other contemporary modes of writing philosophy, this would have been a better and more useful book, although an even longer one. As I see it, the kind of philosophy which stems from Russell and Frege is, like classical Husserlian phenomenology, simply one more attempt to put philosophy in the position which Kant wished it to have—that of judging other areas of culture on the basis of its special knowledge of the "foundations" of these areas. "Analytic" philosophy is one more variant of Kantian philosophy, a variant marked principally by thinking of representation as linguistic rather than mental, and of philosophy of language rather than "transcendental critique," or psychology, as the discipline which exhibits the "foundations of knowledge." This emphasis on language, I shall be arguing in chapters four and six, does not essentially change the Cartesian-Kantian problematic, and thus does not really give philosophy a new self-image. For analytic philosophy is still committed to the construction of a permanent, neutral framework for inquiry, and thus for all of culture.

It is the notion that human activity (and inquiry, the search for knowledge, in particular) takes place within a framework which can be isolated prior to the conclusion of inquiry—a set of presuppositions discoverable a priori—which links contemporary philosophy to the Descartes-

Locke-Kant tradition. For the notion that there is such a framework only makes sense if we think of this framework as imposed by the nature of the knowing subject, by the nature of his faculties or by the nature of the medium within which he works. The very idea of "philosophy" as something distinct from "science" would make little sense without the Cartesian claim that by turning inward we could find ineluctable truth, and the Kantian claim that this truth imposes limits on the possible results of empirical inquiry. The notion that there could be such a thing as "foundations of knowledge" (*all* knowledge—in every field, past, present, and future) or a "theory of representation" (*all* representation, in familiar vocabularies and those not yet dreamed of) depends on the assumption that there is some such a priori constraint. If we have a Deweyan conception of knowledge, as what we are justified in believing, then we will not imagine that there are enduring constraints on what can count as knowledge, since we will see "justification" as a social phenomenon rather than a transaction between "the knowing subject" and "reality." If we have a Wittgensteinian notion of language as tool rather than mirror, we will not look for necessary conditions of the possibility of linguistic representation. If we have a Heideggerian conception of philosophy, we will see the attempt to make the nature of the knowing subject a source of necessary truths as one more self-deceptive attempt to substitute a "technical" and determinate question for that openness to strangeness which initially tempted us to begin thinking.

One way to see how analytic philosophy fits within the traditional Cartesian-Kantian pattern is to see traditional philosophy as an attempt to escape from history—an attempt to find nonhistorical conditions of any possible historical development. From this perspective, the common message of Wittgenstein, Dewey, and Heidegger is a historicist one. Each of the three reminds us that investigations of the foundations of knowledge or morality or language or society may be simply apologetics, attempts to eternalize a certain contemporary language-game, social practice, or self-image. The moral of this book is also historicist, and the three parts into which it is divided are intended to put the notions of "mind," of "knowledge," and of "philosophy," respectively, in historical perspective. Part I is concerned with philosophy of mind, and in chapter one I try to show that the so-called intuitions which lie behind Cartesian dualism are ones which have a historical origin. In chapter two, I try to show how these intuitions would be changed if physiological methods of prediction and control took the place of psychological methods.

Part II is concerned with epistemology and with recent attempts to find "successor subjects" to epistemology. Chapter three describes the genesis of the notion of "epistemology" in the seventeenth century, and its connection with the Cartesian notions of "mind" discussed in chapter one. It presents "theory of knowledge" as a notion based upon a confusion between the justification of knowledge-claims and their causal explanation—between, roughly, social practices and postulated psychological processes. Chapter four is the central chapter of the book—the one in which the ideas which led to its being written are presented. These ideas are those of Sellars and of Quine, and in that chapter I interpret Sellars's attack on "givenness" and Quine's attack on "necessity" as the crucial steps in undermining the possibility of a "theory of knowledge." The holism and pragmatism common to both philosophers, and which they share with the later Wittgenstein, are the lines of thought within analytic philosophy which I wish to extend. I argue that when extended in a certain way they let us see truth as, in James's phrase, "what it is better for us to believe," rather than as "the accurate representation of reality." Or, to put the point less provocatively, they show us that the notion of "accurate representation" is simply an automatic and empty compliment which we pay to those beliefs which are successful in helping us do what we want to do. In chapters five and six I discuss and criticize what I regard as reactionary attempts to treat empirical psychology or philosophy of language as "successor subjects" to epistemology. I argue that only the notion of knowledge as "accuracy of representation" persuades us that the study of psychological processes or of language—qua media of representation—can do what epistemology failed to do. The moral of part II as a whole is that the notion of knowledge as the assemblage of accurate representations is optional—that it may be replaced by a pragmatist conception of knowledge which eliminates the Greek contrast between contemplation and action, between representing the world and coping with it. A historical epoch dominated by Greek ocular metaphors may, I suggest, yield to one in which the philosophical vocabulary incorporating these metaphors seems as quaint as the animistic vocabulary of pre-classical times.

In part III I take up the idea of "philosophy" more explicitly. Chapter seven interprets the traditional distinction between the search for "objective knowledge" and other, less privileged, areas of human activity as merely the distinction between "normal discourse" and "abnormal discourse." Normal discourse (a generalization of Kuhn's notion of "normal science") is any discourse (scientific, political, theological, or whatever) which embodies agreed-upon criteria for reaching agreement; abnormal discourse is any which lacks such criteria. I argue that the attempt (which has defined traditional philosophy) to explicate "rationality" and "objectivity" in terms of conditions of accurate representation is a self-deceptive effort to eternalize the normal discourse of the day, and that, since the Greeks, philosophy's self-image has been dominated by this attempt. In chapter eight I use some ideas drawn from Gadamer and Sartre to develop a contrast between "systematic" and "edifying" philosophy, and to show how "abnormal" philosophy which does not conform to the traditional Cartesian-Kantian matrix is related to "normal" philosophy. I present Wittgenstein, Heidegger, and Dewey as philosophers whose

11

aim is to edify—to help their readers, or society as a whole, break free from outworn vocabularies and attitudes, rather than to provide "grounding" for the intuitions and customs of the present.

I hope that what I have been saying has made clear why I chose "Philosophy and the Mirror of Nature" as a title. It is pictures rather than propositions, metaphors rather than statements, which determine most of our philosophical convictions. The picture which holds traditional philosophy captive is that of the mind as a great mirror, containing various representations—some accurate, some not—and capable of being studied by pure, nonempirical methods. Without the notion of the mind as mirror, the notion of knowledge as accuracy of representation would not have suggested itself. Without this latter notion, the strategy common to Descartes and Kant—getting more accurate representations by inspecting, repairing, and polishing the mirror, so to speak—would not have made sense. Without this strategy in mind, recent claims that philosophy could consist of "conceptual analysis" or "phenomenological analysis" or "explication of meanings" or examination of "the logic of our language" or of "the structure of the constituting activity of consciousness" would not have made sense. It was such claims as these which Wittgenstein mocked in the *Philosophical Investigations,* and it is by following Wittgenstein's lead that analytic philosophy has progressed toward the "post-positivistic" stance it presently occupies. But Wittgenstein's flair for deconstructing captivating pictures needs to be supplemented by historical awareness—awareness of the source of all this mirror-imagery—and that seems to me Heidegger's greatest contribution. Heidegger's way of recounting history of philosophy lets us see the beginnings of the Cartesian imagery in the Greeks and the metamorphoses of this imagery during the last three centuries. He thus lets us "distance" ourselves from the tradition. Yet neither Heidegger nor Wittgenstein lets us see the historical phenomenon of mirror-imagery, the story of the domination of the mind of the West by ocular metaphors, within a social perspective. Both men are concerned with the rarely favored individual rather than with society—with the chances of keeping oneself apart from the banal self-deception typical of the latter days of a decaying tradition. Dewey, on the other hand, though he had neither Wittgenstein's dialectical acuity nor Heidegger's historical learning, wrote his polemics against traditional mirror-imagery out of a vision of a new kind of society. In his ideal society, culture is no longer dominated by the ideal of objective cognition but by that of aesthetic enhancement. In that culture, as he said, the arts and the sciences would be "the unforced flowers of life." I would hope that we are now in a position to see the charges of "relativism" and "irrationalism" once leveled against Dewey as merely the mindless defensive reflexes of the philosophical tradition which he attacked. Such charges have no weight if one takes seriously the criticisms of mirror-imagery which he, Wittgenstein, and Heidegger make. This book has little to add to these criticisms, but I hope that it presents some of them in a way which will help pierce through that crust of philosophical convention which Dewey vainly hoped to shatter.

PART ONE

Our Glassy Essence

CHAPTER I

The Invention of the Mind

1. CRITERIA OF THE MENTAL

Discussions in the philosophy of mind usually start off by assuming that everybody has always known how to divide the world into the mental and the physical—that this distinction is common-sensical and intuitive, even if that between two sorts of "stuff," material and immaterial, is philosophical and baffling. So when Ryle suggests that to talk of mental entities is to talk of dispositions to behave, or when Smart suggests that it is to talk of neural states, they have two strikes against them. For why, if anything like behaviorism or materialism is true, should there be anything like this intuitive distinction?

We seem to have no doubt that pains, moods, images, and sentences which "flash before the mind," dreams, hallucinations, beliefs, attitudes, desires, and intentions all count as "mental" whereas the contractions of the stomach which cause the pain, the neural processes which accompany it, and everything else which can be given a firm location within the body count as nonmental. Our unhesitating classification suggests that not only have we a clear intuition of what "mentality" is, but that it has something to do with non-spatiality and with the notion that even if the body were destroyed the mental entities or states might somehow linger on. Even if we discard the notion of "mind-stuff," even if we drop the notion of *res cogitans* as subject of predication, we seem able to distinguish mind from body nonetheless, and to do so in a more or less Cartesian way.

These purported intuitions serve to keep something like Cartesian dualism alive. Post-Wittgensteinian philosophers who oppose behaviorism and materialism tend to grant to

17

Wittgenstein and Strawson that in some sense there is nothing there but the human organism, and that we must give up the notion of this organism as made out of a bit of *res cogitans* nonspatially associated with a bit of *res extensa*. But, they say, the Cartesian intuition that the mental-physical distinction is unbridgeable by empirical means, that a mental state is no more like a disposition than it is like a neuron, and that no scientific discovery can reveal an identity remains. This intuition seems to them enough to establish an unbridgeable gap. But such neo-dualist philosophers are embarrassed by their own conclusions, since although their metaphysical intuitions seem to be Cartesian, they are not clear whether they are entitled to *have* such things as "metaphysical intuitions." They tend to be unhappy with the notion of a method of knowing about the world prior to and untouchable by empirical science.

In this situation, it is tempting for the dualist to go linguistic and begin talking about "different vocabularies" or "alternative descriptions." This jargon suggests that the dualistic intuition in question is merely one of the differences between ways of talking about the same phenomenon, and thus seems to lead one from something like dualism to something like Spinoza's double-aspect theory. But the question "two descriptions of *what*?" makes this a difficult position to hold onto. To reply "two descriptions of organisms" seems all right until we ask, "Are organisms physical?" or "Is there more to organisms, even human organisms, than the actual and possible dispositions of their parts?" Neo-dualists are usually happy to concede a whole raft of mental states to Ryle, and to say that beliefs, desires, attitudes, and intentions (not to mention skills, virtues, and moods) are all merely ways of talking about organisms, their parts, and the actual and possible movements of those parts. (But they may insist, following Brentano and Chisholm, that no Rylean necessary and sufficient conditions can be provided). But when they come to pains, mental images, and occurrent thoughts—short-term mental states which look,

18

so to speak, event-like rather than disposition-like—they hesitate. And well they should. For the difference between dualism and materialism would vanish if once they said that to describe an organism as in pain is simply one way of talking about a state of its parts. These parts, remember, must be *physical* parts, since once we have Kantized and Strawsonized Descartes the notion of "mental part" will no longer even seem to make sense. What more could a defender of mind-body identity ask for than the admission that talk of how one *feels* is just an alternative way of reporting on how suitable portions of one's anatomy (presumably neurons) *are*?

We thus have the following dilemma: either neo-dualists must construct an epistemological account of how we know a priori that entities fall under two irreducibly distinct ontological species, or else they must find some way of expressing their dualism which relies on neither the notion of "ontological gap" nor that of "alternative description." But before casting about for ways of resolving this dilemma, we should look more closely at the notion of "ontological species" or "ontological gap." What sort of notion is this? Do we have any other examples of ontological gaps? Any other case in which we know a priori that no empirical inquiry can identify two entities? We know, perhaps, that no empirical inquiry can identify two spatio-temporal entities which have different locations, but that knowledge seems too trivial to be relevant. Is there any other case in which we know a priori about natural ontological kinds? The only examples which I can think of are the distinctions between finite and infinite, between human and divine, and between particular and universal. Nothing, we intuit, could cross *those* divides. But these examples do not seem very helpful. We are inclined to say that we do not know what it would be for something infinite to exist. If we try to clarify the orthodox notion of "the divine" we seem to have either a merely negative conception, or else one explicated in terms of the notions of "infinity" and "immateriality."

Since reference to infinity explains the obscure by the more obscure, we are left with immateriality. We feel vaguely confident that if the infinite *could* exist, it, like the universal, could only be exemplified by the immaterial. If it makes any sense to speak of the existence of universals, it would seem that they must exist immaterially, and *that* is why they can never be identified with spatio-temporal particulars. But what does "immaterial" mean? Is it the same thing as "mental"? Even though it is hard to see more in the notion of being "physical" than being "material" or "spatio-temporal," it is not clear that "mental" and "immaterial" are synonyms. If they were, then such disputes as that about the status of universals between conceptualists and realists would look even sillier than they do. Nevertheless, the opposite of "mental" is "physical" and the opposite of "immaterial" is "material." "Physical" and "material" seem synonymous. How can two distinct concepts have synonymous opposites?

At this point we may be tempted to recur to Kant and explain that the mental is temporal but not spatial, whereas the immaterial—the mystery beyond the bounds of sense—is neither spatial nor temporal. This seems to give us a nice neat threefold distinction: the physical is spatio-temporal; the psychological is nonspatial but temporal; the metaphysical is neither spatial nor temporal. We can thus explain away the apparent synonymy of "physical" and "material" as a confusion between "nonpsychological" and "nonmetaphysical." The only trouble is that Kant and Strawson have given convincing arguments for the claim that we can only identify mental states as states of spatially located persons.[1] Since we have given up "mind-stuff," we are bound to take these arguments seriously. This brings us almost full circle, for now we want to know what sense it

[1] See Kant's "Refutation of Idealism" at K.d.r.V. B274ff. and P. F. Strawson, *Individuals* (London, 1959), chap. 2, and *The Bounds of Sense* (London, 1966), pp. 162ff.

makes to say that some states of a spatial entity are spatial and some are not. It is no help to be told that these are its *functional* states—for a person's beauty and his build and his fame and his health are functional states, yet intuition tells us that they are not mental states either. To clarify our intuition, we have to identify a feature shared by our pains and beliefs but not by our beauty or our health. It will not help to identify the mental as that which can survive death or the destruction of the body, since one's beauty can survive death and one's fame can survive the destruction of one's body. If we say that one's beauty or one's fame exists only relationally, in the eyes or the opinion of others, rather than as states of oneself, then we get sticky problems about how to distinguish merely relational properties of persons from their intrinsic states. We get equally sticky problems about a person's unconscious beliefs, which may be discovered only after his death by psycho-biographers, but which are presumably as much his mental states as those beliefs which he was aware of having during his lifetime. There may be a way of explaining why a person's beauty is a nonintrinsic relational property whereas his unconscious paranoia is a nonrelational intrinsic state; but that would seem to be explaining the obscure by the more obscure.

I conclude that we cannot make non-spatiality the criterion of mental states, if only because the notion of "state" is sufficiently obscure that neither the term *spatial state* nor the term *nonspatial state* seems useful. The notion of mental entities as nonspatial and of physical entities as spatial, if it makes any sense at all, makes sense for particulars, for subjects of predication, rather than for the possession of properties by such subjects. We can make some dim sort of pre-Kantian sense out of bits of matter and bits of mind-stuff, but we cannot make any post-Kantian sense out of spatial and nonspatial states of spatial particulars. We get a vague sense of explanatory power when we are told that human bodies move as they do because they are inhabited by ghosts, but none at all when we are told that persons have nonspatial states.

I hope that I have said enough to show that we are not entitled to begin talking about the mind-body problem, or about the possible identity or necessary non-identity of mental and physical states, without first asking what we mean by "mental." I would hope further to have incited the suspicion that our so-called intuition about what is mental may be merely our readiness to fall in with a specifically philosophical language-game. This is, in fact, the view that I want to defend. I think that this so-called intuition is no more than the ability to command a certain technical vocabulary—one which has no use outside of philosophy books and which links up with no issues in daily life, empirical science, morals, or religion. In later sections of this chapter I shall sketch a historical account of how this technical vocabulary emerged, but before doing so, I shall beat some neighboring bushes. These are the possibilities of defining "mental" in terms of the notion of "intentionality" and in terms of the notion of being "phenomenal"—of having a characteristic appearance, an appearance somehow exhaustive of reality.

2. The Functional, the Phenomenal, and the Immaterial

The obvious objection to defining the mental as the intentional is that pains are not intentional—they do not represent, they are not *about* anything. The obvious objection to defining the mental as "the phenomenal" is that beliefs don't feel like anything—they don't have phenomenal properties, and a person's real beliefs are not always what they appear to be. The attempt to hitch pains and beliefs together seems ad hoc—they don't seem to have anything in common except our refusal to call them "physical." We can gerrymander, of course, so as to make pain the acquisition of a belief that one of one's tissues is damaged, construing pain reports as Pitcher and Armstrong construe

22

perceptual reports.[2] But such a tactic still leaves us with something like a dualistic intuition on our hands—the intuition that there is "something more" to being conscious of a pain or a sensation of redness than being tempted to acquire a belief that there is tissue-damage or a red object in the vicinity. Alternatively, we can gerrymander the other way and simply confine the term *mental* to what *does* have phenomenal properties, abandoning beliefs and desires to Armstrong to identify with the physical. But that tactic runs up against the intuition that whatever the mind-body problem is, it is not the feeling-neuron problem. If we expel representations, intentional states, from the mind we are left with something like a problem of the relation between life and nonlife, rather than a mind-body problem.

Still another tactic would be simply to define "mental" disjunctively as "either phenomenal or intentional." This suggestion leaves it entirely obscure how an abbreviation for this disjunction got entrenched in the language, or at least in philosophical jargon. Still, it does direct our attention to the possibility that the various "mental" items are held together by family resemblances. If we consider thoughts—occurrent thoughts, flashing before the mind in particular words—or mental images, then we seem to have something which is a little like a pain in being phenomenal and a little like a belief in being intentional. The words make the thoughts phenomenal and the colors and shapes make the images phenomenal, yet both of them are *of* something in the required intentional sense. If I suddenly and silently say to myself, "Good Lord, I left my wallet on that cafe-table in Vienna," or if I have an image of the wallet on the table, then I am representing Vienna, the wallet, the table, etc.—I have all these as intentional objects. So perhaps we should think of thoughts and mental images as the *paradigmatic*

[2] See George Pitcher, *A Theory of Perception* (Princeton, 1971); D. M. Armstrong, *Perception and the Physical World* (London and New York, 1961) and *A Materialist Theory of the Mind* (London and New York, 1968).

23

mental entities. Then we can say that pains and beliefs get classified as mental through their resemblance to these paradigms, even though the resemblance is in two quite different respects. The relationship between the various candidates for mentality could then be illustrated by the following diagram:

	with phenomenal properties	without phenomenal properties
intentional, representational	occurrent thoughts, mental images	beliefs, desires, intentions
nonintentional, nonrepresentational	raw feels—e.g., pains and what babies have when they see colored objects	"the merely physical"

Suppose for the moment that we settle for this "family resemblance" answer to the question "what makes the mental mental?"—viz., that it is one or another family resemblance to the paradigmatically mental. Now let us turn back to our original question, and ask what makes us fill in the fourth box with "the merely physical?" Does "physical" mean merely "what doesn't fit in the other three boxes?" Is it a notion which is entirely parasitic on that of "mental?" Or does it somehow tie in with "material" and "spatial," and how does it do so?

To answer this, we have to ask two subquestions: "Why is the intentional nonmaterial?" and "Why is the phenomenal nonmaterial?" The first question may seem to have a fairly straightforward answer. If we take "the material" to be "the neural," for example, we can say that no amount of inspection of the brain will reveal the intentional character of the pictures and inscriptions found there. Suppose that all persons struck by the thought "I left my wallet on a cafe-table in Vienna," *in those very English words,* have an identical series of neural events concomitant with the

24

thought. This seems a plausible (though probably false) hypothesis. But it is *not* plausible that all those who acquire the belief that they have left their wallet on a cafe-table in Vienna have this series of events, for they may formulate their belief in quite other words or in quite other language. It would be odd if a Japanese and an English thought should have the same neural correlate. It is equally plausible that all those who suddenly see the same missing wallet on the same distant table in their mind's eye should share a second series of neural events, though one quite different from that correlated with the thinking of the English sentence. Even such neat concomitance would not tempt us to "identify" the intentional and the neurological properties of the thought or the image, any more than we identify the typographical and the intentional properties of the sentence "I left my wallet on a cafe-table in Vienna" when we meet it on the printed page. Again, the concomitance of pictures of wallets on cafe-tables against a Viennese background with certain properties of the surfaces of paper and canvas does not identify the intentional property "being about Vienna" with the arrangement of pigments in space. So we can see why one might say that intentional properties are not physical properties. But, on the other hand, this comparison between neurological and typographical properties suggests that there is no interesting problem about intentionality. Nobody wants to make philosophical heavy weather out of the fact that you can't tell merely from the way it looks what a sentence means, or that you can't recognize a picture of X *as* a picture of X without being familiar with the relevant pictorial conventions. It seems perfectly clear, at least since Wittgenstein and Sellars, that the "meaning" of typographical inscriptions is not an extra "immaterial" property they have, but just their place in a context of surrounding events in a language-game, in a form of life. This goes for brain-inscriptions as well. To say that we cannot observe intentional properties by looking at the brain is like saying that we cannot see a proposition when we look at a Mayan codex—we simply do not know what to look for, because we do not yet know how to relate what we see to a symbol-system. The relation between an inscription—on paper or, given the hypothesized concomitance, in the brain—and what it means is no more mysterious than the relation between a functional state of a person, such as his beauty or his health, and the parts of his body. It is just those parts seen in a given context.

So the answer to the question "Why is the intentional nonmaterial?" is "because any functional state—any state which can only be grasped by relating what is observed to a larger context—is, in a trivial sense, nonmaterial." The problem is in trying to relate this trivial notion of being "nonmaterial"—which means merely something like "not immediately evident to all who look"—with the philosophically pregnant sense of "immateriality." To put it another way, why should we be troubled by Leibniz's point that if the brain were blown up to the size of a factory, so that we could stroll through it, we should not see thoughts? If we know enough neural correlations, we shall indeed see thoughts—in the sense that our vision will reveal to us what thoughts the possessor of the brain is having. If we do not, we shall not, but then if we stroll through *any* factory without having first learned about its parts and their relations to one another, we shall not see what is going on. Further, even if we could find no such neural correlations, even if cerebral localization of thoughts was a complete failure, why would we want to say that a person's thoughts or mental images were nonphysical simply because we cannot give an account of them in terms of his parts? To use an example from Hilary Putnam, one cannot give an account of why square pegs do not fit into round holes in terms of the elementary particles which constitute the peg and the hole, but nobody finds a perplexing ontological gap between macrostructure and microstructure.

I think that we can link the trivial sense of "nonmaterial" (which applies to any functional, as opposed to observable, state) with the pregnant sense of "immaterial" only by resurrecting Locke's view of how meaning attaches to inscriptions—the view which Wittgenstein and Sellars attack. For Locke the meaningfulness—the intentional character— of an inscription was the result of its production by, or encoding of, an idea. An idea, in turn, was "what is before a man's mind when he thinks." So the way to see the intentional as the immaterial is to say that neither a sequence of processes in the brain nor some ink on paper can represent anything unless an idea, something of which we are aware in that "immediate" way in which we are aware of pains, has impregnated it. In a Lockean view, when we walk through Leibniz's factory we do not see thoughts not because, as for Wittgenstein, we cannot yet translate brain-writing, but because we cannot see those invisible (because nonspatial) entities which infuse the visible with intentionality. For Wittgenstein, what makes things representational or intentional is the part they play in a larger context —in interaction with large numbers of other visible things. For Locke, what makes things representational is a special causal thrust—what Chisholm describes as the phenomenon of sentences deriving intentionality from thoughts as the moon derives its light from the sun.[3]

So our answer to the question "How can we convince ourselves that the intentional must be immaterial?" is "First we must convince ourselves, following Locke and Chisholm and *pace* Wittgenstein and Sellars, that intentionality is intrinsic only in phenomenal items—items directly before the mind." If we accept that answer, however, we are still only part of the way to resolving the issue. For since the problem with which we have been wrestling has been caused precisely by the fact that beliefs do not have phenomenal properties, we now have to ask how Locke, following Descartes, can conflate pains and beliefs under the common term *idea*—how he can convince himself that a

[3] Roderick Chisholm, "Intentionality and the Mental" in *Minnesota Studies in the Philosophy of Science* 2 (1958), 533.

belief is something which is "before the mind" in the way in which a mental image is, how he can use the same ocular imagery for mental images and for judgments. I shall discuss the origin of this Cartesian-Lockean use of the term *idea* below. But for the moment I shall pass over the issue and come to the *second* subdivision of the question "Why should the mental be thought of as immaterial?"—namely, why should the *phenomenal* be thought of as immaterial? Why do some neo-dualist philosophers say that how something feels, what it is like to be something, cannot be identical with any physical property, or at least any physical property which we know anything about?

A trivial answer to this question would be that we can know all about something's physical properties and not know how it feels—especially if we can't talk to it. Consider the claim that babies and bats and Martians and God and panpsychistically viewed rocks all may inhabit different phenomenal "quality spaces" from those we inhabit.[4] So they may. But what does this have to do with non-physicality? Presumably those who say that the phenomenal is

---

[4] This claim has been presented very forcefully in Thomas Nagel's "What Is It Like to Be a Bat?" *Philosophical Review* 83 (1974), 435-450. I have learned a great deal from Nagel's work in philosophy of mind, although I disagree heartily with him on almost every point. I think that the difference between our views goes back to the question (raised most sharply by Wittgenstein) of whether "philosophical intuitions" are more than residua of linguistic practices, but I am not sure how this issue is to be debated. Nagel's intuition is that "facts about what it is like to be an X are very peculiar" (p. 437), whereas I think that they look peculiar only if, following Nagel and the Cartesian tradition, we hold that "if physicalism is to be defended, the phenomenological features must themselves be given a physical account" (p. 437). In later sections of this chapter, I try to trace the history of the philosophical language-game in which this claim is at home. For the Davidsonian reasons offered in chapter four, section 4, below, I do not think physicalism subject to such a constraint. Physicalism, I argue there, is probably true (but uninteresting) if construed as predicting every event in every space-time region under some description or other, but obviously false if construed as the claim to say everything true.

nonphysical are not complaining that being told how the atoms of the bat's brain are laid out will not help one feel like a bat. Understanding about the physiology of pain does not help us feel pain either, but why should we expect it to, any more than understanding aerodynamics will help us fly? How can we get from the undoubted fact that knowing how to use a physiological term (e.g., "stimulation of C-fibers") will not necessarily help us use a phenomenological term (e.g., "pain") to an ontological gap between the referents of the two terms? How can we get from the fact that knowing Martian physiology does not help us translate what the Martian says when we damage his tissues to the claim that he has got something immaterial we haven't got? How, to come to the point, do we know when we have two ways of talking about the same thing (a person, or his brain) rather than descriptions of two different things? And why are neo-dualists so certain that feelings and neurons are an instance of the latter?

I think that the only reply such philosophers have to offer is to point out that in the case of phenomenal properties there is no appearance-reality distinction. This amounts to defining a physical property as one which anybody could be mistaken in attributing to something, and a phenomenal property as one which a certain person cannot be mistaken about. (E.g., the person who has the pain cannot be mistaken about how the pain feels.) Given this definition, of course, it is trivially the case that no phenomenal property can be a physical one. But why should this *epistemic* distinction reflect an *ontological* distinction? Why should the epistemic privilege we all have of being incorrigible about how things seem to us reflect a distinction between two realms of being?

The answer presumably has to go something like this: Feelings just *are* appearances. Their reality is exhausted in how they seem. They are pure seemings. Anything that is not a seeming (putting the intentional to one side for the moment) is merely physical—that is, it is something which

29

can appear other than it is. The world comes divided into things whose nature is exhausted by how they appear and things whose nature is not. But if a philosopher gives this answer he is in danger of changing from a neo-dualist into a plain old-fashioned Cartesian dualist, "mind-stuff" and all. For now he has stopped talking about pains as states of people or properties predicated of people and started talking about pains as particulars, a special sort of particular whose nature is exhausted by a single property. Of what could such a particular be made, save mind-stuff? Or, to put it another way, what could mind-stuff be save something out of which such thin, wispy, and translucent things can be made? As long as feeling painful is a property of a person or of brain-fibers, there seems no reason for the epistemic difference between reports of how things feel and reports of anything else to produce an ontological gap. But as soon as there is an ontological gap, we are no longer talking about states or properties but about distinct particulars, distinct subjects of predication. The neo-dualist who identifies a pain with how it feels to be in pain is hypostatizing a property—painfulness—into a special sort of particular, a particular of that special sort whose *esse* is *percipi* and whose reality is exhausted in our initial acquaintance with it. The neo-dualist is no longer talking about how people feel but about feelings as little self-subsistent entities, floating free of people in the way in which universals float free of the instantiations. He has, in fact, modeled pains on universals. It is no wonder, then, that he can "intuit" that pains can exist separately from the body, for this intuition is simply the intuition that universals can exist independently of particulars. That special sort of subject of predication whose appearance *is* its reality—phenomenal pain—turns out to be simply the painfulness of the pain abstracted from the person having the pain. It is, in short, the universal *painfulness* itself. To put it oxymoronically, mental particulars, unlike mental states of people, turn out to be universals.

This then is the answer I want to give to the question: Why do we think of the phenomenal as immaterial? We do so because, as Ryle put it, we insist on thinking of having a pain in ocular metaphors—as having a funny sort of particular before the eye of the mind. That particular turns out to be a universal, a quality hypostatized into a subject of predication. Thus when neo-dualists say that how pains *feel* are essential to what pains *are*, and then criticize Smart for thinking of the causal role of certain neurons as what is essential to pain, they are changing the subject. Smart is talking about what is essential to people being in pain, whereas neo-dualists like Kripke are talking about what is essential for something's being *a pain*. Neo-dualists feel unafraid of the question "What is the epistemological basis for your claim to know what is an essential property of pain?" for they have arranged things so that pains have only *one* intrinsic property—namely, feeling painful—and so the choice of which properties are to count as essential to them is obvious.

Let me now summarize the results of this section. I have said that the only way to associate the intentional with the immaterial is to identify it with the phenomenal, and that the only way to identify the phenomenal with the immaterial is to hypostatize universals and think of them as particulars rather than abstractions from particulars—thus giving them a non-spatio-temporal habitation. It turns out, in other words, that the universal-particular distinction is the *only* metaphysical distinction we have got, the only one which moves anything at all outside of space, much less outside of space-time. The mental-physical distinction then is parasitic on the universal-particular distinction, rather than conversely. Further, the notion of mind-stuff as that out of which pains and beliefs are made makes exactly as much or as little sense as the notion of "that of which universals are made." The battle between realists and conceptualists over the status of universals is thus empty because we have no idea of what a mind is save that it is made of whatever universals are made of. In constructing both a Lockean idea and a Platonic Form we go through exactly the same process—we simply lift off a single property from something (the property of being red, or painful, or good) and then treat it as if it itself were a subject of predication, and perhaps also a locus of causal efficacy. A Platonic Form is merely a property considered in isolation and considered as capable of sustaining causal relations. A phenomenal entity is precisely that as well.

3. The Diversity of Mind-Body Problems

At this point we might want to say that we have dissolved the mind-body problem. For, roughly speaking, all that is needed to find this problem unintelligible is for us to be nominalists, to refuse firmly to hypostatize individual properties. Then we shall not be fooled by the notion that there are entities called pains which, because phenomenal, cannot be physical. Following Wittgenstein, we shall treat the fact that there is no such thing as "a misleading appearance of pain" not as a strange fact about a special ontological genus called the mental, but just as a remark about a language-game—the remark that we have the convention of taking people's word for what they are feeling. From this "language-game" point of view, the fact that a man is feeling whatever he thinks he's feeling has no more ontological significance than the fact that the Constitution is what the Supreme Court thinks it is, or that the ball is foul if the umpire thinks it is. Again following Wittgenstein, we shall treat the intentional as merely a subspecies of the functional, and the functional as merely the sort of property whose attribution depends upon a knowledge of context rather than being observable right off the bat. We shall see the intentional as having no connection with the phenomenal, and the phenomenal as a matter of how we talk. The mind-body problem, we can now say, was merely a result of Locke's unfortunate mistake about how words get meaning, combined with his and Plato's muddled attempt to talk about adjectives as if they were nouns.

As fast dissolutions of philosophical problems go, this one has its points. But it would be silly to think that we had resolved anything by arriving at this diagnosis. It is as if a psychiatrist were to explain to a patient that his unhappiness is a result of his mistaken belief that his mother wanted to castrate him, together with his muddled attempt to think of himself as identical with his father. What the patient needs is not a list of his mistakes and confusions but rather an understanding of how he came to make these mistakes and become involved in these confusions. If we are going to get rid of the mind-body problem we need to be able to answer such questions as the following:

> How did these rather dusty little questions about the possible identity of pains and neurons ever get mixed up with the question of whether man "differed in kind" from the brutes—whether he had dignity rather than merely value?

> Given that people thought that they survived the destruction of their bodies long before Locke and Plato began to make specifically philosophical confusions, haven't we left something out when we treat the mind as simply an assemblage of phenomenal and intentional states?

> Isn't there some connection between our ability to have knowledge and our having minds, and is this accounted for by referring simply to the fact that persons, like inscriptions, have intentional properties?

All these are good questions, and nothing that I have said so far helps answer them. To answer them, I think, nothing will serve save the history of ideas. Just as the patient needs to relive his past to answer his questions, so philosophy needs to relive its past in order to answer *its* questions. So far I have, in the customary manner of contemporary philosophers of mind, been flinging around terms like "phenomenal," "functional," "intentional," "spatial" and the like as if these formed the obvious vocabulary in which to discuss the topic. But of course the philosophers who created the language which gave us the mind-body problem did not use this vocabulary, or anything close to it. If we are to understand how we got the intuitions which make us think that there *must* be a *real*, indissoluble, philosophical problem *somewhere* in the neighborhood, we have to set aside our up-to-date jargon and think in the vocabulary of the philosophers whose books gave us those intuitions. In my Wittgensteinian view, an intuition is never anything more or less than familiarity with a language-game, so to discover the source of our intuitions is to relive the history of the philosophical language-game we find ourselves playing.

The "mind-body problem" which I have just "dissolved" concerns only a few of the notions which, emerging at different points in the history of thought, have intertwined to produce a tangle of interrelated problems. Questions like "How are intentional states of consciousness related to neural states?" and "How are phenomenal properties such as painfulness related to neurological properties?" are parts of what I shall call the "problem of consciousness." This problem is distinct from such pre-philosophical problems about personhood as "Am I really only this mass of flesh and bone?" and from such Greek philosophical problems about knowledge as "How can we have certainty about the changing?" "How can knowledge be of the unchanging?" and "How can the unchanging become internal to us by being known?" Let us call the "problem of personhood" that of what more a human being is than flesh. This problem has one form in the pre-philosophical craving for immortality, and another in the Kantian and romantic assertion of human dignity—but both cravings are quite distinct from problems about consciousness and about knowledge. Both are ways of expressing our claim to be something quite different from the beasts that perish. Let us call the "problem of reason" that of how to spell out the Greek claim that the crucial difference between men and beasts is that we can *know*—that we can know not merely singular facts but universal truths, numbers, essences, the eternal. This problem takes different forms in Aristotle's hylomorphic account of knowing, Spinoza's rationalist account, and Kant's transcendental account. But these issues are distinct both from those about the interrelations between two sorts of things (one spatial and the other nonspatial) and from issues concerning immortality and moral dignity. The problem of consciousness centers around the brain, raw feels, and bodily motions. The problem of reason centers around the topics of knowledge, language, and intelligence—all our "higher powers." The problem of personhood centers around attributions of freedom and of moral responsibility.

In order to sort out some of the relations among these three problems, I shall offer a list of ways of isolating beings which have minds in contrast to the "merely physical"— "the body," "matter," the central nervous system, "nature" or "the subject matter of the positive sciences." Here are some, though hardly all, of the features which philosophers have, at one time or another, taken as marks of the mental:

1. ability to know itself incorrigibly ("privileged access")
2. ability to exist separately from the body
3. non-spatiality (having a nonspatial part or "element")
4. ability to grasp universals
5. ability to sustain relations to the inexistent ("intentionality")
6. ability to use language
7. ability to act freely
8. ability to form part of our social group, to be "one of us"
9. inability to be identified with any object "in the world"

This is a long list, and it could easily be lengthened.[5] But

[5] See Herbert Feigl, *The "Mental" and the "Physical"* (Minneapolis, 1967) for a similar list, and for illuminating comments on the relationships between the various items.

it is important to go through these various suggestions about what it is to have a mind, for each of them has helped philosophers to insist on an unbridgeable dualism between mind and body. Philosophers have constantly seized upon some distinctive feature of human life in order to give our intuition of our uniqueness a "firm philosophical basis." Because these firm bases are so varied, naturalisms and materialisms, when not shrugged off as hopeless attempts to jump a vast ontological (or epistemological, or linguistic) gulf, are often treated as trivially true but pointless. They are pointless, it is explained, because our uniqueness has nothing whatever to do with whichever abyss the naturalist has laboriously filled in, but everything to do with some other abyss which has all the while been gaping just behind his back. In particular, the point is often made that even if we settled all questions about the relation between pains and neurons, and similar questions arising out of incorrigibility—(1) above—we should still have dealt, at best, only with (2) and (3) among the other marks of the mental. We should still have left everything relevant to reason (notably [4], [5] and [6]) and everything relevant to personhood (notably [7], [8] and [9]) as obscure as ever.

I think that this point is quite right, and further, that if it had been appreciated earlier the problem of consciousness would not have loomed so large as it has in recent philosophy. In the sense of having pains as well as neurons, we are on a par with many if not all of the brutes, whereas we presumably share neither reason nor personhood with them. It is only if we assume that possession of *any* nonphysical inner state is somehow, via (3), connected with (4) or (5) that we will think that light shed upon raw feels would reflect off onto representational mental states, and thereby illuminate our capacity to mirror the world around us. Again, only the assumption that life itself (even that of the fetus, the brain-damaged human, the bat, or the caterpillar) has a special sanctity akin to personhood would make us think that understanding raw feels might help us to

36

understand our moral responsibilities. Both assumptions are, however, often made. Understanding why they are made requires an understanding of intellectual history rather than an understanding of the meanings of the relevant terms, or an analysis of the concepts they signify. By sketching a little of the history of discussions of the mind, I hope to show that the problem of reason cannot be stated without a return to epistemological views which no one really wishes to resurrect. Further, I want to supply some ground for a suggestion which I shall develop later: that the problem of personhood is not a "problem" but a description of the human condition, that it is not a matter for philosophical "solution" but a misleading way of expostulating on the irrelevance of traditional philosophy to the rest of culture.

I shall not, however, discuss all the items on the list above in this chapter, but only (2), (3), and (4)—separation from the body, non-spatiality, and the grasp of universals. What I want to say about the other items will come in other chapters. I shall discuss (1)—privileged access—in the following chapter, and I shall be discussing (5) and (6)—intentionality and the ability to use language—in chapters four and six. While the items bearing on personhood—(7), (8), and (9)—will not be discussed separately, I shall be sketching the way in which I think the notion of personhood should be treated in chapter four, section 4, again in chapter seven, section 4, and in chapter eight, section 3. In the present chapter, I want to stick as closely as possible to the question: Why should consciousness seem to have anything to do with reason or with personhood? By sticking to the three topics of grasping universals, separation from the body, and non-spatiality, I shall move toward my conclusion that if we hold these last three historically distinct notions apart, then we shall no longer be tempted by the notion that knowledge is made possible by a special Glassy Essence which enables human beings to mirror nature. Thus we shall not be tempted to think that the possession of an inner life, a stream of consciousness, is relevant to reason. Once consciousness and reason are separated out in this way, then personhood can be seen for what I claim it is—a matter of decision rather than knowledge, an acceptance of another being into fellowship rather than a recognition of a common essence.

4. MIND AS THE GRASP OF UNIVERSALS

There would not have been thought to be a problem about the nature of reason had our race confined itself to pointing out particular states of affairs—warning of cliffs and rain, celebrating individual births and deaths. But poetry speaks of man, birth, and death as such, and mathematics prides itself on overlooking individual details. When poetry and mathematics had come to self-consciousness— when men like Ion and Theaetetus could identify themselves with their subjects—the time had come for something general to be said about knowledge of universals. Philosophy undertook to examine the difference between knowing that there were parallel mountain ranges to the west and knowing that infinitely extended parallel lines never meet, the difference between knowing that Socrates was good and knowing what goodness was. So the question arose: What are the analogies between knowing about mountains and knowing about lines, between knowing Socrates and knowing the Good? When this question was answered in terms of the distinction between the eye of the body and the Eye of the Mind, νοῦς—thought, intellect, insight—was identified as what separates men from beasts. There was, we moderns may say with the ingratitude of hindsight, no particular reason why this ocular metaphor seized the imagination of the founders of Western thought. But it did, and contemporary philosophers are still working out its consequences, analyzing the problems it created, and asking whether there may not be something to it after all. The notion of "contemplation," of knowledge of universal concepts or truths as θεωρία, makes the Eye of the Mind the inescapable model for the better sort of knowledge. But it is fruitless to ask whether the Greek language, or Greek economic conditions, or the idle fancy of some nameless pre-Socratic, is responsible for viewing this sort of knowledge as *looking* at something (rather than, say, rubbing up against it, or crushing it underfoot, or having sexual intercourse with it).[6]

Given this model, and with it the Mind's Eye, what must the mind be? Presumably something as different from the body as invisible parallelness is from visible mountain ridges. Something like that was ready to hand, for poetry and religion suggested that something humanoid leaves the body at death and goes off on its own.[7] Parallelness

[6] Dewey sees the metaphor of the Eye of the Mind as the result of the prior notion that knowledge must be of the unchangeable:

> The theory of knowing is modeled after what was supposed to take place in the act of vision. The object refracts light and is seen; it makes a difference to the eye and to the person having an optical apparatus, but none to the thing seen. The real object is the object so fixed in its regal aloofness that it is a king to any beholding mind that may gaze upon it. A spectator theory of knowledge is the inevitable outcome. (*The Quest for Certainty* [New York, 1960], p. 23)

It is hard to know whether the optical metaphor determined the notion that the object of true knowledge must be eternal and immutable or conversely, but the two notions do seem made for one another. Compare A. O. Lovejoy, *The Great Chain of Being* (Cambridge, Mass., 1936), chap. 2. The quest for certainty and the optical metaphor persist, however, once the notion of immutability and eternality is given up—for example, C. D. Broad's argument to sense-data on the ground that "if nothing elliptical is before my mind, it is very hard to understand why the penny should seem elliptical rather than of any other shape" (*Scientific Thought* [London, 1923], p. 240).

[7] On the connection of ψυχή, shadow, and breath, see C. A. van Peursen, *Body, Soul, Spirit* (Oxford, 1966), p. 88 and chap. 7 passim, together with the passages in Bruno Snell's *Discovery of the Mind* (Cambridge, Mass., 1953) and R. B. Onians's *The Origins of European Thought* (Cambridge, Mass., 1951) to which van Peursen refers. Onians's discussion of the relation between θυμός and ψυχή (pp. 93ff.) makes clear how little connection either notion had with knowing, and how

can be thought of as the very breath of parallels—the shadow remaining when the mountains are no more. The more wispy the mind, the more fit to catch sight of such invisible entities as parallelness. So even Aristotle, who spent his life pouring cold water on the metaphysical extravagances of his predecessors, suggests that there probably is *something* to the notion that the intellect is "separable," even though nothing else about the soul is. Aristotle has been praised by Ryleans and Deweyans for having resisted dualism by thinking of "soul" as no more ontologically distinct from the human body than were the frog's abilities to catch flies and flee snakes ontologically distinct from the frog's body. But this "naturalistic" view of soul did not prevent Aristotle from arguing that since the intellect had the power of receiving the form of, for example, froghood (skimming off the universal from the clearly known particular frog, so to speak) and taking it on itself without thereby becoming a frog, the intellect (νοῦς) must be something very special indeed. It must be something immaterial—even though no such strange quasi-substance need be postulated to explain *most* human activity, any more than it need be postulated to explain the frog's.[8]

---

much with fighting, sex, and movement generally. On the relation of these two notions to νοῦς in the pre-philosophical period, see Snell, chap. I, where Plato's description of νοῦς as "the eye of the soul" is cited and explained by reference to the archaic use of νοεῖν as the grasp of images. For our purposes, the important thing is that it is only when the notion of an immaterial and invisible object of knowledge (as in the knowing of the geometer) comes along that a clear distinction between, as van Peursen says, "inner and outer worlds" gets developed. Cf. van Peursen, pp. 87, 90.

[8] I do not think Aristotle ever explicitly gives this argument for claiming that the intellect is separable (and the difficulty about the relations between the active and the passive intellect in *De Anima* III, 4 make it almost impossible to see whether he intended to). But his followers have assumed that this was the argument which led him to write *De Anima* 408b 19-20 and 413b 25ff., and I have no better suggestion. See Mortimer Adler, *The Difference of Man and the Difference*

Philosophers have often wished that Aristotle had never fallen in with Plato's talk of universals and his spectator theory of knowledge, or that his *Entwicklung* had lasted long enough for such passages as *De Anima* III, 5 and *Metaphysics* XII to be expunged as juvenalia.[9] But once again, there is no point in trying to pin the blame on Aristotle or his interpreters. The metaphor of knowing general truths by internalizing universals, just as the eye of the body knows particulars by internalizing their individual colors and shapes, was, once suggested, sufficiently powerful to become the intellectual's substitute for the peasant's belief in life among the shades. In varied forms, running the gamut between neo-Platonic notions of knowledge as a direct connection with (emanation from, reflection of) the Godhead on the one hand, and down-to-earth neo-Aristotelian hylomorphic accounts of abstraction on the other, the soul as immaterial-because-capable-of-contemplating-universals remained the Western philosopher's answer to the question "Why is man unique?" for some two thousand years.

The tension thus established between the two sides of our being found conventionalized expression in passages like Isabella's "ape and essence" speech:

It Makes (New York, 1967), p. 220, citing 429a 18-b23 as adumbrating the standard Thomistic argument from the hylomorphic explanation of abstraction. For a Deweyan account of "separability" as a "Platonic wild oat," cf. J. H. Randall, *Aristotle* (New York, 1960), and the treatment by Werner Jaeger to which Randall refers. See also Marjorie Grene, *A Portrait of Aristotle* (London, 1963), pp. 243ff. I share Grene's bafflement on the point.

9 For an interesting contrary view, see T. H. Green, "The Philosophy of Aristotle" (in *Collected Works* [London, 1885], III, pp. 52-91). Green takes *De Anima* III, 5 as an advance on both Plato and the *Posterior Analytics* toward the discovery of holism and of the concrete universal. Green also, incidentally, compliments Aristotle (at p. 81) on appreciating the difference between "sensation and the intelligent consciousness of sensation" which Locke fatally ignored. I suggest below, following Kenny, that Locke's mistake was a consequence of Descartes's transformation of the notion of the mind.

> But man, proud man
> Dressed in a little brief authority
> Most ignorant of what he's most assured—
> His glassy essence—like an angry ape,
> Plays such fantastic tricks before high Heaven
> As make the angels weep—who, with our spleens,
> Would all laugh themselves mortal.[10]

Our Glassy Essence—the "intellectual soul" of the scholastics—is also Bacon's "mind of man" which "far from the nature of a clear and equal glass, wherein the beams of things should reflect according to their true incidence . . . is rather like an enchanted glass, full of superstition and imposture, if it be not delivered and reduced."[11] These early seventeenth-century conceits express a division within ourselves which was felt long before the New Science, Descartes's division between thinking and extended substance, the veil of ideas, and "modern philosophy." Our Glassy Essence was not a philosophical doctrine, but a pic-

[10] William Shakespeare, *Measure for Measure*, II, iii, 11. 117-123. See J. V. Cunningham, " 'Essence' and *The Phoenix and the Turtle*," *English Literary History* 19 (1952), p. 266 for the claim that the "glassy essence" here is the "intellectual soul," which is "glassy, for it mirrors God." The O.E.D. does not give this sense of "glassy," but Cunningham is persuasive and is followed by the editors of the *Arden Shakespeare* (to which I owe the reference to Cunningham). Shakespeare here seems to be simply original, rather than using a stock trope. There is apparently no allusion to the "*speculum obscurum*" passage in St. Paul or any other standard notion. For the history of analogies between the soul and a mirror, see Herbert Grabes, *Speculum, Mirror und Looking-Glass* (Tübingen, 1973), pp. 92ff. ("Geistig-Seelisches als Spiegel"). The phrase *man's glassy essence* was first invoked in philosophy by C. S. Peirce in an 1892 essay of that title on the "molecular theory of protoplasm," which Peirce strangely thought important in confirming the view that "a person is nothing but a symbol involving a general idea" and in establishing the existence of "group minds" (cf. *Collected Works*, ed. Charles Hartshorne and Paul Weiss [Cambridge, Mass., 1935], 6.270-271).

[11] Francis Bacon, *Advancement of Learning*, bk. II in *Works*, ed. James Spedding and Robert Ellis (Boston, 1861), VI, 276.

ture which literate men found presupposed by every page they read. It is glassy—mirror-like—for two reasons. First, it takes on new forms without being changed—but intellectual forms, rather than sensible ones as material mirrors do. Second, mirrors are made of a substance which is purer, finer grained, more subtle, and more delicate than most.[12] Unlike our spleen, which, in combination with other equally gross and visible organs, accounted for the bulk of our behavior, our Glassy Essence is something we share with the angels, even though they weep for our ignorance of its nature. The supernatural world, for sixteenth-century intellectuals, was modeled upon Plato's world of Ideas, just as our contact with it was modeled upon his metaphor of vision.

There are few believers in Platonic Ideas today, nor even many who make a distinction between the sensitive and the intellectual soul. But the image of our Glassy Essence remains with us, as does Isabella's lament that we cannot grasp it. A sense of moral failure mixes with a sense of grievance that philosophy—the discipline supremely concerned with "the higher"—has not made us more aware of our own nature. That nature, it is still felt, makes its distinctive character most clearly felt in a certain sort of knowledge—knowledge of the highest and purest things: mathematics, philosophy itself, theoretical physics, anything which contemplates universals. To suggest that there are no universals—that they are *flatus vocis*—is to endanger our uniqueness. To suggest that the mind is the brain is to

12 Cf. ibid., p. 242 for Bacon's claim that "the soul is the simplest of substances." He quotes a Lucretian passage from Vergil in support: *purumque reliquit / aethereum sensum atque auraï simplicis ignem* (Aeneid, VI, 747). The notion that the soul must be made of some very special fine-grained material in order to be capable of knowledge goes back to Anaxagoras. Antiquity wavered between *νοῦς* as utterly incorporeal and as made of some very special, very pure matter. Such wavering was inevitable, given the unimaginability of the non-spatio-temporal and the notion that reason must resemble the non-spatio-temporal forms or truths which it grasps.

43

suggest that we secrete theorems and symphonies as our spleen secretes dark humors. Professional philosophers shy away from these "crude pictures" because they have other pictures—thought to be less crude—which were painted in the later seventeenth century. But the sense that the nature of reason is a "permanent problem" and that anyone who doubts our uniqueness should study mathematics persists. The θυμός which quickened the Homeric heroes, St. Paul's πνεῦμα, and Aquinas's active intellect, are all quite different notions. But for present purposes we can coalesce them, as Isabella does, in the phrase *Glassy Essence*. They are all things which corpses do not have and which are distinctively human. The powers manifested by Achilles were not those of Theaetetus or the Apostles or St. Thomas, but the "intellectual essence" of the scholastics inherited the dualistic notions which gathered force between Homer and Anaxagoras, were given canonical form by Plato, were toned down by Aristotle, and then became entangled (in St. Paul) with a new and determinedly other-worldly religious cult.[13]

[13] The vague common-sense dualism of body and soul which lay ready to hand for Descartes was a product of the vocabulary of vernacular translations of the Bible as much as of anything else. So, in order to see how recent and parochial the Cartesian distinction is, it is worth noting that the authors of the Bible did not have anything much like the Cartesian contrast between "consciousness" and "insensate matter" in mind. On Jewish conceptions and their influence on St. Paul, see Onians, *Origins of European Thought*, pp. 480ff. On St. Paul himself, it is useful to note that, unlike modern writers on philosophy of mind, he does not identify body (σῶμα) with what is buried after death. The latter is σάρξ (flesh) whereas, according to J.A.T. Robinson, "σῶμα is the nearest equivalent of our word 'personality' " (*The Body: A Study in Pauline Theology* [London, 1952], p. 28; contrast Keith Campbell, *Body and Mind* [New York, 1970], p. 2: "Provided you know who *you* are, it is easy to say what your body is: it is what the undertakers bury when they bury you.") As Robinson says (p. 31n.), it is not that σῶμα and σάρξ are distinct *parts* of man but rather "the whole man differently regarded." The notion of man divided into *parts* does not come naturally to non-philosophers even after Plato; see van Peursen, *Body, Soul, Spirit*, chap. 6. For examples of the un-Cartesian ways in which σῶμα, σάρξ, ψυχή, and πνεῦμα are used by Paul, see 1 *Corinthians* 15:35-54.

In the "mirror" images of the Renaissance humanists, the differences between Homer and Augustine, Plotinus and Thomas, were flattened out to produce a vague but emphatic dualism—ape and essence—which everyone knew philosophers were supposed to know about, even though few could guess what they might hope to say about it. Recent philosophy of mind has tended to lump this vague conglomerate—man's Glassy Essence—together with the post-Cartesian notions of "consciousness" or "awareness." In the next section I shall try to show how different they are.

5. ABILITY TO EXIST SEPARATELY FROM THE BODY

The only point in the previous section at which argument intruded was in the mention of the Thomistic (and possibly Aristotelian) inference to the "separable," immaterial character of νοῦς from a hylomorphic conception of knowledge—a conception according to which knowledge is not the possession of accurate *representations* of an object but rather the subject's becoming *identical* with the object. To see the difference between this argument and the various Cartesian and contemporary arguments for dualism, we need to see how very different these two epistemologies are. Both lend themselves to the imagery of the Mirror of Nature. But in Aristotle's conception intellect is not a mirror inspected by an inner eye. It is both mirror and eye in one. The retinal image is *itself* the model for the "intellect which becomes all things," whereas in the Cartesian model, the intellect *inspects* entities modeled on retinal images. The substantial forms of frogness and starness get right into the Aristotelian intellect, and are there in just the same way they are in the frogs and the stars—*not* in the way in which frogs and stars are reflected in mirrors. In Descartes's conception—the one which became the basis for "modern" epistemology—it is *representations* which are in the "mind." The Inner Eye surveys these representations hoping to find some mark which will testify to their fidelity.

45

Whereas skepticism in the ancient world had been a matter of a moral attitude, a style of life, a reaction to the pretensions of the intellectual fashions of the day,[14] skepticism in the manner of Descartes's *First Meditations* was a perfectly definite, precise, "professional" question: How do we know that anything which is mental represents anything which is not mental? How do we know whether what the Eye of the Mind sees is a mirror (even a distorted mirror—an enchanted glass) or a veil? The notion of knowledge as inner representation is so natural to us that Aristotle's model may seem merely quaint, and Cartesian (as opposed to Pyrrhonian "practical") skepticism seems to us so much a part of what it is to "think philosophically" that we are amazed that Plato and Aristotle never confronted it directly. But if we see that the two models—the hylomorphic and the representative—are equally optional, perhaps we can see the inferences to mind-body dualism which stem from each as just as optional.

In an article called "Why Isn't the Mind-Body Problem

[14] See Philip P. Hallie on Greek skepticism as "eudaemonistic practical-wisdom philosophy" whose "doubt, rather than being an instrument for rolling back the veil of sense-experience, is a means of wiping off the excrescences that befoul man's life and lead him into endless, bitter conflicts with his fellow men" (*Scepticism, Man and God* [Middletown, Conn., 1964], p. 7). It is not clear what role the notion of the veil of ideas played in ancient skepticism, but it seems to have been incidental, rather than central in the way in which the Locke-Berkeley-Kant tradition made it central. Charlotte Stough (*Greek Scepticism* [Berkeley, 1969], p. 24) describes Pyrrho as viewing τὸ φαινόμενον as "a curtain between subject and object, screening the real world from his view." However it is not clear that τὸ φαινόμενον is much like a Lockean idea, which is incorrigibly before the mind, purely mental simply because incorrigibly known. The closest ancient thought seems to come to a notion of a class of incorrigibly knowable mental entities is the Stoic doctrine of καταληπτικὴ φαντασία (cf. Stough, pp. 38-40), but this is defined as a representation exactly corresponding to its object and *therefore* compelling assent, which is hardly Locke's notion. See also Josiah B. Gould, "Being, the World and Appearance in Early Stoicism and Some Other Greek Philosophers," *Review of Metaphysics* 27 (1974), 261-288, especially pp. 277ff.

Ancient?"[15] Wallace Matson has noted the principal point which divides Greek from seventeenth-century ways of looking at the separation of mind from body:

> The Greeks did not lack a concept of mind, even of a mind separable from the body. But from Homer to Aristotle, the line between mind and body, when drawn at all, was drawn so as to put the processes of sense perception on the body side. That is one reason why the Greeks had no mind-body problem. Another is that it is difficult, almost impossible, to translate such a sentence as "What is the relation of sensation to mind (or soul)?" into Greek. The difficulty is in finding a Greek equivalent for "sensation" in the sense philosophers make it bear. . . . "Sensation" was introduced into philosophy precisely to make it possible to speak of a conscious state without committing oneself as to the nature or even existence of external stimuli.[16]

One can sum up both of Matson's points by saying that in Greek there is no way to divide "conscious states" or "states of consciousness"—events in an inner life—from events in an "external world." Descartes, on the other hand, used "thought" to cover doubting, understanding, affirming, denying, willing, refusing, imagining, and feeling, and said

[15] Wallace Matson, "Why Isn't the Mind-Body Problem Ancient?" in *Mind, Matter and Method: Essays in Philosophy and Science in Honor of Herbert Feigl*, ed. Paul Feyerabend and Grover Maxwell (Minneapolis, 1966), pp. 92-102.

[16] Matson, "Mind-Body Problem," p. 101. He goes on to argue that neither αἴσθησις nor αἴσθημα will do as an equivalent of "sensation." Φάντασμα is a tempting possibility, but even to translate Aristotle's use of it as "mental image" is not above suspicion, and one could not call a pain a φάντασμα. On the difficulty of interpreting Aquinas's notion of *phantasma*, see Anthony Kenny, "Intellect and Imagination in St. Thomas" in *Aquinas: A Collection of Critical Essays*, ed. Kenny (Garden City, N.Y., 1969), pp. 293-294. The point Matson makes in the final sentence of this quotation is backed up by Thomas Reid's account of the term "sensation." See his *Essays on the Intellectual Powers of Man* (Cambridge, Mass., 1969), p. 249 (and essay II, passim).

that even if I dream that I see light "properly speaking this in me is called feeling, and used in this precise sense that is no other thing than thinking."[17] Once Descartes had entrenched this way of speaking it was possible for Locke to use "idea" in a way which has no Greek equivalent at all, as meaning "whatsoever is the object of the understanding when a man thinks" or "every immediate object of the mind in thinking."[18] As Kenny puts it, the modern use of the

[17] In *Meditation* II Descartes starts by defining a "thing which thinks" as "a mind or soul, or an understanding, or a reason" (*res cogitans, id est, mens, sive animus, sive intellectus, sive ratio*) and quickly goes on to "What is a thing which thinks? It is a thing which doubts, understands, affirms, denies, wills, refuses, *and also imagines and feels*" (italics added; "*Nempe dubitans, intelligens, affirmans, negans, volens, nolens, imaginans quoque, et sentiens*"). Then he continues with the second passage cited above (*hoc est proprie quod in me sentire appelatur; atque hoc praecise sic sumptum nihil aliud est quam cogitare*). All three texts are at pp. 184-186 in *Oeuvres Philosophiques*, ed. Alquié (Paris, 1967), vol. II (pp. 152-153 in vol. I of the Haldane and Ross translation). See also *Principles I*, sec. 9: "By the word *thought* I understand all that of which we are conscious of operating in us (*tout ce qui se fait en nous de telle sorte que nous l'apercevons immédiatement par nous-mêmes*). And that is why not only understanding, willing, imagining, but also feeling (*sentir*) are here the same thing as thought" (*Oeuvres Philosophiques* III, p. 95; Haldane and Ross, I, p. 222). On translating *res cogitans* as "consciousness" see Robert McRae, "Descartes' Definition of Thought" in *Cartesian Studies*, ed. R. J. Butler (Oxford, 1972), pp. 55-70.

[18] The first quotation is from the *Essay* (I, i, 8) and the second from the "Second Letter to the Bishop of Worcester." Immediacy as the mark of the mental (with the criterion of immediacy being incorrigibility) became an unquestioned presupposition in philosophy because of such passages as these. As so often in philosophy, neologistic usage became the mark of an understanding of "distinctively philosophical" topics and issues. Thus we find Hume saying, ". . . all the conclusions, which the vulgar form under this head, are directly contrary to those which are confirmed by philosophy. For philosophy informs us, that everything, which appears to the mind, is nothing but a perception, and is interrupted, and dependent on the mind; whereas the vulgar confound perceptions and objects, and attribute a distinct continued existence to the very things we feel and see" (*Treatise*, I, iv, ii). Jonathan Bennett notes that "Locke's thought is dominated by his attempt to use 'idea'

word *idea* derives through Locke from Descartes, "and Descartes was consciously giving it a new sense . . . it was a new departure to use it systematically for the contents of a human mind."[19] More important, there had been no term,

---

univocally as a key term in his accounts of perception and of meaning —or, in shorthand, his use of 'idea' to cover both sense-data and concepts" and says that this "embodies his substantive mistake, shared with Berkeley and Hume and others in the empiricist tradition, of assimilating the sensory far too closely to the intellectual" (Bennett, *Locke, Berkeley, Hume: Central Themes* [Oxford, 1971], p. 25). This mistake, however, goes back to Descartes and was embodied equally in the rationalist tradition. It is part of what Wilfrid Sellars calls the "framework of givenness" common to both traditions, and has always been the target of those influenced by Hegel. Cf. Sellars's *Science, Perception and Reality* (London and New York, 1963), pp. 127 and 155-156. Sellars's and Bennett's complaints are presaged by H. L. Prichard, and before him by T. H. Green, whom I discuss briefly below in chapter three, section 2.

[19] Anthony Kenny, "Descartes on Ideas" in *Descartes: A Collection of Critical Essays*, ed. Willis Doney (Garden City, N.Y., 1967), p. 226. See Descartes's definitions of "pensée" as "tout ce qui est tellement en nous, que nous en sommes immédiatement connaissants" and of "idée" as "cette forme de chacune de nos pensées, par la perception immédiate de laquelle nous avons connaissance de ses mêmes pensées" (*Replies to Second Objections*, Alquié edition, II, 586). John Yolton, however, takes issue with Kenny (and with Alquié and other commentators who take the traditional line—which I am taking here—that Descartes's doctrine of representative perception was a sharp, and perhaps disastrous, break with the scholastic tradition of direct realism.) In his "Ideas and Knowledge in Seventeenth-Century Philosophy" (*Journal of the History of Philosophy* 13 [1975], 145-165) he cites Descartes's characterization of "idée" as "une manière ou façon de penser" in the *Third Meditation* (Alquié, II, 439) as evidence that Descartes held an "act" theory of ideas which was compatible with scholastic direct realism. Here and in other works Yolton has suggested that the usual story (common to, e.g., Étienne Gilson and J. H. Randall) about the emergence of epistemological skepticism out of a theory of representative perception created by Descartes and Locke may be too simple-minded. A similar line is taken by Brian O'Neil in *Epistemological Direct Realism in Descartes' Philosophy* (Albuquerque, N.M., 1974), pp. 96-97: "Descartes' long struggle was an effort to retain and relate the theory of esse objectivum and the doctrine of simple natures." O'Neil agrees with Jean

even of philosophical art, in the Greek and medieval traditions coextensive with the Descartes-Locke use of "idea."
Nor had there been the conception of the human mind as
an inner space in which both pains and clear and distinct
ideas passed in review before a single Inner Eye. There
were, to be sure, the notions of taking tacit thought, forming resolutions in *foro interno*, and the like.[20] The novelty
was the notion of a single inner space in which bodily and
perceptual sensations ("confused ideas of sense and imagination" in Descartes's phrase), mathematical truths, moral
rules, the idea of God, moods of depression, and all the rest
of what we now call "mental" were objects of quasi-ob-
servation. Such an inner arena with its inner observer had
been suggested at various points in ancient and medieval
thought but it had never been taken seriously long enough
to form the basis for a problematic.[21] But the seventeenth

Wahl that Descartes "ait exprimé les deux conceptions fondamentales
et antinomiques du réalisme," the one based on something like Tho-
mism and the other based on something like a veil of ideas, some of
which guarantee their own accuracy as representations. If Yolton's revisionist readings of Locke and Descartes are correct, then one will
have to look further along in history for the emergence of what is now
thought of as the epistemological problematic created by Descartes.
Here, however, I am going along with Kenny's more familiar account.

[20] See, for example, Plato, *Sophist* 263E.

[21] Adler (*Difference of Man*, pp. 217-218) agrees with Matson that
"within the framework of Aristotelian metaphysics and psychology
there can be no mind-body problem" but claims that "Plato, for example, would have understood Descartes much better than Aristotle could
have, especially the Cartesian separation of mind and body into exis-
tentially distinct substances and the Cartesian view of the mind's inde-
pendence of the body." I would doubt, however, that there is a real
difference between Plato and Aristotle on this point; Matson's point
applies equally well to both. On the other hand, I have to admit that
there is something to Gilson's view that Descartes brings back just those
elements in the Augustinian tradition which Thomas had used Aristotle to criticize. So the Coleridgean choice between Plato and Aristotle
does seem relevant. Further, there are passages in Augustine which are
remarkably close to passages usually cited from Descartes to show the

50

century took it seriously enough to permit it to pose the problem of the veil of ideas, the problem which made epistemology central to philosophy.

Once Descartes had invented that "precise sense" of "feeling" in which it was "no other than thinking," we began to lose touch with the Aristotelian distinction between reason-as-grasp-of-universals and the living body which takes care of sensation and motion. A *new* mind-body distinction was required—the one which we call that "between consciousness and what is not consciousness." This was not a distinction between human faculties but a distinction between two series of events, such that many events in one series shared many characteristics with many events in

originality of his notion of "thinking" to cover both sense and intellect. Gareth Matthews (in "Consciousness and Life," *Philosophy* 52 [1977], 13-26) cites a striking example from *Contra Academicos*, bk. 3, sec. 11, chap. 26 and comments:

> The picture of human beings as having . . . both an "inside" and an "outside" is so commonplace, so (as it may seem to us) commonsensical, that we find it hard to realize how strikingly modern it is. But to appreciate its modernity one need only cast about for statements of it earlier than Descartes. One does find interesting anticipations of it in Augustine, but not much earlier, and not much between the time of Augustine and that of Descartes. (p. 25)

Matthews's point (like Matson's) seems to me a useful corrective to the claim that Ryle was attacking a basic human intuition when he attacked the notion of the ghost in the machine, rather than merely a Cartesian idiosyncrasy. Such a claim is made, for example, by Stuart Hampshire ("Critical Study" of *The Concept of Mind*, *Mind* 59 [1950], 237-255, esp. sec. 2). On the other hand, Hampshire's criticism is strengthened by the suggestion (made to me in conversation by Michael Frede) that the apparent novelty of Cartesian doctrines of representative perception and of human beings' "inner space" is mitigated if one reads Hellenistic philosophy and appreciates the role of the Stoics in Renaissance thought. If Frede is right, and especially if Yolton is also right on the issues discussed above in note 19, then there are many more continuities in the history of philosophic discussion of these topics than the story I am telling (which is borrowed from the Gilson-Randall historiographical tradition) would allow.

51

the other, while nonetheless differing *toto caelo* because one was an event in extended, and the other in nonextended, substance. It was more like a distinction between two worlds than like a distinction between two sides, or even parts, of a human being. The "Ideal World" of philosophers like Royce inherits the prestige and the mystery of the Glassy Essence of the Renaissance, but it is self-contained in a way in which a part of a man could never be.[22] To show that mind was imaginable apart from body was thus an entirely different project from that found in the tradition which stemmed from Aristotle. In Aristotle, the faculty which received universals without embodying them in matter was "separable" and it was hard (without some help from extra-philosophical concerns, such as Christianity) to say whether one should view it as a special power which the body had, a separate substance attached to each mature human body, or perhaps a single substance which was somehow shared among as many men and angels as there happened to be. Aristotle vacillated between the first and second options, with the second having the usual attrac-

[22] See Royce's description of Cartesian subjectivism as "The Rediscovery of the Inner Life" (the title of chapter III of his *The Spirit of Modern Philosophy* [New York, 1892]) and as opening the way to an understanding that the real world must be "mental" (the conclusion he draws triumphantly in chapter XI). See also chapter I of Lovejoy's *The Revolt Against Dualism* (La Salle, Ill., 1930), in which Lovejoy insists, against those who would dethrone Descartes, that the veil of ideas is a problem which arises for all who hold

> the primary and most universal faith of man, his inexpugnable realism, his two-fold belief that he is on the one hand in the midst of realities which are not himself nor mere obsequious shadows of himself, a world which transcends the narrow confines of his own transient being; and, on the other hand, that he can himself somehow reach beyond those confines and bring these external existences within the compass of his own life, yet without annulment of their transcendence. (p. 14)

To Aristotle, Aquinas, Dewey, or Austin this "realism" would seem as artificial and farfetched as Royce's idealism.

tions offered by the possibility of surviving death. Medieval philosophy vacillated between the second and third. But in all these disputes the controversy was not about the survival of "consciousness" but about the indestructibility of *reason*.[23] Once mind is no longer synonymous with reason,

[23] Thus Augustine leads off his treatise "On the Immortality of the Soul" with what he regards as the simplest and most decisive argument of all: the soul is immortal because it is the subject (i.e., the seat) of science, which is eternal. In chapter II, for example, he says: "The human body is mutable and reason is immutable. For all which does not exist always in the same mode is mutable, but that two and two are four exists always in the same mode. . . . This sort of reasoning, then, is immutable. Therefore, reason is immutable" (*Concerning the Teacher* and *On the Immortality of the Soul*, trans. George Leckie [New York, 1938], p. 61). Between Plato's *Phaedo* and the seventeenth century, the standard *philosophical* argument for immortality had always revolved around our ability to do what beasts cannot—know unchanging truths rather than just particular facts. Even Descartes, although he opened the floodgates to an entirely new conception of the difference between mind and body, was inclined to backtrack to the standard position and say that the body was responsible for all the actions which we share with brutes—for example, flight from danger. Thus in the *Fourth Responses* he says that reflex action occurs "without the aid of mind," and that this is no more a marvel than that "light reflected from the body of a wolf in the eyes of a sheep should be capable of exciting a motion of flight" (*Oeuvres Philosophiques*, ed. Alquié, II, 671; Haldane and Ross, II, 104). But his treatment of feeling as a sort of thinking would seem to force him into the paradoxical claim (which neither Aristotle nor Augustine would have any reason to make) that the feeling of terror which accompanies our flight has no parallel within the sheep. See the argument in a letter to Henry More (February 5, 1649) at p. 885 of vol. III of the Alquié edition. In such passages as this, the ambiguity of "thought" between "reasoning" and "consciousness" comes to a head. Descartes needs the former sense to avoid paradox and to maintain a link with the tradition, and the latter sense to establish a dualism of extended and nonextended substance. For a review of relevant Cartesian texts and a good account of the impact of Descartes's view on later philosophy, see Norman Malcolm, "Thoughtless Brutes," *Proceedings and Addresses of the American Philosophical Association* 46 (1973), 5-20. Malcolm, however, thinks that my question of why Descartes repackaged pains and thoughts so as

then something other than our grasp of universal truths must serve as the mark of mind.

If we look in Descartes for a common factor which pains, dreams, memory-images, and veridical and hallucinatory perceptions share with concepts of (and judgments about) God, number, and the ultimate constituents of matter, we find no explicit doctrine. Descartes tells us that we have a clear grasp of the distinction between the extended and the non-extended, and so we do (in the same trivial sense in which we might claim a clear grasp of the distinction between the finite and the infinite), but this does not help with the borderline cases (sensory grasp of particulars) which are, as it happens, the heart of the matter. For it is just the status of the "confused ideas of sense and imagination" which makes the difference between mind-as-reason and mind-as-consciousness.

The answer I should like to give to the question "What common factor did Descartes find?" is "indubitability," that is, the fact that pains, like thoughts and most beliefs, are such that the subject cannot doubt that he has them, whereas doubt is possible about everything physical. If we give this answer, then we can see what Royce called "Descartes's rediscovery of the inner life" as the discovery of the true

---

to include them within the same substance is answered by saying that what is common to imagining, willing, sensing, feeling, etc. is that in all of them "there is an object of awareness." (Malcolm, "Descartes's Proof That His Essence Is Thinking" in *Descartes: A Collection of Critical Essays*, ed. Willis Doney, p. 317n.) In other words, Malcolm thinks that intentionality is sufficient to unite all the things which Descartes wants to unite under *cogitatio* and *pensée*. I do not think that this will work for pains. In any case it runs together the genuine intentionality of linguistic representations and the pseudo-intentionality (as Sellars calls it) of sensations which Aquinas kept separate. It is just this coalescence by Descartes which needs explanation. Or, to put it another way, what needs explanation is just the origin of the notion of "awareness" in the phrase "object of awareness." On the distinction between genuine and pseudo-intentionality, see Sellars, "Being and Being Known" in *Science, Perception and Reality*.

essence of consciousness—that there is no distinction between appearance and reality, whereas everywhere else there is. The trouble with offering this answer, however, is that it is never explicitly given by Descartes himself. So the best I can do to justify it is to say that *something* is needed to explain Descartes's repackaging of the various items which Aristotle and Aquinas had separated, that nothing else seems to do, and that indubitability was so close to the heart of the author of the *First Meditation* that it seems a natural motive for his conceptual revolution.

Margaret Wilson has noted that we can find in Descartes an argument for mind-body dualism (a dualism drawn along the revisionist lines I have been describing) which is a simple "argument from doubt." This argument says that what we can doubt exists cannot, by Leibniz's law, be identical with what we cannot doubt exists. As Wilson says, this argument is "universally recognized to be fallacious."[24] It is fallacious, if for no other reason, because Leibniz's law does not apply to intentional properties. But, Wilson continues, the argument for dualism in the *Sixth Meditation* is *not* a version of this fallacious argument. It turns instead on the notion of "a complete thing" (which seems the same as the notion of "substance" in the sense of the term in which Descartes will admit only three substances—thought, extension, and God). The crucial premise is "I can clearly and distinctly understand that something can be a complete thing if it has χ (a psychological property) even if it lacks ϕ (a physical property)" (p. 14).

I think that Wilson's analysis is right, and that she is also right when she says that this argument as a whole "is no better than the distinction between clear and distinct perception and 'mere' perception," concerning which she doubts whether "recent essentialists' appeals to intuition" are on better ground (p. 14). In my view, however, the prin-

---

[24] See Margaret Wilson, "Descartes: the Epistemological Argument for Mind-Body Distinctness," *Nous* 10 (1976), 7-8. I am much indebted to Wilson for careful and helpful comments on a draft of this chapter.

cipal question raised by her analysis is how Descartes managed to convince himself that something which included
both pains and mathematical knowledge was "a complete
thing" rather than two things. This in turn reduces to the
question of how he was able to give "*penser*" the extended
sense of "consciousness" while still seeing it as the name of
a separate substance, in the way in which νοῦς and *intellectus* had been made familiar as the names of separate
substances. In my view, as I have said, "essentialist intuitions" and "clear and distinct perceptions" are always appeals to linguistic habits entrenched in the language by our
predecessors. So what needs explanation is how Descartes
was able to convince himself that his repackaging was
"intuitive."

Granted that the "argument from doubt" has no merit,
I think that nevertheless it is one of those cases of "finding
bad reasons for what we believe on instinct" which serves as
a clue to the instincts which actually do the convincing.
The hunch in question here was, I think, that the indubitably known mathematical truths (once their proofs had
been worked through so as to make them clearly and distinctly perceived with a sort of "phenomenal" vividness
and non-discursiveness) and the indubitable momentary
states of consciousness had something in common—something permitting them to be packaged inside of one substance. Thus Descartes says:

> Now as to what concerns ideas, if we consider them only
> in themselves and do not relate them to anything else
> beyond themselves, they cannot properly speaking be
> false; for whether I imagine a goat or a chimera, it is not
> the less true that I imagine the one rather than the
> other.[25]

Speaking of the imaginary beings created by painters, he
says that even if

[25] *Meditation III*, Alquié edition, ɪɪ, 193.

their work represents a thing purely fictitious and absolutely false, it is certain all the same that the colors
of which this is composed are necessarily real. And for
the same reason, although these general things (*generalia*)
such as eyes, a head, hands, and so on, may be imaginary,
it is nevertheless necessary that there be some more simple
and universal (*quaedam aduc magis simplicia et universalia*) things out of which all these are made—just as
out of colors all the images of things (*rerum imagines*),
whether true or false, which are in our thought (*quae in
cogitatione nostra sunt*) are made.[26]

In these passages, I think Descartes is dimly envisaging a
similarity between the "simple natures" which we know in
mathematical physics (which may be the *quaedam simplicia
et universalia* in question) and the colors themselves. Colors,
in his official, Galilean, metaphysical view, are secondary
qualities waiting upon analysis into simples, but epistemologically they seem, like pain, to have the same sort of primitive inescapability as the simple natures themselves. He
could not make the analogy explicit without setting his
foot on the road toward Lockean empiricism. But neither
could he give it up without falling back into the old Aristotelian distinctions between the sensitive and the intellectual souls. This would have brought back all the pre-
Galilean metaphysics which he wanted to avoid, not to
mention a hylomorphic epistemology impossibly difficult
to reconcile with the explanatory power of Galilean mechanics.[27] In this difficult situation, he allowed, I think,

[26] *Meditation I*, Alquié edition, II, 179.
[27] Thus the following remark of A.G.A. Balz:

I think Descartes would have liked to assert that the intellect alone
is the thinking thing, the unextended immaterial soul substance, attributing to the body imagination, sense, and feeling. But if the pain,
caused by the knife, is not a property of the knife as a constellation
of modes of matter, it cannot be a property of that constellation of
modes of matter that is the human body. So perforce pain and all the
remainder of our immediate experience must be dumped into the

most of the work of changing the notion of "mind" to be done under the table, not by any explicit argument but simply by verbal maneuvers which reshuffled the deck slightly, and slightly differently, at each passage in which the mind-body distinction came to the fore.[28]

If I am right in thinking that Descartes's badly argued hunch, the one which made him able to see pains and thoughts as modes of a single substance, was that indubitability was the common factor they shared with nothing physical, then we can see him as working his way around toward a view in which indubitability is no longer the mark of eternality, but rather of something for which the Greeks had no name—consciousness. Whereas previous philosophers had more or less followed Plato in thinking that only the eternal was known with certainty, Descartes was substituting "clear and distinct perception"—that is, the sort of unconfused knowledge gained by going through a process of analysis—for "indubitability" as a mark of eternal truths. *This left indubitability free to serve as a criterion of the mental.* For although the thought that I am in pain does not count as a clear and distinct perception, it can no more be successfully doubted than the thought that I exist. Whereas Plato and the tradition had made the lines between confusion and clarity, dubitability and indubitability, and the mind and the body coincide, Descartes was

---

soul substance. ("Concerning the Thomistic and Cartesian Dualisms: A Rejoinder to Professor Mourant," *Journal of Philosophy* 54 [1957], 387.)

[28] Such unconscious sleight-of-hand, when practiced by men of Descartes's boldness of imagination, is an occasion for gratitude rather than censure. No great philosopher has avoided it, and no intellectual revolution could succeed without it. In "Kuhnian" terminology, no revolution can succeed which employs a vocabulary commensurable with the old, and thus none can succeed by employing arguments which make unequivocal use of terms shared with the traditional wisdom. So bad arguments for brilliant hunches must necessarily precede the normalization of a new vocabulary which incorporates the hunch. Given that new vocabulary, better arguments become possible, although these will always be found question-begging by the revolution's victims.

now rearranging them. The result was that from Descartes on we have to distinguish between the special metaphysical ground for our certainty about our inner states ("nothing is closer to the mind than itself") and the various epistemological reasons which ground our certainties about anything else. This is why, once this distinction was drawn clearly, and once Descartes's own confusion between certainty that something exists and certainty about its nature was dissipated, empiricism began to edge out rationalism. For our certainty that our concept of "painful" or "blue" signifies something real edges out our certainty that we have a clear and distinct perception of such simple natures as "substance," "thought," and "motion." With Lockean empiricism, foundationalist epistemology emerged as the paradigm of philosophy.[29]

Descartes himself was forever trying to hold on to standard Platonic and scholastic distinctions with one hand while deconstructing them with the other. Thus we find him, when challenged by Hobbes,[30] using the pineal gland to

[29] The discovery of the possibility of an empiricist foundationalism is connected with what Ian Hacking has described in *The Emergence of Probability* (Cambridge, Cambridge University Press, 1975) as the invention of the notion of "evidence" in the modern sense—a notion which was a prerequisite for foundationalist projects, and a fortiori for empiricism. This invention, as well as the eventual triumph of empiricism, was connected with the distinction between the high and low sciences (cf. Hacking, p. 35, and T. S. Kuhn, *The Essential Tension* [Chicago, 1978], chap. 3). A fuller account of these Cartesian shifts would bring these themes together.

[30] See his claim that Hobbes confuses ideas properly so-called with "les images des choses matérielles depeinte en la fantasie corporelle," the latter being the pineal gland, in *Replies to Third Objections*, Alquié edition, II, 611. Margaret Wilson, in "Cartesian Dualism" (in *Descartes: Critical and Interpretive Essays*, ed. Michael Hooker, [Baltimore, 1978]) suggests, on the basis of such passages, that we should be cautious about attributing to him the view that "we clearly and distinctly perceive our sensations apart from any physical state or occurrence." Caution is indeed called for, but this is not to say that there is a way of making Descartes's denial of this claim consistent with the more "mainline" dualistic passages in the *Meditations*. (This essay of Wilson's also makes the useful point that Descartes himself, unlike

reintroduce the distinction between the sensitive and intellective souls, and using it again to recreate the standard Pauline association between the passions and the flesh in *The Passions of the Soul.* But this dissimulation was laughed out of court by, for example, Spinoza, who saw clearly that a confused, but purely mental, idea could do everything which animal spirits or "la fantasie corporelle" could do.[31] Once such second-generation Cartesians, who viewed Descartes himself as having one foot still implanted in the scholastic mud, had purified and "normalized" Cartesian doctrine, we got the full-fledged version of the " 'idea' idea," the one which made it possible for Berkeley to think of extended substance as a hypothesis of which we had no need. This thought could never have occurred to a pre-Cartesian bishop, struggling with the flesh rather than with intellectual confusion. With this full-fledged " 'idea' idea" there came the possibility of philosophy as a discipline which centered around, of all things, epistemology, rather than around God and morality.[32] Even for Descartes himself, the

---

Gassendi, Hobbes, and Spinoza, did not believe in psychophysical parallelism and thus did adopt the view that nonphysical forces operated in the mind which made it impossible to predict thoughts physiologically.)

[31] See Spinoza, *Ethics,* the first and last paragraphs of part III and the discussion of animal spirits in the preface to part v.

[32] This full-fledged " 'idea' idea" (blandly presupposed by Hume in the passage cited in note 18 above) is the one Reid despairingly protested against; in this protest he was preceded by Arnauld and succeeded in later centuries by T. H. Green and by John Austin. John Yolton has pointed out to me a passage in Arnauld's *Des vraies et des fausses idées* (Oeuvres, Paris and Lausanne, 1780, vol. 39, p. 190) which brings in the mirror-imagery (going back to Plato, *Republic* 510a) that I have been treating as the original sin of epistemology:

Since all men were at first infants, and since they then were occupied only with their bodies and with the things which their senses encountered, they spent a long time without knowing of any other sight (*vue*) than the corporeal, which they attribute to their eyes. They could not avoid noticing two facts. The first is that it is necessary that the object be before our eyes if we are to see it. This is

matter of the relation between body and soul was not something for philosophy; philosophy had, so to speak, risen above the practical wisdom sought by the ancients and had become professional, almost as professional as mathematics, whose subject symbolized the indubitability characteristic of the mind. "It is only in daily life and ordinary discourse, abstaining from meditating and studying matters which excite the imagination, that one learns to grasp (*concevoir*) the union of body and soul . . . that union which everyone experiences without philosophizing."[33] The Cartesian change from mind-as-reason to mind-as-inner-arena was not the triumph of the prideful individual subject freed from scholastic shackles so much as the triumph of the quest for certainty over the quest for wisdom. From that time forward, the way was open for philosophers either to attain the rigor of the mathematician or the mathematical physicist, or to explain the appearance of rigor in these fields, rather than to help people attain peace of mind. Science, rather than living, became philosophy's subject, and epistemology its center.

6. DUALISM AND "MIND-STUFF"

I can summarize the result of the previous section by saying the notion of the "separation between mind and

---

what they call presence (*présence*) and this makes them regard the presence of the object as a necessity for sight. The second fact is that we sometimes see visible things in mirrors, or in water, or in other things which represent them. Thus they believe, wrongly, that they do not then see the things themselves, but only their images."

Compare Austin on "the philosophers' use of 'directly perceive' " (*Sense and Sensibilia* [Oxford, 1962], p. 19) and on mirror-images (ibid., pp. 31, 50). For a valuable survey of post-Cartesian accounts of what Descartes should have meant by "idea" (including Arnauld's last-ditch attempt to treat ideas as acts, in the manner of Brentano, Husserl, and G. E. Moore), see Robert McRae, " 'Idea' as a Philosophical term in the 17th Century," *Journal of the History of Ideas* 26 (1965), 175-190.

[33] Letter to Princess Elizabeth, June 28, 1643 (Alquié edition, III, 45), cited in van Peursen, *Body, Soul, Spirit*, p. 25.

body" means different things, and is proved by different philosophical arguments, before and after Descartes. The hylomorphic epistemology which thought of grasping universals as instancing in one's intellect what the frog instanced in its flesh was, thanks to the rise of mathematical physics, being replaced by a law-event framework which explained froghood as possibly a merely "nominal" essence. So the notion of reason as a faculty of grasping universals was not available for use in a premise proving the distinctness of the mind from the body. The notion which would define what could "have a distinct existence from the body" was one which would draw a line between the cramps in one's stomach and the associated feeling in one's mind.

I have suggested that the only criterion which will draw this line is indubitability—that closeness to the Inner Eye which permits Descartes to say (in a sentence which would have astonished Isabella and antiquity) that "nothing is easier for the mind to know than itself."[34] But this may seem strange, since the obvious Cartesian candidate for such a mark would seem to be non-spatiality. Descartes insists over and over again that we can separate mind from "extended substance," thereby viewing it as nonextended substance. Further, the first and most common-sensical rebuttal offered to contemporary philosophers who suggest that pains might be identical with brain processes is drawn straight from Descartes: viz., pains "in" amputated limbs are nonspatial—the argument being that if they had *any* spatial location they would be in an arm, but since there is no arm, they must be of a quite different ontological sort.

---

[34] This passage occurs in a splendid *non sequitur* following the example of the piece of wax in *Meditation* ii: since even bodies are not known *"proprie"* by sense or imagination but only by intellect, it is clear that *nihil facilius aut evidentius mea mente posse a me percipi* (Alquié, II, 192; Haldane and Ross, I, 157). The argument depends upon confusion between the *cogito* as proof of my existence and as isolation of my essence.

Philosophers still insist that "it *makes no sense at all* to locate the occurrence of a thought at some place within your body,"[35] and they tend to attribute this insight to Descartes. But, as I have argued in section 2 above, we would hardly think of a thought or a pain as a *thing* (a particular distinct from a person, rather than a state of a person) which was not locatable unless we already had the notion of a nonextended substance of which it might be a portion. No intuition that pains and thoughts are nonspatial antedates, or can ground an argument for, the Cartesian notion of the mind as a distinct substance (a nonspatial one). There is, however, more to be said about how the notion of "nonspatial substance," and thus of "mindstuff," entered philosophy, and thus about why contemporary philosophy of mind finds itself talking about *pains* and *beliefs* rather than *people having* pains or beliefs. Going over this further material will, I hope, make clearer how very different *Cartesian* dualism is from the "dualism" of contemporary discussions.

We need to bear in mind that the nonspatial substance which Kant and Strawson reject as an incoherent notion was a seventeenth-century notion, and that it is a commonplace of intellectual history that strange things happened to the notion of "substance" in that century. For Aristotle, and still for St. Thomas, the paradigm of a substance was an individual man or frog. Detached parts of men or frogs were, like clumps of turf or pailsful of water, dubious borderline cases—they were "capable of existing separately" in one sense (spatial separation), but they did not have the functional unity or "nature" which proper substances should have. Aristotle, when worried about such cases, was wont to dismiss them as "mere potencies"—as neither accidents, like the frog's color, nor proper actuali-

---

[35] Jerome Shaffer, *Philosophy of Mind* (Englewood Cliffs, N.J., 1968), p. 48; cf. Norman Malcolm, "Scientific Materialism and the Identity Theory," *Dialogue* 3 (1964), 115-125.

ties, like the living, leaping frog itself.[36] Descartes pretends
that he is using "distinct substance" in the standard sense
of "capable of separate existence," but he does not mean
either spatial separation *or* functional unity.[37] He means
something like "capable of having everything else disappear
[or be "thought away"] and still being around."[38] This
definition of "capacity for separate existence" fits the One,
the Platonic Ideas, and Aristotle's Unmoved Movers, but
almost nothing else. Given such a definition, it is hardly
surprising that there should turn out to be, at most, only
three substances—God, mind, and matter. Nor is it surprising that Malebranche and Berkeley should begin to have
doubts about the third candidate, and Spinoza about both
third and second. It would not have occurred to Aristotle
to think that frogs, stars, and men were simply so many accidents of one big substance merely on the ground that if

[36] Cf. *Metaphysics* 1040b, 5-10 on "heaps." I discuss the tension between Aristotle's criteria for being a substance—"separate existence"
and "unity"—in "Genus as Matter," in *Exegesis and Argument: Studies
in Greek Philosophy in Honor of Gregory Vlastos*, ed. Edward N. Lee
et al. (Dordrecht, 1973).

[37] Descartes thinks that a human hand, whether or not detached, is
a perfectly good example of substance. Cf. *Fourth Responses* (Alquié,
II, 663; Haldane and Ross, II, 99), where he says that the sense in which
a hand is an "incomplete substance" is unimportant and is merely a
matter of "not forming a whole distinct from every other thing" (*en un
autre sens on les peut appeler incomplètes, non qu'elles aient rien
d'incomplet en tant qu'elles sont des substances, mais seulement en tant
qu'elles se rapportent à quelqu'autre substance avec laquelle elles com-
posent un tout par soi et distinct de tout autre*). There is, however, a
tension in Descartes between the view that any material thing (a hand,
a dust mote) is a substance and the notion (clear in Spinoza) that these
things are only modes of a larger substance (e.g., matter-as-a-whole).

[38] This definition gives Descartes trouble since it suggests the Spinoza-
istic view that God, on whom everything else must be thought to
depend, is the only substance. The point is discussed by L. J. Beck,
The Metaphysics of Descartes (Oxford, 1965), p. 110, who says: "The
apparent inconsistency in using the word *substantia*, or even *res*, to
connote the self of the *Cogito* is due, in no small measure, to trying to
put new wine into old bottles, to express the Cartesian doctrine in the
technical language of the schools."

we imagine all the other bodies in the world (e.g., earth and air) annihilated, the frog and the human could hardly be imagined to survive. But precisely this notion of one big substance was what was needed to provide a "philosophical foundation" of Galilean mechanics while heaping scorn on traditional hylomorphic explanations.[39] When matter-as-all-the-atoms- (or vortices) -put-together replaced matter-as-potentiality, it was promoted to the rank of substance (absorbing all the old nonhuman Aristotelian substances into itself) and left only Aristotle's "pure actuality" (the νοῦς which is the Unmoved Movers and may not be distinct from the "separable" νοῦς in individual men) as a possible rival in that rank.[40]

We contemporary inheritors of the Cartesian distinction between mind and matter have lost touch with the notion of "substance" in its seventeenth-century definition. The notion of existence a se was never intelligible to the vulgar, and Kant succeeded in making it unintelligible even to professional philosophers. So when we assent to the claim that there is an obvious distinction between a category of things which can exist in space and another category of things which cannot, we are not assenting to Descartes's claim that mind and matter are distinct entities "which depend on nothing else for their existence." Many contemporary philosophers who agree that it is nonsense to

39 Cf. E. A. Burtt, *Metaphysical Foundations of Modern Physical Science* (Garden City, N.Y., 1955), chap. IV. At p. 117 Burtt says, "The fact is, and this is of central importance for our whole study, *Descartes' real criterion is not permanence but the possibility of mathematical handling*; in his case, as with Galileo, the whole course of his thought from his adolescent studies on had inured him to the notion that we know objects only in mathematical terms." The resulting distinction between primary and secondary qualities supplies the motive to regard paradigmatic Aristotelian substances as merely modes of *res extensa*.

40 Cf. *Fourth Responses* (Alquié, II, 662; Haldane and Ross, II, 98) where Descartes says that "*concevoir pleinement*" and "*concevoir que c'est une chose complète*" are synonymous, a point which he thinks helps explain how we grasp that soul and body are two substances.

speak of the location of a pain or a thought nevertheless insist, *pace* Descartes, that a stream of consciousness without a body is unimaginable. Such philosophers are content to think of mental entities as states of persons rather than "bits of ghostly stuff," and to let nonlocatability be a sign of the adjectival status of states rather than of the peculiar makeup of certain particulars. Since a man's build, personality, weight, hilarity, or charm is not capable of being pinpointed in space, why should his beliefs and desires be? So it seems plausible to say that Descartes's insight was merely a recognition of the difference between parts of persons or states of those parts (e.g., cramps of their stomachs) on the one hand and certain states of the whole person on the other, misleadingly stated in a corrupted scholastic vocabulary as a distinction of "substance."

This account of what it means to say that the mind is nonspatial provides a convenient way of simultaneously stating and dissolving *one* mind-body problem. For few people are worried by an ontological gap between what is signified by names and what is signified by adjectives. However, like most behaviorist-style solutions to the mind-body problem, this one has difficulties with thoughts and raw feels—events as opposed to dispositions. It is easy to view beliefs and desires and moods as (in Ryle's phrase) "traits of intellect and character" which require no nonmaterial medium as substrate but only the man himself. It is harder to think of raw feels, mental images, and thoughts this way.[41] They suggest an immaterial stream of consciousness rushing invisibly and intangibly through the interstices of the brain, perhaps—

[41] The point is made in various ways by Hampshire, Austin, and Ayer in their respective reviews of *The Concept of Mind* reprinted in *Ryle: A Collection of Critical Essays*, ed. O. P. Wood and George Pitcher (Garden City, N.Y., 1970). For ways of extending Ryle's methods to perceptions and the associated raw feels, see Pitcher, *A Theory of Perception*. On perceptions as dispositions to belief, and the discussion of "adverbial materialism," see James Cornman, *Materialism and Sensations* (New Haven, 1971). See also Richard Rorty, "Incorrigibility as the Mark of the Mental," *Journal of Philosophy* 67 (1970), 406-409.

because it seems so natural to regard them as things rather than states of things. So contemporary philosophers, returning to an Aristotelian and vulgar notion of "thing" instead of Descartes's sophisticated and extravagant notion of "substance," are inclined to split the difference between Aristotle and Descartes. That is, they think that Aristotle neglected certain particulars—for example, pains and raw feels—whereas Descartes pointlessly took them to be accidents of one big nonextended substance, just as he took frogs and atoms to be accidental configurations of one big extended substance called Matter. This permits contemporary philosophers to have mental entities without the soul, and thus without appearing to be haunted by the Invisible and Intangible Man of religious belief (a notion which they read into Descartes—not without some encouragement from Descartes himself).

This dualism based on "separate existence from the body" —a fourth sort—is quite different from the dualism between a person and his ghost, or between a person and his Aristotelian passive intellect, or between *res cogitans* and *res extensa*. But it is also a partial dualism—as partial, in equal and opposite ways, as that of the ancients. Whereas the ancients took only the universal-grasping part of Descartes's nonextended substance as "separately existing," contemporary dualists (conceding beliefs, desires, and the like to Ryle as ways of speaking of dispositions) take only event-like candidates for mentality as "separately existing." Whereas Thomists, for example, accuse Descartes of having pointlessly endowed sense with the immateriality which is the prerogative of reason, contemporary dualists accuse him of having pointlessly endowed mathematical knowledge and decisions on conduct with the immaterial thinghood which belongs to pains, after-images, and occurrent thoughts. For the ancients, the mind was most obviously capable of separate existence when it contemplated the unchanging and was itself unchanging. For the moderns, it is most obviously so capable when it is a blooming, buzzing collection of raw

67

feels.[42] Whoever is right, it is clear that neither ancients nor moderns share Descartes's "clear and distinct perception" of the separability of *all* the items he lumped together under "thinking."

Descartes's only improvement on the Homeric notion of an Invisible and Intangible Man was to strip the intruder of humanoid form. By thus making the possible intruders among bodies less easily identifiable, he made them more philosophical. They were more philosophical in that, like the νοῦς of Aristotle and the Glassy Essence of Isabella, they were not shady homunculi, but rather essentially unpicturable entities. Since to be concerned with philosophical matters was to be concerned with that which the eye cannot see nor the ear hear, both seventeenth-century nonextended substance and contemporary nonlocatable thoughts and feels were thought to be more philosophically respectable than the ghosts for whose peace religious believers pray. But contemporary philosophers, having updated Descartes, can be dualists without their dualism making the slightest difference to any human interest or concern, without interfering with science or lending any support to religion. For insofar as dualism reduces to the bare insistence that pains and thoughts have no places, nothing whatever hangs on the distinction between mind and body.

Let me now remind the reader of the course I have followed in this chapter. In sections 1–2 I argued that we could make no sense of the notion of "mental entities" as a distinct ontological genus without invoking the notion of "phenomenal entities" such as pains, entities whose being was exhausted by the single property of, for example, painfulness. I claimed that the real problem was not to abjure such

[42] "Whereas, for Plato, rational thoughts were the paradigmatic activities of the soul, such lowly events as itches, toothaches, and twinges are now among those typically mentioned in philosophical discussion as mental events" (Jaegwon Kim, "Materialism and the Criteria of the Mental," *Synthese* 22 [1971], 336).

INVENTION OF THE MIND

hypostatized universals but to explain why anyone had taken them seriously, and how they came to seem relevant to discussions of the nature of personhood and of reason. I hope that sections 3–6 have given an idea of how I think these historical questions can be answered (although I am painfully aware of the lacunae in the story I have told). My answer to the question "Why do we tend to lump the intentional and the phenomenal together as 'the mental'?" is that Descartes used the notion of the "incorrigibly known" to bridge the gap between them. So I now need to spell out more fully my own anti-Cartesian, Wittgensteinian, view of the nature of "our privileged access to the mental." In the following chapter, therefore, I put aside personhood and reason, and discuss consciousness almost exclusively. I shall try to show that the purportedly metaphysical "problem of consciousness" is no more and no less than the epistemological "problem of privileged access," and that once this is seen questions about dualism versus materialism lose their interest.

CHAPTER II

Persons Without Minds

1. THE ANTIPODEANS

Far away, on the other side of our galaxy, there was a planet on which lived beings like ourselves—featherless bipeds who built houses and bombs, and wrote poems and computer programs. These beings did not know that they had minds. They had notions like "wanting to" and "intending to" and "believing that" and "feeling terrible" and "feeling marvelous." But they had no notion that these signified *mental* states—states of a peculiar and distinct sort—quite different from "sitting down," "having a cold," and "being sexually aroused." Although they used the notions of believing and knowing and wanting and being moody of their pets and their robots as well as of themselves, they did not regard pets or robots as included in what was meant when they said, "We all believe . . ." or "We never do such things as. . . ." That is to say, they treated only members of their own species as *persons*. But they did not explain the difference between persons and non-persons by such notions as "mind," "consciousness," "spirit," or anything of the sort. They did not *explain* it at all; they just treated it as the difference between "us" and everything else. They believed in immortality for themselves, and a few believed that this would be shared by the pets or the robots, or both. But this immortality did not involve the notion of a "soul" which separated from the body. It was a straightforward matter of bodily resurrection followed by mysterious and instantaneous motion to what they referred to as "a place above the heavens" for good people, and to a sort of cave, beneath the planet's surface, for the wicked. Their philosophers were concerned primarily with four topics: the nature of Being, proofs of the existence of a Benevolent and

Omnipotent Being who would carry out arrangements for the resurrection, problems arising out of discourse about nonexistent objects, and the reconciliation of conflicting moral intuitions. But these philosophers had not formulated the problem of subject and object, nor that of mind and matter. There was a tradition of Pyrrhonian skepticism, but Locke's "veil of ideas" was unknown, since the notion of an "idea" or "perception" or "mental representation" was also unknown. Some of their philosophers predicted that the beliefs about immortality which had been central in earlier periods of history, and which were still held by all but the intelligentsia, would someday be replaced by a "positivistic" culture purged of all superstitions (but these philosophers made no mention of an intervening "metaphysical" stage).

In most respects, then, the language, life, technology, and philosophy of this race were much like ours. But there was one important difference. Neurology and biochemistry had been the first disciplines in which technological breakthroughs had been achieved, and a large part of the conversation of these people concerned the state of their nerves. When their infants veered toward hot stoves, mothers cried out, "He'll stimulate his C-fibers." When people were given clever visual illusions to look at, they said, "How odd! It makes neuronic bundle G-14 quiver, but when I look at it from the side I can see that it's not a red rectangle at all." Their knowledge of physiology was such that each well-formed sentence in the language which anybody bothered to form could easily be correlated with a readily identifiable neural state. This state occurred whenever someone uttered, or was tempted to utter, or heard, the sentence. This state also sometimes occurred in solitude and people reported such occasions with remarks like "I was suddenly in state S-296, so I put out the milk bottles." Sometimes they would say things like "It looked like an elephant, but then it struck me that elephants don't occur on this continent, so I realized that it must be a mastodon." But they would also

71

sometimes say, in just the same circumstances, things like "I had G-412 together with F-11, but then I had S-147, so I realized that it must be a mastodon." They thought of mastodons and milk bottles as objects of beliefs and desires, and as causing certain neural processes. They viewed these neural processes as interacting causally with beliefs and desires—in just the same way as the mastodons and milk bottles did. Certain neural processes could be deliberately self-induced, and some people were more skillful than others in inducing certain neural states in themselves. Others were skilled at detecting certain special states which most people could not recognize in themselves.

In the middle of the twenty-first century, an expedition from Earth landed on this planet. The expedition included philosophers, as well as representatives of every other learned discipline. The philosophers thought that the most interesting thing about the natives was their lack of the concept of mind. They joked among themselves that they had landed among a bunch of materialists, and suggested the name Antipodea for the planet—in reference to an almost forgotten school of philosophers, centering in Australia and New Zealand, who in the previous century had attempted one of the many futile revolts against Cartesian dualism in the history of Terran philosophy. The name stuck, and so the new race of intelligent beings came to be known as Antipodeans. The Terran neurologists and biochemists were fascinated by the wealth of knowledge in their field which the Antipodeans exhibited. Since technical conversation on these subjects was conducted almost entirely in offhand references to neural states, the Terran experts eventually picked up the ability to report their own neural states (without conscious inference) instead of reporting their thoughts, perceptions, and raw feels. (The physiologies of the two species were, fortunately, almost identical.) Everything went swimmingly, except for the difficulties met by the philosophers.

The philosophers who had come on the expedition were,

as usual, divided into two warring camps: the tender-minded ones who thought philosophy should aim at Significance, and the tough-minded philosophers who thought that it should aim at Truth. The philosophers of the first sort felt that there was no real problem about whether the Antipodeans had minds. They held that what was important in understanding other beings was a grasp of their mode of being-in-the-world. It became evident that, whatever *Existentiale* the Antipodeans were using, they certainly did not include any of those which, a century earlier, Heidegger had criticized as "subjectivist." The whole notion of "the epistemological subject," or the person as spirit, had no place in their self-descriptions, nor in their philosophies. Some of the tender-minded philosophers felt that this showed that the Antipodeans had not yet broken out of Nature into Spirit, or, more charitably, had not yet progressed from Consciousness to Self-Consciousness. These philosophers became town-criers of inwardness, attempting to bully the Antipodeans across an invisible line and into the Realm of Spirit. Others, however, felt that the Antipodeans exhibited the praiseworthy grasp of the union of πόλεμος and λόγος which was lost to Western Terran consciousness through Plato's assimilation of οὐσία to ἰδέα. The Antipodean failure to grasp the notion of mind, in the view of this set of philosophers, showed their closeness to Being and their freedom from the temptations to which Terran thought had long since succumbed. In the contest between these two views, equally tender-minded as both were, discussion tended to be inconclusive. The Antipodeans themselves were not much help, because they had so much trouble translating the background reading necessary to appreciate the problem—Plato's *Theaetetus*, Descartes's *Meditations*, Hume's *Treatise*, Kant's *Critique of Pure Reason*, Hegel's *Phenomenology*, Strawson's *Individuals*, etc.

The tough-minded philosophers, as usual, found a much more straightforward and clean-cut question to discuss. They did not care what the Antipodeans thought about themselves, but rather focused on the question: Do they in fact have minds? In their precise way, they narrowed this question down to: Do they in fact have sensations? It was thought that if it became clear whether they had, say, sensations of pain, as well as stimulated C-fibers, when touching hot stoves, everything else would be plain sailing. It was clear that the Antipodeans had the same behavioral dispositions toward hot stoves, muscle cramps, torture, and the like as humans. They loathed having their C-fibers stimulated. But the tough-minded philosophers asked themselves: Does their experience contain the same phenomenal properties as ours? Does the stimulation of C-fibers feel painful? Or does it feel some other, equally awful, way? Or does feeling not come into it at all? These philosophers were not surprised that the Antipodeans could offer noninferential reports of their own neural states, since it had been learned long since that psychophysiologists could train human subjects to report alpha-rhythms, as well as various other physiologically describable cortical states. But they felt baffled by the question: Are some phenomenal properties being detected by an Antipodean who says, "It's my C-fibers again—you know, the ones that go off every time you get burned or hit or have a tooth pulled. It's just awful."?

It was suggested that the question could only be answered experimentally, and so they arranged with the neurologists that one of their number should be wired up to an Antipodean volunteer so as to switch currents back and forth between various regions of the two brains. This, it was thought, would also enable the philosophers to insure that the Antipodeans did not have an inverted spectrum, or anything else which might confuse the issue. As it turned out, however, the experiment produced no interesting results. The difficulty was that when the Antipodean speech center got an input from the C-fibers of the Earthling brain it always talked only about its C-fibers, whereas when the Earthling speech center was in control it always talked only about pain. When the Antipodean speech center was asked what the C-fibers felt like it said that it didn't quite get the notion of "feeling," but that stimulated C-fibers were, of course, terrible things to have. The same sort of thing happened for the questions about inverted spectra and other perceptual qualities. When asked to call off the colors on a chart, both speech centers called off the usual color-names in the same order. But the Antipodean speech center could also call off the various neuronic bundles activated by each patch on the chart (no matter which visual cortex it happened to be hooked up to). When the Earthling speech center was asked what the colors were like when transmitted to the Antipodean visual cortex, it said that they seemed just as usual.

This experiment seemed not to have helped. For it was still obscure whether the Antipodeans had pains. It was equally obscure whether they had one or two raw feels when indigo light streamed onto their retinas (one of indigo, and one of neural state C-692)—or whether they had no raw feels at all. The Antipodeans were repeatedly questioned about how they knew it was indigo. They replied that they could see that it was. When asked how they knew they were in C-692, they said they "just knew" it. When it was suggested to them that they might have unconsciously inferred that it was indigo on the basis of the C-692 feel, they seemed unable to understand what unconscious inference was, or what "feels" were. When it was suggested to them that they might have made the same inference to the fact that they were in state C-692 on the basis of the raw feel of indigo, they were, of course, equally baffled. When they were asked whether the neural state appeared indigo, they replied that it did not—the *light* was indigo—and that the questioner must be making some sort of category mistake. When they were asked whether they could imagine having C-692 and not seeing indigo, they said they could not. When asked whether it was a conceptual truth or an empirical generalization that these two experiences went together, they replied that they were not sure how to tell the difference. When asked

75

whether they could be wrong about whether they were seeing indigo, they replied that they of course could, but could not be wrong about whether they seemed to be seeing indigo. When asked whether they could be wrong about whether they were in state C-692, they replied in exactly the same way. Finally, skillful philosophical dialectic brought them to realize that what they could not imagine was seeming to see indigo and failing to seem to be in state C-692. But this result did not seem to help with the questions: "Raw feels?" "Two raw feels or one?" "Two referents or one referent under two descriptions?" Nor did any of this help with the question about the way in which stimulated C-fibers appeared to them. When they were asked whether they could be mistaken in thinking that their C-fibers were stimulated, they replied that of course they could—but that they could not imagine being mistaken about whether their C-fibers seemed to be stimulated.

At this point, it occurred to someone to ask whether they could detect the neural state which was the concomitant of "seeming to have their C-fibers stimulated." Antipodeans replied that there was, of course, the state T-435 which was the constant neural concomitant of the utterance of the sentence "My C-fibers seem to be stimulated," state T-497 which went with "It's just as if my C-fibers were being stimulated," state T-293 which went with "Stimulated C-fibers!" and various other neural states which were concomitants of various other roughly synonymous sentences—but that there was no further neural state which they were aware of in addition to these. Cases in which Antipodeans had T-435 but no stimulation of C-fibers included those in which, for example, they were strapped to what they were falsely informed was a torture machine, a switch was theatrically turned on, but nothing else was done.

Discussion among the philosophers now switched to the topic: Could the Antipodeans be mistaken about the T-series of neural states (the ones which were concomitants of understanding or uttering sentences)? Could they seem to be having T-435 but not really be? Yes, the Antipodeans said, cerebroscopes indicated that sort of thing occasionally happened. Was there any explanation of the cases in which it happened—any pattern to them? No, there did not seem to be. It was just one of those odd things that turned up occasionally. Neurophysiology had not yet been able to find another sort of neural state, outside the T-series, which was a concomitant of such weird illusions, any more than for certain perceptual illusions, but perhaps it would someday.

This answer left the philosophers still in difficulties on the question of whether the Antipodeans had sensations of pain, or anything else. For there now seemed to be nothing which the Antipodeans were incorrigible about except how things seemed to them. But it was not clear that "how things seemed to them" was a matter of what raw feels they had, as opposed to what they were inclined to say. If they had the raw feel of painfulness, then they had minds. But a raw feel is (or has) a phenomenal property—one which you cannot have the illusion of having (because, so to speak, having the illusion of it is itself to have *it*). The difference between stimulated C-fibers and pains was that you could have the illusion of stimulated C-fibers (could have, e.g., T-435) without having stimulated C-fibers, but could not have the illusion of pain without having pain. There was nothing which the Antipodeans could not be wrong about except how things seemed to them. But the fact that they could not "merely seem to have it seem to them that . . ." was of no interest in determining whether they had minds. The fact that "seems to seem . . ." is an expression without a use is a fact about the notion of "appearance," not a tip-off to the presence of "phenomenal properties." For the appearance-reality distinction is not based on a distinction between subjective representations and objective states of affairs; it is merely a matter of getting something wrong, having a false belief. So the Antipodeans' firm grasp of the former distinction did not help philosophers tell whether to ascribe the latter to them.

2. PHENOMENAL PROPERTIES

Coming back now to the present, what *should* we say about the Antipodeans? The first thing to do, presumably, is to look more closely at the notion of "phenomenal property," and in particular at the disanalogy between apprehending a physical phenomenon in a misleading way and apprehending a mental phenomenon in a misleading way. Kripke's account of the distinction sums up the intuition on which defenders of dualism have usually relied, so we may begin a closer look by trying to apply his terminology:

> Someone can be in the same epistemic situation as he would be if there were heat, even in the absence of heat, simply by feeling the sensation of heat; and even in the presence of heat, he can have the same evidence as he would have in the absence of heat simply by lacking the sensation S. No such possibility exists in the case of pain or in other mental phenomena. To be in the same epistemic situation that would obtain if one had a pain *is* to have a pain; to be in the same epistemic situation that would obtain in the absence of a pain *is* not to have a pain. . . . The trouble is that the notion of an epistemic situation qualitatively identical to one in which the observer had a sensation S simply *is* one in which the observer had that sensation. The same point can be made in terms of the notion of what picks out the reference of a rigid designator [an expression which designates the same object in all the possible worlds in which it designates at all]. In the case of identity of heat with molecular motion the important consideration was that although "heat" is a rigid designator, the reference of that designator was determined by an accidental property of the referent, namely the property of producing in us the sensation S. . . . Pain, on the other hand, is not picked out by one of its accidental properties; rather it is picked out by the property of being pain itself, by its immediate phenomenological quality. Thus pain, unlike heat, is not only rigidly

designated by "pain" but the reference of the designator is determined by an essential property of the referent. Thus it is not possible to say that although pain is necessarily identical with a certain physical state, a certain phenomenon can be picked out in the same way we pick out pain without being correlated with that physical state. If any phenomenon is picked out in exactly the same way that we pick out pain, then that phenomenon *is* pain.[1]

These considerations suggest that the real question is: Do the Antipodeans pick out mental phenomena by accidental properties? If we assume for the moment that they *do* have pains, could they perhaps miss the "immediate phenomenological quality" and note only the accidental feature of being constantly accompanied by stimulated C-fibers? Or, if they cannot exactly *miss* an immediate phenomenological quality, might they perhaps fail to have a name for it, and thus fail to pick out the entity that has the quality by an essential property? To put it another way, since the Antipodeans do *not* pick out pain "in exactly the same way that we pick out pain," can we conclude that whatever they have it is *not* pain? Is one's epistemic relation to one's raw feels necessary as well as sufficient to establish the existence of the raw feel in question? Or should we say that actually they *do* pick out pain in exactly the way that we do—because when they say, "Ooh! Stimulated C-fibers!" they feel exactly what we feel when we say, "Pain!"? Actually, perhaps, they were feeling pain and calling that feeling "the state of seeming to have one's C-fibers stimulated," and they are in the same epistemic situation relative to seeming to have their C-fibers stimulated as we are in seeming to see something red, and to all other such incorrigible states.

1 Saul Kripke, "Naming and Necessity" in *Semantics of Natural Language*, ed. Donald Davidson and Gilbert Harman (Dordrecht, 1972), pp. 339-340. For criticism of Kripke's discussion of dualism and materialism, see Fred Feldman, "Kripke on the Identity Theory," and William Lycan, "Kripke and the Materialists," both in *Journal of Philosophy* 71 (1974), 665-689.

It now looks as if what we need is some quite general
criterion for deciding when two things are "really" the same
thing described in two different ways. For there seems
nothing distinctive about the present conundrum which
makes it depend upon the peculiarities of the mental. If
we agree that what counts in deciding whether the Antipodeans have raw feels is incorrigibility—the inability to
have an illusion of . . .—the general problem about alternative descriptions will still prevent us from applying this
criterion and thus resolving the issue. This problem is not
one which is going to receive a neat, clear-cut, readily ap-
plicable solution. For nothing general will resolve every
tension between saying,

> You're talking about X's all right, but practically every-
> thing you say about them is false

and saying instead,

> Since practically nothing you say is true of X's, you can't
> be talking about X's.

But let us put aside this difficulty for the moment (returning to it in chapter six) and consider the still more depress-
ing point that anyone who even tried to state general
criteria for assimilating or distinguishing referents of expressions would need some general ontological categories—
some firm, if coarse, way of blocking things out—just to get
started. It would help, in particular, to have a distinction
between mental entities and physical entities. But the problem about the Antipodeans puts this whole distinction in
doubt. To see why it does so, suppose that there are no
criteria for "mental phenomenon" save Kripke's epistemic
one.[2] This supposition identifies "the mental" with raw
feels, passing thoughts, and mental images. It excludes such

[2] I defended a qualified form of this supposition in "Incorrigibility
as the Mark of the Mental," *Journal of Philosophy* 67 (1970), 399-424.
See also Jaegwon Kim, "Materialism and the Criteria of the Mental,"
Synthese 22 (1972), 323-345, esp. 336-341.

things as beliefs, moods, and the like (which, though indubitably "higher," are nonetheless not parts of our incorrigibly reportable inner life, and hence not such as to encourage the Cartesian kind of distinction between two ontological realms). The supposal amounts, in other words, to the claim that (1) it is sufficient for being a mental state that the thing in question be incorrigibly knowable by its possessor, and (2) we do not literally attribute any nonphysical states (e.g., beliefs) to beings which fail to have some such incorrigibly knowable states. (This conforms to Antipodean practice, as well as to our intuition that dogs have nonphysical states simply by virtue of having pains, whereas computers do not, even by virtue of offering us novel and exciting truths.) On this supposition, then, there will be *nothing* to answer to the question "When they report that their C-fibers seem to be firing, are they reporting a feeling (perhaps the same feeling that we report by "pain!") or are they just making the noises which are triggered by their neurons being in certain states?" And if this is so, since the role played in our lives by reports of feelings is the same as the role played in Antipodean lives by reports of neurons, we face the further question: Are *we* reporting feelings or neurons when *we* use "pain"?

To see that this is a real issue, consider the implications of the identity of functional role. If it is the case that the Antipodeans have the entire range of culture that we do, if they are as intentional in their discourse and as self-consciously aesthetic in their choice of objects and persons as we, if their yearning for moral excellence and immortality is as great, they are likely to think our philosophers' interest in whether they have minds is a bit parochial. Why, they wonder, does it make such a difference? Why, they may ask us, do *we* think that we have these odd things called "feels" and "minds"? Now that they have taught us micro-neurology, cannot we see that talk of mental states was merely a place-holder for talk of neurons? Or, if we really do have some funny extra states besides the neurological ones, are they really all that important? Is the possession of such states really the basis for a distinction between ontological categories?

These last sets of questions illustrate how lightly the Antipodeans take the controversy which, among Terran philosophers, is the hard-fought issue between materialists and epiphenomenalists. Further, the success of Antipodean neurology, not only in the explanation and control of behavior but in supplying the vocabulary for the Antipodean self-image, shows that none of the other Terran theories about "the relation between mind and body" can even get a look-in. For parallelism and epiphenomenalism can only be differentiated on some non-Humean view of causation—some view according to which there is a causal mechanism to be discovered which will show which way causal lines run. But nobody, not even the most diehard Cartesian, imagines that when a molecule-by-molecule account of the neurons is before us (as, *ex hypothesi*, it is before the Antipodeans) there will still be a place to look for further causal mechanisms. (What would "looking" amount to?) So even if we abandon Hume, we are still in no position to be parallelist, except on some a priori ground according to which we "just know" that the mental is a self-contained causal realm. As for interactionism, the Antipodeans would not dream of denying that beliefs and desires, for example, interact causally with irradiations of the retina, movements of the arm, and so on. But they view talk of such an interaction not as yoking different ontological realms but as a handy (because brief) reference to function rather than to structure. (It is as philosophically unproblematic as a transaction between a government and an individual. No set of necessary and sufficient conditions stated in terms of just who did what to whom can be given for a remark about such a transaction, any more than for remarks about beliefs caused by radiations and movements caused by beliefs—but who would have thought they could?) Interaction would only be of interest if a neural discharge were swerved from its course by a raw feel, or drained of some of its power by a raw feel, or something of the sort. But the Antipodean neurologists have no need of such hypotheses.

If there is no way of explaining to the Antipodeans our problems and theories about mind and body—no way of making them see that this is the paradigm case of an ontological divide—we ought to be prepared to face up to the possibility that the "materialist" Antipodeans (as opposed to the more charitable "epiphenomenalist" ones) are right: we have just been reporting neurons when we thought we were reporting raw feels. It was just a happenstance of our cultural development that we got stuck so long with placeholders. It is as if, while perfecting many sublunary disciplines, we had never developed astronomy and had remained pre-Ptolemaic in our notions of what was above the moon. We would doubtless have many complicated things to say about holes in the black dome, movements of the dome as a whole, and the like—but once we were clued in we could redescribe what we had been reporting easily enough.

At this point, however, there is a familiar objection to be dealt with. It is expressed in such remarks as the following:

> . . . in the case of stabbing pains, it is not possible to hold that the micro-picture is the real picture, that perceptual appearances are only a coarse duplication, for in this case we are dealing with the perceptual appearances themselves, which cannot very well be a coarse duplicate of themselves.[3]

It is all very well to claim that hurtfulness is how activity of the C-fibers in the cortex appears, that the smell of onion is how the shape of onion molecules appears to a human with a normal nasal system. . . . This deals with the pain, smell or color apprehended and, relegating it to the category of appearance, renders it ontically neutral.

[3] Richard Brandt, "Doubts about the Identity Theory," in *Dimensions of Mind*, ed. Sidney Hook (New York, 1961), p. 70.

But it leaves us with a set of *seemings*, acts of imperfect apprehension, in which the phenomenal properties are grasped. So we must ask the new question: Is it possible that things can *seem to be* in a certain way to a merely material system? Is there a way in which acts of imperfect apprehension can be seen to be ontically neutral?

. . . The materialist account of real men can find no place for the fact that our imperfect apprehension is by phenomenal property and not by, for example, beliefs just spontaneously arising.[4]

This objection common to Brandt and Campbell seems at first blush to be that one can only misdescribe things if one is not a "merely material system"—for such systems cannot have things appear to them differently from what they are. But this will not do as it stands, for, as I suggested earlier, the distinction between reality and appearance seems merely the distinction between getting things right and getting things wrong—a distinction which we have no trouble making for simple robots, servo-mechanisms, etc. To make the objection plausible we must say that "appearance" in the present context is a richer notion—one which has to be explicated by the notion of "phenomenal property." We must hold some principle like:

(P) Whenever we make an incorrigible report on a state of ourselves, there must be a property we are presented with which induces us to make the report.

But this principle, of course, enshrines the Cartesian notion that "nothing is closer to the mind than itself," and involves an entire epistemology and metaphysics, a specifically dualistic one.[5] So it is not surprising, once we have encapsu-

[4] Keith Campbell, *Body and Mind* (New York, 1960), pp. 106-107, 109.

[5] George Pitcher has worked out an account of the linguistic behavior we display in reporting pains without using such a premise. Pitcher takes pains to be reports of damaged peripheral tissue, whereas the Antipodeans take them to be reports of states of the central nervous

lated this view in the notion of "phenomenal property," that "the materialist account . . . can find no place for the fact that our imperfect apprehension is by phenomenal property."

Still, we must ask whether there is some pre-philosophical intuition which is preserved in (P) and which can be separated from the Cartesian picture. What exactly is the difference between misdescribing something like a star and misdescribing something like a pain? Why does the former seem obviously possible and the latter unimaginable? Perhaps the answer goes something like this. We expect the star to look the same even after we realize that it is a faraway ball of flame rather than a nearby hole, but the pain ought to feel different once we realize that it is a stimulated C-fiber, for the pain *is* a feeling, as the star is *not* a visual appearance. If we give this answer, however, we are still stuck with the notion of "feeling" and with the puzzle about whether the Antipodeans have any feelings. What, we must ask, is the difference between feeling a pain and simply reacting to a stimulated C-fiber with the vocable "pain," avoidance-behavior, and the like? And here we are inclined to say: no difference at all from the outside, but all the difference in the world from the inside. The difficulty is that there will

system. In his view, it is a mistake to think of the common-sense concept of pain as the concept of a mental particular. I would want to say that it *is* the concept of a mental particular, but claim that his analysis of the epistemological status of pains applies, *mutatis mutandis*, equally well wherever one stands on this question. See Pitcher, "Pain Perception," *Philosophical Review* 79 (1970), 368-393. Pitcher's general strategy is a defense of direct realism and is also found in his *A Theory of Perception* (Princeton, 1971) and in D. M. Armstrong, *Perception and the Physical World* (London and New York, 1961) and *A Materialist Theory of the Mind* (London and New York, 1968). This strategy seems to me essentially right, and enough to show that the mental-particular view is optional. But I am dubious about Pitcher's and Armstrong's metaphilosophical stance, which would make this view a philosopher's misconstrual of what we believe, rather than a correct account of what we believe (but need not continue to believe).

never be any way in which we can explain this difference to the Antipodeans. The materialist Antipodeans think that we don't have any feelings, because they do not think there is such a thing as "feeling." The epiphenomenalist Antipodeans think that there may be such things, but cannot imagine why we make such a fuss about having them. The Terran philosophers who think that Antipodeans do have feelings but don't know it have reached the terminal stage of philosophizing mentioned by Wittgenstein: they just feel like uttering an inarticulate sound. They cannot even say to the Antipodeans that "it's different for us on the inside" because the Antipodeans do not understand the notion of "inner space"; they think "inside" means "inside the skull." *There*, they rightly remark, it *isn't* different. The Terran philosophers who think that the Antipodeans don't have feelings are in a better position only because they feel it beneath their dignity to argue with mindless beings about whether they have minds.

We seem to be getting nowhere with pursuing the objection offered by Brandt and Campbell. Let us try another tack. In the materialist view, every appearance of anything is going to be, in reality, a brain-state. So, it would seem, the materialist is going to have to say that the "coarse" duplicate of a brain-state (the way stimulated C-fibers feel) is going to be another brain-state. But, we may then say, let that other brain-state be the referent of "pain" rather than the stimulated C-fibers. Every time the materialist says "but that's just our description of a brain-state," his opponent will reply, "Okay, let's talk about the brain-state which is the 'act of imperfect apprehension' of the first brain-state."[6] And so the materialist seems to be pressed ever backward— with the mental cropping up again wherever error does. It is as if man's Glassy Essence, the Mirror of Nature, only became visible to itself when slightly clouded. A neural

---

[6] I owe this way of putting the Brandt-Campbell point to Thomas Nagel.

system can't have clouds but a mind can. So minds, we conclude, cannot be neural systems.

Consider now how the Antipodeans would view "acts of imperfect apprehension." They would see them not as cloudy portions of the Mirror of Nature but as a result of learning a second-rate language. The whole notion of incorrigibly knowable entities, as opposed to being incorrigible about how entities seem to be—the notion of "seemings" as themselves a kind of entity—strikes them as a deplorable way of speaking. The whole Terran vocabulary of "acts of apprehension," "cognitive states," "feelings," etc. strikes them as an unfortunate turn for a language to have taken. They see no way of getting us out of it except by proposing that we raise some of our children to speak Antipodean and see whether they don't do as well as a control group. The Antipodean materialists, in other words, see our notion of "mind and matter" as a reflection of an unfortunate linguistic development. The Antipodean epiphenomenalists are baffled by the question "What is the neural input to the Terrestrial speech center which produces pain reports as well as C-fiber reports?" Those Terrestrial philosophers who think that Antipodeans do have feelings think that the Antipodean language is "inadequate to reality." Those Terrestrial philosophers who think that the Antipodeans don't have feelings rest their case on a theory of language-development according to which the first things named are the things "better known to us"—raw feels—so that the absence of a name for feeling entails the absence of feeling.

To sharpen the issue a bit further, perhaps we may drop from consideration the Antipodean epiphenomenalists and the Terrestrial skeptics. The former's problem about the neurology of pain reports seems insoluble; if they are to continue charitably to ascribe states to Earthmen which are unknown to Antipodeans they will have to swallow a whole dualistic system, irrefutable by further empirical inquiry, in order to explain our linguistic behavior. As for the Terran skeptic's claim that the Antipodeans have no raw feels, this is based entirely on the a priori dictum that one cannot have a raw feel and lack a word for it. Neither intellectual position—the extreme charity of the Antipodean epiphenomenalist and the parochial distrust of the Terrestrial skeptic—is attractive. We are left with the Antipodean materialist saying "They think they have feelings but they don't" on the one hand and Terrestrial philosophers saying "They have feelings but don't know it" on the other hand. Is there a way out of this impasse, given that every empirical result (brain-switching, etc.) seems to weigh equally on both sides? Are there powerful philosophical methods which will cut through the problem and either settle it or offer some happy compromise?

3. Incorrigibility and Raw Feels

One philosophical method which will do no good at all is "analysis of meanings." Everybody understands everybody else's meanings very well indeed. The problem is that one side thinks there are too many meanings around and the other side too few. In this respect the closest analogy one can find is the conflict between inspired theists and uninspired atheists. An inspired theist, let us say, is one who "just knows" that there are supernatural beings which play certain explanatory roles in accounting for natural phenomena. (They are not to be confused with natural theologians—who offer the supernatural as the best explanation of these phenomena.) Inspired theists have inherited their picture of the universe as divided into two great ontological realms—the supernatural and the natural—along with their language. The way they talk about things is inextricably tied up with—or at least strikes them as inextricably tied up with—references to the divine. The notion of the supernatural does not strike them as a "theory" any more than the notion of the mental strikes us as a "theory." When they encounter atheists they view them as people who don't know what's going on, although they admit that atheists seem able to predict and control natural phenomena very nicely indeed. ("Thank heaven," they say, "that we are not as those natural theologians are, or we too might lose touch with the real.") The atheists view these theists as having too many words in their language and too many meanings to bother about. Enthusiastic atheists explain to inspired theists that " all there *really* is is . . . ," and the theists reply that one should realize that there are more things in heaven and earth. . . . And so it goes. The philosophers on both sides may analyze meanings until they are blue in the face, but all such analyses are either "directional" and "reductive" (e.g., "noncognitive" analyses of religious discourse, which are the analogue of "expressive" theories of pain reports) or else simply describe alternative "forms of life," culminating in nothing more helpful than the announcement: "This language-game is played." The theists' game is essential to their self-image, just as the image of man's Glassy Essence is essential to the Western intellectual's, but neither has a larger context available in which to evaluate this image. Where, after all, would such a context come from?

Well, perhaps from philosophy. When experiment and "meaning analysis" fail, philosophers have traditionally turned to system-building—inventing a new context on the spot, so to speak. The usual strategy is to find a compromise which will enable both those who favor Occam's Razor (e.g., materialists, atheists) and those who cling to what they "just know" to be viewed indulgently as having achieved "alternate perspectives" on some larger reality which philosophy has just adumbrated. Thus some tenderminded philosophers have risen above the "warfare between science and theology" and seen Bonaventure and Bohr as possessing different, noncompetitive "forms of consciousness." The question "consciousness of *what?*" is answered by something like "the world" or "the thing-in-itself" or "the sensible manifold" or "stimulations." It does not matter which of these is offered, since all are terms of art designed to name entities with no interesting features save placid neutrality. The analogue of this tactic among tough-minded philosophers of mind is neutral monism, in which the mental and the physical are seen as two "aspects" of some underlying reality which need not be described further. Sometimes we are told that this reality is intuited (Bergson) or is identical with the raw material of sensation (Russell, Ayer), but sometimes it is simply postulated as the only means of avoiding epistemological skepticism (James, Dewey). In no case are we told anything about it save that "we just know what it's like" or that reason (i.e., the need to avoid philosophical dilemmas) requires it. Neutral monists like to suggest that philosophy has discovered, or should look for, an underlying substrate, in the same way in which the scientist has discovered molecules beneath elements, atoms beneath molecules, and so on. But in fact the "neutral stuff" which is neither mental nor physical is not found to have powers or properties of its own, but simply postulated and then forgotten about (or, what comes to the same thing, assigned the role of ineffable datum).[7] This tactic cannot help in coping with the question which the tough-minded Terrestrial philosophers raised

[7] Urging that philosophers need to do more than this, Cornelius Kampe has suggested that the mind-body identity theory will make sense only if we provide "a theoretical framework (or an ontology for the common idiom) of such a type as to provide a link for the two diverse phenomena whose identity is asserted." His motive for this revival of neutral monism is his belief that making sense of an identity theory requires that "the subjective-objective distinction must be abandoned, as must the privileged status of first-person introspective reports." Such a change, he says, would "drastically affect the logic of our language." I think Kampe is right that giving up the subjective-objective distinction would have such a drastic effect, but wrong in thinking that giving up privileged access would. As I think Sellars has shown, and as I have been arguing here, the subjective-objective distinction (the notion of "seems") can get along quite well without the notions of "mind," "phenomenal property," etc. (Cf. Kampe, "Mind-Body Identity: A Question of Intelligibility," *Philosophical Studies* 25 [1974], 63-67.)

90

about the Antipodeans: Do they have raw feels or don't they?

The problem about the Antipodeans can be summarized as follows:

1. It is essential to raw feels that they be incorrigibly knowable

together with

2. There is nothing which the Antipodeans think themselves incorrigible about

seems to leave us either with

3. The Antipodeans do not have raw feels

or with

4. The Antipodeans do not know about their own incorrigible knowledge.

The trouble with (3) is that the Antipodeans have pretty much the behavior, physiology, and culture that we do. Further, we can train Antipodean infants to report raw feels, and take themselves to be incorrigible about them. These considerations seem to drive us toward (4). But (4) sounds silly, and needs at least to be softened to

4'. The Antipodeans do not know about their own capacity for incorrigible knowledge

which is a little odd but at least has a few parallels. (Compare "John XXIII had to be convinced by argument of his own infallibility upon succeeding to the papacy.") However, if we press (4'), the teachability of Antipodean infants seems to leave us up in the air between

5. The Antipodeans can be taught to recognize their own raw feels

and

91

5'. The Antipodeans can be taught, thanks to the presence of neural concomitants of raw feels, to simulate reports of raw feels without actually having any.

One might hope to resolve this new dilemma by finding a bilingual Antipodean. But the bilingual does not have "inside" knowledge about the meanings of the foreign expressions; he just has the same sort of theory which the lexicon-maker has. Consider an adult Antipodean who has come to speak English. He says, "I am in pain" or the Antipodean for "My C-fibers are firing," depending on which he's speaking. If a Terran interlocutor tells him that he really isn't in pain he points out that the remark is a deviant utterance, and claims privileged access. When Antipodean interlocutors show him that his C-fibers aren't in fact firing he says something like "That's funny; they certainly seem to be. That's why I told the Terrans I was in pain," or perhaps something like "That's funny; I'm certainly in what the Terrans call 'pain,' and that never happens except when my C-fibers are firing." It is hard to see that he would have any strong preference for either locution, and harder to see that philosophers could make anything out of a preference if he had one. Once again, we seem driven to the rhetorical question "But what does it *feel* like?"—to which the bilingual Antipodean replies, "It feels like pain." When asked, "Doesn't it also feel like C-fibers?" he explains that there is no concept of "feeling" in Antipodean, and so it would not occur to him to say that he *felt* his C-fibers firing, although of course he is aware of it whenever they do.

If this seems paradoxical, it is presumably because we think that "noninferential awareness" and "feeling" are pretty well synonymous. But pointing this out is no help. If we treat them as synonymous, then of course Antipodean *does* have the concept of a state called "feeling," but it still doesn't have the concept of "feelings" as intentional objects of knowledge. Antipodean has the verb but not the noun, so to speak. An accommodating Antipodean can note that his language can express the notion of "state such that one cannot be mistaken in thinking one is in it"—namely, the state of it seeming to one that . . .—but still be puzzled about whether these states are the same things as the pains and other raw feels in which the Terrans are so interested. On the one hand, it seems all they *could* be talking about, for he remembers having learned to say "pain" when and only when his C-fibers seem to be firing. On the other hand, the Terrans insist that there is a difference between being in a state such that it seems to one that one is . . . and having a raw feel. The former state is an epistemic position toward something about which doubt is possible. The latter state automatically puts one in an epistemic position toward something about which doubt is impossible.

So the dilemma seems to boil down to this: We must affirm or deny

6. any report of how something seems to one is a report of a raw feel.

The only ground for affirming it seems to be that it is a corollary of the converse of (1), that is:

7. It is essential to whatever is incorrigibly knowable that it be a raw feel.

But (7) is just a form of the principle invoked by the Brandt-Campbell objection above, viz.:

(P) Whenever we make an incorrigible report on a state of ourselves, there must be a property which we are presented with which induces us to make the report

and in this principle everything turns on the notion "presented with"—a notion which harks straight back to the metaphors of the "Eye of the Mind," "presence to consciousness," and the like, which are in turn derived from the initial image of the Mirror of Nature—of knowledge as a set of immaterial representations. If we adopt this principle, then, oddly enough, we can no longer be skeptics: the Antipodeans automatically have raw feels. We *must* choose (5) over (5'). Since we do not contest that it seems to some Antipodean that his stomach is cramped or his C-fibers firing, and since we grant incorrigibility to such reports, we must grant that he has some raw feels which are the "basis" for his seems-statements and which he could be trained to report by learning an appropriate vocabulary. But this means, paradoxically enough, that a species of behaviorism is entailed by the very principle that incarnates the Cartesian image of the Eye of the Mind—the very image which has often been accused of leading to the "veil of ideas" and to solipsism. We should only be able to be skeptics and assert (5')—that simulation might be all the Antipodeans could do—by holding that when the Antipodeans made seems-statements they were not really meaning what we meant by them, and that the deviance, in Antipodean, of the expression "You may be mistaken in saying that it seems to you that your C-fibers are firing" does not suffice to show that the Antipodeans have any incorrigible knowledge. That is, we should have to reconstrue the behavior which we initially took to be exhibited, and base our skepticism about their raw feels on a more general skepticism about their possession of knowledge (or of some kinds of knowledge). But it is difficult to see how we could make skepticism about this plausible except on some antecedent conviction that they were mindless—a conviction which would a fortiori rule out raw feels. So skepticism here will have to be groundless and Pyrrhonian.[8] On the other

[8] I want to distinguish between "mere," or Pyrrhonian, skepticism and the specifically "Cartesian" form of skepticism which invokes the "veil of ideas" as a justification for a skeptical attitude. "Pyrrhonian" skepticism, as I shall use the term, merely says, "We can never be certain; so how can we ever know?" "Veil of ideas" skepticism, on the other hand, has something more specific to say, viz., "Given that we shall never have certainty about anything except the contents of our own minds, how can we ever justify an inference to a belief about anything else?" For a discussion of the intertwining of these two forms of

94

hand, if we deny (6)—if we disengage seeming from the having of mental states and abandon the Cartesian pictures —then we have to face up to the possibility that we ourselves never had any feelings, any mental states, any minds, any Glassy Essence. This paradox seems so overwhelming as to drive us right back to (P) and the Mirror of Nature. So the problem comes down to a choice among three troubling possibilities. We have to either share our Glassy Essence with any being which seems to speak a language containing seems-statements, or become Pyrrhonian skeptics, or else face up to the possibility that this essence was never ours. If we grant (7) above—the premise which makes being a raw feel essential to being an object of incorrigible knowledge—then we must admit either (a) that the Antipodean language, just by virtue of containing some incorrigible reports, is about raw feels, or (b) that we shall never know whether the Antipodeans speak a language just because we shall never know whether they have raw feels, or (c) that the whole issue about raw feels is a fake because the example of the Antipodeans shows that we never had any raw feels ourselves.

These three possibilities correspond roughly to three standard positions in the philosophy of mind—behaviorism, skepticism about other minds, and materialism. Rather than adopt any of these three, however, I suggest that we deny (7), and with it (P). That is, I suggest that we abandon the notion that we possess incorrigible knowledge by virtue of a special relation to a special kind of object called "mental objects." This suggestion is a corollary of Sellars's attack on the Myth of the Given. I shall present that attack in more detail in chapter four, but here I merely note that this myth is the notion that such epistemic relations as "direct knowledge" or "incorrigible knowledge" or "certain knowledge" are to be understood on a causal, para-mechan-

---

skepticism, see Richard Popkin, *The History of Scepticism from Erasmus to Descartes* (New York, 1964).

ical model, as a special relation between certain objects and the human mind which enables knowledge to take place more easily or naturally or quickly. If we think of incorrigible knowledge simply as a matter of social practice —of the absence of a normal rejoinder in normal conversation to a certain knowledge-claim—then no principle like (7) or (P) will seem plausible.

In the last two sections I have been treating "mental object" as if it were synonymous with "incorrigibly knowable object," and thus as if to have a mind were the same thing as having incorrigible knowledge. I have disregarded immateriality and the ability to abstract, which were discussed in chapter one, and intentionality, which will be discussed in chapter four. My excuse for pretending that the mind is nothing but a set of incorrigibly introspectible raw feels, and that its essence is this special epistemic status, is that the same pretense is current throughout the area called "philosophy of mind." This area of philosophy has come into existence in the thirty years since Ryle's *The Concept of Mind*. The effect of that book was to make issues about minds and bodies turn almost entirely on the cases which resisted Ryle's own logical behaviorist attempt to dissolve Cartesian dualism—namely, raw feels. Wittgenstein's discussion of sensations in *Philosophical Investigations* seemed to offer the same sort of attempt at dissolution. Thus many philosophers have taken it for granted that "the mind-body problem" was the question of whether raw feels could be viewed as dispositions to behave. Thus the only possibilities have seemed to be the ones I have just cited: (a) granting that Ryle and Wittgenstein were right, and that there are no mental objects, (b) saying that they were wrong, and that therefore Cartesian dualism stands intact, with skepticism about other minds a natural consequence, and (c) some form of mind-brain identity theory, according to which Ryle and Wittgenstein were wrong, but Descartes is not thereby vindicated.

The effect of setting up the issues in this way is to focus

on pains, while paying less attention to the side of the mind which is, or should be, of more concern to epistemology—beliefs and intentions. (The balance has been somewhat redressed in recent years thanks to philosophers of mind who try to build bridges with empirical psychology. Their work will be discussed in chapter five.) But it is still the case that "the mind-body problem" is thought of primarily as a problem about pains, and the distinctive point about pains is just the one mentioned by Kripke—that there seems no such thing as an appearance-reality distinction in regard to our knowledge of them. In fact, as I have tried to show in chapter one, this is only one of several "mind-body problems," each of which has contributed to the fuzzy notion that there is something especially mysterious about man which makes him capable of knowing, or of certain special sorts of knowing.

For the remainder of this chapter, however, I shall try to support my claim that we should drop (P) and thus be neither dualists, skeptics, behaviorists, nor "identity-theorists." I do not know how to argue against (P) directly, since the claim that incorrigible knowledge is a matter of being presented with a phenomenal property is not so much a claim as an abbreviation for an entire theory—a whole set of terms and assumptions which center around the image of mind as mirroring nature, and which conspire to give sense to the Cartesian claim that the mind is naturally "given" to itself. It is this image itself which has to be set aside if we are to see through the seventeenth-century notion that we can understand and improve our knowing by understanding the workings of our mind. I hope to show the difference between setting it aside and adopting any of the positions which presuppose this image. So the remainder of this chapter is devoted to behaviorism, skepticism, and the mind-body identity theory, in an attempt to differentiate my position from each of these. In the concluding section of the chapter—"Materialism without Identity"—I attempt to say something more positive, but this attempt needs to

97

be linked up with the discussion of other "mind-body problems" in chapter one in order to appear plausible.

4. BEHAVIORISM

Behaviorism is the doctrine that talk of "inner states" is simply an abbreviated, and perhaps misleading, way of talking of dispositions to behave in certain ways. In its Rylean or "logical" form—with which I shall be concerned in what follows—its central doctrine is that there is a necessary connection between the truth of a report of a certain raw feel and a disposition to such-and-such behavior. One motive for holding this view is a distrust of what Ryle called "ghosts in machines," the Cartesian picture of people, and another is the desire to prevent the skeptic about other minds from raising the question of whether the person writhing on the floor has feels of the sort which the skeptic himself would have when he writhes. In the logical behaviorist view, reports of such feels are to be taken not to refer to nonphysical entities, and perhaps not to any entities at all save to the writhing or the disposition to writhe.

This doctrine has been attacked on the ground that there seems no way to fill in a description of the requisite disposition to behave without giving infinitely long lists of possible movements and noises. It has also been attacked on the ground that whatever "necessity" there is in the area is not a matter of "meaning" but simply an expression of the fact that we customarily explain certain behavior by reference to certain inner states—so that the necessity is no more "linguistic" or "conceptual" than that which connects the redness of the stove to the fire within. Finally, it has been attacked as the sort of philosophical paradox which would only occur to a mind obsessed with instrumentalist or verificationist dogma—eager to reduce all unobservables to observables in order to avoid any risk of believing in something unreal.

All these criticisms are, I think, quite justified. The classic statements of logical behaviorism do indeed presuppose just the distinctions between observation and theory and between language and fact which philosophers would, as I shall argue in chapter four, do well to give up. But the feeling that the behaviorist is on to something remains. One point which he has going for him is that it seems absurd to suggest that we might someday, after years of fruitful conversation with the Antipodeans, have ground for saying, "Ah, no raw feels; so no minds; so no language, and not persons after all." The suggestion that we might find ourselves compelled to say that they had no raw feels makes us ask whether we can even imagine what such a compulsion could be like. It also makes us realize that even if we somehow were so compelled, we should almost certainly not draw the suggested inferences. On the contrary, we might begin to share the Antipodeans' bewilderment about why we had cared so much about this question. We should begin to appreciate the quizzical attitude which the Antipodeans adopt toward the whole topic—the same attitude with which the Polynesians viewed missionaries' preoccupation with the question "Are these descendants of Shem or of Ham?" The behaviorist's strong point is that the more one tries to answer them the more pointless the tough-minded philosopher's questions "Minds or no minds?" "Raw feels or no raw feels?" seem to become.

But this good point begins to go bad as soon as it is put as a thesis about "necessary connections" established by "analysis of meanings." Ryle's insight was frustrated by the positivistic epistemology he inherited. Instead of saying that incorrigible knowledge was just a matter of what practices of justification were adopted by one's peers (the position which I shall call "epistemological behaviorism" in chapter four), he was led to say that a certain type of behavior formed a necessary and sufficient condition for the ascription of raw feels, and that this was a fact about "our language." He then was confronted by a stubborn problem. The fact that our language licensed the inference to the presence of such feels made it difficult, without falling back on materialism, to deny that there really were ghostly entities to report. Thus the two motives behind logical behaviorism came into conflict, since the desire to find a "logical" barrier to skepticism about other minds seems to lead back toward dualism. For if we take the notion that a given linguistic practice, a given piece of behavior, is enough (*pace* the skeptic) to show the necessity of raw feels within, in whatever sense raw feels exist, then it seems necessary to say that our conversational experience with the Antipodeans entails that they have raw feels in whatever sense *we* have raw feels. That is, it seems necessary to adopt the following view:

> (P′) The ability to speak a language which includes incorrigible seems-statements entails the presence of raw feels in speakers of that language, in whatever sense raw feels are present in *us*.

It is easy to heap ridicule on the notion that we can discover the truth of such a claim by doing something called "analyzing meanings."[9] It seems easy to say (with the skeptic) that we might have the ability without the feels. But it is hard, as Wittgenstein and Bouwsma have made clear, actually to tell a coherent story about what we have imagined. Despite this, (P′) has a certain plausibility. The reason it is plausible is that it is, once again, a corollary of:

> (P) Whenever we make an incorrigible report on a state of ourselves, there must be a property with which we are presented which induces us to make this report—

a principle vital to the image of the Mirror of Nature. It is the picture according to which "appearance" is not just mistaken belief but mistaken belief generated by a particu-

---

[9] For a sample of such ridicule, see Hilary Putnam, "Brains and Behavior" in *Mind, Language and Reality*, vol. ii (Cambridge, 1975).

lar mechanism (a misleading thing getting before the Eye of the Mind) which makes the connection between behavior and raw feel seem so necessary. It is the picture according to which three things are involved when a person gets something wrong (or, by extension, right): the person, the object he is talking about, and the inner representation of that object.

Ryle thought that he had eschewed this picture, but that he was unable to do so is shown by his attempt to show, paradoxically and fruitlessly, that there were no such things as incorrigible reports. Ryle was afraid that if there were any such reports, then something like (P) would have to be true in order to explain their existence. For he thought that if there were such a thing as an ability to make incorrigible noninferential reports on inner states, this would show that someone who knew nothing of behavior could know everything about inner states, and thus that Descartes was right after all. He rightly criticized the usual Cartesian account of introspection as a piece of "para-optics," but he did not have another account available and thus was forced into the impossible position of having to deny the phenomenon of privileged access altogether. He devoted the least convincing chapter of *The Concept of Mind* ("Self-Knowledge") to the paradoxical claim that "the sorts of things that I can find out about myself are the same as the sorts of things that I can find out about other people, and the methods of finding them out are much the same."[10] The result was that many philosophers who agreed that Ryle had shown that beliefs and desires were not inner states agreed also that he had left raw feels untouched, and thus that a choice still had to be made between dualism and materialism.[11]

10 Gilbert Ryle, *The Concept of Mind* (New York, 1965), p. 155. The reference to "para-optics" is at p. 159.

11 Sellars's "Empiricism and the Philosophy of Mind" (in *Science, Perception and Reality* [London and New York, 1963]) took the first step beyond Ryle. Sellars showed that even though the fact that be-

To put Ryle's mistake in other words, he believed that if one could show a "necessary connection" between ascriptions of behavioral dispositions and ascriptions of inner states, then one would have shown that there were really no inner states. But this instrumentalist *non sequitur* can be avoided, as can (P), while preserving the antiskeptical point that the behavior of the Antipodeans is quite enough evidence to warrant the attribution to them of as much or as little of an inner life as we ourselves possess. The metaphysical inference which the behaviorist is tempted to make—the inference that there is no Glassy Essence within —is, in isolation, as implausible as any other instrumentalist claim. (Compare: "There are no positrons; there are just dispositions on the part of electrons to. . . ." "There are no electrons; there are just dispositions on the part of macroscopic objects to. . . ." "There are no physical objects; there are just dispositions on the part of sense-contents to. . . .") Stripped of its pretensions to rigor, the behaviorist position simply comes down to reminding us that the notion of raw

---

havior is evidence for raw feels is "built into the very logic" of concepts of raw feels, this does not mean that there can be no raw feels, any more than the parallel point about macro-phenomena and micro-entities dictates the operationalist claims that there can be no micro-entities. Sellars there said what Ryle should have said in his chapter on "Self-Knowledge" but did not—viz., that introspective reporting was no more mysterious than any other noninferential report, and did not require the Myth of the Given (and thus did not require para-optics) for its explanation. Unfortunately, however, Sellars did not draw the conclusion that, as Armstrong was later to say, there was no such thing as "logically privileged access" but only "empirically privileged access" (Armstrong, *A Materialist Theory of the Mind* [London, 1968], p. 108). This point, which is vital to the view I am presenting in this book, is suggested by everything Sellars says, but Quine's attack on the logical-empirical distinction was required to make it possible to get around the shibboleth of "logically necessary connections" which Ryle had built into the philosophy of mind. As I suggest in chapter four, Sellars has never quite been able to swallow Quineanism full strength, and his talk of "the very logic of these concepts" was unfortunately in the Rylean tradition.

feel only has a role in the context of a picture which connects certain sorts of behavior (introspective reports) with others (reports of physical objects) in terms of a certain image of what human beings (not just their minds) are like. The behaviorist is looking at the social role of the notion of "pain" and not attempting to burrow behind it to the ineffable phenomenological quality which pains have. The skeptic has to insist that it is this quality—which you only know of from your own experience—which counts. The reason why the behaviorist keeps edging himself into the paradoxical metaphysical position of denying that there are nondispositional mental causes for behavioral dispositions is put by Wittgenstein as follows:

> How does the philosophical problem about mental processes and states and about behaviorism arise?—The first step is the one that altogether escapes notice. We talk of processes and states and leave their nature undecided. Sometime perhaps we shall know more about them—we think. But that is just what commits us to a particular way of looking at the matter. For we have a definite concept of what it means to learn to know a process better. (The decisive movement in the conjuring-trick has been made, and it was the very one that we thought quite innocent.)[12]

Alan Donagan provides an admirable gloss on this passage, saying that

> the Cartesians . . . transformed the grammatical facts which we summed up in the proposition that sensation is non-dispositional and private into the grammatical fiction that sensations are states or processes in a private, and hence non-material, medium.

The behaviorists, on the other hand,

12 Ludwig Wittgenstein, *Philosophical Investigations* (London and New York, 1953), pt. I, sec. 308.

whether moved by the barrenness of much introspectionist psychology, by the philosophical difficulties of
Cartesianism, or by other considerations, began by denying that the private Cartesian processes in their non-
material medium exist at all.

Wittgenstein cleared up the matter, Donagan thinks, by
allowing "that sensations are private non-dispositional accompaniments of the behavior by which they are naturally
expressed," but refusing "to recognize those accompaniments as processes that can be named and investigated independently of the circumstances that produce them, and
the behavior by which they are naturally expressed."[13]

I think that Donagan's pithy account of the common difficulty of behaviorists and dualistic skeptics about other
minds is right, but that it can be clarified and carried one
step further. The notion of a "private, . . . non-material
medium" is obscure because it suggests that we have a notion of what it is like to have a Glassy Essence—a metaphysical grasp of what nonextended substance is like—which is
independent of the epistemic criterion of the mental. If we
neglect this notion and press Wittgenstein's phrase "a definite concept of what it means to learn to know a process
better" we can get a diagnosis of what Donagan calls the
"opposite and complementary errors"[14] of behaviorism and
Cartesianism which avoids reference to the metaphysical
("non-material," ghostly) nature of raw feels.

The basic epistemological premise which both schools
share, and which forms their notion of "knowing better," is
the doctrine of the Naturally Given, that is:

Knowledge is either of the sort of entity naturally suited
to be immediately present to consciousness, or of entities
whose existence and properties are entailed by entities of

[13] All four quotations are from Alan Donagan, "Wittgenstein on
Sensation," *Wittgenstein: The Philosophical Investigations: A Collection of Critical Essays,* ed. George Pitcher (New York, 1966), p. 350.
[14] Ibid., p. 349.

the first sort (and which are thus "reducible" to those of the first sort).

The Cartesians thought that the only sorts of entities which were naturally suited to be directly present to consciousness were mental states. The behaviorists, at their epistemological best, thought that the only sort of entities directly present to consciousness were states of physical objects. The behaviorists prided themselves on escaping the notions of our Glassy Essence and the Inner Eye but they remained true to Cartesian epistemology in retaining the notion of an Eye of the Mind which got some things firsthand. Science, in this view, infers to other things entailed by "ground-floor" entities, and philosophy then reduces these other things back down again. The behaviorists gave up the notion that "nothing is better known to the mind than itself" but they kept the notion that some things were naturally knowable directly and others not, and the metaphysical corollary that only the first were "really real." This doctrine—that the most knowable was the most real—which George Pitcher has dubbed the "Platonic Principle,"[15] added to the principle of the Naturally Given, produced either an idealistic or panpsychist reduction of the physical to the mental, or a behaviorist or materialist reduction in the other direction. The choice between the two sorts of reduction depends, I think, not so much on difficulties in psychology or philosophy but on one's general notion of what wisdom is like, and thus of what philosophy is good for. Is it to emphasize the aspects of man reached by public methods of common conversation and scientific inquiry? Or rather a personal and inarticulate sense of "something far more deeply interfused"? This choice has little to do with philosophical argument or with the image of the Mirror of Nature. But the image—and particularly the metaphor

15 Cf. Pitcher, *Theory of Perception*, p. 23 and Plato, *Republic* 478B: "So if the real is the object of knowledge, then the object of belief must be something other than the real."

105

of the Inner Eye—serves the purposes of both disputants equally well, which is why debate between them has been so lengthy and so inconclusive. Both have a clear sense of what is best known, and knowing a process means either knowing it *that* way, or else showing that it "really is nothing but" something else which *is* known that way.

If we look at the controversy between the behaviorist and the skeptic about other minds from the Antipodean point of view, the first thing we realize is there is no place for the "Naturally Given." There is, to be sure, a place for the notion of "direct knowledge." This is simply knowledge which is had without its possessor having gone through any conscious inference. But there is no suggestion that some entities are especially well suited to be known in this way. What we know noninferentially is a matter of what we happen to be familiar with. Some people (those who sit in front of cloud-chambers) are familiar with, and make noninferential reports of, elementary particles. Others are familiar with diseases of trees, and can report "another case of Dutch elm disease" without performing any inferences. All Antipodeans are familiar with the states of their nerves, and all Terrans with their raw feels. The Antipodeans do not suggest that there is something suspiciously metaphysical or ghostly about raw feels—they just do not see the point of talking about such things instead of talking about one's nerves. Nor, of course, does it help if the Terrans explain that though (putting aside the possibility of unconscious inference) perhaps anything *can* be known noninferentially it does not follow that anything except certain naturally suitable entities can be known *incorrigibly*. For the Antipodeans do not have the notion of *entities* known incorrigibly but only of *reports* (seems-statements) which are incorrigible and which may be about *any* sort of entity. They understand that the Terrans do have the former notion, but they are baffled why they think they need it, although they can see how, in ignorance of neurology, a lot of strange notions might have become current.

106

5. Skepticism about Other Minds

When we turn to the skeptic about other minds—the person who emphasizes that there can be inner states without behaviorial accompaniments—we again have a perfectly sound intuition blown up into a paradox. The sound intuition is just that raw feels are as good particulars as tables or archangels or electrons—as good inhabitants of the world, as good candidates for ontological status. The question "Do the Antipodeans have raw feels?" is no fishier or more "metaphysical" than the question "Do they have red blood?" or "Do they have the moral sense?" Further, we do indeed have a special, superior way of knowing about our own raw feels—we have privileged access to private entities.

This good point begins to turn bad, however, when the principle of the Naturally Given suggests that since raw feels are so very well known indeed, they must be entities of a very special sort—processes in a private "non-material medium," perhaps. It turns bad, so to speak, when more is made of man's Glassy Essence than the fact that man's knowledge is a Mirror of Nature, and when the question arises "What kind of special and marvelous material, or non-material, could do that mirroring?" There is nothing wrong, so to speak, with saying that people have to be pretty special to know so much more than the beasts of the field; even the Antipodeans say the same. But when we try to go from

1. We know our minds better than we know anything else

to

2. We could know all about our minds even if we knew nothing else

to

3. Knowing whether something has a mind is a matter of knowing it as it knows itself

107

then we can never say why we should not be solipsists. The transition from (1) to (2) is made natural, though not necessitated, by the principle of the Naturally Given and the metaphor of the Inner Eye. For if we think of the Eye simply turning inward and spotting a raw feel, the whole complex of social institutions and behavioral manifestations which surround reports of such raw feels seems irrelevant. Just because it is irrelevant, we are impelled to move from (2) to (3)—all we shall ever know about our fellows (if we have any), we now say wistfully, is their behavior and their social position. We shall never know how it is with them within, if indeed there is any "within" there. The effect of this is that we stop thinking of our friends and neighbors as people and start thinking of them as husks surrounding a mysterious thing (the Glassy Essence, the private nonmaterial medium) which only professional philosophers, perhaps, can describe but which we know (or hope) is there. The notion that introspection is a glimpse into another ontological realm is not (and here the Wittgensteinians are quite right) something which becomes obvious when we actually do some introspecting. No haunting sense of spying on the uncanny comes over us when we turn the Eye of the Mind inward. The notion that we are doing so is a product of the epistemological notions which let us slide from (1) to (2) to (3). Here, as elsewhere, epistemology precedes, and tempts us into, metaphysics.

But the artificial uncanniness produced by too much epistemology should not lead us (and here some Wittgensteinians are quite wrong) to think that there can be nothing inside at all. Nor should we think our privileged access to our own mental states is a mystery requiring either metaphysical defense or skeptical destruction. The force of the skeptic's original sound intuition can be brought out by emphasizing this last point. I shall do so by taking a critical look at Wittgensteinian arguments that mental entities have a sort of diminished ontological responsibility, and that the whole notion of "private" entities and of privileged

108

access to them is somehow misguided. It has been emphasized by Strawson that Wittgenstein had two distinct sorts
of "hostility"—one to privacy and one to immediacy. The
latter, I think, was crucially important, but the former was
entirely misguided.[16]

Consider the famous passage in which Wittgenstein says
that a sensation "is not a *something*, but not a *nothing*
either! The conclusion was only that a nothing would
serve just as well as a something about which nothing could
be said."[17] This directs attention to the paradoxical thing
about the skeptic's claim—the insistence that it is the "special incommunicable felt qualities" of inner states which
matter. But if we distinguish between the claim that

We have privileged access to our own pains

and the claim that

We know which mental states we are in purely by virtue
of their special felt qualities

we can avoid the paradox and let a sensation be as much a
something as a table. The former claim merely says that
there is no better way of finding out whether somebody is in
pain than by asking him, and that nothing can overrule his

16 Cf. P. F. Strawson, "Review of Wittgenstein's *Philosophical Investigations*" in the anthology cited in note 13, p. 62. I have argued
elsewhere that we can save Wittgenstein's epistemological insights,
which center around the impossibility of learning the meaning of
words without antecedent "stage-setting," without getting caught up
in a hostility to privacy which led Wittgenstein to the edge of behaviorism and which led some of his followers over the edge. In the view I
would recommend, Wittgenstein's critique of "pure ostensive definition"
can be generalized into Sellars's doctrine that we cannot know the
meaning of one word without knowing the meaning of a lot of others,
and thus can be used to show what is wrong with the notion of the
Eye of the Mind, without drawing any metaphysical corollaries. See my
"Wittgenstein, Privileged Access, and Incommunicability," *American
Philosophical Quarterly* 7 (1970), 192–205 and "Verificationism and
Transcendental Arguments," *Nous* 5 (1971), 3-14.

17 Wittgenstein, *Philosophical Investigations*, pt. I, sec. 304.

own sincere report. The latter says that the mechanism which makes this privilege possible is his inspection of the "phenomenological properties" of his own mental states. To get from the first claim to the second we need the Cartesian model of self-knowledge as analogous to observation—the image of the Inner Eye—and the notion that stomach cramps, for example, are not Naturally Given in the way in which the feelings produced by stomach cramps are. This is the notion which, brought to bear on the Antipodeans, produces the notion that they can't be directly acquainted with their C-fibers but must be making an "unconscious" inference from "special, felt qualities."

If we drop the notion that the only way in which we can have "direct knowledge" of an entity is by being acquainted with its "special, felt, incommunicable qualities," then we can have privileged access without paradox. We can drop this notion if, with Wittgenstein, we note that unless there were such a thing as typical pain behavior we would never be able to teach a child the meaning of, for example, "toothache." More generally, we can note that the way in which the pre-linguistic infant knows that it has a pain is the way in which the record-changer knows the spindle is empty, the plant the direction of the sun, and the amoeba the temperature of the water. But this way has no connection with what a language-user knows when he knows what pain is—that it is mental rather than physical, typically produced by injured tissues, etc. The mistake which Wittgenstein exposed was to assume that we learn what a pain is in the second sense by casting linguistic garb over our knowledge of what pain is in the first sense—by clothing our direct acquaintance with special felt, incommunicable qualities in words (thus rendering ourselves forever skeptical about whether the same incommunicable quality is being named when our friends use the same word). The notion that knowledge in the first sense—the sort manifested by behavioral discrimination—is the "foundation" (rather than simply one possible causal antecedent) of knowledge in the second sense is itself one more product of the Cartesian model. For as long as it is thought that the Naturally Given is known through and through simply by being seen by the Inner Eye, it will seem odd to suggest that the behavior and environment which we must know about in order to *use* the word "pain" in ordinary conversation should have anything to do with what "pain" *means*. The image of the Mental Eye, combined with the notion that language consists of names of the Naturally Given plus abbreviations for instrumentalistic criteria for detecting the presence of all entities not Naturally Given, produces skepticism. For these assumptions guarantee that the facts about behavior and environment of which behaviorists and Wittgensteinians make much should seem irrelevant to the "essence" of pain. For that essence is determined simply by what is *named*.[18]

From the Antipodean point of view, the notion of "private entities"—entities about which only one person has incorrigible knowledge—is strange but not incomprehensible. It strikes the Antipodeans as clear but pointless. What *would* strike them as unintelligible is the notion of entities so private, so to speak, that knowledge of them is not only privileged but incommunicable. These indeed, they might say, are not entities at all. Contrariwise, the Wittgensteinian temptation to suggest that sensations have some sort of halfway existence between nothings and somethings—that they "drop out" of the world like the beetles-in-boxes of Wittgenstein's famous analogy—comes from running to-

[18] One might argue about whether Wittgenstein's views on sensations were a corollary of his views about meaning, or whether the epistemological views reflected in the former entail his philosophy of language. I do not think that such an argument would be fruitful. As I shall suggest in chapter six, there is no particular reason to view philosophy of language as "prior" to other parts of philosophy. In particular, I do not think that disputes about the "theory of reference" (which I discuss in section 4 of chapter six) help to illuminate the issue which Kripke raises about the essence of pain in the passage cited in section 2 of this chapter. Questions about rigid designation leave questions about essence wide open.

111

gether the notions of incorrigibility and incommunicability. If we assimilate the two, and realize the skeptical implications of incommunicability, then we will indeed be skeptical about privileged access to private entities. But this skepticism will not be the sort the Antipodeans have. They are skeptical because they think such entities and such access are *de trop*, not because they think that the notions of them are "conceptual confusions."

Traditional Cartesian skeptics about other minds are of still a third sort. They just doubt whether other people have, for example, pains. This skepticism is no more refutable and no more interesting than skepticism about whether the table exists when there is no one about to perceive it. It is, after all, quite possible that tables vanish when nobody is around. It is quite possible that our companions always simulate pain-behavior without ever having any pains. It is quite possible that the world is a very different sort of place than we imagine. But this kind of skepticism would never have occupied philosophers' attention if it were not for the notion of the Naturally Given, and the consequent suggestion that everything (our friend's mind, as well as his table and his body) which is not a fragment of our own Inner Mirror—a part of our own Glassy Essence—is just a "posit," "an inference," "a construction," or something equally dubious which requires metaphysical system-building (Descartes, Kant) or discoveries about "our language" (Russell, Ayer) for its defense. Such redescriptions of reality or language are supposed to show that it is *impossible* for the skeptic to doubt what he doubts without making some wholesale intellectual mistake—"misunderstanding the nature of matter" (Kant) or "misunderstanding the logic of our language" (Ayer). But it is not impossible, it is just pointless, unless some further reason for doubt is given other than that certainty cannot be had.

We should not think that philosophers of the seventeenth century misunderstood the nature of the mind by, so to speak, systematically distorting ordinary language (Ryle).

Nor should we think that since the naive metaphysics of common sense generates skeptical problems we need to replace it by, say, a neutral monism (Spinoza), or a panpsychism (Whitehead, Hartshorne), or a materialism (Smart). The seventeenth century did not "misunderstand" the Mirror of Nature or the Inner Eye any more than Aristotle misunderstood natural motion or Newton gravity. They hardly *could* misunderstand it, since they invented it. The charge that this set of images inaugurated an era of philosophy which centered around epistemological skepticism is sound enough, but it is important to see that this was *not* because other minds were somehow especially susceptible to skepticism. They are no more susceptible than anything else that is outside one's own mind. The seventeenth century gave skepticism a new lease on life because of its epistemology, not its philosophy of mind. Any theory which views knowledge as accuracy of representation, and which holds that certainty can only be rationally had about representations, will make skepticism inevitable.

The veil-of-ideas epistemology which took over philosophy in the seventeenth century transformed skepticism from an academic curiosity (Pyrrhonian skepticism) and a concrete and local theological issue (the authority of the church versus that of the individual reader of Scripture) into a cultural tradition.[19] It did so by giving rise to a new philosophical genre—the system which brings subject and object together again. This reconciliation has been the goal of philosophical thought ever since. Ryle and Wittgenstein are misleading when they say that there must be something wrong with the seventeenth-century picture which has held us captive, on the ground that in ordinary life we have no difficulty telling what has a mind and what doesn't, nor

[19] See Popkin, *Scepticism from Erasmus to Descartes* and Maurice Mandelbaum, *Philosophy, Science, and Sense-Perception* (Baltimore, 1964) for discussions of various factors which contributed to the formation of this tradition. For a more radical interpretation, see Jacques Maritain, *The Dream of Descartes* (New York, 1944).

113

whether tables persist out of sight. It is as if we said that the imitation of Christ cannot be a suitable ideal because in ordinary life we have no trouble recognizing the bounds placed on love by prudence and self-interest. The images which generate philosophical (and poetic) traditions are not likely to be attended to outside the study, just as the counsels of perfection which religion proffers are not likely to be noticed on weekdays. If philosophy is an attempt to see how "things, in the largest sense of the term, hang together, in the largest sense of the term," then it will always involve the construction of images which will have characteristic problems and will beget characteristic genres of writing. One may wish to say, as I do, that the seventeenth-century image is outworn—that the tradition which it inspired has lost its vitality. But that is quite a different criticism from saying that this tradition misunderstood something or failed to solve a problem. Skepticism and the principal genre of modern philosophy have a symbiotic relationship. They live one another's death, and die one another's life. One should see philosophy neither as achieving success by "answering the skeptic," nor as rendered nugatory by realizing that there is no skeptical case to be answered. The story is more complicated than that.

6. Materialism without Mind-Body Identity

Like the behaviorist and the skeptic about other minds, the materialist has a sound intuition which becomes paradoxical when stated in the vocabulary of the tradition to which it is a reaction. Encouraged by reflection on the Antipodeans, the materialist thinks it likely that reference to neurological microstructures and processes may replace reference to short-term mental states (sensations, thoughts, mental images) in the explanation of human behavior. (If he is wise, he does not think the same for beliefs, desires, and other long-term—and not incorrigibly knowable—mental states, but is content to view them as properties of persons rather than of minds, in the manner of Ryle.) Not content with this plausible prediction, however, he wishes to say something metaphysical. The only thing to be said seems to be that "mental states are nothing but neural states." But this sounds paradoxical. So he tries various tactics to mitigate the paradox. One such tactic is to say that the nature of the mind has so far been misunderstood, and that once we understand it correctly we shall see that it is not paradoxical to say that it may turn out to be the nervous system. Behaviorism is one form of this tactic, and it is compatible with materialism in the sense that the claim:

When we talk about mental events we are really talking about behavioral dispositions

though not compatible with:

When we talk about mental events we are really talking about neural events

is compatible with:

There are, however, other things relevant to prediction and explanation of behavior than the systematic inter-relationships of dispositions with events in the external world, and among these are the neural events which sometimes cause the onset of such dispositions.

It has been customary in recent discussions, however, to take behaviorism and materialism as two quite different ways—mild and violent, respectively—of modifying the seventeenth-century picture of the mind. In this spirit, materialists have fastened on those mental entities most recalcitrant to Ryle's dispositional analyses—the raw feels, the passing thoughts, the mental images—and tried to show that these are to be construed, roughly, as "whatever it is which *causes* the onset of certain behavior or behavioral dispositions." This so-called topic-neutral analysis of the mind (by, especially, J.J.C. Smart and David Armstrong) runs into trouble, however, over the intuitive distinction

between "whatever mental state it is which causes the onset . . . " and "whatever physical state it is which causes the
onset. . . ." To put it another way, the intuition that there
is some difference between materialism and parallelism
makes us feel that there is something misleading, or at least
incomplete, in topic-neutral accounts of what makes the
mental mental. Or, to put it still another way, if our notion
of "mind" is what topic-neutral analyses say it is, it is very
hard to explain the existence of a mind-body problem.[20]
We may say that the lack of a fine-grained neurological account promoted the notion that there is something distinctive about the mind—that it must be something ghostly—
but this tactic simply splits the traditional notion of the
mental into two parts: the causal role and the Glassy Essence believed to play this causal role. Topic-neutral analyses obviously cannot capture, and do not want to capture,
the latter. But it seems mere gerrymandering to split our
concept of a "mental state" into the portion which is compatible with materialism and the portion which is not, and
then say that only the former is "essential" to the concept.[21]

We can put the attempt at "topic-neutral" analyses in
perspective by seeing it as one way to get around the following argument for dualism:

1. Some statements of the form "I just had a sensation of
   pain" are true
2. Sensations of pain are mental events
3. Neural processes are physical events
4. "Mental" and "physical" are incompatible predicates
5. No sensation of pain is a neural event
6. There are some nonphysical events

[20] See M. C. Bradley's "Critical Notice" of J.J.C. Smart's *Philosophy
and Scientific Realism, Australasian Journal of Philosophy* 42 (1964),
262–283, on this point. My own "Incorrigibility as the Mark of the
Mental," *Journal of Philosophy* 67 (1970), 399-424, begins with a discussion of this point, and was inspired by Bradley's review of Smart.

[21] Doing so is the inverse of Kripke's Cartesian claim that the "immediate phenomenological quality" of pain is essential to it.

Ryleans, and some Wittgensteinians, taking mentality to consist in accessibility to privileged access, and indulging what Strawson calls "a hostility to privacy," deny (2). Panpsychists have denied (3).[22] "Reductive" materialists such as Smart and Armstrong, who offer "topic-neutral" analyses of mentalistic terms, challenge (4). "Eliminative" materialists like Feyerabend and Quine deny (1). This last position claims the advantage over the "reductive" version of not having to offer revisionary "analyses" of terms, and thus not having to get involved with dubious notions such as "meaning" and "analysis." It does not say that we have been misleadingly calling neural processes "sensations," but merely that there are no sensations. Nor does it say that the meaning of the term *sensation* can be analyzed in such a way as to produce such unexpected results as the denial of (4). It is fully "Quinean" and wholly anti-Rylean in the sense that it happily accepts all the things which the dualist would like to construe the man in the street as saying, and merely adds, "So much the worse for the man in the street."

This position seems to hold out hope of a sense in which the materialists' metaphysical claim "Mental states are nothing but neural states" can be cheaply bought. For now it can be defended without the need to do anything as laborious or as shady as "philosophical analysis." We can say that although in one sense there just are no sensations, in another sense what people *called* "sensations," viz., neural states, do indeed exist. The distinction of senses is no more sophisticated than when we say that the sky does not exist,

[22] Hartshorne and Whitehead are perhaps the clearest examples in recent philosophy. I have argued against Whitehead's version of this doctrine in "The Subjectivist Principle and the Linguistic Turn" in *Alfred North Whitehead: Essays on His Philosophy*, ed. George Kline (Englewood Cliffs, N.J., 1963). A panpsychist view is also suggested by Thomas Nagel's proposal for an "objective phenomenology" which would "permit questions about the physical basis of experience to assume a more intelligible form" ("What Is It Like to Be a Bat?" *Philosophical Review* 83 [1974], 449). However, in both Hartshorne and Nagel, panpsychism tends to merge with neutral monism.

117

but that there is something which people call the sky (the appearance of a blue dome as a result of refracted sunlight) which does exist (although, as the prevalence of the Brandt-Campbell objection discussed in section 2 shows, the analogy cannot be pressed so as to make a mental state the "appearance" of a neural state). So it looks as if the argument for dualism above can be handled by saying that all the dualist is entitled to is the following premise:

    1′. Some statements of the form "I just had a sensation of pain" are as properly taken as true as "The sky is overcast" and "The sun is rising," but none of them *is* true.

If we substitute (1′) for (1) in the argument, then we will substitute the following for (2):

    2′. If there were any sensations of pain, they would be mental events

and then draw the conclusion:

    6′. The things which people have been calling "sensations" are physical (and, specifically, neural) events.

We can then conclude that although there are no mental events, the things which people have called mental events are physical events, even though "mental" and "physical" are as incompatible as "rising above the horizon" and "standing still."

This attempt at a cheap version of the identity of minds and brains will work well enough if we refrain from pressing questions about criteria of identity of reference, just as topic-neutral analyses will work well enough if we refrain from pressing questions about identity of meaning. I do not, however, think that there are criteria for the identity of either which are useful in philosophically controversial cases. So I do not think that "eliminative materialism" is a more plausible version of the thesis of mind-brain identity than "reductive materialism." When we try to make sense of any claim of the form "There aren't really any X's; what you have been talking about are nothing but Y's," it is always possible to object that (a) "X" refers to X's, and (b) we cannot refer to what does not exist. So to get around this standard criticism the eliminative materialist would have to say either that "sensation" does not refer to sensations, but to nothing at all, or that "refer" in the sense of "talk about" is not subject to (b). Either line is defensible, and I defend the second in discussing the notion of reference in connection with the so-called problem of conceptual change in chapter six below. But since I think that the reductive and eliminative versions of the identity theory are both merely awkward attempts to throw into current philosophical jargon our natural reaction to an encounter with the Antipodeans, I do not think that the difference between the two should be pressed. Rather, they should both be abandoned, and with them the notion of "mind-body identity." The proper reaction to the Antipodean story is to adopt a materialism which is not an identity theory in *any* sense, and which thus avoids the artificial notion that we must wait upon "an adequate theory of meaning (or reference)" before deciding issues in the philosophy of mind.[23]

23 This is not to say that the controversies surrounding the reductive and eliminative forms of the identity theory have been pointless. On the contrary, I think that they have been very useful, and particularly so because of their interplay with questions in the philosophy of language. But I think that the upshot of this interplay has been, first, to bolster Quine's view that the notion of "sameness of meaning" cannot be invoked to solve philosophical problems where the notion of "coextensive" has failed, and, second, to show that the sense of "really talking about" used in such discussions as that about materialism is not interestingly connected with the Fregean notion of reference (in which one cannot refer to what does not exist). (The latter point is argued in chapter six.) Having adopted an eliminative materialist position some years ago ("Mind-Body Identity, Privacy and Categories," *Review of Metaphysics* 19 [1965], 25-54), I am very grateful to the people whose criticisms of this article eventually led me to what I hope is a clearer understanding of the issues. I am especially indebted to publications by, or conversations with, Richard Bernstein, Eric Bush,

This amounts to saying, once again, that the materialist should stop reacting to stories such as that about the Antipodeans by saying metaphysical things, and confine himself to such claims as "No predictive or explanatory or descriptive power would be lost if we had spoken Antipodean all our lives." It is pointless to ask whether the fact that cerebroscopes correct Antipodean reports of inner states shows that they are not *mental* states, or shows rather that mental states are really neural states. It is pointless not just because nobody has any idea how to resolve the issue, but because nothing turns on it. The suggestion that it *has* a clear-cut answer depends upon the pre-Quinean notion of "necessary and sufficient conditions built into our language" for the application of the terms "sensation," "mental," and the like, or upon some similar essentialism.[24] Only a philosopher with a lot invested in the notion of "ontological status" would need to worry about whether a corrigibly re-

---

David Coder, James Cornman, David Hiley, William Lycan, George Pappas, David Rosenthal, Steven Savitt, and Richard Sikora. The reader interested in following up the similarities and differences between reductive and eliminative materialism might consult Cornman, *Materialism and Sensations* (New Haven, 1971), Lycan and Pappas, "What Is Eliminative Materialism?" *Australasian Journal of Philosophy* 50 (1972), 149-159, Bush, "Rorty Revisited," *Philosophical Studies* 25 (1974), 33-42, and Hiley, "Is 'Eliminative Materialism' Materialism?" *Philosophy and Phenomenological Research* 38 (1978), 325-337.

[24] I injudiciously invoked such a notion in "Incorrigibility as the Mark of the Mental," cited in note 20 above. I there concluded that the development of due respect for cerebroscopes would mean the discovery that there had never been any mental events. But this is overdramatized, and tries to establish more of a difference between eliminative and reductive materialism than (as Lycan and Pappas have shown) there really is. I have been greatly helped to see the flaws in my earlier view by correspondence with David Coder concerning his "The Fundamental Error of Central State Materialism," *American Philosophical Quarterly* 10 (1973), 289-298, and with David Rosenthal concerning his "Mentality and Neutrality," *Journal of Philosophy* 73 (1976), 386-415.

portable pain was "really" a pain or rather a stimulated C-fiber.[25]

If we stop asking questions about what counts as "mental" and what does not, and instead recall that incorrigibility is all that is at issue in puzzles about the Antipodeans, then we can see the argument for dualism offered above as an over-dramatized version of the following argument:

1. Some statements of the form "I just had a sensation of pain" are true
2'. Sensations of pain are incorrigibly reportable
3'. Neural events are not incorrigibly reportable
4'. Nothing can be both corrigibly and incorrigibly reportable
5. No sensation of pain is a neural event

Here the temptation to avoid (5) by denying (1) is much less great, for (4') is more easily criticized than (4). It is hard to say that "mental" really means "something that might turn out to be physical," just as it is hard to say that "criminal behavior" really means "behavior which might turn out to be innocent." That is why detailed attempts at topic-neutral analysis in hopes of denying (4) seem foredoomed. But it is relatively easy to deny (4') and say that something can be corrigibly reportable (by those who know neurology)

25 But this is not to say that the Antipodeans would have no impact on philosophy. The disappearance of psychology as a discipline distinct from neurology, and similar cultural developments, might eventually free us from the image of the Mirror of Nature much more effectively than philosophers' identity theories. Outside of philosophy, there would be a bit of "blurring" in ordinary speech (a bit of "not knowing *what* to say" when the sincere introspector defied the cerebroscope), but common sense, language, and culture have survived worse muddles than this. Compare, for example, conversations between moralistic judges and psychiatrists who produce a case history to show that "criminal" is inappositely applied to the accused's behavior. Nobody but an overzealous philosopher would think that there was an essence of "crime" determined by looking at, for example, "our language" and capable of resolving judges' dilemmas.

121

and incorrigibly reportable (by those who don't), as easy as to say, "Something can be treated rather than punished (by those who understand psychology) and punished rather than treated (by those who don't)." For in both these latter examples we are talking about social practices rather than "intrinsic properties of the entities in question" or "the logic of our language." It is easy to imagine different social practices in regard to the same objects, actions, or events, depending upon the degree of intellectual and spiritual development of the culture in question ("higher" stages of development being, *pace* Hegel, those in which Spirit is less self-conscious). So by denying (4') we seem to open the way for denying (5), and saying that "sensation" and "brain process" are just two ways of talking about the same thing.

Having earlier heaped scorn on both neutral monists and identity theorists, I may now seem to be edging into their camp. For the question now arises: Two ways of talking about *what*? Something mental or something physical? But here, I think, we have to resist our natural metaphysical urge, and *not* reply, "A third thing, of which both mentality and physicality are aspects." It would be better at this point to abandon argument and fall back on sarcasm, asking rhetorical questions like "What is this mental-physical contrast anyway? Whoever said that anything one mentioned had to fall into one or other of two (or half-a-dozen) ontological realms?" But this tactic seems disingenuous, since it seems obvious (once the psychology departments stop doing experiments with questionnaires and slide shows, and just do it all with cerebroscopes) that "the physical" has somehow triumphed.

But what did it triumph over? The mental? What was that? The practice of making incorrigible reports about certain of one's states? That seems too small a thing to count as an intellectual revolution. Perhaps, then, it triumphed over the sentimental intellectual's conviction that there was a private inner realm into which publicity, "scientific method," and society could not penetrate. But this is not right either. The secret in the poet's heart remains unknown to the secret police, despite their ability to predict his every thought, utterance, and movement by monitoring the cerebroscope which he must wear day and night. We can know which thoughts pass through a man's mind without understanding them. Our inviolable uniqueness lies in our poetic ability to say unique and obscure things, not in our ability to say obvious things to ourselves alone.

The real difficulty we encounter here is, once again, that we are trying to set aside the image of man as possessor of a Glassy Essence, suitable for mirroring nature with one hand, while holding on to it with the other. If we could ever drop the whole cluster of images which Antipodeans do not share with us, we would not be able to infer that matter had triumphed over spirit, science over privacy, or anything over anything else. These warring opposites are notions which do not make sense outside of a cluster of images inherited from the Terran seventeenth century. No one except philosophers, who are professionally obligated to take these images seriously, will be scandalized if people start saying, "The machine told me that it didn't really hurt—it only, very horribly, seemed to." Philosophers are too involved with notions like "ontological status" to take such developments lightly, but no other part of culture is. (Consider the fact that *only* philosophers remain perplexed about how one can have unconscious motives and desires.) Only the notion that philosophy should provide a permanent matrix of categories into which every possible empirical discovery and cultural development can be fitted without strain impels us to ask unanswerable questions like "Would this mean that there were no minds?" "Were we wrong about the nature of the mind?" "Were the Antipodeans right in saying, 'There never were any of those things you called "raw feels" '?"

Finally, the same overambitious conception of philosophy, stemming from the same set of seventeenth-century

123

images, is responsible for materialists' fears that unless
cerebral localization and "philosophical analysis" cooper-
ate to "identify" the mind and the body, then "the unity of
science" is endangered. If we follow Sellars in saying that
science is the measure of all things, then we shall not worry
about cerebral localization turning out to be a flop, much
less about materialist "analyses" of our everyday mentalistic
vocabulary succumbing to counter-examples. We shall not
interpret either failure as showing that science has all the
while been riding on two horses—one solid and one ghostly
—which may start galloping off in opposite directions at any
moment. Science's failure to figure out how the brain works
will cause no more danger to science's "unity" than its
failure to explain mononucleosis, or the migration of butterflies, or stockmarket cycles. Even if neurons turn out to
"swerve"—to be buffeted by forces as yet unknown to science—Descartes would not be vindicated. To think otherwise is to commit the fallacy of *omne ignotum pro spectro*
—taking everything one cannot understand to be a ghost,
something known in advance to be beyond the reach of science, and which must therefore be despairingly handed over
to philosophy.[26] If we do not think of philosophy as supply-

[26] This point can be made a bit more precisely by using Meehl and
Sellars's distinction between "physical₁," ("an event or entity is physical₁
if it belongs in the space-time network") and "physical₂," ("an event or
entity is physical₂ if it is definable in terms of theoretical primitives adequate to describe completely the actual states though not necessarily
the potentialities of the universe before the appearance of life"). This
distinction (drawn in "The Concept of Emergence," *Minnesota Studies
in the Philosophy of Science*, I [1956], 252) can be multiplied to distinguish "physical₁," from appropriate senses of "physical_n," defined in
terms of "the universe before the appearance of linguistic behavior"
(". . . of intentional action," "of beliefs and desires," etc.). For any
such distinction, the point to be emphasized is that science's failure to
explain something in terms of physical_n (for *n* greater than *1*) entities
does *nothing* to show that the explanation must be in terms of non-
physical₁ entities. The point is put to good use by Geoffrey Hellman
and Frank Thompson in "Physicalism: Ontology, Determination and
Reduction," *Journal of Philosophy* 72 (1975), 551-564 and "Physicalist

ing a permanent ontological frame for any possible scientific result (consisting, e.g., of categories like "mental" and "physical") we shall not think of science's failure as a vindication of Descartes, any more than we regard science's failure to explain the origin of the first living cell as a vindication of Aquinas. If the neurons do swerve, or if the brain works holistically rather than atomistically, this does not help show that we do, after all, have clear and distinct ideas of "the mental" and "the physical." These so-called ontological categories are simply the ways of packaging rather heterogenous notions, from rather diverse historical sources, which were convenient for Descartes's own purposes. But his purposes are not ours. Philosophers should not think of his artificial conglomerate as if it were a discovery of something preexistent—a discovery which because "intuitive" or "conceptual" or "categorical" sets permanent parameters for science and philosophy.

7. Epistemology and "the Philosophy of Mind"

I hope that the two chapters on the "mind-body problem" which the reader has just finished have persuaded him of at least the following points:

Unless we are willing to revive Platonic and Aristotelian notions about grasping universals, we shall not think that knowledge of general truths is made possible by some special, metaphysically distinctive, ingredient in human beings.

Unless we wish to revive the seventeenth century's somewhat awkward and inconsistent use of the Aristotelian notion of "substance" we shall not make sense of the notion of two ontological realms—the mental and the physical.

Materialism," *Nous* 11 (1977), 309-346. Their version of "materialism without identity" should be compared with Davidson's in his "Mental Events" (discussed in chapter four below).

Unless we wish to affirm what I have called Principle (P)—roughly, the claim that a distinctive metaphysical property of "presence to consciousness" grounds some of our noninferential reports of our states—we shall not be able to use the notion of "entities whose appearance exhausts their reality" to bolster the mental-physical distinction.

The notion that there is a problem about mind and body originated in the seventeenth century's attempt to make "the mind" a self-contained sphere of inquiry. The idea was to offer a para-mechanical account of mental processes which, somehow, would underwrite some claims to knowledge and disallow other claims. The paradigm of the "epistemological turn" taken by philosophy in the seventeenth century was what Kant called "the physiology of the human understanding of the celebrated Mr. Locke"—a causal account of mental processes which is supposed to criticize and justify knowledge-claims. To get this notion off the ground required the Cartesian replacement of the ancient and medieval problem of reason by the modern problem of consciousness. If what I have been saying in the past two chapters is right, the persistence of notions like the "mind-body problem" and "the philosophy of mind" is due to the persistence of the notion that there is some link between the older notions of reason or personhood and the Cartesian notion of consciousness. Part II of this book attempts to dissolve the modern version of the problem of reason— the notion that there is a problem about the possibility or extent of accurate representation which is the concern of a discipline called "epistemology." Insofar as it succeeds, this attempt frees us from the notion of human knowledge as an assemblage of representations in a Mirror of Nature, and thus reinforces the claim of part I that we can do without the notion of our Glassy Essence. If knowledge is not a matter of accuracy of representations, in any but the most trivial and unproblematic sense, then we need no inner mirror, and there is thus no mystery concerning the relation of that mirror to our grosser parts.

Even if the problems of consciousness and reason are both dissolved, however, that of personhood might seem to remain intact, since this notion draws on our moral intuitions, intuitions which seem unlikely to be merely the results of misguided Greek or seventeenth-century attempts to construct models of knowing or of the mind. Insofar as personhood is discussed in this book, it is in part III, in connection with the notion of "philosophy." There I try to show how the peculiarly philosophical project of picking out which entities are persons, and therefore possess moral dignity, on the basis of some "objective criterion"—for example, their possession of a Glassy Essence—is a confusion between, roughly, science and ethics. Part III tries to suggest a way of viewing our moral consciousness which avoids this idea.

Parts II and III thus pick up the notions which I listed in chapter one, section 3, above as "marks of the mental" but have not discussed in part I. They suggest ways of handling these notions—for example, intentionality, moral dignity—once the notion of a special mental ingredient— our Glassy Essence—is dropped. So I hope that some of the doubts which have emerged in the reader's mind in the course of part I, and some of the questions which may have been left dangling, will be resolved in the remainder of the book.

PART TWO

Mirroring

CHAPTER III

The Idea of a "Theory of Knowledge"

1. EPISTEMOLOGY AND PHILOSOPHY'S SELF-IMAGE

The notion that there is an autonomous discipline called "philosophy," distinct from and sitting in judgment upon both religion and science, is of quite recent origin. When Descartes and Hobbes denounced "the philosophy of the schools" they did not think of themselves as substituting a new and better kind of philosophy—a better theory of knowledge, or a better metaphysics, or a better ethics. Such distinctions among "fields of philosophy" were not yet drawn. The idea of "philosophy" itself, in the sense in which it has been understood since the subject became standardized as an academic subject in the nineteenth century, was not yet at hand. Looking backward we see Descartes and Hobbes as "beginning modern philosophy," but they thought of their own cultural role in terms of what Lecky was to call "the warfare between science and theology." They were fighting (albeit discreetly) to make the intellectual world safe for Copernicus and Galileo. They did not think of themselves as offering "philosophical systems," but as contributing to the efflorescence of research in mathematics and mechanics, as well as liberating intellectual life from ecclesiastical institutions. Hobbes defined "philosophy" as "such knowledge of effects of appearances, as we acquire by true ratiocination from the knowledge we have first of their causes of generation."[1] He had no wish to distinguish what he was doing from something else called "science." It was not until after Kant that our modern philosophy-science distinction took hold. Until the power of the

---

[1] Thomas Hobbes, *De Corpore*, chap. I, sec. 2.

churches over science and scholarship was broken, the energies of the men we now think of as "philosophers" were directed toward demarcating their activities from religion. It was only after that battle had been won that the question of separation from the sciences could arise.

The eventual demarcation of philosophy from science was made possible by the notion that philosophy's core was "theory of knowledge," a theory distinct from the sciences because it was their *foundation*. We now trace that notion back at least to Descartes's *Meditations* and Spinoza's *De Emendatione Intellectus*, but it did not achieve self-consciousness until Kant. It did not become built into the structure of academic institutions, and into the pat, unreflective self-descriptions of philosophy professors, until far into the nineteenth century. Without this idea of a "theory of knowledge," it is hard to imagine what "philosophy" could have been in the age of modern science. Metaphysics—considered as the description of how the heavens and the earth are put together—had been displaced by physics. The secularization of moral thought, which was the dominating concern of European intellectuals in the seventeenth and eighteenth centuries, was not then viewed as a search for a new metaphysical foundation to take the place of theistic metaphysics. Kant, however, managed to transform the old notion of philosophy—metaphysics as "queen of the sciences" because of its concern with what was most universal and least material—into the notion of a "most basic" discipline—a *foundational* discipline. Philosophy became "primary" no longer in the sense of "highest" but in the sense of "underlying." Once Kant had written, historians of philosophy were able to make the thinkers of the seventeenth and eighteenth centuries fall into place as attempting to answer the question "How is our knowledge possible?" and even to project this question back upon the ancients.[2]

[2] On the difference between histories of philosophy written before and after Kant, see Maurice Mandelbaum, "On the Historiography of

A "THEORY OF KNOWLEDGE"

This Kantian picture of philosophy as centered in epistemology, however, won general acceptance only after
Hegel and speculative idealism had ceased to dominate the
intellectual scene in Germany. It was only after people
like Zeller began saying that it was time to stop throwing
up systems and to get down to the patient labor of sorting
out the "given" from the "subjective additions" made by

Philosophy," *Philosophy Research Archives*, vol. II (1976); John Passmore's article on "Historiography of Philosophy" in *The Encyclopedia
of Philosophy* (New York, 1967); Lucien Braun, *Histoire de l'Histoire
de la Philosophie* (Paris, 1973), esp. chap. 5; Victor Cousin, *Introduction à l'Histoire de la Philosophie* (Paris, 1868), douzième leçon, "Des
Historiens de la Philosophie." Mandelbaum (p. 713) says of the fre-
quency with which the concept of the history of philosophy was discussed in the last decade of the eighteenth century in Germany that
"I believe it to be the case—although my documentation is insufficient
to make this more than a conjecture—that this discussion must have
been instigated through the impact of Kant's work in that period: by
the sense that his system was at one and the same time an end and a
new beginning." All these writers emphasize the contrast between
Brucker's *Historia Critica Philosophiae* of 1742-1767 and the histories
of Tiedemann (*Geist der spekulativen Philosophie*, 1791-1797) and
Tennemann (*Geschichte der Philosophie*, 1789-1819). Brucker devotes
about one-tenth of his space to the modern "syncretic philosophers"
(i.e., those who do not fit into one of the ancient schools) and includes
(besides the now standard sequence consisting of Bacon, Descartes,
Hobbes, Spinoza, etc.) some twenty-odd other figures (e.g., Machiavelli,
Kepler, Boyle). These are dropped from consideration by Tiedemann,
who originates the canonical short list of "great modern philosophers."
Tennemann tells us that "the history of philosophy is the exhibition
of the successive stages in the development of philosophy, the exhibition of the strivings of Reason to realize the idea of a science of the
ultimate bases and laws of Nature and of Freedom," having previously
told us that reason begins with the faculty of "unifying the manifold
of representations," and continues from there to the ultimate unification of scientific thought. (*Geschichte der Philosophie*, vol. I, Leipzig, 1798, pp. xxix, xxvi.) His history of philosophy already has the
"dramatic" quality which we associate with Hegel's. He gives us both
a canon of those who are to count as philosophers, based on how closely
their work can be thought to resemble Kant's, and the notion of
progress in philosophy from the ancients to the moderns.

133

the mind that philosophy could be thoroughly professionalized.[3] The "back to Kant" movement of the 1860s in Germany was also a "let's get down to work" movement—a way
of separating the autonomous nonempirical discipline of
philosophy from ideology on the one hand and from the
rising science of empirical psychology on the other. The
picture of "epistemology-and-metaphysics" as the "center of
philosophy" (and of "metaphysics" as something which
emerges out of epistemology rather than vice versa), which
was established by the neo-Kantians, is the one built into
philosophy curricula today.[4] The expression *theory of
knowledge* itself attained currency and respectability only
after Hegel had gone stale. The first generation of Kant's
admirers used *Vernunftkritik* as a handy label for "what

[3] Cf. Edouard Zeller, "Über Bedeutung und Aufgabe der Erkenntnistheorie" in *Vorträge und Abhandlungen,* Zweite Sammlung (Leipzig,
1877), p. 495. Zeller's essay is one of a long sequence since Kant which
announces that the day of the philosophical amateur is over and that
the professionals are now in charge. For a later version, see G. J. Warnock, *English Philosophy Since 1900* (London, 1958), p. 171: ". . .
philosophy has only rather recently achieved professional status" and
p. 172: ". . . it is only quite recently that the subject matter, or rather
the tasks, of philosophy have come to be clearly distinguished from
those of other disciplines." (Warnock is speaking of the period 1900-
1958.) I do not know the earliest appearance of such claims, but note
Ernst Reinhold's use of the term *Philosophen von Profession* to contrast with the *alle wissenschaftlich Gebildete* for whom his *Handbuch
der allgemeinen Geschichte der Philosophie* is intended. (*Handbuch
. . .* , Erster Theil, Gotha, 1828, p. v) The *Einleitung* to Reinhold's
history is useful for confirming Mandelbaum's claim (cf. note 2 above)
about the relation of Kantian thought to the replacement of "chronicles
of the opinions of the philosophers" by "history of philosophy" in the
modern sense.

[4] As I shall be arguing in more detail below, especially in chapter
six, the contemporary notion of philosophy of language as "first philosophy" is not so much a change from the older claim that epistemology
was "first" as a minor variant upon it. The central claim of philosophy
since Kant has been that the "possibility of representing reality" was
what needed explanation, and for this project the difference between
mental and linguistic representations is relatively unimportant.

134

Kant did," and the words *Erkenntnislehre* and *Erkenntnistheorie* were invented a bit later (in 1808 and 1832 respectively).[5] But Hegel and idealistic system-building had by then intervened to obscure the question "What is the relation of philosophy to other disciplines?" Hegelianism produced an image of philosophy as a discipline which somehow both completed and swallowed up the other disciplines, rather than *grounding* them. It also made philosophy too popular, too interesting, too important, to be properly professional; it challenged philosophy professors to embody the World-Spirit, rather than simply getting on with their *Fach*. The essay of Zeller's which (according to Mauthner) "first raised the term 'Erkenntnistheorie' to its present academic dignity,"[6] ends by saying that those who believe that we can spin all the sciences out of our own spirit may continue on with Hegel, but anyone saner should recognize that the proper task of philosophy (once the notion of the thing-in-itself, and thus the temptations of idealism, are rejected) is to establish the objectivity of the knowledge-claims made in the various empirical disciplines.

5 Cf. Hans Vaihinger, "Über den Ursprung des Wortes 'Erkenntnistheorie,'" *Philosophische Monatshefte*, vol. XII (Leipzig, 1876), pp. 84-90 for the history of the term. Vaihinger presents the view, which most neo-Kantians seemed to share, and which I am adopting here, that Locke was the first to "have a clear consciousness that all metaphysical and ethical discussion must be preceded by epistemological investigations," and that what Descartes and Spinoza said along these lines was merely occasional and unsystematic (p. 84). I am indebted for the reference to Vaihinger (as well as for other references and for many enlightening ideas) to an unpublished paper by Ian Hacking on the rise of epistemology as a discipline.

6 Fritz Mauthner, *Wörterbuch der Philosophie* (Munich and Leipzig, 1910), s.v. "Erkenntnistheorie," vol. 1, p. 296: "ein ausschliesslich deutscher Ausdruck, von Reinhold der Sohne (nach Eisler) geprägt, aber erst durch Zeller zu seiner jetzigen akademischen Würde promoviert." The same claim for Zeller is made by Vaihinger, "Wortes 'Erkenntnistheorie,'" p. 89. Vaihinger's article is both a report on, and an example of, the new "professionalized" self-image which neo-Kantian philosophers were in the course of creating.

135

This will be done by the appropriateness of the a priori contributions brought to bear in perception.[7] *Erkenntnistheorie* thus appears in 1862 as a way out from both "idealism" and "speculation." Fifteen years later, Zeller notes there is no longer any need to point out the proper role of *Erkenntnistheorie*, since this is now commonly accepted, especially by "our younger colleagues."[8] Thirty years further on, William James would bemoan "the gray-plaster temperament of our bald-headed young Ph.D.'s, boring each other at seminaries, writing those direful reports of literature in the *Philosophical Review* and elsewhere, fed on 'books of reference' and never confounding 'Aesthetik' with 'Erkenntnistheorie.' "[9]

In this chapter I want to trace some of the crucial stages in the transition from the campaigns of Descartes and Hobbes against "the philosophy of the schools" to the nineteenth century's reestablishment of philosophy as an autonomous, self-contained, "scholastic," discipline. I shall try to back up the claim (common to Wittgenstein and Dewey) that to think of knowledge which presents a "problem," and about which we ought to have a "theory," is a product of viewing knowledge as an assemblage of representations—a view of knowledge which, I have been arguing, was a product of the seventeenth century. The moral to be drawn is that if this way of thinking of knowledge is optional, then so is epistemology, and so is philosophy as it has understood itself since the middle of the last century. The story I shall be telling about how philosophy-as-epistemology attained self-certainty in the modern period will go like this:

Descartes's invention of the mind—his coalescence of beliefs and sensations into Lockean ideas—gave philosophers new ground to stand on. It provided a field of inquiry which seemed "prior" to the subjects on which the ancient

[7] Zeller, "Erkenntnistheorie," pp. 494-495.
[8] Ibid., p. 496.
[9] William James, *Letters*, ed. Henry James (Boston, 1920), p. 228 (letter to George Santayana of May 2, 1905).

philosophers had had opinions. Further, it provided a field within which *certainty*, as opposed to mere *opinion*, was possible.

Locke made Descartes's newly contrived "mind" into the subject matter of a "science of man"—moral philosophy as opposed to natural philosophy. He did this by confusedly thinking that an analogue of Newton's particle mechanics for "inner space" would somehow be "of great advantage in directing our Thoughts in the search of other Things"[10] and would somehow let us "see, what Objects our Understandings were, or were not fitted to deal with."[11]

This project of learning more about what we could know and how we might know it better by studying how our mind worked was eventually to be christened "epistemology." But before the project could come to full self-consciousness, a way had to be found of making it a *nonempirical* project. It had to be a matter of armchair reflection, independent of physiological discoveries and capable of producing necessary truths. Whereas Locke had retained the new inner space of research—the workings of the newly invented Cartesian mind—he had not been able to hold onto Cartesian certainty. Locke's "sensualism" was not yet a suitable candidate for the vacant position of "queen of the sciences."

Kant put philosophy "on the secure path of a science" by putting outer space inside inner space (the space of the constituting activity of the transcendental ego) and then claiming Cartesian certainty about the inner for the laws of what had previously been thought to be outer. He thus reconciled the Cartesian claim that we can have certainty only about our ideas with the fact that we already had certainty—a priori knowledge—about what seemed not to be ideas. The Copernican revolution was based on the notion that we can only know about objects a priori if we "constitute" them, and Kant was never troubled by the question of how we could have apodictic knowledge of these "constitut-

10 John Locke, *Essay* I, 1, i.
11 Ibid., "Epistle to the Reader."

ing activities," for Cartesian privileged access was supposed to take care of that.[12] Once Kant replaced the "physiology of the human understanding of the celebrated Mr. Locke" with (in Strawson's words) "the mythical subject of transcendental psychology," "epistemology" as a discipline came of age.

Besides raising "the science of man" from an empirical to an a priori level, Kant did three other things which helped philosophy-as-epistemology to become self-conscious and self-confident. First, by identifying the central issue of epistemology as the relations between two equally real but irreducibly distinct sorts of representations—"formal" ones (concepts) and "material" ones (intuitions)—he made it possible to see important continuities between the new epistemological problematic and problems (the problems of reason and of universals) which had bothered the ancients and the medievals. He thereby made it possible to write "histories of philosophy" of the modern sort. Second, by linking epistemology to morality in the project of "destroying reason to make room for faith" (that is, destroying Newtonian determinism to make room for the common moral consciousness), he revived the notion of a "complete philosophical system," one in which morality was "grounded" on something less controversial and more scientific. Whereas the ancient schools had each had a view of human virtue designed to match their view of what the world was like, Newton had preempted views on the latter subject. With Kant, epistemology was able to step into metaphysics' role of guarantor of the presuppositions of morality. Third, by taking everything we say to be about something we have

12 See K.d.r.V., Bxvi-xvii: The supposition that "objects must conform to our knowledge," Kant says, "agrees better with the supposition that it should be possible to have knowledge of objects a priori, determining something in regard to them prior to their being given." The question of how we know what conditions they must conform to—how to validate knowledge-claims made from the transcendental standpoint—is discussed neither here nor elsewhere in the first Critique.

"constituted," he made it possible for epistemology to be thought of as a foundational science, an armchair discipline capable of discovering the "formal" (or, in later versions, "structural," "phenomenological," "grammatical," "logical," or "conceptual") characteristics of any area of human life. He thus enabled philosophy professors to see themselves as presiding over a tribunal of pure reason, able to determine whether other disciplines were staying within the legal limits set by the "structure" of their subject matters.[13]

2. LOCKE'S CONFUSION OF EXPLANATION WITH JUSTIFICATION

The "epistemological turn" taken by Descartes might not have captured Europe's imagination had it not been for a crisis of confidence in established institutions, a crisis expressed paradigmatically in Montaigne. But we should distinguish traditional Pyrrhonian skepticism about our ability to attain certainty from the new veil-of-ideas skepticism which Descartes made possible by carving out inner space. Traditional skepticism had been troubled principally by the "problem of the criterion"—the problem of validating procedures of inquiry while avoiding either circularity or dogmatism. This problem, which Descartes thought he had solved by "the method of clear and distinct ideas," had little to do with the problem of getting from inner space to outer space—the "problem of the external world" which

---

[13] Kant's fondness for jurisprudential metaphors has often been remarked. It is also found in the neo-Kantians. See, for example, Zeller's "Über die Aufgabe der Philosophie und ihre Stellung zu den übrigen Wissenschaften" (*Vorträge und Abhandlungen*, Zweite Sammlung, pp. 445-466). In the course of sketching the philosopher's pretensions as overseer of culture, he speaks of the *Rechtstitel* which each discipline should secure from philosophy and says that "there is no branch of human knowledge of which the roots do not reach down into philosophical terrain, for all science springs from the knowing spirit and borrows its laws from that spirit's procedures" (p. 465).

became paradigmatic for modern philosophy.[14] The idea of a "theory of knowledge" grew up around this latter problem—the problem of knowing whether our inner representations were accurate. The idea of a discipline devoted to "the nature, origin, and limits of human knowledge"—the textbook definition of "epistemology"—required a field of study called "the human mind," and that field of study was what Descartes had created. The Cartesian mind simultaneously made possible veil-of-ideas skepticism and a discipline devoted to circumventing such skepticism.

This is not to say, however, that the invention of the Cartesian mind is a *sufficient* condition for the development of epistemology. That invention gave us the notion of inner representations, but this notion would not have given rise to epistemology without the confusion I attributed to Locke—the confusion, of which Descartes was largely innocent, between a mechanistic account of the operations of our mind and the "grounding" of our claims to knowledge. This is what T. H. Green was to call

the fundamental confusion, on which all empirical psychology rests, between two essentially distinct questions—

[14] The uneasy relations between these two forms of skepticism are illustrated by section XII of Hume's *Enquiry Concerning Human Understanding*, "Of the Academical or Sceptical Philosophy." Hume wants to distinguish the skepticism of Descartes's *First Meditation* (which he thought hyperbolical and impossible) both from his own veil-of-ideas skepticism based on the view that "nothing can ever be present to the mind but an image or perception" (David Hume, *Philosophical Works* [Boston and Edinburgh, 1854], vol. 4, p. 173) and from Pyrrhonism, or *excessive* skepticism (p. 183). He was anxious to separate the second from the third and to insist that one not take the merely "professional" and "technical" skepticism of the "new way of ideas" seriously. Hume did not think of himself as finding new arguments to support Sextus; rather he was anxious to show that the skeptical outcome of Locke's project showed not (as Kant and Russell were to believe) the need for a new and better sort of epistemology but the need to appreciate the unimportance of epistemology and the importance of sentiment. On Pyrrhonism in the period before Descartes, see Richard Popkin, *History of Scepticism from Erasmus to Descartes* (New York, 1964).

one metaphysical, What is the simplest element of knowledge? the other physiological, What are the conditions in the individual human organism in virtue of which it becomes a vehicle of knowledge?[15]

Green's distinction between an "element of knowledge" and "the conditions of the organism" reminds us that a claim to knowledge is a claim to have justified belief, and that it is rarely the case that we appeal to the proper functioning of our organism as a *justification*. Granted that we sometimes justify a belief by saying, for example, "I have good eyes," why should we think that chronological or compositional "relations between ideas," conceived of as *events* in inner space, could tell us about the logical relations between *propositions*? After all, as Sellars says:

> In characterizing an episode or a state as that of *knowing*, we are not giving an empirical description of that episode or state; we are placing it in the logical space of reasons, of justifying and being able to justify what one says.[16]

How was it that Locke should have committed what Sellars calls "a mistake of a piece with the so-called 'naturalistic fallacy' in ethics," the attempt to "analyze epistemic facts without remainder into non-epistemic facts"?[17] Why should he have thought that a causal account of how one comes to have a belief should be an indication of the justification one has for that belief?

The answer, I think, is that Locke, and seventeenth-century writers generally, simply did *not* think of knowledge as justified true belief. This was because they did not think of knowledge as a relation between a person and a proposi-

---

15 T. H. Green, *Hume and Locke* [Green's "Introductions" to Hume's *Treatise*], ed. Ramon Lemos (New York, 1968), p. 19.

16 Wilfrid Sellars, *Science, Perception and Reality* (London and New York, 1963), p. 169.

17 Ibid., p. 131. For a development of Sellars's point, with application to recent phenomenalisms, see Michael Williams, *Groundless Belief* (Oxford, 1977), esp. chap. 2.

tion. *We* find it natural to think of "what S knows" as the collection of propositions completing true statements by S which begin "I know that. . . ." When we realize that the blank may be filled by such various material as "this is red," "e = mc²," "my Redeemer liveth," and "I shall marry Jane," we are rightly skeptical of the notion of "the nature, origin, and limits of human knowledge," and of a "department of thought" devoted to this topic. But Locke did not think of "knowledge that" as the primary form of knowledge. He thought, as had Aristotle, of "knowledge of" as prior to "knowledge that," and thus of knowledge as a relation between persons and objects rather than persons and propositions. Given that picture, the notion of an examination of our "faculty of understanding" makes sense, as does the notion that it is fitted to deal with some sorts of objects and not with others. It makes even more sense if one is convinced that this faculty is something like a wax tablet upon which objects make *impressions*, and if one thinks of "having an impression" as in itself a *knowing* rather than a causal antecedent of knowing.

It was just the notion of an "impression" upon which Reid—the great eighteenth-century enemy of the " 'idea' idea"—fastened, to be followed by Green in the following century, and by a host of others (H. A. Prichard, Wilfrid Sellars, J. L. Austin, Jonathan Bennett) in our own. Reid says:

> There is no prejudice more natural to man, than to conceive of the mind as having some similitude to body in its operations. Hence, men have been prone to imagine, that as bodies are put in motion by some impulse or impression made upon them by contiguous bodies; so the mind is made to think and to perceive by some impression made upon it, or some impulse given to it by contiguous bodies.[18]

[18] Thomas Reid, *Essays on the Intellectual Powers of Man*, reprinted with an introduction by Baruch Brody (Cambridge, Mass., 1969), p. 100.

142

Green, in a passage following the one quoted from him above, says that only through the confusion between elements of knowledge (propositions) and physiological conditions can "any idea be described as an 'impression' at all. . . . A metaphor, interpreted as a fact, becomes the basis of (Locke's) philosophical system."[19] Sellars (speaking of Hume rather than Locke) diagnoses a confusion between:

1. An impression of a red triangle as a red and triangular item which is immediately and noninferentially known to exist and to be red and triangular.

[and]

2. An impression of a red triangle as a knowing that a red and triangular item exists.[20]

All three criticisms are protests against the notion that a quasi-mechanical account of the way in which our immaterial tablets are dented by the material world will help us know what we are entitled to believe.

Locke presumably thought himself justified in running together the two senses of "impression" distinguished by Sellars because he thought the dents in our quasi-tablet to be (as Ryle puts it) self-intimating. Thus he says: ". . . imprinting, if it signify any thing, being nothing else, but the making certain Truths to be perceived. For to imprint anything on the Mind without the Mind's perceiving it, seems to me hardly intelligible."[21] It is as if the *tabula rasa* were perpetually under the gaze of the unblinking Eye of the Mind—nothing, as Descartes said, being nearer to the mind than itself. If the metaphor *is* unpacked in this way, however, it becomes obvious that the imprinting is of less interest than the observation of the imprint—all the knowing gets done, so to speak, by the Eye which observes the

19 Green, *Hume and Locke*, p. 11.
20 Wilfrid Sellars, *Philosophical Perspectives* (Springfield, Ill., 1967), p. 211.
21 Locke, *Essay*, I, 2, v.

imprinted tablet, rather than by the tablet itself. Locke's success, accordingly, depended upon *not* unpacking the metaphor, on leaving intact the ambiguity between the quasi-red-and-triangular quasi-object in inner space and knowledge that such an object was there. Whereas Aristotle had not had to worry about an Eye of the Mind, believing knowledge to be the *identity* of the mind with the object known, Locke did not have this alternative available. Since for him impressions were *representations*, he needed a faculty which was *aware* of the representations, a faculty which *judged* the representations rather than merely *had* them—judged that they existed, or that they were reliable, or that they had such-and-such relations to other representations. But he had no room for one, for to postulate such a faculty would have intruded a ghost into the quasi-machine whose operation he hoped to describe. He kept just enough of Aristotle to retain the idea of knowledge as consisting of something object-like entering the soul,[22] but not enough to avoid either skeptical problems about the accuracy of representations or Kantian questions about the difference between intuitions with and without the "I think." To put it another way, the Cartesian conglomerate *mind* which Locke took for granted resembled Aristotelian νοῦς just enough to give a traditional flavor to the notion of "impression" and departed from it just enough to make Humean skepticism and Kantian transcendentalism possible. Locke was balancing awkwardly between knowledge-as-identity-with-object and knowledge-as-true-judgment-about-object, and the confused idea of "moral philosophy" as an empirical "science of man" was possible only because of this transitional stance.[23]

[22] Reid thought that Aristotle, in his doctrine of phantasms, had begun the descent down the slippery slope which led to Hume. Cf. *Essays*, p. 133.

[23] In his groundbreaking *The Emergence of Probability* (Cambridge, 1975), Ian Hacking suggests that the idea of *evidence*, as a relation of confirmation holding between propositions, was just begin-

Still another way of describing the tension in Locke's thought is to see it as pulled on one side toward physiology and on another side toward Aristotle. Reid and Green, once again, agree in this diagnosis. Reid says of Descartes that

> he sometimes places the ideas of material objects in the brain . . . yet he sometimes says, that we are not to conceive the images or traces in the brain to be perceived as if there were eyes in the brain; these traces are only occasions on which, by the laws of the union of soul and body, ideas are excited in the mind. . . . Descartes seems to have hesitated between the two opinions, or to have passed from the one to the other. Mr. Locke seems, in like manner, to have wavered between the two; sometimes representing the ideas of material things as being in the brain, but more frequently as in the mind itself.[24]

Green, discussing Locke's "ideas of reflection," speaks of his "confusion of thought and matter in the imaginary cerebral tablet" and says that

> Locke disguises the difficulty from himself and his reader by constantly shifting both the receptive subject and the impressive matter. We find the "tablet" perpetually receding. First it is the "outward part" or bodily organ. Then it is the brain. . . . Then it is the perceptive mind, which takes an impression of the sensation or has an idea of it. Finally, it is the reflective mind. . . .[25]

The reason for the shuffling which Reid and Green criticize is that if (like Aristotle and Locke) one tries to model *all*

---

ning to emerge in the seventeenth century. If Hacking is right, then this fact sheds considerable light on the various awkward blendings of propositional and (purported) nonpropositional knowledge in the work of the British empiricists. See especially Hacking's remarks on Locke, Berkeley, and Hume in chapter 19.

[24] Reid, *Essays*, pp. 147-148.
[25] Green, *Hume and Locke*, p. 11; cf. also p. 163.

knowledge on sense-perception, then one will be torn between the literal way in which part of the body (e.g., the retina) can have the same quality as an external object and the metaphorical way in which the person as a whole has, for example, froghood "in mind" if he has views about frogs. The notion of an "immaterial tablet" splits the difference between simple physiological fact and speculative metaphor, and any philosophy which uses it will be torn both ways. It is precisely the choice of sense-perception as a model, and in particular of ocular imagery, which makes both Aristotle and Locke attempt to reduce "knowledge that"—justified true belief in propositions—to "knowledge of" construed as "having in mind." Since Locke views himself as an up-to-date scientist he would love to cash the "tablet" metaphor in physiological terms. Since he cannot, shuffling is his only option. When he shuffles back toward Aristotle, he begins to talk about a "reflective mind" which is very un-tablet-like indeed.

However, the most important shuffle in Locke's treatment of knowledge is not between brain and νοῦς but, as I have said, between knowledge as something which, being the simple *having* of an idea, can take place without judgment, and knowledge as that which results from forming justified judgments. This is the shuffle which Kant detected as the basic error of empiricism—the error most vigorously expressed in his criticism of the confusion of "a succession of apprehensions with an apprehension of succession," but which bears equally upon the confusion between merely having two "juxtaposed" ideas—froghood and greenness— and "synthesizing" these into the judgment "Frogs are usually green." Just as Aristotle has no clear way to relate grasping universals to making judgments, no way to relate the receptivity of forms into the mind to the construction of propositions, neither has Locke. This is the principal defect of *any* attempt to reduce "knowledge that" to "knowledge of," to model knowing on seeing.

This defect in Locke was thought by Green, and by most

writers in epistemology in the nineteenth century, to have been made good by Kant. Green sums up his own basic criticism of British empiricism in the following passage:

Locke's empiricism becomes invincible as soon as it is admitted that qualified things are "found in nature" without any constitutive action of the mind. As the only effective way of dealing with Locke is to ask—After abstraction of all that he himself admitted to be the creation of thought, what remains to be merely found?—so Hume must be met *in limine* by the question whether, apart from such ideas of relation as according to his own showing are not simple impressions, so much as the singular proposition is possible. If not, then the singularity of such proposition does not consist in any singleness of presentation to sense.[26]

The phrase "constitutive action of the mind" is the tip-off to Green's own view of the matter, which is summed up in the slogan of the British Idealists: Only Thought Relates. They viewed this doctrine as an abbreviation of Kant's slogan that "intuitions without concepts are blind." Kant's discovery was supposed to have been that there are no "qualified things"—no objects—prior to "the constitutive action of the mind." An object—something of which several predicates are true—is thus always a result of synthesis.

With Kant, the attempt to formulate a "theory of knowledge" advanced half of the way toward a conception of knowledge as fundamentally "knowing that" rather than "knowing of"—halfway toward a conception of knowing which was *not* modeled on perception. Unfortunately, however, Kant's way of performing the shift still remained within the Cartesian frame of reference; it was still phrased as an answer to the question of how we could get from inner space to outer space. His paradoxical answer was that outer space was constructed out of the *Vorstellungen* which

26 Ibid., pp. 185-186.

147

inhabited inner space. Nineteenth-century attempts to preserve the insight that knowledge is a relation to propositions
rather than to objects while avoiding Kantian paradox also
remained within the Cartesian frame, and thus were "ideal-
isms." The only object of which they could conceive was
one constituted by the synthesis of Lockean ideas, and thus
they devoted themselves to identifying the ensemble of such
objects with the thing-in-itself. So in order to understand
the idea of "epistemology" as the twentieth century inherited it, we need to turn from Locke's confusion between
explanation and justification to Kant's confusion between
predication (saying something about an object) and synthesis (putting representations together in inner space).

3. Kant's Confusion of Predication with Synthesis

For a person to form a predicative judgment is for him
to come to believe a sentence to be true. For a Kantian transcendental ego to come to believe a sentence to be true is for
it to relate representations (*Vorstellungen*) to one another:
two radically distinct sorts of representations, concepts on
the one hand and intuitions on the other. Kant provided a
framework for understanding the confusing seventeenth-
century intellectual scene when he said that "Leibniz intel-
lectualized appearances, just as Locke . . . sensualized all
concepts of the understanding."[27] He thereby created the
standard version of "the history of modern philosophy"
according to which pre-Kantian philosophy was a struggle
between "rationalism," which wanted to reduce sensations
to concepts, and "empiricism," which wanted the inverse
reduction. Had Kant instead said that the rationalists
wanted to find a way of replacing propositions about
secondary qualities with propositions which somehow did
the same job but were known with certainty, and that the
empiricists opposed this project, the next two centuries of
philosophical thought might have been very different. For

[27] *K.d.r.V.* A271, B327.

if the "problem of knowledge" had been stated in terms of the relations between propositions and the degree of certainty attaching to them, rather than in terms of putative *components* of propositions, we might not have inherited our present notion of "the history of philosophy. "According to standard neo-Kantian historiography, from the time of the *Phaedo* and *Metaphysics Z* through Abelard and Anselm, Locke and Leibniz, and right down to Quine and Strawson reflection which was distinctively *philosophical* has concerned the relation between universals and particulars. Without this unifying theme, we might not have been able to see a continuous problematic, discovered by the Greeks and worried at continuously down to our own day, and thus might never have had the notion of "philosophy" as something with a twenty-five-hundred-year history. Greek thought and seventeenth-century thought might have seemed as distinct both from each other and from our present concerns as, say, Hindu theology and Mayan numerology.

For better or worse, however, Kant did not take this pragmatic turn. He talked about inner representations rather than sentences. He simultaneously gave us a history of our subject, fixed its problematic, and professionalized it (if only by making it impossible to be taken seriously as a "philosopher" without having mastered the first *Critique*). He did so by building into our conception of a "theory of knowledge" (and thus our conception of what distinguished philosophers from scientists) what C. I. Lewis called "one of the oldest and most universal philosophical insights," viz.:

> There are, in our cognitive experience, two elements; the immediate data, such as those of sense, which are presented or given to the mind, and a form, construction, or interpretation, which represents the activity of thought.[28]

The "insight," however, is neither old nor universal. It is no older than the notion that we possess something called

28 Lewis, *Mind and the World-Order* (New York, 1956), p. 38.

"cognitive experience." The term *experience* has come to be the epistemologists' name for their subject matter, a name for the ensemble of Cartesian *cogitationes*, Lockean ideas. In this sense, "experience" is a term of philosophical art (quite distinct from the everyday use, as in "experience on the job," in which it is equivalent to ἐμπειρία). Lewis's claim that when we look at this ensemble we find it falling into two kinds makes it sound as if the man in the street, untutored in philosophy, could simply be asked to turn his mental eye inward and notice the distinction. But a man who does not know that Locke used "experience" to include only "ideas of sensation and reflection" and to exclude judgments, and that Kant used it to cover "both the object and the method of knowledge, the combination, in accordance with the laws of thought, of all functions of knowledge,"[29] may be baffled about what he is supposed to look *at*, much less what distinction he is to notice.

Strawson repeats Lewis's claim when he says "the duality of general concepts . . . and particular instances of general concepts encountered in experience" is a "fundamental duality, inescapable in any philosophical thinking about experience or empirical knowledge."[30] This version is less misleading than Lewis's, simply because it includes the word *philosophical*. For the reason this duality is inescapable in *philosophical* thinking about experience is just that those who do not find it do not call themselves "philosophers." We can only explain what "philosophical thinking about experience" is by reference to the sort of thing which Kant did. Psychologists can go on about stimuli and responses, but

[29] Heinrich Ratke, *Systematisches Handlexikon zu Kants Kritik der Reinen Vernunft* (Hamburg, 1929), p. 62: "Erfahrung bezeichnet sowohl den *Gegenstand* als die *Methode* der Erkenntnis, den denkgesetzlichen Zusammenhang aller Funktionen der Erkenntnis." Kant's usage is, indeed, such that no definition less fuzzy and less richly ambiguous than Ratke's could do it justice. On the philosophic sense of "experience," see John Dewey, *Experience and Nature* (New York, 1958), p. 11.

[30] P. F. Strawson, *The Bounds of Sense* (London, 1966), p. 20.

this is *blosse Naturalismus*, and does not count as "philosophical." Common sense can talk about experience in its banal way—pondering whether we have had enough experience with something to make a judgment about it, for example, but this too is not philosophical. Thought is only *philosophical* if, like Kant's, it looks for causes of, rather than merely reasons for, claims to empirical knowledge, and if the resulting causal account is compatible with anything which psychological inquiry might come up with.[31] Philosophical thinking of the sort which finds this duality inescapable is supposed to do more than just tell us that normally we have knowledge when we have justified true belief, referring us to common sense and common practice for details about what counts as justification. It is supposed to explain *how knowledge is possible*, and to do that in some a priori way which both goes beyond common sense and yet avoids any need to mess about with neurons, or rats, or questionnaires.

Given these somewhat exiguous requirements and no knowledge of the history of philosophy we might well be puzzled about just what was wanted and about where to begin. Such puzzlement can only be alleviated by getting the hang of terms like "Being versus Becoming," "sense versus intellect," "clear versus confused perceptions," "simple versus complex ideas," "ideas and impressions," "concepts and intuitions." We will thereby get into the epistemological language-game, and the professional form of life called

---

[31] It may seem shocking to call Kant's account "causal," but the notion of "transcendental constitution" is entirely parasitical on the Descartes-Locke notion of the mechanics of inner space, and Kant's self-deceptive use of "ground" rather than "cause" should not be permitted to obscure this point. If we eliminate from Kant what Strawson calls "the mythical subject of transcendental psychology" we can make no sense of the Copernican revolution. I have discussed Strawson's version of what remains of Kant once one forgets the Copernican revolution in "Strawson's Objectivity Argument," *Review of Metaphysics* 24 (1970), 207-244.

"philosophy." When we begin our philosophical meditations we do not, as Lewis and Strawson suggest, inevitably stumble across the intuition-concept distinction. Rather, we would not know what counted as "experience," much less as being *philosophical* about it, unless we had mastered that distinction. For, once again, the notion of a "theory of knowledge" will not make sense unless we have confused causation and justification in the manner of Locke, and even then it will seem fuzzy until we have isolated some entities in inner space whose causal relations seem puzzling. "Concepts" and "intuitions" are exactly the entities required. If Kant had gone straight from the insight that "the singular proposition" is not to be identified with "the singularity of a presentation to sense" (nor, for that matter, to intellect) to a view of knowledge as a relation between persons and propositions, he would not have needed the notion of "synthesis." He might have viewed a person as a black box emitting sentences, the justification for these emissions being found in his relation to his environment (including the emissions of his fellow black boxes). The question "How is knowledge possible?" would then have resembled the question "How are telephones possible?" meaning something like "How can one build something which does that?" Physiological psychology, rather than "epistemology," would then have seemed the only legitimate follow-up to the *De Anima* and the *Essay Concerning Human Understanding*.

It is important, however, before leaving Kant behind, to ask *how* he contrived to make the concept-intuition distinction look both plausible and intriguingly problematic. To understand this, we must notice that the Kantian "synthesis" required for a judgment differs from the Humean "association of ideas" in being a relation which can hold only between ideas of two different sorts—general ideas and particular ideas. .The notions of "synthesis" and the concept-intuition distinction are thus tailor-made for one another, both being invented to make sense of the paradoxical but unquestioned assumption which runs through the first *Critique*—the assumption that manifoldness is "given" and that unity is made. That assumption is spelled out in the claim that inner space does contain something like what Hume found there, a collection of "singular presentations to sense," but that these "intuitions" cannot be "brought to consciousness" unless "synthesized" by a second set of representations (unnoticed by Hume)—the concepts—which enter into one-many relations with batches of intuitions. Unofficially, to be sure, the reason for this assumption is that it is required by the strategy of the Copernican revolution, to insure that objects will conform to our knowledge rather than be able to demand conformity from us.[32] But officially, it is used as a premise in the "Transcendental Deduction" to argue that the "Copernican" strategy works. The "Deduction" is supposed to show that we can only be conscious of objects constituted by our own synthesizing activity. Officially, then, we are supposed just to *see* that

of all representations, *combination* is the only one which cannot be given through objects. . . . For where the understanding has not previously combined, it cannot dissolve, since only as having been combined *by the understanding* can anything that allows of analysis be given to the faculty of representation.[33]

But how, if we have not read Locke and Hume, do we know that the mind is presented with a diversity? Why should we think that sensibility "in its original receptivity"[34] presents us with a manifold, a manifold which, however, "cannot be represented as a manifold"[35] until the under-

---

[32] *K.d.r.V.*, Bxvii.   [33] Ibid., B130.   [34] Ibid., A100.

[35] Ibid., A99. According to the *Transcendental Aesthetic*, of course, the manifold is spatio-temporal from the outset. But the *Analytic* contradicts this (cf., e.g., A102, B160n), and the argument of the *Analogies* would not go through unless the doctrine of the *Aesthetic* were abandoned. Cf. Robert Paul Wolff, *Kant's Theory of Mental Activity* (Cambridge, Mass., 1963), pp. 151ff. on this point.

standing has used concepts to synthesize it? We cannot intro-spect and see that it does, because we are never conscious of unsynthesized intuitions, nor of concepts apart from their application to intuitions. The doctrine that we are not so conscious is precisely Kant's advance in the direction of taking knowledge to be of propositions rather than of objects—his step away from the attempts of Aristotle and Locke to model knowing on perceiving. But if it is not an evident pre-analytic fact that such a manifold exists, how can we use the claim that sensibility presents us with a manifold as a premise? How, in other words, do we know that a manifold which cannot be represented as a manifold *is* a manifold? More generally, if we are going to argue that we can only be conscious of synthesized intuitions, how do we get our information about intuitions prior to synthesis? How, for instance, do we know that there is more than one of them?[36]

This last question can be answered by saying that if there were only one then synthesis would be unnecessary. But this just leads us around a rather small circle. What we want to know is whether concepts *are* synthesizers, and it is no help to be told that they couldn't be unless there were a lot of intuitions awaiting synthesis. At this point, I think, we must confess that "intuition" and "concept," in their Kantian senses, are susceptible only of contextual defini-tions; like "electron" and "proton," they have sense only as elements in a theory which hopes to explain something. But with that admission, of course, we snap the last links to Locke's and Descartes's appeals to that special certainty with which we are aware of "what is closest to our minds" and "easiest for us to know." The assumption that diversity

[36] Suppose a mystic tells us that intuition presents us with unity—the white radiance of eternity—whereas conceptual thinking (like a dome of many-colored glass) breaks this up into a multiplicity. How could we decide whether he or Kant was right about whether unity was correlated with receptivity or with spontaneity? How could it matter?

is found and unity made turns out to have its *sole* justification in the claim that only such a "Copernican" theory will explain our ability to have synthetic a priori knowledge.[37] But if we view the whole Kantian story about synthesis as *only* postulated to explain the possibility of synthetic a priori knowledge, if we accept the claim that the quasi-psychological goings-on described in the "Deduction" have no introspective ground, we shall no longer be tempted by the "Copernican" strategy. For the claim that knowledge of necessary truths about made ("constituted") objects is more intelligible than about found objects depends upon the Cartesian assumption that we have privileged access to the activity of making. But on the interpretation of Kant just given, there is no such access to our constituting activities. Any mystery which attaches to our knowledge of necessary truths will remain. For postulated theoretical entities in inner space are not, by being inner, any more useful than such entities in outer space for explaining how such knowledge can occur.

4. KNOWLEDGE AS NEEDING "FOUNDATIONS"

It may be objected to my treatment of Kant that there is, in fact, a pre-analytic distinction between intuitions and concepts, one as old as Plato. Sensory intuitions, one could argue, are identified first of all as the source of knowledge of contingent truths, and concepts as the source of knowledge of necessary truths. The conflict between rationalism and empiricism, in this view, is not, as I have been claiming, Kant's invidious way of describing his predecessors in terms

[37] To put the point another way, Kant's own transcendental idealism cuts the ground out from under the "Transcendental Deduction" —for either the machinery (synthesis) and the raw material (concepts, intuitions) described in the "Deduction" are noumenal, or they are phenomenal. If phenomenal, then, contrary to the premises of the "Deduction," we can be aware of them. If noumenal, then nothing (including what the "Deduction" says) can be known of them.

of his own new distinction, but is as old as the discovery of
the dramatic difference between mathematical truth and
more humdrum truths. I have been speaking as if the familiar oppositions between sense and intellect, confused and
clear ideas, etc., were all parts of a modern artifact called
"theory of knowledge." But, even if one grants that the
"philosophical" sense of "experience" is a modern artifact,
surely the Greek distinction between sense and intellect was
a genuine discovery, as much a discovery as that of the
rigorous provability of geometrical truth? And surely Kant
was asking a good question when he asked how necessary
(e.g., mathematical) truth was possible?

This objection gives me a chance to introduce a final
point to round out my account of the origin and nature of
the idea of a "department of thought concerned with the
origin and nature of human knowledge." Plato, in my view,
did not discover the distinction between two kinds of entities, either inner or outer. Rather, as I have remarked
earlier, he was the first to articulate what George Pitcher
has called the "Platonic Principle"—that differences in
certainty must correspond to differences in the objects
known.[38] This principle is a natural consequence of the
attempt to model knowledge on perception and to treat
"knowledge of" as grounding "knowledge that." If it is
assumed that we need distinct faculties to "grasp" such
different objects as bricks and numbers (as we have distinct
sense-organs for colors and for smells) then the discovery of
geometry will seem to be the discovery of a new faculty
called νοῦς. This in turn will generate the problem of reason
discussed in chapter one.

It is so much a part of "thinking philosophically" to be
impressed with the special character of mathematical truth
that it is hard to shake off the grip of the Platonic Principle.
If, however, we think of "rational certainty" as a matter of
victory in argument rather than of relation to an object

[38] Cf. chapter two, note 15.

156

known, we shall look toward our interlocutors rather than to our faculties for the explanation of the phenomenon. If we think of our certainty about the Pythagorean Theorem as our confidence, based on experience with arguments on such matters, that nobody will find an objection to the premises from which we infer it, then we shall not seek to explain it by the relation of reason to triangularity. Our certainty will be a matter of conversation between persons, rather than a matter of interaction with nonhuman reality. So we shall not see a difference in kind between "necessary" and "contingent" truths. At most, we shall see differences in degree of ease in objecting to our beliefs. We shall, in short, be where the Sophists were before Plato brought his principle to bear and invented "philosophical thinking": we shall be looking for an airtight case rather than an unshakable foundation. We shall be in what Sellars calls "the logical space of reasons" rather than that of causal relations to objects.[39]

The major point I wish to make about the necessary-contingent distinction is just that the notion of "foundations of knowledge"—truths which are certain because of their causes rather than because of the arguments given for them —is the fruit of the Greek (and specifically Platonic) analogy between perceiving and knowing. The essential feature of the analogy is that knowing a proposition to be true is to be identified with being caused to do something by an object. The object which the proposition is about *imposes* the proposition's truth. The idea of "necessary truth" is just the idea of a proposition which is believed because the "grip" of the object upon us is ineluctable. Such a truth is necessary in the sense in which it is sometimes necessary to believe that what is before our eyes looks red—there is a

[39] For a sympathetic account of the Sophists, and pre-Platonic thought generally, which accords with this view, see Laszlo Versényi, *Socratic Humanism* (New Haven, 1963). See also Heidegger's discussion of Protagoras in *The Question Concerning Technology and Other Essays*, trans. William Lovitt (New York, 1977), pp. 143-147.

power, not ourselves, which compels us. The objects of mathematical truths will not *let* themselves be misjudged or misreported. Such paradigmatically necessary truths as the axioms of geometry are supposed to have no need of justification, of argument, of discussion—they are as undiscussable as the command of Zeus shaking the lightning, or of Helen beckoning to her bed. (Putatively rational ἀνάγκη is, so to speak, just a sublimated form of brute βία.)

The notion of "concept" can, if one likes, be thought of as "the source of knowledge of necessary truths," but this does not mean that Lewis and Strawson are right in thinking that the concept-intuition distinction is pre-analytically given. It is merely the modern version of a set of optional metaphors—the ones chosen by Plato, the ones which have become definatory of "philosophical thinking." Plato's primary distinction was not between two kinds of entities in inner space, two sorts of inner representations. Although he toyed with "inner space" metaphors (as in the aviary image of the *Theaetetus* and in his use of "in the soul" [ἐν τῇ ψυχῇ]), and at times approximated Descartes's imagery of the Eye of the Mind inspecting various—more or less compelling— inner pictures, his thought was essentially "realistic." The Platonic distinction to which mathematical truth gave rise was metaphysical rather than epistemological—a distinction between the worlds of Being and of Becoming. What corresponds to the metaphysical distinctions on the "divided line" of *Republic* vi are distinctions not between kinds of nonpropositional inner representations, but between grades of certainty attaching to propositions. Plato did not focus on the idea of nonpropositional inner entities, but rather on that of the various parts of the soul and of the body being compelled in their respective ways by their respective objects. Plato, like Descartes, based a model of man on the distinction between two sorts of truth, but these were two quite different models. More important, however, the idea that the existence of mathematical truth requires some such explanatory model is not something pre-analytic, given at

158

the beginning of philosophical reflection. It is a product of the choice of a certain set of metaphors for talking about knowledge, the perceptual metaphors which underlie both Platonic and modern discussions.[40]

So much, then, for the objection with which I began this section. I want now to enlarge on the point that the idea of "foundations of knowledge" is a product of the choice of perceptual metaphors. To recapitulate, we can think of knowledge as a relation to propositions, and thus of justification as a relation between the propositions in question and other propositions from which the former may be inferred. Or we may think of both knowledge and justification as privileged relations to the objects those propositions are about. If we think in the first way, we will see no need to end the potentially infinite regress of propositions-brought-forward-in-defense-of-other-propositions. It would be foolish to keep conversation on the subject going once everyone, or the majority, or the wise, are satisfied, but of course we *can*. If we think of knowledge in the second way, we will want to get behind reasons to causes, beyond argument to compulsion from the object known, to a situation in which argument would be not just silly but impossible, for anyone gripped by the object in the required way will be *unable* to doubt or to see an alternative. To reach that point is to reach the foundations of knowledge. For Plato, that point was reached by escaping from the senses and opening up the faculty of reason—the Eye of the Soul—to the World of Being. For Descartes, it was a matter of turning the Eye of the Mind from the confused inner representations to the clear and distinct ones. With Locke, it was a matter of reversing Descartes's directions and seeing "singular presentations to sense" as what should "grip" us—what we cannot and should not wish to escape from. Before Locke, it would not have occurred to anyone to look for foundations for knowledge in the realm of the senses. Aristotle, to

40 It is perhaps obvious that my discussion of Platonic ocular metaphors is indebted to both Dewey and Heidegger.

be sure, had remarked that we cannot be in error about how things appear to us, but the idea of basing knowledge on appearances would have struck both him and Plato as absurd. What we want to have as an object of knowledge is precisely what is not an appearance, and the idea of propositions about one sort of object (the appearances) being *evidence* for propositions about another sort of object (what is really there) would not have made sense to either of them.

After Descartes, however, the appearance-reality distinction began to slip out of focus, and was replaced by the inner-outer distinction. The question "How can I escape from the realm of appearance?" was replaced by the question "How can I escape from behind the veil of ideas?" To this question, Locke had an answer: Make the same use of your certainty about how things appear to your senses as Plato made of the axioms of geometry—use them as premises to infer everything else (only inductively, rather than, as in Plato, deductively). This answer looked good only until Hume got to work on it, but it had a certain innocent charm. It satisfied the same need to be gripped, grasped, and compelled which Plato had felt, yet "simple ideas of sensation" seemed less pretentious and more up-to-date than Platonic Forms. By the time of Kant, therefore, it looked as if there were two alternative foundations for knowledge —one had to choose between the interiorized version of the Forms, Cartesian clear and distinct ideas, on the one hand, and Humean "impressions" on the other. In both cases, one was choosing objects to be compelled by. Kant, in rejecting both these putative objects as essentially incomplete and powerless to compel unless combined with one another in "synthesis," was the first to think of the foundations of knowledge as propositions rather than objects. Before Kant, an inquiry into "the nature and origin of knowledge" had been a search for privileged inner representations. With Kant, it became a search for the rules which the mind had set up for itself (the "Principles of the Pure Understanding"). This is one of the reasons why Kant was thought to have led us from nature to freedom. Instead of seeing ourselves as quasi-Newtonian machines, hoping to be compelled by the right inner entities and thus to function according to nature's design for us, Kant let us see ourselves as deciding (noumenally, and hence unconsciously) what nature was to be allowed to be like.

Kant did not, however, free us from Locke's confusion between justification and causal explanation, the basic confusion contained in the idea of a "theory of knowledge." For the notion that our freedom depends on an idealistic epistemology—that to see ourselves as "rising above mechanism" we have to go transcendental and claim to have "constituted" atoms and the void ourselves—is just Locke's mistake all over again. It is to assume that the logical space of giving reasons—of justifying our utterances and our other actions—needs to stand in some special relationship to the logical space of causal explanation so as to insure either an accord between the two (Locke) or the inability of the one to interfere with the other (Kant). Kant was right in thinking accord was senseless and interference impossible, but wrong in thinking that establishing the latter point required the notion of the "constitution" of nature by the knowing subject. Kant's advance in the direction of a propositional rather than a perceptual view of knowledge went only halfway because it was contained within the framework of causal metaphors—"constitution," "making," "shaping," "synthesizing," and the like.

The difference between the "mainstream" Anglo-Saxon tradition and the "mainstream" German tradition in twentieth-century philosophy is the expression of two opposed stances toward Kant. The tradition which goes back to Russell dismissed Kant's problem about synthetic a priori truths as a misunderstanding of the nature of mathematics, and thus viewed epistemology as essentially a matter of updating Locke. In the course of this updating, epistemology was separated off from psychology by being viewed as a study of the evidential relations between basic and nonbasic propositions, and these relations were viewed as a matter of "logic" rather than of empirical fact. In the German tradition, on the other hand, the defense of freedom and spirituality through the notion of "constitution" was retained as the distinctive mission of the philosopher. Logical empiricism and, later, analytic philosophy were dismissed by most German (and many French) philosophers as not "transcendental," and therefore neither methodologically sound nor properly edifying. Even those with the gravest doubts about most Kantian doctrines never doubted that something like his "transcendental turn" was essential. On the Anglo-Saxon side, the so-called linguistic turn was thought to do the job of demarcating philosophy from science, while freeing one of any vestiges of, or temptation to, "idealism" (which was thought the besetting sin of philosophy on the Continent).

On both sides of the Channel, however, most philosophers have remained Kantian. Even when they claim to have "gone beyond" epistemology, they have agreed that philosophy is a discipline which takes as its study the "formal" or "structural" aspects of our beliefs, and that by examining these the philosopher serves the cultural function of keeping the other disciplines honest, limiting their claims to what can be properly "grounded." The great exceptions to this neo-Kantian consensus are, once again, Dewey, Wittgenstein, and Heidegger. In connection with the topic of this section—the notion of "foundations" of knowledge as based on an analogy with the compulsion to believe when staring at an object—it is Heidegger who is especially important. For Heidegger has tried to show how the epistemological notion of "objectivity" derives from, as he puts it, the Platonic "identification of $\phi\acute{v}\sigma\iota\varsigma$ with $\iota\delta\acute{\epsilon}a$"—of the reality of a thing with its presence before us.[41] He is concerned to explore the way in which the West became obsessed with the notion of our primary relation to objects as analogous

[41] Martin Heidegger, *Introduction to Metaphysics*, trans. Ralph Manheim (New Haven, 1959), p. 185.

to visual perception, and thus to suggest that there could be other conceptions of our relations to things. The historical roots of the Aristotle-Locke analogy of knowledge to perception are beyond the scope of this book, but we can at least take from Heidegger the idea that the desire for an "epistemology" is simply the most recent product of the dialectical development of an originally chosen set of metaphors.[42]

To describe this development as a linear sequence is of course simplistic, but perhaps it helps to think of the original dominating metaphor as being that of having our beliefs determined by being brought face-to-face with the object of the belief (the geometrical figure which proves the theorem, for example). The next stage is to think that to understand how to know better is to understand how to improve the activity of a quasi-visual faculty, the Mirror of Nature, and thus to think of knowledge as an assemblage of accurate representations. Then comes the idea that the way to have accurate representations is to find, within the Mirror, a special privileged class of representations so compelling that their accuracy cannot be doubted. These privileged foundations will be the foundations of knowledge, and the discipline which directs us toward them—the theory of knowledge—will be the foundation of culture. The theory of knowledge will be the search for that which compels the mind to belief as soon as it is unveiled. Philosophy-as-epistemology will be the search for the immutable structures within which knowledge, life, and culture must be contained—structures set by the privileged representations which it studies. The neo-Kantian consensus thus appears as the end-product of an original wish to substitute *confrontation* for *conversation* as the determinant of our belief.

In part III I try to show how things look if conversation is thought sufficient and the search for confrontation abandoned, and thus if knowledge is *not* conceived of as rep-

---

[42] Martin Heidegger, *The End of Philosophy*, ed. and trans. Joan Stambaugh (New York, 1973), p. 88.

resentations in the Mirror of Nature. In the next three chapters, however, I shall try first (in chapter four) to sketch the shape the neo-Kantian consensus took in twentieth-century philosophy, and the confusion into which one form of this consensus—"analytic philosophy"—has recently fallen. This will involve describing, and defending, Quine's and Sellars's attacks on the notion of privileged representation. In chapters five and six I take up two putative "successor subjects" to philosophy-as-epistemology—empirical psychology and philosophy of language, respectively—which remain within the neo-Kantian consensus by taking philosophy to be, paradigmatically, the study of representing.

CHAPTER IV

Privileged Representations

1. APODICTIC TRUTH, PRIVILEGED REPRESENTATIONS, AND
ANALYTIC PHILOSOPHY

At the end of the nineteenth century, philosophers were
justifiably worried about the future of their discipline. On
the one hand, the rise of empirical psychology had raised
the question "What do we need to know about knowledge
which psychology cannot tell us?"[1] Ever since Descartes's
attempt to make the world safe for clear and distinct ideas
and Kant's to make it safe for synthetic a priori truths,
ontology had been dominated by epistemology. So the
"naturalization" of epistemology by psychology suggested
that a simple and relaxed physicalism might be the only
sort of ontological view needed. On the other hand, the
tradition of German idealism had declined—in England
and America—into what has been well described as "a
continuation of Protestantism by other means." The idealists purported to save the "spiritual values" which physicalism seemed to neglect by invoking Berkeleian arguments to
get rid of material substance and Hegelian arguments to
get rid of the individual ego (while resolutely ignoring
Hegel's historicism). But few took these high-minded efforts seriously. The earnest reductionism of Bain and Mill
and the equally earnest romanticism of Royce drove
aesthetical ironists like James and Bradley, as well as social

[1] This question has echoed through our own century, in ways described in the following chapter. Psychology was born out of philosophy in the confused hope that we might get back behind Kant and
recapture Lockean innocence. Ever since, psychologists have vainly protested their neglect by neo-Kantian philosophers (of both the analytic
and the phenomenological sorts).

165

reformers like the young Dewey, to proclaim the unreality of traditional epistemological problems and solutions. They were provoked to radical criticisms of "truth as correspondence" and "knowledge as accuracy of representations," thus threatening the entire Kantian notion of philosophy as metacriticism of the special disciplines. Simultaneously, philosophers as various as Nietzsche, Bergson, and Dilthey were undermining some of the same Kantian presuppositions. For a time, it seemed as if philosophy might turn away once and for all from epistemology, from the quest for certainty, structure, and rigor, and from the attempt to constitute itself a tribunal of reason.

The spirit of playfulness which seemed about to enter philosophy around 1900 was, however, nipped in the bud. Just as mathematics had inspired Plato to invent "philosophical thinking," so serious-minded philosophers turned to mathematical logic for rescue from the exuberant satire of their critics. The paradigmatic figures in this attempt to recapture the mathematical spirit were Husserl and Russell. Husserl saw philosophy as trapped between "naturalism" and "historicism," neither of which offered the sort of "apodictic truths" which Kant had assured philosophers were their birthright.[2] Russell joined Husserl in denouncing the psychologism which had infected the philosophy of mathematics, and announced that logic was the essence of philosophy.[3] Driven by the need to find something to be

[2] Cf. Edmund Husserl, "Philosophy as Rigorous Science," in *Phenomenology and the Crisis of Philosophy*, ed. and trans. Quentin Lauer (New York, 1965), p. 120. In this essay (published in 1910), Husserl analyzed both naturalism and historicism as forms of skepticism and relativism. See, for example, pp. 76-79, 122. He began his criticism of naturalism by repeating the attack on psychological conceptions of logic made in his *Logical Investigations*. (Cf. pp. 8off. on naturalism's self-refutation through its reduction of norms to fact.)

[3] Bertrand Russell ended the chapter called "Logic as the Essence of Philosophy" in his *Our Knowledge of the External World* (London, 1914) with the following claims:

The old logic put thought in fetters, while the new logic gives it

apodictic about, Russell discovered "logical form" and Husserl discovered "essences," the "purely formal" aspects of the world which remained when the nonformal had been "bracketed." The discovery of these privileged representations began once again a quest for seriousness, purity, and rigor,[4] a quest which lasted for some forty years. But, in the end, heretical followers of Husserl (Sartre and Heidegger) and heretical followers of Russell (Sellars and Quine) raised the same sorts of questions about the possibility of apodictic truth which Hegel had raised about Kant. Phenomenology gradually became transformed into what Husserl despairingly called "mere anthropology,"[5] and "ana-

---

wings. It has, in my opinion, introduced the same kind of advance into philosophy as Galileo introduced into physics, making it possible at last to see what kinds of problems may be capable of solution, and what kinds must be abandoned as beyond human powers. And where a solution appears possible, the new logic provides a method which enables us to obtain results that do not merely embody personal idiosyncrasies, but must command the assent of all who are competent to form an opinion.

For my present purposes, the standard charge (made, e.g., by Dummett and by Anscombe) that Russell confused the specifically semantical doctrines of Frege and Wittgenstein, which *did* spring from the new logic, with epistemological doctrines which did not, is irrelevant. The charge is fair enough, but without this very confusion the analytic movement either would not have got off the ground, or would have been quite a different thing. Only in the last two decades has a clear distinction between "linguistic philosophy" and "philosophy of language" begun to be made. See chapter six, section 1, for more on this distinction.

4 See Russell, *Our Knowledge of the External World*, p. 61 (in the American edition [New York, 1924]), and Husserl, *Phenomenology*, pp. 110-111.

5 See Herbert Spiegelberg, *The Phenomenological Movement*, 2d ed. (The Hague, 1965), I, 275-283, and David Carr's "Translator's Introduction" to Edmund Husserl, *The Crisis of European Sciences and Transcendental Phenomenology* (Evanston, 1970), pp. xxv-xxxviii. See also Ryle's reaction to *Sein und Zeit*, exemplifying the kinship between Anglo-Saxon projects influenced by Russell and Husserl's original project: "It is my personal opinion that qua First Philosophy Phenomenology is at present heading for bankruptcy and disaster and will end either in self-ruinous Subjectivism or in a windy Mysticism"

lytic" epistemology (i.e., "philosophy of science") became increasingly historicist and decreasingly "logical" (as in Hanson, Kuhn, Harré, and Hesse). So, seventy years after Husserl's "Philosophy as Rigorous Science" and Russell's "Logic as the Essence of Philosophy," we are back with the same putative dangers which faced the authors of these manifestoes: if philosophy becomes too naturalistic, hard-nosed positive disciplines will nudge it aside; if it becomes too historicist, then intellectual history, literary criticism, and similar soft spots in "the humanities" will swallow it up.[6]

The full story of the splendors and the miseries of phenomenology and analytic philosophy is, obviously, far beyond the scope of this book. The story I want to tell in this chapter is merely how the notion of two sorts of representations—intuitions and concepts—fell into disrepute in the latter days of the analytic movement. I have been claiming that the Kantian picture of concepts and intuitions getting together to produce knowledge is needed to give sense to the idea of "theory of knowledge" as a specifically philosophical discipline, distinct from psychology. This is

---

(*Mind*, 1929; cited by Spiegelberg, I, 347). Ryle's prescient point was that the coming of "existential phenomenology" meant the end of phenomenology as "rigorous science."

[6] I think that in England and America philosophy has already been displaced by literary criticism in its principal cultural function—as a source for youth's self-description of its own difference from the past. Cf. Harold Bloom, *A Map of Misreading* (New York, 1975), p. 39:

> The teacher of literature now in America, far more than the teacher of history or philosophy or religion, is condemned to teach the presentness of the past, because history, philosophy and religion have withdrawn as agents from the Scene of Instruction, leaving the bewildered teacher of literature at the altar, terrifiedly wondering whether he is to be sacrifice or priest.

This is roughly because of the Kantian and antihistoricist tenor of Anglo-Saxon philosophy. The cultural function of teachers of philosophy in countries where Hegel was not forgotten is quite different, and closer to the position of literary critics in America. See my "Professionalized Philosophy and Transcendentalist Culture," *Georgia Review* 30 (1976), 757-769.

equivalent to saying that if we do not have the distinction between what is "given" and what is "added by the mind," or that between the "contingent" (because influenced by what is given) and the "necessary" (because entirely "within" the mind and under its control), then we will not know what would count as a "rational reconstruction" of our knowledge. We will not know what epistemology's goal or method could be. These two distinctions were attacked at intervals throughout the history of the analytic movement. Neurath had questioned Carnap's appeal to the given, for example, and doubts had often been expressed about Russell's notion of "knowledge by acquaintance" and Lewis's "expressive language." These doubts only came to a head, however, in the early 1950s, with the appearance of Wittgenstein's *Philosophical Investigations*, Austin's mockery of "the ontology of the sensible manifold," and Sellars's "Empiricism and the Philosophy of Mind." The distinction between the necessary and the contingent—revitalized by Russell and the Vienna Circle as the distinction between "true by virtue of meaning" and "true by virtue of experience"—had usually gone unchallenged, and had formed the least common denominator of "ideal language" and "ordinary language" analysis. However, also in the early fifties, Quine's "Two Dogmas of Empiricism" challenged this distinction, and with it the standard notion (common to Kant, Husserl, and Russell) that philosophy stood to empirical science as the study of structure to the study of content. Given Quine's doubts (buttressed by similar doubts in Wittgenstein's *Investigations*) about how to tell when we are responding to the compulsion of "language" rather than that of "experience," it became difficult to explain in what sense philosophy had a separate "formal" field of inquiry, and thus how its results might have the desired apodictic character. For these two challenges were challenges to the very idea of a "theory of knowledge," and thus to philosophy itself, conceived of as a discipline which centers around such a theory.

169

In what follows, I shall confine myself to discussing two radical ways of criticizing the Kantian foundations of analytic philosophy—Sellars's behavioristic critique of "the whole framework of givenness" and Quine's behavioristic approach to the necessary-contingent distinction. I shall present both as forms of holism. As long as knowledge is conceived of as accurate representing—as the Mirror of Nature—Quine's and Sellars's holistic doctrines sound pointlessly paradoxical, because such accuracy requires a theory of privileged representations, ones which are automatically and intrinsically accurate. So the response to Sellars on givenness and Quine on analyticity is often that they have "gone too far"—that they have allowed holism to sweep them off their feet and away from common sense. In order to defend Sellars and Quine, I shall be arguing that their holism is a product of their commitment to the thesis that justification is not a matter of a special relation between ideas (or words) and objects, but of conversation, of social practice. Conversational justification, so to speak, is naturally holistic, whereas the notion of justification embedded in the epistemological tradition is reductive and atomistic. I shall try to show that Sellars and Quine invoke the same argument, one which bears equally against the given-versus-nongiven and the necessary-versus-contingent distinctions. The crucial premise of this argument is that we understand knowledge when we understand the social justification of belief, and thus have no need to view it as accuracy of representation.

Once conversation replaces confrontation, the notion of the mind as Mirror of Nature can be discarded. Then the notion of philosophy as the discipline which looks for privileged representations among those constituting the Mirror becomes unintelligible. A thoroughgoing holism has no place for the notion of philosophy as "conceptual," as "apodictic," as picking out the "foundations" of the rest of knowledge, as explaining which representations are "purely given" or "purely conceptual," as presenting a "canonical notation" rather than an empirical discovery, or as isolating "trans-framework heuristic categories." If we see knowledge as a matter of conversation and of social practice, rather than as an attempt to mirror nature, we will not be likely to envisage a metapractice which will be the critique of all possible forms of social practice. So holism produces, as Quine has argued in detail and Sellars has said in passing, a conception of philosophy which has nothing to do with the quest for certainty.

Neither Quine nor Sellars, however, has developed a new conception of philosophy in any detail. Quine, after arguing that there is no line between science and philosophy, tends to assume that he has thereby shown that science can replace philosophy. But it is not clear what task he is asking science to perform. Nor is it clear why natural science, rather than the arts, or politics, or religion, should take over the area left vacant. Further, Quine's conception of science is still curiously instrumentalist. It is based on a distinction between "stimuli" and "posits" which seems to lend aid and comfort to the old intuition-concept distinction. Yet Quine transcends both distinctions by granting that stimulations of sense-organs are as much "posits" as anything else. It is as if Quine, having renounced the conceptual-empirical, analytic-synthetic, and language-fact distinctions, were still not quite able to renounce that between the given and the postulated. Conversely, Sellars, having triumphed over the latter distinction, cannot quite renounce the former cluster. Despite courteous acknowledgment of Quine's triumph over analyticity, Sellars's writing is still permeated with the notion of "giving the analysis" of various terms or sentences, and with a tacit use of the distinction between the necessary and the contingent, the structural and the empirical, the philosophical and the scientific. Each of the two men tends to make continual, unofficial, tacit, heuristic use of the distinction which the other has transcended. It is as if analytic philosophy could not be written without at least *one* of the

171

two great Kantian distinctions, and as if neither Quine nor Sellars were willing to cut the last links which bind them to Russell, Carnap, and "logic as the essence of philosophy."

Analytic philosophy *cannot*, I suspect, be written without one or the other of these distinctions. If there are no intuitions into which to resolve concepts (in the manner of the *Aufbau*) nor any internal relations among concepts to make possible "grammatical discoveries" (in the manner of "Oxford philosophy"), then indeed it is hard to imagine what an "analysis" might be. Wisely, few analytic philosophers any longer try to explain what it is to offer an analysis. Although there was a great deal of metaphilosophical literature in the 1930s and 1940s under the aegis of Russell and Carnap, and another spate of such literature in the 1950s which took the *Philosophical Investigations* and *The Concept of Mind* as paradigms,[7] there is now little attempt to bring "analytic philosophy" to self-consciousness by explaining how to tell a successful from an unsuccessful analysis. The present lack of metaphilosophical reflection within the analytic movement is, I think, symptomatic of the sociological fact that analytic philosophy is now, in several countries, the entrenched school of thought. Thus in these countries *anything* done by philosophers who employ a certain style, or mention certain topics, counts (*ex officiis suis*, so to speak) as continuing the work begun by Russell and Carnap. Once a radical movement takes over the establishment against which it revolted, there is less need for methodological self-consciousness, self-criticism, or a sense of location in dialectical space or historical time.

I do not think that there any longer exists anything identifiable as "analytic philosophy" except in some such stylistic or sociological way. But this is not a disparaging remark, as if some legitimate expectation had been disap-

[7] I attempted to summarize this literature, up through 1965, in the introduction to *The Linguistic Turn*, ed. Richard Rorty (Chicago, 1967).

pointed. The analytic movement in philosophy (like any movement in any discipline) worked out the dialectical consequences of a set of assumptions, and now has little more to do. The sort of optimistic faith which Russell and Carnap shared with Kant—that philosophy, its essence and right method discovered at last, had finally been placed upon the secure path of a science—is not something to be mocked or deplored. Such optimism is possible only for men of high imagination and daring, the heroes of their times.

2. EPISTEMOLOGICAL BEHAVIORISM

The simplest way to describe the common features of Quine's and Sellars's attacks on logical empiricism is to say that both raise behaviorist questions about the epistemic privilege which logical empiricism claims for certain assertions, qua reports of privileged representations. Quine asks how an anthropologist is to discriminate the sentences to which natives invariably and wholeheartedly assent into contingent empirical platitudes on the one hand and necessary conceptual truths on the other. Sellars asks how the authority of first-person reports of, for example, how things appear to us, the pains from which we suffer, and the thoughts that drift before our minds differs from the authority of expert reports on, for example, metal stress, the mating behavior of birds, or the colors of physical objects. We can lump both questions together and simply ask, "How do our peers know which of our assertions to take our word for and which to look for further confirmation of?" It would seem enough for the natives to know which sentences are unquestionably true, without knowing which are true "by virtue of language." It would seem enough for our peers to believe there to be no better way of finding out our inner states than from our reports, without their knowing what "lies behind" our making them. It would also seem enough for *us* to know that our peers have this acquiescent attitude.

173

That alone seems sufficient for that inner certainty about our inner states which the tradition has explained by "immediate presence to consciousness," "sense of evidence," and other expressions of the assumption that reflections in the Mirror of Nature are intrinsically better known than nature itself. For Sellars, the certainty of "I have a pain" is a reflection of the fact that nobody cares to question it, not conversely. Just so, for Quine, the certainty of "All men are animals" and of "There have been some black dogs." Quine thinks that "meanings" drop out as wheels that are not part of the mechanism,[8] and Sellars thinks the same of "self-authenticating non-verbal episodes."[9] More broadly, if assertions are justified by society rather than by the character of the inner representations they express, then there is no point in attempting to isolate *privileged* representations.

Explaining rationality and epistemic authority by reference to what society lets us say, rather than the latter by the former, is the essence of what I shall call "epistemological behaviorism," an attitude common to Dewey and Wittgenstein. This sort of behaviorism can best be seen as a species of holism—but one which requires no idealist metaphysical underpinnings. It claims that if we understand the rules of a language-game, we understand all that there is to understand about why moves in that language-game are made (all, that is, save for the extra understanding obtained from inquiries nobody would call epistemological—into, for example, the history of the language, the structure of the brain, the evolution of the species, and the political or cultural ambiance of the players). If we are behaviorist in this sense, then it will not occur to us to invoke either of the traditional Kantian distinctions. But

[8] For an interpretation of Quine as attacking the explanatory utility of the "philosophical notion of meaning," see Gilbert Harman, "Quine on Meaning and Existence, I," *Review of Metaphysics* 21 (1967), 124-151, esp. 125, 135-141.

[9] Wilfrid Sellars, *Science, Perception and Reality* (London and New York, 1963), p. 167.

174

can we just go ahead and be behaviorist? Or, as Quine's and Sellars's critics suggest, doesn't behaviorism simply beg the question?[10] Is there any reason to think that fundamental epistemic notions *should* be explicated in behavioral terms?

This last question comes down to: Can we treat the study of "the nature of human knowledge" just as the study of certain ways in which human beings interact, or does it require an ontological foundation (involving some specifically philosophical way of describing human beings)? Shall we take "S knows that p" (or "S knows noninferentially that p," or "S believes incorrigibly that p," or "S's knowledge that p is certain") as a remark about the status of S's reports among his peers, or shall we take it as a remark about the relation between subject and object, between nature and its mirror? The first alternative leads to a pragmatic view of truth and a therapeutic approach to ontology (in which philosophy can straighten out pointless quarrels between common sense and science, but not contribute any arguments of its own for the existence or inexistence of something). Thus for Quine, a necessary truth is just a statement such that nobody has given us any interesting alternatives which would lead us to question it. For Sellars, to say that a report of a passing thought is incorrigible is to say that nobody has yet suggested a good way of predicting and controlling human behavior which does not take sincere first-person contemporary reports of thoughts at face-value. The second alternative leads to "ontological" explanations of the relations between minds and meanings, minds and immediate data of awareness, universals and particulars, thought and language, consciousness and brains, and so on. For philosophers like Chisholm and Berg-

10 For this sort of criticism of Quine's behaviorism, see H. P. Grice and P. F. Strawson, "In Defense of a Dogma," *Philosophical Review* 65 (1956), pp. 141-156. For such criticisms of Sellars, see Roderick Chisholm's criticisms of his claims about intentionality, in their correspondence printed in *Minnesota Studies in the Philosophy of Science* 2 (1958), pp. 521ff.

mann, such explanations *must* be attempted if the realism of common sense is to be preserved. The aim of all such explanations is to make truth something more than what Dewey called "warranted assertability": more than what our peers will, *ceteris paribus*, let us get away with saying. Such explanations, when ontological, usually take the form of a redescription of the object of knowledge so as to "bridge the gap" between it and the knowing subject. To choose between these approaches is to choose between truth as "what it is good for us to believe" and truth as "contact with reality."

Thus the question of whether we can be behaviorist in our attitude toward knowledge is not a matter of the "adequacy" of behaviorist "analyses" of knowledge-claims or of mental states. Epistemological behaviorism (which might be called simply "pragmatism," were this term not a bit overladen) has nothing to do with Watson or with Ryle. Rather, it is the claim that philosophy will have no more to offer than common sense (supplemented by biology, history, etc.) about knowledge and truth. The question is not whether necessary and sufficient behavioral conditions for "S knows that p" can be offered; no one any longer dreams they can. Nor is the question whether such conditions can be offered for "S sees that p," or "It looks to S as if p," or "S is having the thought that p." To be behaviorist in the large sense in which Sellars and Quine are behaviorist is not to offer reductionist analyses, but to refuse to attempt a certain sort of explanation: the sort of explanation which not only interposes such a notion as "acquaintance with meanings" or "acquaintance with sensory appearances" between the impact of the environment on human beings and their reports about it, but uses such notions to explain the reliability of such reports.

But, once again, how are we to decide whether such notions are needed? It is tempting to answer on the basis of an antecedent decision about the nature of human beings—a decision on whether we need such notions as "mind," "stream of consciousness," and the like to describe them. But this would be the wrong answer. We can take the Sellars-Quine attitude toward knowledge while cheerfully "countenancing" raw feels, a priori concepts, innate ideas, sense-data, propositions, and anything else which a causal explanation of human behavior might find it helpful to postulate.[11] What we *cannot* do is to take knowledge of these "inner" or "abstract" entities as *premises* from which our knowledge of other entities is normally inferred, and without which the latter knowledge would be "ungrounded." The difference is between saying that to know a language is to be acquainted with the meanings of its terms, or that to see a table is to have a rectangular sense-impression, and explaining the *authority* of tokens of "All men are animals" or "That looks like a table" by virtue of the prior (internal, private, nonsocial) authority of a knowledge of meanings or of sense-impressions. Behaviorism in epistemology is a matter not of metaphysical parsimony, but of whether authority can attach to assertions by virtue of relations of "acquaintance" between persons and, for example, thoughts, impressions, universals, and propositions. The difference between the Quine-Sellars and the Chisholm-Bergmann outlooks on these matters is not the difference between lush and spare landscapes, but more like the difference between moral philosophers who think that rights and responsibilities are a matter of what society bestows and those who think that there is something inside a man which society "recognizes" when it makes its bestowal. The two schools of moral philosophy do not differ on the point that human beings have rights worth dying for. They differ rather about whether, once we have

11 I defend this claim when I discuss empirical psychology in chapter five. Sellars and Quine themselves, unfortunately, do not see the matter in this carefree way. For criticism of Quine's flight from intentions, see section 4 below. This criticism can be applied, *mutatis mutandis*, to Sellars's insistence on the claim that "the scientific image" excludes intentions; but Sellars's point is more subtle, and is involved with his Tractarian notion of picturing, criticized below in chapter six, section 5.

understood when and why these rights have been granted or denied, in the way in which social and intellectual historians understand this, there is more to understand. They differ, in short, about whether there are "ontological foundations for human rights," just as the Sellars-Quine approach differs from the empiricist and rationalist traditions about whether, once we understand (as historians of knowledge do) when and why various beliefs have been adopted or discarded, there is something called "the relation of knowledge to reality" left over to be understood.

This analogy with moral philosophy lets us focus the issue about behaviorism in epistemology yet again: the issue is not adequacy of explanation of fact, but rather whether a practice of justification can be given a "grounding" in fact. The question is not whether human knowledge in fact has "foundations," but whether it makes sense to suggest that it does—whether the idea of epistemic or moral authority having a "ground" in nature is a coherent one. For the pragmatist in morals, the claim that the customs of a given society are "grounded in human nature" is not one which he knows how to argue about. He is a pragmatist because he cannot see what it would be like for a custom to be so grounded. For the Quine-Sellars approach to epistemology, to say that truth and knowledge can only be judged by the standards of the inquirers of our own day is not to say that human knowledge is less noble or important, or more "cut off from the world," than we had thought. It is merely to say that nothing counts as justification unless by reference to what we already accept, and that there is no way to get outside our beliefs and our language so as to find some test other than coherence.

To say that the True and the Right are matters of social practice may seem to condemn us to a relativism which, all by itself, is a *reductio* of a behaviorist approach to either knowledge or morals. I shall take up this charge in discussing historicism, in chapters seven and eight. Here I shall simply remark that only the image of a discipline—philosophy—which will pick out a given set of scientific or moral views as more "rational" than the alternatives by appeal to something which forms a permanent neutral matrix for all inquiry and all history, makes it possible to think that such relativism must automatically rule out coherence theories of intellectual and practical justification. One reason why professional philosophers recoil from the claim that knowledge may not have foundations, or rights and duties an ontological ground, is that the kind of behaviorism which dispenses with foundations is in a fair way toward dispensing with philosophy. For the view that there is no permanent neutral matrix within which the dramas of inquiry and history are enacted has as a corollary that criticism of one's culture can only be piecemeal and partial—never "by reference to eternal standards." It threatens the neo-Kantian image of philosophy's relation to science and to culture. The urge to say that assertions and actions must not only cohere with other assertions and actions but "correspond" to something apart from what people are saying and doing has some claim to be called *the* philosophical urge. It is the urge which drove Plato to say that Socrates' words and deeds, failing as they did to cohere with current theory and practice, nonetheless corresponded to something which the Athenians could barely glimpse. The residual Platonism which Quine and Sellars are opposing is not the hypostatization of nonphysical entities, but the notion of "correspondence" with such entities as the touchstone by which to measure the worth of present practice.[12]

12 Unfortunately, both men tend to substitute correspondence to physical entities, and specifically to the "basic entities" of physical science (elementary particles, or their successors). Sellars's (and Jay Rosenberg's) attempt to salvage *something* from the Platonic notion of knowledge as accuracy of picturing is criticized below (chapter six, section 5). My own attitude is Strawson's (and Heidegger's): "The correspondence theory requires, not purification, but elimination." (P. F. Strawson, "Truth," reprinted in *Truth*, ed. George Pitcher [Englewood Cliffs, N.J., 1964], p. 32)—or, more mildly, it requires separation from epistemology and relegation to semantics. (See Robert Brandom,

179

I am claiming, in short, that the Quine-Sellars attack on the Kantian notion of two sorts of representations—intuitions "given" to one faculty, and concepts (or meanings) "given" to another—is not the attempt to substitute one sort of account of human knowledge for another, but an attempt to get away from the notion of "an account of human knowledge." It amounts to a protest against an archetypal philosophical problem: the problem of how to reduce norms, rules, and justifications to facts, generalizations, and explanations.[13] For this reason, we will not find neutral metaphilosophical ground on which to argue the issues Quine and Sellars raise. For they are not offering an "account" to be tested for "adequacy" but pointing to the futility of offering an "account." To refuse, as both do, to justify assertions by appeal to behavioristically unverifiable episodes (in which the mind recognizes its own direct acquaintance with an instantiation of blueness or with the meaning of "blue") is just to say that justification must be holistic. If we are not to have a doctrine of "knowledge by acquaintance" which will give us a foundation, and if we do not simply deny that there is such a thing as justification, then we will claim with Sellars that "science is rational not because it has a *foundation*, but because it is a self-correcting enterprise which can put *any* claim in jeopardy,

---

"Truth and Assertability," *Journal of Philosophy* 73 [1976], pp. 137-149.)

13 Cf. Sellars's claim that "the idea that epistemic facts can be analyzed without remainder—even 'in principle'—into nonepistemic facts, whether phenomenal or behavioural, public or private, with no matter how lavish a sprinkling of subjunctives and hypotheticals is, I believe, a radical mistake—a mistake of a piece with the so-called 'naturalistic fallacy' in ethics" (*Science, Perception and Reality*, p. 131). I would argue that the importance of Sellars's approach to epistemology is that he sees the true and interesting irreducibility in the area not as between one sort of particular (mental, intentional) and another (physical) but as between descriptions on the one hand and norms, practices, and values on the other. (See note 17 below.)

though not *all* at once."[14] We will say with Quine that knowledge is not like an architectonic structure but like a field of force,[15] and that there are no assertions which are immune from revision. We will be holistic not because we have a taste for wholes, any more than we are behaviorist because of a distaste for "ghostly entities," but simply because justification has always *been* behavioristic and holistic. Only the professional philosopher has dreamed that it might be something else, for only he is frightened by the epistemological skeptic. A holistic approach to knowledge is not a matter of antifoundationalist polemic, but a distrust of the whole epistemological enterprise. A behavioristic approach to episodes of "direct awareness" is not a matter of antimentalistic polemic, but a distrust of the Platonic quest for that special sort of certainty associated with visual perception. The image of the Mirror of Nature—a mirror more easily and certainly seen than that which it mirrors—suggests, and is suggested by, the image of philosophy as such a quest.

If what I have been saying so far is sound, there is no way to argue for the views of Sellars and Quine except by replying to their critics. There is no neutral ground on which to stand and show that they have overcome, respectively, "the given" and "the analytic" in a fair fight. The best we can do is to disentangle the pure form of their criticisms of the tradition from various extraneous issues which their critics (and, to some extent, Quine and Sellars themselves) have introduced, and thereby perhaps to mitigate the paradoxical air of their doctrines. In the next section, I shall take up Sellars's attack on the Myth of the Given, and try to disentangle it from the "unfair to babies" implications of the claim that there is no such thing as pre-linguistic awareness. Next, I shall take up Quine's attack on the distinction between language and fact and try to disentangle

14 Sellars, *Science, Perception and Reality*, p. 170.
15 W.V.O. Quine, *From a Logical Point of View* (Cambridge, Mass., 1953), p. 42.

181

it from Quine's unhappy reductionist claims about the "indeterminacy" of translation and of the *Geisteswissenschaften*. When Sellars's and Quine's doctrines are purified, they appear as complementary expressions of a single claim: that no "account of the nature of knowledge" can rely on a theory of representations which stand in privileged relations to reality. The work of these two philosophers enables us to unravel, at long last, Locke's confusion between explanation and justification, and to make clear why an "account of the nature of knowledge" can be, at most, a description of human behavior.

3. Pre-Linguistic Awareness

In "Empiricism and the Philosophy of Mind," Sellars formulates "psychological nominalism" as the view that

> *all* awareness of *sorts, resemblances, facts*, etc., in short all awareness of abstract entities—indeed, all awareness even of particulars—is a linguistic affair. According to it, not even the awareness of such sorts, resemblances, and facts as pertain to so-called immediate experience is presupposed by the process of acquiring the use of language.[16]

The existence of raw feels—pains, whatever feelings babies have when looking at colored objects, etc.—is the obvious objection to this doctrine. To counter this objection, Sellars invokes the distinction between awareness-as-discriminative-behavior and awareness as what Sellars calls being "in the logical space of reasons, of justifying and being able to justify what one says" (p. 169). Awareness in the first sense is manifested by rats and amoebas and computers; it is simply reliable signaling. Awareness in the second sense is manifested only by beings whose behavior we construe as the utterance of sentences with the intention of justifying the utterance of other sentences. In this latter sense awareness is justified true belief—knowledge—but in the former

16 Sellars, *Science, Perception and Reality*, p. 160.

sense it is ability to respond to stimuli. The bulk of "Empiricism and the Philosophy of Mind" is an argument that such ability is a causal condition for knowledge but not a *ground* for knowledge. This view has as a corollary that knowledge of particulars or of concepts is not temporally prior to knowledge of propositions (but always an abstraction from the latter), and thus that empiricist accounts of language-learning and of the nonpropositional basis for propositional knowledge are inevitably misguided. The crucial premise of this argument is that there is no such thing as a justified belief which is nonpropositional, and no such thing as justification which is not a relation between propositions. So to speak of our acquaintance with redness or with an instantiation of redness as "grounding" (as opposed to being a causal condition of) our knowledge that "this is a red object" or that "redness is a color" is always a mistake.

Children and photoelectric cells both discriminate red objects, but pre-linguistic children are thought to "know what red is" in some sense in which photoelectric cells do not. But how can the child know what pain is if all awareness of anything "is a linguistic affair?" Here Sellars needs another distinction. This time it is between "knowing what X is like" and "knowing what sort of thing an X is." The latter involves being able to link the concept of Xness up with other concepts in such a way as to be able to justify claims about X's. On Sellars's Wittgensteinian view, in which to have a concept is to use a word, these two abilities are the same ability. It follows that we cannot have one concept without having many, nor can we come "to have a concept of something because we have noticed that sort of thing"; for "to have the ability to notice a sort of thing is already to have the concept of that sort of thing" (p. 176). But to "notice a sort of thing" is to notice under a description, not just to respond discriminatively to it. What, then, is it to know *what* pain is like without knowing or noticing what *sort* of thing it is?

It is just to *have* pain. The snare to avoid here is the notion that there is some inner illumination which takes place only when the child's mind is lighted up by language, concepts, descriptions, and propositions, and does not take place when the child inarticulately wails and writhes. The child *feels* the same thing, and it feels just the *same* to him before and after language-learning. Before language, he is said to *know* the thing he feels just in case it is the sort of thing which in later life he will be able to make noninferential reports about. That latent ability is what sets him apart from the photoelectric cell, not his greater sensitivity. Thus he may respond directly to a lack of oxygen in the air, the overly rapid motion of molecules, kinky alpha-rhythms in his brain, and so on, but he is not said to "know what they are" unless and until he comes to grasp the relevant vocabulary. But suffocation, heat, ecstasy, pain, fire, redness, parental hostility, mother love, hunger, loudness, and the like, are "known" pre-linguistically, or so ordinary speech would have it. They are known just by being *had* or felt. They are known without being able to be placed in classes, or related in any other way to anything else.

There is no reason for Sellars to object to the notion of "knowing what pain (or redness) is like," for this would only support the Myth of the Given, and contradict psychological nominalism, if there were some connection between knowing what pain feels like and knowing what sort of thing pain is. But the only connection is that the former is an insufficient and unnecessary causal condition for the latter. It is insufficient for the obvious reason that we can know what redness is like without knowing that it is different from blue, that it is a color, and so on. It is unnecessary because we can know all that, and a great deal more, about redness while having been blind from birth, and thus *not* knowing what redness is like. It is just false that we cannot talk and know about what we do not have raw feels of, and equally false that if we cannot talk about them we may

184

nevertheless have justified true beliefs about them. What is special about language is not that it "changes the quality of our experience" or "opens up new vistas of consciousness" or "synthesizes a previously unconscious manifold" or produces any other sort of "inner" change. All that its acquisition does is to let us enter a community whose members exchange justifications of assertions, and other actions, with one another.[17]

So Sellars may be taken as saying to traditional empiricism: knowing what things are like is not a matter of being justified in asserting propositions. To this, the empiricist is likely to reply, as have Roderick Firth and others, that such a view confuses concepts with words.[18] Sellars,

[17] Cf. ibid., p. 169: "The essential point is that in characterizing an episode or a state as that of *knowing*, we are not giving an empirical description of that episode or state; we are placing it in the logical space of reasons, of justifying and being able to justify what one says."

[18] See Roderick Firth, "Coherence, Certainty, and Epistemic Priority," reprinted in *Empirical Knowledge*, ed. Roderick Chisholm and Robert Swartz (Englewood Cliffs, N.J., 1973). Firth attempts to resolve a problem created by the "coherence theory of concepts": viz., since "we cannot fully understand 'looks red' unless we possess the contrasting concept 'is red,' then it would seem that it is *not* logically possible to have the concept 'looks red' [as C. I. Lewis's doctrine of "sense meaning" would require] before we have the concept 'is red' " (p. 461). Firth says that

the underlying paradox is easily dissolved if we do not confuse concepts with the words used to express them. It is a genetic fact, but a fact with philosophical implications, that when a child first begins to use the word "red" with any consistency he applies it to things that *look* red to him. . . . To call this a "primitive form" of the concept "looks red" is to acknowledge that in some sense the child cannot *fully* understand adult usage until he is able to distinguish things that merely look red from things that really are red; but we must not suppose that the child somehow *loses* his primitive concept when he acquires a more sophisticated one. (pp. 461-462)

For a more detailed polemic against the Ryle-Wittgenstein-Sellars identification of having concepts with using words, see Brand Blanshard's *Reason and Analysis* (La Salle, Ill., 1962), chap. IX. Something like Firth's notion of a "primitive concept" recurs in a criticism of Sellars

Wittgenstein, and others who "exaggerate" the importance of language are said to beg the question in favor of psychological nominalism by assuming that to have a concept is to have the use of a word. Sellars can rejoin with the following dilemma: either grant concepts to anything (e.g., record-changers) which can respond discriminatively to classes of objects, or else explain why you draw the line between conceptual thought and its primitive predecessors in a different place from that between having acquired a language and being still in training. This dilemma highlights the fact that traditional notions of givenness have run together raw feels and ability to discriminate, using the lack of the first to eliminate machines and include babies, and then using the presence of the second to make what babies have resemble propositional knowledge. The argument between Sellars and his critics on this point boils down to: Shall we take conceptualization as a matter of classification or of justification? Sellars can say that he will give up the term *concept* to those who wish to endow record-changers or their protoplasmic counterparts with concepts, as long as he can have some other term to indicate what we have when we can place classifications in relation to other classifications in the way language-users do when they argue about what class a given item should fall in. Once again, Sellars falls back on saying that justification is a matter of social practice, and that everything which is not a matter of social practice is no help in understanding the *justification* of human knowledge, no matter how helpful it may be in understanding its *acquisition*. The naturalistic and the genetic fallacies have, Sellars thinks, combined in traditional empiricism to produce the view that we would be in a better position to congratulate ourselves on accurately mirroring nature (or to lament our failure) if we could only bring to consciousness the stages of our childhood develop-

---

by William S. Robinson, "The Legend of the Given," in *Action, Knowledge and Reality*, ed. H.-N. Castañeda (Indianapolis, 1975), pp. 83-108.

ment. Confused by Descartes's conflation of thought and feeling, bemused by the virgin innocence of Locke's wax tablet, and frightened by the fact that if truth is in the whole then certainty is nowhere, empiricists have fastened on "what red feels like" as the key to our knowledge of the natural world. For Sellars, this is like fastening on what the baby feels like when its feeding is delayed as the key to the common moral consciousness.

To sum up, Sellars's psychological nominalism is not a theory of how the mind works, nor of how knowledge is born in the infant breast, nor of the "nature of concepts," nor of any other matter of fact. It is a remark about the difference between facts and rules, a remark to the effect that we can only come under epistemic rules when we have entered the community where the game governed by these rules is played. We may balk at the claim that knowledge, awareness, concepts, language, inference, justification, and the logical space of reasons all descend on the shoulders of the bright child somewhere around the age of four, without having existed in even the most primitive form hitherto. But we do not balk at the thought that a cluster of rights and responsibilities will descend on him on his eighteenth birthday, without having been present in even the most primitive form hitherto. The latter situation is, to be sure, more clear-cut than the former, since there is no mark of the former occasion save some adult's casual remark (e.g., "the kid knows what he's talking about"). But in both cases what has happened is a shift in a person's relations with others, not a shift inside the person which now *suits* him to enter such new relationships. It is not as if we might be *mistaken* in thinking that a four-year-old has knowledge but that no one-year-old does, any more than we might be *mistaken* in taking the statute's word for the fact that eighteen-year-olds can marry freely whereas seventeen-year-olds cannot. It may be *injudicious* to take the prattle of certain four-year-olds seriously, just as it may have been injudicious to have set the age of legal responsibility so low, but no greater

187

understanding of how knowledge (or responsibility) "works" will decide such matters.

Thus Sellars should not be expected to offer arguments for a "theory of the relation between language and thought," for thoughts are inner episodes which may or may not (depending on the needs of empirical psychology) be thought of as necessarily linked to language, to brain-states, or to various other things. As an *epistemologist*, Sellars is not offering a theory about inner episodes. Rather, he is noting that the traditional, nonbehaviorist notion of "epistemology" is the confusion of an account of such episodes with an account of the right to make certain assertions. This is to adopt the view that philosophy (and, specifically, "philosophy of mind") cannot, by supplying a loftier critical point of view, reinforce or diminish the confidence in our own assertions which the approval of our peers gives us. Sellars's psychological nominalism does not stem from behaviorism as a thesis about what the mind is or is not. It stems only from epistemological behaviorism in the sense defined above, a sense indistinguishable from epistemological holism. To be behaviorist in this sense is simply to "divide through" by any and all mental events and faculties and to view our practices of justifying assertions as not needing empirical or "ontological" ground.[19]

Having reverted yet again to the community as source of epistemic authority, I shall end this section by reemphasizing that even the nonconceptual, nonlinguistic knowledge of what a raw feel is like is attributed to beings on the basis of their potential membership in this com-

[19] I shall be claiming in chapter eight that this attitude toward the relation between philosophy of mind and epistemology (or, more largely, between any scientific or metaphysical description of man on the one hand and any remark about the justification for his actions— linguistic or otherwise—on the other) is central to Wittgenstein's efforts in the *Investigations*. I think that, like Sellars's own application of the distinction between describing men and judging them, it is a natural corollary of the *Tractatus's* rigorous separation of fact-stating from all other (e.g., ethical) uses of language.

munity. Babies and the more attractive sorts of animal are credited with "having feelings" rather than (like photoelectric cells and animals which no one feels sentimental about —e.g., flounders and spiders) "merely responding to stimuli." This is to be explained on the basis of that sort of community feeling which unites us with anything humanoid. To be humanoid is to have a human face, and the most important part of that face is a mouth which we can imagine uttering sentences in synchrony with appropriate expressions of the face as a whole.[20] To say, with common sense, that babies and bats know what pain and red are like, but not what the motion of molecules or the change of seasons is like, is just to say that we can fairly readily imagine them opening their mouths and remarking on the former, but not on the latter. To say that a gadget (consisting of a photoelectric cell hitched up to a tape recorder) which says "red!" when and only when we shine red light on it *doesn't* know what red is like is to say that we cannot readily imagine continuing a conversation with the gadget. To say that we just don't *know* whether androids who have been manufactured out of protoplasm (and are all ready to go except for the speech center, which is about to be installed) know what red is like is not to confess scientific or philosophical bafflement concerning the nature of subjectivity.[21] It is merely to say that things with roughly human faces which look as if they might someday be conversational partners are usually credited with "feelings," but that if we know too much about how these things

[20] For a good explication of the force and ramifications of Wittgenstein's view that the human body is the best picture of the human soul, see Virgil Aldrich, "On What It Is Like to Be a Man," *Inquiry* 16 (1973), 355-366. See also Stuart Hampshire, *Thought and Action* (London, 1959), chap. 1.

[21] See Hilary Putnam, "Robots: Machines or Artificially Created Life?" reprinted in *Modern Materialism*, ed. J. O'Connor (New York, 1969), esp. p. 262: ". . . the question: Are robots conscious? calls for a decision, on our part, to treat robots as fellow members of our linguistic community, or not to so treat them."

189

have been put together we may be loath to think of them as even potential partners.[22]

This view of the attribution of pre-linguistic awareness— as a courtesy extended potential or imagined fellow-speakers of our language—has as a corollary that moral prohibitions against hurting babies and the better looking sorts of animals are not "ontologically grounded" in their posses- sion of feeling. It is, if anything, the other way around. The moral prohibitions are expressions of a sense of community based on the imagined possibility of conversation, and the attribution of feelings is little more than a reminder of these prohibitions. This can be seen by noticing that no- body except philosophers of mind cares whether the raw feel of pain or redness is different for koalas than for us, but that we all care quite a bit about a koala when we see it writhing about. This fact does not mean that our or the koala's pain "is nothing but its behavior"; it just means that writhing is more important to our ability to imagine the koala asking us for help than what is going on inside the koala. Pigs rate much higher than koalas on intelligence tests, but pigs don't writhe in quite the right humanoid way, and the pig's face is the wrong shape for the facial expressions which go with ordinary conversation. So we send pigs to slaughter with equanimity, but form societies for the protection of koalas. This is not "irrational," any more than it is irrational to extend or deny civil rights to the moronic (or fetuses, or aboriginal tribes, or Martians). Rationality, when viewed as the formation of syllogisms based on discovery of "the facts" and the application of

[22] This does not mean that we are *right* to be loath, nor that we are wrong. I merely want to call attention to the traditional fear that biologists or psychologists, in their attitude toward their fellow men, may "murder to dissect." We *are* tempted, when we are particularly good at predicting something's behavior on the basis of its internal structure, to be "objective" about it—that is, to treat it as an *en-soi* rather than a *pour-soi* and "one of us." Philosophers have, I think, nothing much to say about when this temptation is justified or unjusti- fied. Novelists and poets, however, do.

190

such principles as "Pain should be minimized" or "Intelligent life is always more valuable than beautiful unintelligent beings," is a myth. Only the Platonic urge to say that every moral sentiment, and indeed every emotion of any sort, should be based on the recognition of an objective quality in the recipient makes us think that our treatment of koalas or whites or Martians is a "matter of moral principle." For the "facts" which must be discovered to apply the principle are, in the case of the koala's or the white's "feelings," not discoverable independently of sentiment.[23] The emotions we have toward borderline cases depend on the liveliness of our imagination, and conversely. Only the notion that in philosophy we have a discipline able to give good reasons for what we believe on instinct lets us think that "more careful philosophical analysis" will help us draw a line between coldness of heart and foolish sentimentality.

This claim that animals' knowledge of what some things are like has little to do with justified true belief, but a lot to do with morals, follows naturally from the Sellarsian notion that the inside of people and quasi-people is to be explained by what goes on outside (and, in particular, by their place in our community) rather than conversely. Ever since Descartes made methodological solipsism the mark of rigorous and professional philosophical thinking, philosophers have wanted to find the "ground" of cognition,

23 It is notorious that moral philosophers are of little help in deciding what is to count as a moral agent, as having dignity rather than value, as among the beings whose happiness is to be maximized, as one of those one must take one's chance on turning out to be while still behind the veil of ignorance, etc. Sellars discusses the topic briefly and inconclusively in terms of the question of whether all members of an epistemic community are members of an ethical community— whether "the intersubjective intention to promote epistemic welfare implies the intersubjective intention to promote welfare *sans phrase*" (*Science and Metaphysics* [London and New York, 1968], p. 225). For the effect of holism on meta-ethics and on the Platonic urge just mentioned, see J. B. Schneewind, "Moral Knowledge and Moral Principles" in *Knowledge and Necessity*, ed. G. A. Vesey (London and New York, 1970).

191

morality, aesthetic taste, and anything else that matters within the individual. For how could there be anything in societies which individuals had not put there? Only since Hegel have philosophers begun toying with the notion that the individual apart from his society is just one more animal. The antidemocratic implications of this view, not to mention its historicist and relativist implications, have made it difficult for Hegelian modes of thought to have any impact on the hard core of analytic philosophy—epistemology, philosophy of language, and philosophy of mind. But Sellars's "Empiricism and the Philosophy of Mind"— self-described as "incipient *Meditations Hegeliènnes*"[24]— succeeds in prying raw feels and justified true belief apart and depriving raw feels of their status as privileged representations. It thereby shows how behaviorism in epistemology can avoid the confusion between explanation and justification which made empiricist epistemology seem possible and necessary. In chapters seven and eight I shall try to show how the emphasis on the priority of the public to the private which results from repudiating empiricism paves the way for further Hegelian and Heideggerian projects of deconstruction.

4. THE " 'IDEA' IDEA"

Having argued that Sellars's attack on the Myth of the Given is compatible with kindness to babies and animals and thus with the common moral consciousness, I now want to argue that Quine's attack on the " 'idea' idea" and the distinction between language and fact is compatible with the intellectual respectability of the *Geisteswissenschaften*. Quine's doctrines of the "indeterminacy of translation" and the "inscrutability of reference" have led him to claim that there is no "matter of fact" involved in attributions of meaning to utterances, beliefs to people, and aspirations to cultures. I think that here again some distinctions will take

---

[24] Sellars, *Science, Perception and Reality*, p. 148.

care of putative counter-intuitive consequences of epistemological behaviorism, letting us see it as clearing the ground
for morality and high culture rather than depriving them
of "objective truth."

What Quine calls the " 'idea' idea" is the view that language is the expression of something "inner" which must
be discovered before we can tell what an utterance means,
or interpret the linguistic behavior of utterers (e.g., attribute beliefs, desires, and cultures to them). To abandon
this idea is at once to abandon the logical-empiricist notion
of "truth in virtue of meaning" and the sometime Oxonian
notion of "conceptual truth," since there are no meanings
or concepts from which truths might be read off. This attitude toward the concept of "concept" makes it possible to
dismiss Kant's distinction between necessary truths (which
can be determined by looking at concepts alone [analytic
truth] or pure concepts and pure forms of intuition alone
[synthetic a priori truth]) and contingent truths (which require reference to empirical intuitions). But Quine regards
concepts and meanings as merely one species of intentions, and he wishes to obliterate *all* intentions. Thus, admitting that "means," "believes," and "desires," for example, have no behavioristic equivalents (as Brentano and
Chisholm, in an effort to preserve some kernel of truth in
traditional mind-body dualism, had also attempted to
show), Quine concludes that this shows that the notions of
"belief" and "desire" are (for "scientific" purposes) as
dispensable as those of "concept" and "intuition":

> One may accept the Brentano thesis either as showing the
> indispensability of intentional idioms and the im-
> portance of an autonomous science of intention, or as
> showing the baselessness of intentional idioms and the
> emptiness of a science of intention. My attitude, unlike
> Brentano's, is the second. To accept intentional usage
> at face value is, we saw, to postulate translation rela-
> tions as somehow objectively valid though indeterminate

193

in principle relative to the totality of speech dispositions. Such postulation promises little gain in scientific
insight if there is no better ground for it than that the
supposed translation relations are presupposed by the
vernacular of semantics and intention.[25]

Quine thinks this anti-intentionalism of a piece with his
polemic against analyticity. But it is not. The author of
"Two Dogmas of Empiricism" *should* have said that concepts and meanings are harmless if posited to give explanations of our behavior, and become harmful only when
treated as the source of a special kind of truth and of a
special sort of authority for certain assertions. In particular,
we would expect him to say that the reasons normally given
for translating languages one way rather than another (or
for ascribing one set of beliefs and desires rather than an
odd alternative which would predict the same linguistic
behavior) are justified simply by their internal coherence,
and that such practices as translation and ascription of
intentional states are justified by their social utility. Quine
grants the utility, but he thinks it philosophically important to insist that the sort of truth proffered in such
remarks as " 'Hund' is German for 'dog,' " and "Robinson
believes in God" is not the sort of truth which expresses
"matter of fact."[26] He thus offers us a distinction between
truth by convenience and truth by correspondence, so to
speak, rather than the old positivist distinction between

[25] W.V.O. Quine, *Word and Object* (Cambridge, Mass., 1960), p. 221.
[26] See *Words and Objections: Essays on the Work of W. V. Quine*,
ed. Donald Davidson and Jaakko Hintikka (Dordrecht, 1969), p. 303,
where Quine says:

Consider . . . the totality of truths of nature, known and unknown,
observable and unobservable, past and future. The point about indeterminacy of translation is that it withstands even all this truth,
the whole truth about nature. This is what I mean by saying that,
where indeterminacy of translation applies, there is no real question of right choice; there is no fact of the matter even to *within*
the acknowledged under-determination of a theory of nature.

194

truth by convention and truth confirmed by sensory experience. Truths about meanings and beliefs and propositions are, somehow, not really truths in the full sense of the term—just as the positivists used to say that necessary truths were not really "about the world."

The holism and pragmatism of "Two Dogmas" would seem to make this distinction between two sorts of truth as difficult to maintain as the older distinctions which Quine is concerned to attack. Many critics of Quine have noted this point, and have diagnosed his insistence on this distinction as a hangover of traditional empiricism.[27] I agree with most of these criticisms, and shall not attempt to summarize or synthesize them (beyond noting that such critics unite in remarking that any sort of "indeterminacy" which we can find in translation will show up, equally harmlessly, in the *Naturwissenschaften*). But by examining the notion of "inscrutability of reference" we may get some understanding of the "empiricist" intuitions which make Quine persist in talk of "correspondence," and which hold him back from the Hegelian implications of his own behaviorism and holism.

Quine summarizes the argument of his "Ontological Relativity" by saying:

27 The best-known criticism of this sort is Noam Chomsky's "Quine's Empirical Assumptions" in *Words and Objections*. The point is most convincingly made, however, by Hilary Putnam in "The Refutation of Conventionalism," *Nous* 8 (1974), 38: "If the adoption of one system of analytical hypotheses rather than another permits a great simplification of such sciences as neurophysiology, psychology, anthropology, etc., then why should we not say that what we mean by 'translation' is *translation according to the manuals that have this property?*" Putnam rightly diagnoses Quine's doctrine of the special indeterminacy of translation as following from a kind of essentialism. It is, roughly, one in which we know in advance that what cannot be put in the vocabulary of the physics of the day is so inessential as to be merely "in the eye of the beholder," a matter of subjective convenience. See also Christopher Boorse, "The Origins of the Indeterminacy Thesis," *Journal of Philosophy* 72 (1975), 369-387, and Richard Rorty, "Indeterminacy of Translation and of Truth," *Synthese* 23 (1972), 443-462.

What makes sense is to say not what the objects of a theory are, absolutely speaking, but how one theory of objects is interpretable or reinterpretable in another. . . . What our present reflections are leading us to appreciate is that the riddle about seeing things upside down, or in complementary colors, should be taken seriously and its moral applied widely. The relativistic thesis to which we have come is this, to repeat: it makes no sense to say what the objects of a theory are, beyond saying how to interpret or reinterpret that theory in another. . . . Talk of subordinate theories and their ontologies *is* meaningful but only relative to the background theory with its own primitively adopted and ultimately inscrutable ontology.[28]

One would think this relativistic thesis the natural and happy result of the approach to knowledge and science which Quine shares with Sellars, were it not for the disturbing phrase "primitively adopted and ultimately inscrutable ontology." On a full-blooded holistic view, the question "Are we *really* referring to rabbits or rabbit-stages? formulae or Gödel numbers?" would be regarded neither as senseless, nor as sensible only when relativized to a background language,[29] but as like "Are we really talking about nations or about groups of individual persons?" or "Are we really talking about witches or about hallucinatory psychotics?" The latter questions have a sense if we give them a sense—that is, if something further depends upon the answer. It is easy to imagine situations in which sense would be given to them; it is harder, but not impossible, for the rabbit-versus-rabbit-stage case. But Quine is not

[28] W.V.O. Quine, *Ontological Relativity and Other Essays* (New York, 1969), pp. 50-51.

[29] See ibid., pp. 47ff. Hartry Field has shown that Quine's notion of "relativization to a background language" and "taking reference at face value" are incompatible with his general line of argument. See his "Quine and the Correspondence Theory," *Philosophical Review* 83 (1974), 207ff. But this difficulty is not relevant to my present purposes.

interested in the question of *that* way of giving sense. His claims about indeterminacy and inscrutability are not supposed to tie in with the needs of science or practice. Admitting that linguists never dream of taking advantage of indeterminacy to translate the short expressions normally uttered when rabbits break cover as "another rabbit-stage!" Quine says:

> The implicit maxim guiding his [the linguist's] choice of "rabbit" . . . is that an enduring and relatively homogenous object, moving as a whole against a contrasting background, is a likely reference for a short expression. . . . The maxim is his own imposition, toward settling what is objectively indeterminate. It is a very sensible imposition, and I would recommend no other. But I am making a philosophical point.[30]

A "philosophical point" in this sense is, at a minimum, one that has no relevance to deciding how the world is. Quine teeters between the older positivist view that such points are disreputably "metaphysical" and the more Oxonian philosophy-as-therapy view that such peculiarly philosophical points serve as antidotes to a πρῶτον ψεῦδος such as the " 'idea' idea." We might, however, take this particular philosophical point as offering an antidote against, if anything, the notions of "ontology" and of "reference." That is, we might fall back on the more old-fashioned view that just as the behaviorist approach to "truth by virtue of meaning" in "Two Dogmas" left us with no notion of "sameness of meaning" save (as Harman says) the commonsensical and philosophically uninteresting one in which "The president went to Vietnam" and "Johnson went to Vietnam" mean the same thing, so the behaviorist approach to "ontology" of "Ontological Relativity" leaves us with no notion of "sameness of reference" save the common-sensical and philosophically uninteresting one in which talk about rabbit-stages and talk about rabbits are talk about the same

[30] Quine, *Ontological Relativity*, p. 34.

197

things (in different ways).[31] The philosophical notion of "reference" seems to Quine to contrast with that of meaning because:

> Reference, extension, has been the firm thing; meaning, intension, the infirm. The indeterminacy of translation now confronting us, however, cuts across extension and intension alike. The terms "rabbit," "undetached rabbit part," and "rabbit stage" differ not only in meaning; they are true of different things. Reference itself proves behaviorally inscrutable.[32]

But this relative firmness was itself merely the product of Quine's claim that intensions, for which there were no criteria of identity, were flabbier entities than extensions, for which there were. The problem about identity-conditions for intensions boils down, Quine thinks, to that of how "two eternal sentences should be related in order that, where 'p' and 'q' stand for them, we be entitled to say that [p] is the same proposition as [q] rather than another."[33] But to think that this question can be answered is to think, Quine says, that there is some synonymy relation which makes a sentence of one language the right translation of a sentence of another.[34]

We have now, however, come full circle. The firmness of reference is what it is because of a putative contrast with an infirmness about meaning. But this infirmness is only present if translation is indeterminate in some way in which physics is not. So if we accept the standard criticisms of Quine's "double" indeterminacy of translation (an indeterminacy which differs from that of physical theory in

---

[31] The example of common-sensical sameness of meaning comes from Harman, "Quine," p. 142. For more on the distinction between the common-sensical and the philosophical senses of "talking about" or referring, see my "Realism and Reference," *Monist* 59 (1976), 321-340, and chapter six, section 4.

[32] Quine, *Ontological Relativity*, p. 35.

[33] Quine, *Word and Object*, p. 200.

[34] Ibid., p. 206.

that there is no "matter of fact" in the former case), then we have no reason for being startled at reference's faring no better, and no reason for thinking that the behavioral inscrutability of reference leads to any conclusions save "so much the worse for reference" or "rabbit-stages and rabbits are just the same things." Since "reference" here means a specifically philosophical notion, whose inscrutability is a specifically philosophical point which depends upon holding rabbits and rabbit-stages further apart than any scientific or practical need would hold them, we might feel entitled to adopt the same insouciant attitude toward this inscrutability which Quine adopts toward the specifically philosophical notion of synonymy and toward Brentano's thesis of the irreducibility of the intentional.

We should indeed adopt this attitude,[35] but not before looking more closely at Quine's vacillation on the subject of ontology. To say that the philosophical notion of reference is one we can well do without is, as Quine would agree, to say that ontology is also. Since it is because of a concern for ontology that Quine takes reference seriously, it will help to see how hard it is for him to reconcile this concern with his holistic claim that there is no "first philosophy" higher than and prior to ordinary scientific inquiry.[36] This latter view would seem to incline him toward Sellars's view that "science is the measure of all things, of what is that it is, and of what is not that it is not."[37] Nevertheless, Quine claims that the practical indispensability of intentional idioms should not blind us to the fact that:

If we are limning the true and ultimate structure of reality, the canonical scheme for us is the austere scheme that knows no quotation but direct quotation and no

35 I argue again for doing so in chapter seven.

36 See "On Carnap's Views on Ontology" in Quine, *Ways of Paradox* (New York, 1968) and "Epistemology Naturalized" in *Ontological Relativity*.

37 The phrase is from Sellars, *Science, Perception and Reality*, p. 173.

propositional attitudes but only the physical constitutions and behavior of organisms.[38]

This project, he claims, is continuous with that of science because:

> Each elimination of obscure constructions or notions that we manage to achieve, by paraphrase into more lucid elements, is a clarification of the conceptual scheme of science. The same motives that impel scientists to seek ever simpler and clearer theories adequate to the subject matter of their special sciences are motives for simplification and clarification of the broader framework shared by all the sciences. . . . The quest of a simplest, clearest overall pattern of canonical notation is not to be distinguished from a quest of ultimate categories, a limning of the most general traits of reality. Nor let it be retorted that such constructions are conventional affairs not dictated by reality; for may not the same be said of a physical theory? True, such is the nature of reality that one physical theory will get us around better than another; but similarly for canonical notations. (p. 161)

The catch, of course, comes in knowing what "obscurity" and "clarity" are. The *Geisteswissenschaften*, Quine thinks, employ notions which are so unclear that we must simply rub them out when limning the structure of reality. All is clear, however, in the physical sciences save when these invoke numbers, functions, properties, etc., in which case we interpret these as sets, an interpretation which the physical scientist can regard with sublime indifference. But the unclarity of "belief," "meaning," "translates as . . . ," etc. are irredeemable; there is nothing on hand in set theory to replace them with; they can survive only on grounds of practical convenience.[39]

[38] Quine, *Word and Object*, p. 221.

[39] Harman ("Quine," p. 126) puts a more charitable interpretation upon Quine's views on these matters. According to Harman,

> It is not that he thinks intensional objects, propositions or meanings, are a *queer* kind of entity (as one might believe that electrons must

Why, however, do "believes in . . ." and "translates as . . ." owe more to the necessities of practice than "is the same electron as . . ." and "is the same set as . . ."? Why do the *Naturwissenschaften* limn reality while the *Geisteswissenschaften* merely enable us to cope with it? What is it that sets them apart, given that we no longer think of any sort of statement having a privileged epistemological status, but of all statements as working together for the good of the race in that process of gradual holistic adjustment made famous by "Two Dogmas of Empiricism"? Why should not the unit of empirical inquiry be the whole of culture (including both the *Natur-* and the *Geisteswissenschaften*) rather than just the whole of physical science?

Trying to answer these rhetorical questions leads us to a genuine contradiction in Quine's view. It comes out most clearly in a passage in which he is trying to argue that the practical dictates of translation have no epistemological implications:

> "Save logical truth" is conventional in character because of the indeterminacy of translation. . . . The very want of determinacy puts a premium on adhering to this strong and simple rule as a partial determinant. . . . "Save logical truth" is both a convention and a wise one. And we see also that it gives logical truth no epistemological status distinct from that of any obvious truths of a so-called factual kind.[40]

---

be a queer kind of entity). His complaint is not that intensional objects, as something abstract, offend his sensibilities in the way that they no doubt offend the sensibilities of Nelson Goodman. . . . Quine's argument . . . is that the various views in that cluster [which invoke such entities] are theories that don't explain what they purport to explain. So his attitude toward intensional objects is similar to his attitude toward phlogiston or the ether (or witches).

Quine seems blandly to endorse Harman's interpretation at *Words and Objections*, p. 296. But I do not think that this interpretation can be reconciled with many of the arguments in *Word and Object* and elsewhere, although I agree that it represents the attitude which Quine *should* have adopted.

40 *Words and Objections*, p. 318.

But if conventionality depends upon a *special* indeterminacy of translation, then we may *not* say, as Quine does in a passage quoted previously, that physical theory is a "conventional affair not dictated by reality." If the permanence of logical truth is merely a practical rule, rather than an insight into the nature of reality, then if physical theory *is* such an insight, it cannot also be a practical rule.

To sum up his vacillations, we may note that Quine wants to assert all the following:

1. There is such a thing as ontology, governed by "scruples about what objects one may assume" and based on a distinction between "irresponsible reification and its opposite."[41]

2. There is no special epistemological status which any sentence has apart from its role in the maintaining that "field of force" which is human knowledge and whose aim is coping with sensory irradiations.

3. So there is no such thing as direct acquaintance with sense-data or meanings which would give inviolability to reports by virtue of their correspondence to reality, apart from their role in the general scheme of belief.

4. So epistemology and ontology never meet, since our scruples about what objects to assume are not dictated by our acquaintance with either universals or particulars.

5. But there is nevertheless a distinction to be made between those parts of the web of belief which express matters of fact and those which do not, and ontology insures that we can detect this difference.

If he is to assert (5) as well as (1)-(4), Quine must give a sense to the distinction between "matter of fact" and "convention" which has no links with the usual instrumentalist-phenomenalist distinction—that between what we are really acquainted with and what we "posit" to cope with stimuli.

[41] Quine, *Word and Object*, pp. 119-120.

202

The only way he can do so, as far as I can see, is simply to pick out the elementary particles of contemporary physics as paradigmatically matter-of-factual and explain that the sense in which there is no matter of fact about meanings or beliefs is that different things can be said about what a sentence means or a man believes without any implications for the movements of these particles. This tactic makes his preference for physics over psychology, and thus his concern about "irresponsible reification," purely aesthetic. Further, it will not work. For alternative biochemical (e.g.) as well as alternative psychological theories will be compatible with all and only the same movements of the same particles. Unless and until there is a genuine deduction of all true nomological statements from the laws of physics (which no one seriously expects), there will be no complaint to be made about intentions which cannot be made about mitochondria.[42]

[42] Dagfinn Føllesdal ("Meaning and Experience" in *Mind and Language*, ed. S. Guttenplan [Oxford, 1975]) suggests a way of construing Quine's indeterminacy thesis designed to show that "Quine's position is more interesting if his ontological bias towards physicalism is regarded as a consequence of a more fundamental epistemological bias towards empiricism." (p. 33) The suggestion is that

. . . all the truths there are, are included in the theory of nature. As we noted earlier, in our theory of nature we try to account for *all* our experiences. And the only entities we are justified in assuming are those that are appealed to in the simplest theory that accounts for all this evidence. These entities and their properties and interrelations are all there is to the world, and all there is to be right or wrong about. All truths about these are included in our theory of nature. In translation we are not describing a further realm of reality, we are just correlating two comprehensive theories concerning all there is. (p. 32)

However, I do not see how we can tell when we have stopped describing and started correlating descriptions. Or, to put it in another way, I do not see how we can mark off "nature" from something else save by finding some sense of "account for all our experiences" in which something less than the whole of culture can account for all our experiences.

An alternative way of tracing the indeterminacy thesis to empiri-

Quine is led into these difficulties, I think, by an attempt to preserve the view which he, like Sellars, inherits from Carnap and ultimately from Wittgenstein's *Tractatus*: the view that the world can be "completely described" in an extensional language. It is intensionality rather than intentionality which is the real bugbear, for only the non-truth-functional character of intentional discourse makes its presumed subject more disreputable than, say, irreducibly bio-chemical talk of mitochondria. Reducibility to talk of particles is only a cover for reducibility to truth-functional discourse. The particles do not matter, but logical form does. The lack of clear identity-conditions for intentions is a disaster not because of some ghostliness which ensues, but simply because this lack leaves certain sentences non-extensional. But if this is so, then we can achieve Quine's ends without employing his means. We can do so by granting that the world *can* be completely described in a truth-functional language, while simultaneously granting that pieces of it can also be described in an intensional one, and simply refraining from invidious comparisons between

cism is offered by John McDowell ("Truth Conditions, Bivalence, and Verificationism" in *Truth and Meaning*, ed. G. Evans and J. McDowell [Oxford, 1976]). McDowell thinks that Quine may be asserting "a version, not quite happily formulated, of the strong verificationist objection to realism in a theory of meaning." (p. 65) This objection is that to construe an assertion's truth as "underdetermined by what is observable" would, if we construed the statement "realistically," require us to attribute to the speaker "a conception of truth as being independent of what is observable." (p. 64) Since the latter is, for the verificationist, absurd, it shows that we must not construe the statement "realistically." This strategy, however, seems to involve finding a sense for "determination by what is observable" which would keep biology and exclude translation, and, once again, I do not see how this is to be done. So I conclude that the tension between (4) and (5) remains, despite the attempts of friendly critics of Quine to reformulate his point in a way that renders it safe from Chomsky's criticism that the only indeterminacy in the area is the familiar underdetermination of theory by observation (a criticism which both Føllesdal and McDowell refer to, and wish to circumvent).

these modes of description. To say that it can be *completely* described is to use a notion of completeness defined in terms of spatio-temporal extent, not in terms of either explanatory power or practical convenience. If we could not refer to intentions, we might be hard put to it to cope with the world, but we should—for whatever this is worth—still be able to describe every bit of it, and even make an accurate prediction about the content of any space-time region of any desired minuteness.

The way to apply this point to the vocabulary of beliefs and desires has been shown by Davidson, who puts the matter in terms of a distinction between homonomic and heteronomic generalizations:

On the one hand, there are generalizations whose positive instances give us reason to believe the generalization itself could be improved by adding further provisos and conditions stated in the same general vocabulary as the original generalization. Such a generalization points to the form and vocabulary of the finished law; we may say that it is a *homonomic* generalization. On the other hand there are generalizations which when instantiated may give us reason to believe there is a precise law at work, but one that can be stated only by shifting to a different vocabulary. We may call such generalizations *heteronomic*.

I suppose most of our practical lore (and science) is heteronomic. This is because a law can hope to be precise, explicit, and as exceptionless as possible only if it draws its concepts from a comprehensive closed theory. . . . Confidence that a statement is homonomic, correctible within its own conceptual domain, demands that it draw its concepts from a theory with strong constitutive elements. . . .

Just as we cannot intelligibly assign a length to any object unless a comprehensive theory holds of objects of that sort, we cannot intelligibly attribute any proposi-

205

tional attitude to an agent except within the framework of a viable theory of his beliefs, desires, intentions, and decisions.[43]

Davidson goes on to say that purported psychophysical laws are like "All emeralds are grue." They combine terms taken from disparate vocabularies. We may talk about emeroses and grueness, or about emeralds and greenness, but not about both at once (at least not if we want a useful comprehensive theory). Even so, we may talk about actions and beliefs, or about movements and neurons, but not (comprehensively) both at once. But there is an obvious sense, in the former example, in which we are talking about *the same things*, whichever set of predicates we choose. Even so, Davidson says, in the latter case. The difference in choice of vocabularies is not a mark of the difference between the real and the ontologically disreputable, nor of that between the factual and the mythical, but is on all fours with the difference between talking of the activities of nations-as-such and talking of the activities of ministers and generals, or between talking of mitochondria as such and talking of the elementary particles they contain. We may usefully and truly say things like "If Asquith had remained prime minister, England would have lost," or "If there had been a few more neutrons in there, the mitochondrion would not have survived," or "If we had just stuck in an electrode in the right place in the cortex, he would never have decided he was Napoleon," or "If we could get hold of an emerose, we should have just the right shade of green," but we cannot (so far as we know now, at least) develop such heteronomic remarks into laws which are parts of comprehensive theories. Nor, on the other hand, need we see such heteronomic remarks as crossing the line between ontological realms—in particular, the realm of the factual and the realm of the nonfactual. In Davidson's view of the relation between different explanatory

[43] Donald Davidson, "Mental Events" in *Experience and Theory*, ed. L. Foster and J. W. Swanson (Amherst, Mass., 1970), pp. 94-96.

vocabularies, there is no reason *whatever* for thinking that those vocabularies which lend themselves to truth-functional formulations "limn the true and ultimate structure of reality" in a way in which intensional vocabularies do not. The extensional-intensional distinction turns out to have no more and no less philosophical interest than the distinction between nations and people: it is capable of inciting reductionist emotion, but not capable of providing a special reason for embarking on reductionist projects.

Davidson's distinction gives us a way of seeing that an intentional vocabulary is just one more vocabulary for talking about portions of a world which can, indeed, be completely described without this vocabulary. We can share Carnap's intuition that the movement of anything can be predicted on the basis of the movement of elementary particles, and that if we simply kept track of all those particles we would be keeping track of (though *not* explaining) all that there is, without speaking, with Quine, of "the baselessness of intentional idioms and the emptiness of a science of intention." One vocabulary—that of particle physics—may work for *every* portion of the universe, whereas talk of mitochondria, emeroses, cabinet ministers, and intentions is called for only here and there. But the distinction between the universal and the specific is not the distinction between the factual and the "empty," still less that between the real and the apparent, or the theoretic and the practical, or nature and convention.

Davidson, however, links his own project to Quine's in a misleading way when he says that "the heteronomic character of general statements linking the mental and the physical traces back to this central role of translation in the description of all propositional attitudes, and to the indeterminacy of translation,"[44] and also when he cites with approval Quine's remark that "Brentano's thesis of the irreducibility of intentional idioms is of a piece with the thesis of indeterminacy of translation."[45] Both remarks sug-

44 Ibid., p. 97.
45 Ibid., p. 97n., quoting Quine, *Word and Object*, p. 221.

gest that the relation between statements which offer translations and behaviorese is *special* in some way that the relation between statements about mitochondria and those about elementary particles is not. Both suggest Quine's odd doctrine of the "double" indeterminacy of translation. But if what I have been saying is right, irreducibility is always *just* irreducibility, and never a clue to "ontological" differences. There are *lots* of vocabularies in the language within which one might expect to get a comprehensive theory phrased in homonomic generalizations, and science, political theory, literary criticism, and the rest will, God willing, continue to create more and more such vocabularies. To abandon the notion that in philosophy we have a discipline which guards against "irresponsible reification" and systematizes our "scruples about what objects one may assume" would be to take irreducibility in our stride and thus to judge each such vocabulary on pragmatic or aesthetic grounds alone. Quine's strictures against Carnap's attempt to divide philosophy from science are just what is needed to help us realize that there is no such discipline, and thus just what is needed to see that the *Geisteswissenschaften* would have not become more *wissenschaftlich*, or more ontologically respectable, if Brentano and Dilthey had turned out to be wrong about their irreducibility. Unfortunately, however, Quine's enduring conviction that symbolic logic must somehow have "ontological implications" leads him to make more of translation, intentionality, and the " 'idea' idea" than needs to be made.

I have devoted this long section to arguing that Quine's attack on "truth by virtue of meaning" as an explanation of putatively necessary truths should not be confused with his attack on "meanings" as ideas in the mind, ideas which determine the accuracy of translations in a way that linguistic behavior cannot. The former is indeed a pseudo-explanation; there are, for the holistic reasons given in "Two Dogmas," no *privileged* representations. But Quine's distrust of privileged representations leads him to distrust *all* representations, to distrust the " 'idea' idea" itself. Yet ideas in the mind are no more or less disreputable than neurons in the brain, mitochondria in the cells, passions in the soul, or moral progress in history. The damage done by the " 'idea' idea" in modern philosophy was done by the pseudo-explanation of epistemic authority through the notion of "direct acquaintance" by the "Eye of the Mind" with mental entities such as sense-data and meanings. But this is epistemological damage, not ontological damage. If I am right in the criticisms of Quine I have been making (and in the general line I am taking in this book) the only way in which one can do *ontological* damage is to block the road of inquiry by insisting on a bad old theory at the expense of a good new theory. It may be claimed that nineteenth-century introspectionist psychology did briefly block the road of inquiry, but even if that were so it would be quite a different thing from saying that the *Geisteswissenschaften* are preventing us from seeing reality plain, or that their shady ontology must be tolerated for the sake of practical ends. The lesson of epistemological behaviorism is just that there is no "philosophical point" to be made about translation or intentionality, nor about any other "ontological" subject. Rather, it helps us see that explanatory power is where we find it, and that the philosophical attempt to distinguish between "scientific" and "unscientific" explanations is needless.

5. EPISTEMOLOGICAL BEHAVIORISM, PSYCHOLOGICAL BEHAVIORISM, AND LANGUAGE

In the previous chapter I said that the epistemological tradition confused the causal process of acquiring knowledge with questions concerning its justification. In this chapter I have presented Sellars's criticism of the Myth of the Given and Quine's criticism of the notion of truth by virtue of meaning as two detailed developments of this more general criticism. If we accept these criticisms, and therefore drop the notion of epistemology as the quest, initiated by Descartes, for those privileged items in the field of consciousness which are the touchstones of truth, we are in a position to ask whether there still remains something for epistemology to be. I want to urge that there does not. To understand the matters which Descartes wanted to understand—the superiority of the New Science to Aristotle, the relations between this science and mathematics, common sense, theology, and morality—we need to turn outward rather than inward, toward the social context of justification rather than to the relations between inner representations. This attitude has been encouraged in recent decades by many philosophical developments, particularly those stemming from Wittgenstein's *Philosophical Investigations* and from Kuhn's *Structure of Scientific Revolutions*. Some of these developments will be canvassed in chapters seven and eight. Before doing so, however, I shall discuss two attempts to preserve something from the Cartesian tradition, attempts which may seem to shed some doubt on our ability simply to drop the image of the Mirror of Nature altogether.

The first of these attempts is the revolt against logical behaviorism in the philosophy of psychology, leading to the development of explanations of behavior in terms of inner representations without, necessarily, any linkup with the justification of beliefs and actions. I have already said that once explanation and justification are held apart there is no reason to object to explanation of the acquisition of knowledge in terms of representations, and that such explanations can be offered without resuscitating the traditional "mind-body problem." But I think that the defense of such explanations against Ryle and Skinner can easily be distorted into a rehabilitation of the traditional seventeenth-century philosophical problematic, and thus I shall devote chapter five to a discussion of such defenses. My aim will be to disassociate empirical psychology from the remnants of epistemology by defending it against both Wittgensteinian criticisms and Chomskyan compliments.

The second attempt to preserve something from the Cartesian tradition which I shall discuss is the effort, within recent philosophy of language, to specify "how language hooks onto the world," thus creating an analogue of the Cartesian problem of how thought hooks onto the world. An attempt to use the notions of the reference of terms and the truth of sentences to aid in understanding the matters which troubled Descartes seems to me doomed to failure, but such a program is very tempting. Because language is a "public" Mirror of Nature, as thought is a "private" one, it seems that we should be able to reformulate a great many Cartesian and Kantian questions and answers in linguistic terms, and thereby rehabilitate a lot of standard philosophical issues (e.g., the choice between idealism and realism). I devote chapter six to various efforts at such rehabilitation, and argue that semantics should be kept as pure of epistemology as should psychology.

Once both the inner representations needed in psychological explanation and the word-world relations needed by semantics to produce a theory of meaning for natural languages are seen as irrelevant to issues of justification, we can see the abandonment of the search for privileged representations as the abandonment of the goal of a "theory of knowledge." The urge toward such a theory in the seventeenth century was a product of the change from one paradigm of understanding nature to another, as well as of the change from a religious to a secular culture. Philosophy as a discipline capable of giving us a "right method of seeking truth" depends upon finding some permanent neutral framework of all possible inquiry, an understanding of which will enable us to see, for example, why neither Aristotle nor Bellarmine was justified in believing what he believed. The mind as Mirror of Nature was the Cartesian tradition's response to the need for such a frame-

211

work. If there are no privileged representations in this mirror, then it will no longer answer to the need for a touchstone for choice between justified and unjustified claims upon our belief. Unless some other such framework can be found, the abandonment of the image of the Mirror leads us to abandon the notion of philosophy as a discipline which adjudicates the claims of science and religion, mathematics and poetry, reason and sentiment, allocating an appropriate place to each. In chapters seven and eight I develop this point further.

CHAPTER V

Epistemology and Empirical Psychology

1. SUSPICIONS ABOUT PSYCHOLOGY

The line of thought I have called "epistemological behaviorism" has produced a prejudice against the notion of
"mental entities" and "psychological processes." A certain
picture of man's higher faculties, common to Descartes
and Locke, has been gradually erased by the work of such
writers as Dewey, Ryle, Austin, Wittgenstein, Sellars, and
Quine. However, this picture—the one which gave rise to
the seventeenth-century notion of a "veil of ideas," and thus
to epistemological skepticism—has not been replaced by
a new and clearer picture. On the contrary, there is widespread fratricidal disagreement among anti-Cartesians
about what, if anything, to say about the mind. Ryle's
magic word "disposition" is no longer in favor, but more
up-to-date notions such as "functional state" are offered as
substitutes. Anything smacking of either Skinnerian methodological behaviorism or Rylean "logical" behaviorism
is looked at askance, but it is agreed that there must be some
way of avoiding such reductive efforts without falling back
into the sort of dualism which engendered the traditional
"problems of modern philosophy." The counter-intuitive
consequences of behaviorism, reductively interpreted, are
illustrated by Malcolm's polemic against much recent work
by psychologists:

> Thus, it is the facts, the circumstances surrounding the
> behavior, that give it the property of expressing recogni-
> tion. This property is not due to something that goes on
> inside.
> It seems to me that if this point were understood by

philosophers and psychologists, they would no longer have a motive for constructing theories and models for recognition, memory, thinking, problem solving, understanding, and other "cognitive processes."[1]

If we follow out this line of thought, we can decide that the whole empirical science of psychology is based on a mistake, and that there is no middle ground for research between common-sensical explanations of behavior on the one hand and neurophysiology on the other. The notion that there is a middle ground for psychology to investigate will, in this view, be a product of Malcolm's "myth of cognitive processes and structures"—what Ryle called "Descartes' Myth." Malcolm seems inclined to take the matter to this point, for example, in his description of the Chomskyan notion of an "internalized system of rules" as typical of the root mistake of the "traditional theory of Ideas," viz.:

> The assumption . . . that in speaking a person must be *guided*. There must be something at hand that shows him how to speak, how to put words together grammatically and with coherent sense. . . . What is being explained is knowledge—both knowing that and knowing how. The presence in him of the structure of the language or of its system of rules is supposed to account for this knowledge —to explain *how* he knows. (p. 389)

If we once see that "our understanding of human cognitive powers is not advanced by replacing the stimulus-response mythology with a mythology of inner guidance systems" (p. 392), Malcolm thinks, we shall not think that there are *any* explanations to be looked for in this area.

It is certainly true that the model of the mind which led Descartes and Locke to construct the "traditional philosophical problems" was built into the terminology of the

[1] Norman Malcolm, "The Myth of Cognitive Processes and Structures," in *Cognitive Development and Epistemology*, ed. Theodore Mischel (New York and London, 1971), p. 387.

214

young science of psychology.[2] It would be surprising if the overthrow of this model did not have some effect upon work in that science. Yet it would be equally surprising if a discipline now several generations away from its philosophical origins should be unable to stand on its own feet. There must, we suspect, be psychological research programs which cannot be endangered by a philosophical criticism of the vocabularies used by their designers.

Wittgensteinian criticisms (like Malcolm's) of such programs often seem based on a fallacious move from

1. The meaning of terms referring to the mental is to be explained in terms of behavior (where "behavior" is short-hand for "functions relating circumstances and stimuli to behavior") rather than by interior ostension

to

2. Psychology can concern itself only with empirical correlations between bits of behavior and external circumstances.

The inference, as successive critics of Ryle have pointed out, has no greater force than the parallel inference made by operationalist philosophers of science about physics.[3] Fodor, for example, remarks that the psychologist is quite prepared to admit that certain features in behavior and in the social matrix are necessary conditions for the occurrence of thoughts, recognitions, emotions, etc., but he urges that there may be lots of equally necessary "inner" conditions as well.[4] So if the psychological investigator has sense enough to avoid *defining*, for example, "act of recognition" in terms of purely inner events, presumably he can take

[2] See, for example, J. C. Flugel and Donald J. West, *A Hundred Years of Psychology* (London, 1964), chapters one and two.

[3] The point was first made, I believe, by Albert Hofstader in "Professor Ryle's Category-Mistakes," *Journal of Philosophy* 47 (1951), 257-270.

[4] Jerry Fodor, "Could There Be a Theory of Perception?" *Journal of Philosophy* 63 (1966), 371.

advantage of behavior and surroundings to identify his data. What more than this can be required to avoid the charge of mythologizing? It might, of course, turn out that there were no "intervening variables" worth postulating, but this could presumably only be discovered a posteriori, by trying and failing. As P. C. Dodwell says, replying to Malcolm:

> On Malcolm's view, psychologists would have to restrict themselves to investigations of simple empirical relationships such as that which might obtain between memory and sleep deprivation. But it is extremely difficult to see how this restriction could be justified. The factors which psychologists investigate in human memory *are* empirical relationships, although usually of a more complicated sort than the one just mentioned. Who, then, should make the decision on which empirical relationships are to be cleared for investigation? Not philosophers, surely.[5]

This reply seems to me entirely convincing, but we can nevertheless profit from considering the reasons why a reductive operationalism has seemed so much more palatable for psychology than for physics. Why have philosophers begrudged psychologists the right to dream up whatever theoretical entities and processes might help them to explain our behavior? One such reason has already been given: the confusion between the claims labeled (1) and (2) above. This confusion rested upon the fear, found in Husserl and Dilthey as well as in Wittgensteinians like Winch and Kenny, that subjecting human behavior to mechanistic explanation in terms of "psychological processes" would obscure the distinction between persons and things, between the human reality studied by the *Geisteswissenschaften* and the rest of reality studied by the *Naturwissenschaften*. More will be said in later chapters about that distinction, but for

[5] P. C. Dodwell, "Is a Theory of Conceptual Development Necessary?" in *Cognitive Development and Epistemology* (cited in note 1 above), p. 382.

now we may be content with Dodwell's reply. Fear of mechanism and loss of personhood is a ground for suspicion of *all* the behavioral sciences, and does not catch what philosophers have found especially dubious about psychology. The more directly relevant reasons for suspicion are those which suggest that psychologists should be *more* mechanistic rather than less, that they should cut straight through the mental to the neurophysiological.

The first reason is simply the urge toward unified science, which is not so much the urge to reduce the Many to the One as the conviction that seventeenth-century science discovered that everything could be explained by atoms and the void, and that philosophy has a moral duty to preserve this insight. This conviction, however, has been softened by a dim awareness of quantum mechanics, so that an ontological respect for insensate matter has been replaced by a sociological respect for professors of physics. Philosophers' references to "the physical" are now standardly accompanied by a note explaining that any entity will count as "physical" which is invoked by the "physical sciences." Before Quine, when "reduction" was still the heart of the logical-empiricist program, philosophers thought themselves able to make actual contributions to the unification of science by "analyzing the meanings" of terms used in sociology, psychology, etc. Since Quine's attack on meaning, however, the need to reduce everything to whatever-physicists-will-countenance has been replaced by a still vaguer feeling that the sciences other than physics become "more scientific" when they can replace functional descriptions of theoretical entities (e.g., "gene") with structural descriptions (e.g., "DNA molecule"). This feeling is evanescent in cases like sociology and economics, where nobody wants to press for the physical realization of postulated theoretical entities, but it persists in psychology, whose theoretical entities have roughly the sort of concreteness which invites replacement by neurophysiology. But why, given Quinean reasons for thinking that no interesting necessary and suf-

217

ficient conditions for the application of the terms of one discipline can be given in the terms of another, should we be so impatient for such replacement? No one thought that genetics involved appeal to dubious entities because DNA was a long time coming. So what accounts for the instinctive feeling that psychologists are blocking the road of inquiry?

To answer this, we must turn to a second reason for suspicion of postulated mental entities and processes. We may call this, following Ryle, the fear of ghosts. The thought that by countenancing the mental, even temporarily, we are losing the scientific spirit, comes from two sources. The first, which I discussed in chapter one, is the confusion of the post-Cartesian conception of "consciousness" with the pre-philosophical notion of the soul as what leaves the body at death. The second is the epistemological argument that introspectibility carries with it privileged access, and that since such epistemic privilege must be based on an ontological difference (mental entities being intrinsically better known to their possessors than anything physical could be known to anyone), we must deny the existence of the mental-qua-introspectable on pain of making part of our knowledge of reality depend upon unverifiable reports. Such an argument is rarely offered so boldly, but something like it underlies a great deal of both positivistic and Wittgensteinian hostility to the mental.[6] However, just as the notion of the "unity of science" as a program for philosophical research cannot survive Quine's attack on "meaning," so this epistemological argument cannot survive Sellars's treatment of "givenness." In Sellars's account of immediate knowledge, introspection is a learned ability, and the dark suspicion that subjects will turn out to introspect whatever the experimenter tells them they ought to be able to introspect is largely justified. For our immediate knowledge

[6] See, for example, Malcolm's "expression theory" of first-person mentalistic reports, based on a passage in the *Philosophical Investigations*.

of mental events is not, according to Sellars, a mark of distinct ontological status, and the incorrigibility of first-person reports, like all matters concerning epistemic status, is a sociological rather than a metaphysical concern. But giving up the special ghostly status which had been supposed to make privileged access possible redeems the methodological respectability of appeals to introspection. For we can now see that teaching people to introspect thoughts, or nostalgia, or blood-pressure, or kinky alpha-rhythms, is simply a matter of utilizing connections within the organism—presumably the connections between the speech center and the rest of the nervous system—as scientific instruments. The fact that such training must take its point of departure from intersubjectively available circumstances is enough to insure that nothing sneaky is going on. The "subjectivity" and "unscientific" character of introspective reports are thus no more philosophically significant than the defects of spectroscopes. Once "subjective reports" are seen as a matter of heuristic convenience, rather than of permitting someone's unsupported word to refute a promising scientific hypothesis, we can clear away the unfortunate associations of introspectionist psychology with rationalism's appeal to clear and distinct ideas and Protestantism's appeal to the individual conscience.

I conclude that the Quinean and Sellarsian arguments I have outlined in the preceding chapter also serve to clear psychology of the standard suspicions which empiricistic and physicalistic philosophers have brought against it. The suspicions which come from the other direction—from the need to preserve human uniqueness, free will, and the integrity of the *Geisteswissenschaften*—will be discussed in chapters seven and eight. In the present chapter, I shall stick to the question: Can we find any relevance to traditional philosophical problems concerning *knowledge* in actual or expected results of empirical psychological research? Since I wish to say that these "philosophical prob-

219

lems" should be dissolved rather than solved, it is predictable that I should give a negative answer. But this negative answer needs considerable defense, since many philosophers who have been impressed by the arguments against privileged representations marshaled by Quine and Sellars nevertheless want to replace traditional "foundationalist" epistemology by the use of psychological results to produce a general theory of inner representations. I shall be arguing that such a "new epistemology" can offer nothing relevant to issues of justification, and that consequently it has no relevance to the cultural demands which led to the emergence of epistemology in the seventeenth and eighteenth centuries. Nor, consequently, can it aid in maintaining the image of philosophy as a discipline which stands apart from empirical inquiry and explains the relevance of the results of such inquiry to the rest of culture.

To make this point I shall discuss two suggestions current in the recent philosophical literature, all of which attribute to psychology a greater degree of philosophical importance than I think it deserves. The first is Quine's suggestion that psychology can investigate the "relations between theory and evidence" which used to be the subject matter of epistemology. In section 2 I shall argue that these relations cannot be restated in psychological terms. The second is the claim that the analogies between program states of computers and psychological states of persons and between "hardware" states of computers and neurophysiological states of bodies give a new and interesting sense to the notion that our knowledge consists of an "inner representation" of the world. This claim has been developed in greatest detail by Fodor; in sections 3 and 4 I shall be arguing that Fodor runs together a sense of "representation" in which representations may be judged accurate or inaccurate, and another in which they may not. These two senses, I hold, mark out the respective domains of epistemology and psychology.

220

2. The Unnaturalness of Epistemology

In an essay called "Epistemology Naturalized," Quine reviews the various embarrassments confronting efforts to provide a "foundation for science" and finally considers Wittgenstein's sardonic attitude toward this enterprise:

> Carnap and the other logical positivists of the Vienna Circle had already pressed the term "metaphysics" into pejorative use, as connoting meaninglessness; and the term "epistemology" was next. Wittgenstein and his followers, mainly at Oxford, found a residual philosophical vocation in therapy: in curing philosophers of the delusion that there were epistemological problems.
>
> But I think that at this point it may be more useful to say rather that epistemology still goes on, though in a new setting and a clarified status. Epistemology, or something like it, simply falls into place as a chapter of psychology and hence of natural science. It studies a natural phenomenon, viz., a physical human subject. This human subject is accorded a certain experimentally controlled input—certain patterns of irradiation in assorted frequencies, for instance—and in the fullness of time the subject delivers as output a description of the three-dimensional external world and its history. The relation between the meager input and the torrential output is a relation that we are prompted to study for somewhat the same reason that always prompted epistemology; namely, in order to see how evidence relates to theory, and in what ways one's theory of nature transcends any available evidence.[7]

Consider first Quine's claim that the motive behind epistemology has always been "to see how evidence relates to theory, and in what ways one's theory of nature transcends any available evidence." Most intellectual historians have

---

[7] W. V. O. Quine, *Ontological Relativity and Other Essays* (New York, 1969), pp. 82-83.

found it striking that what we now call the "theory of knowledge" plays so little part in the thought of writers before the seventeenth century. In Quine's account of epistemology, it is hard to see why this should be so. We might suggest that the need for a choice between radically distinct theories about planets and ballistic missiles became intense in the time of Galileo and Descartes, and that consequently the mind of the West was newly struck with the way in which "one's theory of nature transcends any available evidence." But this suggestion is rather thin. There were plenty of competing theories about the heavens in ancient and medieval times, but we have to rummage about quite a bit to find anything called "epistemology" in Plato and Aristotle, if epistemology means noting the gaps between theory and evidence and comparing ways of crossing those gaps. We can fasten with glad cries upon some passages in the *Theaetetus* and the *De Anima*; neo-Kantian historians of Greek philosophy like Zeller often have. But little to the purpose will turn up elsewhere in the fourth century, and practically nothing in the *Posterior Analytics* (where Aristotle, who knew all about controversy between competing scientific theories, and competed with the best of them, discusses the status and methodology of science). When Cartesianism burst upon a startled world in the seventeenth century, it was not because a new view was being offered about long-debated questions concerning the relations between theory and evidence. It was rather because questions were being taken seriously which, as Gilson remarked with some indignation, the scholastics had been too sensible to ask.[8]

---

[8] "From the point of view of medieval philosophy, Descartes plays the role of the *indisciplinatus*—someone who takes pride in insisting, no matter what discipline is in question, on the same degree of certainty, no matter how inappropriate. In a word, Descartes no longer recognizes an intermediary between the true and the false; his philosophy is the radical elimination of the notion of 'the probable.'" (Étienne Gilson, *Études sur le Role de la Pensée Médiévale dans la Formation du Système Cartésien* [Paris, 1930], p. 235.)

To understand why the seventeenth century became intrigued with the relation between theory and evidence, we need to ask why Descartes's fantasies captured Europe's imagination. As Quine says: "Epistemologists dreamed of a first philosophy, firmer than science and serving to justify our knowledge of the external world."[9] But why did everybody suddenly start dreaming the same dream? Why did the theory of knowledge become something more than the languid academic exercise of composing a reply to Sextus Empiricus? The dream of a first philosophy firmer than science is as old as the *Republic*, and we may agree with Dewey and Freud that the same primordial urges lie behind both religion and Platonism. But that does not tell us why anyone should think that first philosophy consists in, of all things, epistemology.

It may seem heavy-handed to press Quine's phrases in this way. I am doing so nevertheless because I think that understanding modern philosophy requires a more radical break with the tradition than Quine wants to make, or than is needed for his purposes. His genial "Don't let's throw out epistemology—let's let it be psychology" line is entirely reasonable if our aim is to show what in empiricism can be saved once we throw out the dogmas. But if we want to know why anybody thought it worthwhile, much less exciting or morally obligatory, to be an empiricist, we have to step back from the whole subject and press questions which Quine can safely neglect. To help achieve this distance, I turn now to some of the things Quine says about psychology. I want to show how very remote any psychological discovery of the sort he envisages will be from any concern with the foundations of science or with the relation between theory and evidence.

The link between empirical psychology of perception and empiricist epistemology is, I think, provided largely by the loose use of such words as "evidence," "information," and

9 W. V. O. Quine, "Grades of Theoreticity," in *Experience and Theory*, ed. L. Foster and J. W. Swanson (Amherst, Mass., 1970), p. 2.

"testimony." This use permits Quine to say things like "The nerve endings . . . are the place of input of unprocessed information about the world"[10] and "It is simply the stimulations of our sensory receptors that are best looked upon as the input to our cognitive mechanism."[11] Suppose we ask: Could psychology discover that it is not at the retina (the first nerve cells to be troubled by light rays) that information begins to be processed? Could it discover that it is actually in the lens, or perhaps only just where the optic nerve merges into the visual cortex? Could it discover that everything up to the latter point was not information but just electricity? Presumably not, since it is hard to see what would count as an experimental criterion of "information" or "processing." Quine, however, writes as if there *could* be such criteria. He notes that epistemology has always been torn between two criteria for being "datal": "causal proximity to the physical stimulus" and "the focus of awareness." But, he says:

> The dilemma is dissolved, and the strain relieved, when we give up the dream of a first philosophy firmer than science. If we are seeking only the causal mechanism of our knowledge of the external world, and not a justification of that knowledge in terms prior to science, we can settle after all for a theory of vision in Berkeley's style based on color patches in a two-dimensional field. . . . We can look upon man as a black box in the physical world, exposed to externally determinable stimulatory forces as input and spouting externally determinable testimony about the external world as output. Just which of the inner workings of the black box may be tinged with awareness is as may be.[12]

10 Ibid., p. 3.

11 Quine, "Epistemology Naturalized," in *Ontological Relativity*, p. 84.

12 Quine, "Grades of Theoreticity," in *Experience and Theory*, pp. 2-3.

But if we forget justification and look for causal mechanisms, we are certainly not going to be talking about color patches in a two-dimensional visual field. We shall have no use for the distinction between what is given and what is inferred, and no need for the notion of a "visual field" to hold the former. We may talk about irradiated patches on a two-dimensional retina or pulses in the optic nerve, but this will be a matter of choosing a black box, not of discovering touchstones for inquiry. Quine dissolves a dilemma only by changing the motive of inquiry. If one were only interested in causal mechanisms, one would never have worried one's head about awareness. But the epistemologists who dreamed the dream Quine describes were not only interested in causal mechanisms. They were interested in making, for example, an invidious distinction between Galileo and the professors who refused to look through his telescope.

If there are indeed no experimental criteria for where the real data come, then Quine's suggestion that we give up the notion of "sense data" and speak causally of nerve endings and epistemologically of observation sentences[13] does not resolve a dilemma which has plagued epistemology. Rather it lets epistemology wither away. For if we have psychophysiology to cover causal mechanisms, and the sociology and history of science to note the occasions on which observation sentences are invoked or dodged in constructing and dismantling theories, then epistemology has nothing to do. We would think that this result would be congenial to Quine, but in fact he resists it. The resistance is clearest when he rebukes such writers as Polanyi, Kuhn, and Hanson for wanting to drop the notion of observation altogether.[14] Quine thinks this a perfectly good notion, and wants to reconstruct it in terms of intersubjectivity. He defines an "observation sentence" as "one on which all speakers of the language give the same verdict when given the

[13] Ibid., p. 3.
[14] Ibid., p. 5; cf. "Epistemology Naturalized," p. 87.

same concurrent stimulation. To put the point negatively, an observation sentence is one that is not sensitive to differences in past experience within the speech community."[15] Quine thinks that by excluding the blind, the insane, and a few more "occasional deviants" (p. 88n.) we can tell which are the sentences which "depend on present sensory stimulation and on no stored information beyond what goes into understanding the sentence" (p. 86). This amounts to defining "present sensory stimulation" in terms of the uncontroversiality of certain sentences. Quine thinks that this preserves the force of the empiricist insight while abandoning the notions about meaning which are associated with the " 'idea' idea."

I think Quine is right in taking this line in order to preserve what was true in empiricism, for doing so makes it quite clear that if anything "replaces" epistemology it is the history and sociology of science, and is certainly not psychology. But this is not Quine's reason. Consider another passage about "data":

> What to count as observation now can be settled in terms of the stimulation of sensory receptors, let consciousness fall where it may.
>
> In the old anti-psychologistic days the question of epistemological priority was moot. What is epistemologically prior to what? Are Gestalten prior to sensory atoms . . . ? Now that we are permitted to appeal to physical stimulation, the problem dissolves; A is epistemologically prior to B if A is causally nearer than B to the sensory receptors. Or, what is in some ways better, just talk explicitly in terms of causal proximity to sensory receptors and drop the talk of epistemological priority. (pp. 84-85)

What is puzzling is that we have defined "observation sentence" in terms of the *consensus gentium*; we can divide observation from theory without knowing or caring which bits of our body are the sensory receptors, much less how far down the nerves the "processing" begins. We do not

[15] Quine, "Epistemology Naturalized," pp. 86-87.

need any psychophysiological account of causal mechanisms to isolate what is intersubjectively agreeable—we just do this in ordinary conversation. So presumably psychology has nothing to tell us about causal proximity which is worth knowing by those who wish to continue "epistemology in a psychological setting." To put it another way, once we have picked out the observation sentences conversationally rather than neurologically, further inquiry into "how evidence relates to theory" would seem to be a matter for Polanyi, Kuhn, and Hanson. For what could psychology add to their accounts of how scientists form and discard theories? Quine says of them that

> . . . some iconoclastic philosophers of science have taken to questioning the notion of observation only now that it ceases to present a problem. Theirs is, I think, a delayed reaction against the dubiety of the old notion of datum. Now that we have thrown off the old dream of a first philosophy, let us exult rather in our new access to unproblematical concepts. Neural input is one, and observation sentence as just now defined is another.[16]

But these concepts, where unproblematic, are not new. As electricity, neural input is not new; as "information" it is problematic. The notion of "observation sentence" as Quine has defined it is as old as the first lawyer who asked a witness, "But what did you actually see?" If we are to exult over anything, it is that we are no longer asking certain questions—not that we have found something new to do or some new terms in which to think. Quine has told us that we gave up bothering about consciousness when we gave up rational reconstruction. But he seems to be bringing it right back again by explicating observationality in terms of intersubjectivity. So he should either let Polanyi, Kuhn, and Hanson say that "observation" is just a matter of what we can agree on these days, or he should show how psychological discoveries can make something more of this notion. If

---

16 Quine, "Grades of Theoreticity," pp. 4-5.

they cannot, then defining "dependence on present sensory stimulation" in terms of intersubjectivity will just be invoking an old epistemological honorific to no psychological purpose.

My discussion of Quine has pressed his words with tiresome literalness. Quine probably does not care about the fate of the word "epistemology." What he does care about, perhaps, is his Deweyan position that science and philosophy are continuous—not to be viewed as having different methods or subjects. He is opposed to loose Oxonian talk about "philosophy as the analysis of concepts," and he associates Wittgenstein and "therapeutic positivism" with this sort of talk. I have been suggesting that we emphasize rather what Dewey and Wittgenstein have in common— their view that a natural quest for understanding has been run together, by modern philosophers, with an unnatural quest for certainty. In this view, the hopes and fears which psychology at various times inspired among philosophers are equally misguided.[17] To say with Wisdom and Bouwsma that "epistemology" is a collection of obsessive concerns with certainty to be dissolved by therapy, and to say with Quine that epistemological impulses should be satisfied by psychological results, may both be viewed as ways of saying: We can have psychology or nothing.

[17] See Ludwig Wittgenstein, *Philosophical Investigations* (London, 1953), p. 232, on "the confusion and barrenness of psychology": "The existence of the experimental method makes us think we have the means of solving the problems which trouble us; though problem and method pass each other by." See also Dewey's warnings about the movement which was eventually to become the "behavioristic psychology" which Quine admires: "The older dualism between sensation and idea is repeated in the current dualism of peripheral and central structures and functions; the older dualism of body and soul finds a distinct echo in the current dualism of stimulus and response . . ."; again, ". . . sensation as stimulus does not mean any particular psychical *existence*. It means simply a function, and will have its value shift according to the special work requiring to be done." ("The Reflex Arc Concept in Psychology," in *The Early Works of John Dewey*, vol. 5 [Carbondale, 1972], pp. 96, 107.)

If it were not that one of my concerns in this book is to ask why we have such a phenomenon as "philosophy" in our culture, the matter could be left at that. But for this historical question the difference between nothing and psychology is important. Dewey emphasized the religious and social motives behind the non-"scientific" aspects of philosophy, and joined his insistence on the continuity between philosophy and science with an invidious distinction between what philosophy had been and what it should become. Quine is reluctant to flirt with a genetic fallacy, and genially disposed to see himself and Locke as fellow-inquirers into "the relation between theory and evidence": Locke, he thinks, was misled by a bad theory of meaning, but we moderns may now be led aright (toward psychology) by a good one. But this geniality hides precisely what is important for historical understanding: Locke's concern about the skeptic's suggestion that our subjective modes of apprehension might hide reality from us, and Quine's refusal to be troubled by skepticism at all.

Quine's remoteness from skeptical concerns is shown by his assimilation of elements of experience to elements of knowledge, and of explanation to justification. Psychology, by finding the elements of experience, explains knowledge. Epistemology, by (putatively) finding elements of knowledge, justifies nonelementary knowledge. Nobody would want "human knowledge" (as opposed to some particular theory or report) justified unless he had been frightened by skepticism. Nobody would assimilate epistemology to psychology unless he were so little frightened by skepticism as to regard "grounding human knowledge" as a bit of a joke. So, though we may heartily agree with Quine that if there are discoveries to be made about human knowledge they are likely to come from psychology, we can also sympathize with the view which Quine attributes to Wittgenstein: The thing to do with epistemology is to "cure philosophers of the delusion that there were epistemological problems." Such therapy does not separate philosophy from science: it takes philosophy to be just common sense or science mobilized to provide "reminders for a particular purpose."[18]

3. PSYCHOLOGICAL STATES AS GENUINE EXPLANATIONS

To get a psychological theory which *would* say something about the relation between theory and evidence we need, at a minimum, one which will reproduce "internally" the ordinary "public" justification of assertions by circumstances and other assertions. We need, in other words, mental entities which can bear the same relations to public assertions and to one another as do premises and conclusions in speeches, as the testimonies of witnesses to the charges in law courts, and so on. But whenever a psychological theory is proposed which answers to this need, the cry of "infinite regress" is likely to be raised. Thus we find Malcolm saying:

> If we say that the way in which a person knows that something in front of him is a dog is by seeing that the creature "fits" his Idea of a dog, then we need to ask "How does he know that this is an example of fitting?" What guides his judgment here? Does he not need a second-order Idea which shows him what it is like for something to fit an Idea? That is, will he not need a model of *fitting?* . . . An infinite regress has been generated and nothing has been explained.[19]

The difficulty, made familiar by Ryle, is that if we are not content to take "He sees it" as a sufficient justification for

[18] Wittgenstein, *Philosophical Investigations*, p. 50.

[19] Malcolm, "Myth of Cognitive Processes," p. 391. Compare Ryle, *The Concept of Mind* (New York, 1949), chap. 7, and Wittgenstein, *Philosophical Investigations*, pp. 213-215. See also John Passmore, *Philosophical Reasoning* (London, 1961), chap. 2 ("The Infinite Regress Argument"), where he discusses Ryle's use of the argument. I have compared Wittgenstein's and Peirce's anti-Cartesian employment of this argument in "Pragmatism, Categories, and Language," *Philosophical Review* 49 (1961), 197-223.

the man's knowing that there is a dog before him, then we shall not be able to take anything else as a justification either. For insofar as a mentalistic account provides merely a causal explanation of recognition by sight, it does not seem to answer the question "How does he know?" It does not tell us anything about the man's *evidence* for his view, but only about his coming to hold it. On the other hand, insofar as it does offer a justification of the original public knowledge-claim, it provides an occasion to press for further justification.

Fodor criticizes Ryle's claim that nothing "para-mechanical" could improve our understanding of perceptual recognition, and remarks that "the appealing simplicity of Ryle's position is purchased by begging precisely the sorts of question theories of perception and learning have traditionally attempted to answer."[20] He proceeds to argue that "some simple story about learned associations" will not do to answer these questions:

> But if what the various ways of performing "Lillibulero" have in common is something abstract, it would appear to follow that the system of expectations that constitutes one's recipe for hearing the song must be abstract in the same sense. . . .
> . . . The relevant expectations must be complicated and abstract, since perceptual identities are surprisingly independent of physical uniformities among stimuli. Since it is precisely this perceptual "constancy" that psychologists and epistemologists have traditionally supposed unconscious inferences and other para-mechanical transactions will be needed to explain, it seems relevant to remark that Ryle's treatment has begged all the issues that constancy raises. (pp. 377-378)

We may agree with Fodor that if there *are* "issues that constancy raises" then Ryle has begged them. But Ryle

[20] Fodor, "Could There Be a Theory of Perception?" *Journal of Philosophy* 63 (1966), 375.

could easily reply that the notion of "complicated and abstract expectations" (e.g., a set of unconscious inferences involving reference to some rules, or some abstract paradigms) is what makes it appear that there are issues here. Perhaps only the picture of a little man in the mind, applying rules drawn up in nonverbal but still "abstract" terms, makes us ask "How is it done?" Had we not had this picture imposed on us, Ryle can say, we would respond with something like "It's only possible because of having a complicated nervous system—doubtless some physiologist will someday tell us just how it works." The notion of nonphysiological "models" would not occur, in other words, if we did not already have the whole Cartesian bag of tricks in hand.

This reply can be restated a bit more precisely. Suppose we agree with Fodor that recognition of similarity among potentially infinite differences is recognition of something "abstract"—Lillibulerohood, say. What does it mean to say that "one's recipe for hearing the song must be abstract in the same sense"? Presumably that it must be able to distinguish similarity among potentially infinite differences. But then there is no use for the notion of "*non*-abstract recipe," since *any* recipe must be able to do this. The possible qualitative variations among the ingredients for a batch of chocolate chip cookies are also potentially infinite. So if we are to talk about "complicated sets of expectations" (or "programs" or "systems of rules") at all, we shall always be talking about something "abstract"—precisely as abstract, in fact, as the characteristic whose recognition (or the task whose accomplishment) we wish to explain. But then we are in a dilemma: either the acquisition of these sets of expectations or rules requires the postulation of new sets of expectations or rules, or they are unacquired. If the former horn is grasped, Malcolm's infinite regress really will be generated by Fodor's principle that recognition of the abstract requires use of the abstract, for what holds of recognition should hold of acquisition. If we grasp the latter horn, then we seem to be back with Ryle: to say that people have an unacquired ability to recognize similarity among infinite differences is hardly to say anything explanatory about "the issues that constancy raises."

So, Ryle can conclude, these issues are either "conceptual" issues about the sufficient conditions for the ordinary application of terms like "recognize," or else issues about physiological mechanisms. The latter sort of issue involves no problems about regresses, since nobody thinks that "constancy" requires postulating "abstract" mechanisms in photoelectric cells or tuning forks. Yet is there any difference between middle C and "Lillibulerohood," save that we have dubbed the former a "concrete acoustic quality" and the latter an "abstract similarity?" We could specify a thousand accidental features (timbre, volume, presence of light, color of the object emitting the sound) which the tuning fork ignores, just as the Lillibulero-recognizer does. Since the abstract-concrete distinction is as relative to a given data-base as the complex-simple distinction, it looks as if, in saying that psychological explanation requires reference to abstract entities, we are simply claiming that explaining the sort of thing mammals can do requires reference to different—*categorically* different—sorts of things from explaining what amoebas, tuning forks, cesium atoms, and stars can do. But how do we know that? And what does "categorically" mean here? Once again, Ryle can say that if we did not already have the Cartesian picture (of an Inner Eye looking at the rules posted on the walls of the mental arena), we should not know what to make of the claim.

So much for the strength of the infinite-regress argument. Now consider the sort of rejoinder to it which would be made by someone like Dodwell, who argues that nonphysiological model-building is, a priori, neither good nor bad, but is to be justified by its fruits. Dodwell is impressed by the analogy between brains and computers: "The single most powerful influence on psychologists' ideas about cognitive processes at present is the nexus of concepts which

233

has been developed for computer programming."[21] Nevertheless, he admits:

> It might be argued that the computer analogy is trivial, because a program merely codifies a set of operations which are like cognitive operations, but no more *explains* thinking than does writing down a set of rules for solving arithmetic problems. . . . To say that a computer program can "explain" thinking, then, would have about the same force as to say that a set of logical formulas "explain" the laws of correct deductive argument. (pp. 371-372)

To this argument he replies that the computer analogy only has force once one distinguishes levels:

> . . . explanations of what goes on in problem solving by a computer can be given at different levels. . . . The *implementation* of a program has to be explained in terms of computer hardware, just as, presumably, the implementation of thinking has in some sense to be explained by processes which actually occur in the central nervous system. The subroutines by which particular computations are made can be explained by reference to the "machine language" and the step-by-step algorithms by which solutions are found. . . . The principle of the subroutine operation is not itself to be understood and explained just by examining the hardware, in just the same way that the point of multiplication tables could not be grasped by examining the brain. Similarly, an understanding of how the subroutines themselves work does not explain the principle of solving problems in terms of a sequence of steps. . . . For that, one must look at the executive process, which in the machine embodies the overall organization and goal of the program, and in the human being a less clearly understood "goal directedness." (p. 372)

[21] Dodwell, "Is a Theory of Conceptual Development Necessary?" p. 370.

234

The importance of levels is illustrated, for example, by the fact that experimentation may give us reason to say that we recognize visual patterns by a template-matching process rather than a feature-extraction process (p. 379). To say this is neither a "conceptual" remark (about "the executive process") nor a "physiological" one (about "hardware"), but it may be genuinely explanatory nonetheless. The notion of "subroutine" seems to give us just what psychology needs—an explanation of what the middle ground between common sense and physiology might be good for.

But how does this notion help us avoid an infinite-regress argument? Presumably Malcolm and Ryle would urge that either "templates" or abstract ideas of the features extracted (depending upon which model one picks) themselves produce the same problems as the "constancy" they are supposed to explain. But Dodwell can reply that they would only do this if they were supposed to be answers to such general questions as "How is abstraction (recognition, constancy) possible?" To such questions, he can say, there is *no* answer, except the pointless remark that nature has evolved suitable hardware to get the job done. For any of Dodwell's models will indeed be anthropomorphic, in the sense of envisaging a little inferrer in the brain checking his (or its) templates or ticking off features. This inferrer's powers of abstraction or recognition will be as problematic as those of his host, and it does not make them less so to say that he (or it) is a little machine rather than a little man.[22]

---

[22] This would be doubted by some psychologists. Gregory, citing with approval Helmholtz's notion of "unconscious inferences" involved in perception, says that

> we must be clear that there is no "little man inside" doing the arguing, for this leads to intolerable philosophical difficulties. Helmholtz certainly did not think this, but his phrase "unconscious inferences" and his description of perceptions as "unconscious conclusions" did perhaps suggest, at the time, to people unfamiliar with computers, some such unacceptable idea. But our familiarity with computers should remove temptation towards confusion of this kind. For we no

Anthropomorphic models here are no more misleading than the programmer's anthropomorphic remark that "the machine won't understand the problem if you use Polish notation, because it only knows about. . . ." To complain that "templates"—like Locke's "ideas"—are a reduplication of the explanandum is like claiming that the particles which make up the Bohr atom are a reduplication of the billiard balls whose behavior they help explain. It turns out to be fruitful to postulate little billiard balls inside big ones, so why not postulate little people inside big ones (or little rats inside big rats)? Every such "model" is, in Sellars's phrase, accompanied by a "commentary" which lists the features of the modeled entity "abstracted from" in the model.[23] It seems reasonable to suggest that the implicit commentary on all anthropomorphic models in psychology goes something like this:

> As long as we stay on the level of subroutines we shall feel free to talk anthropomorphically about inferences and other operations "unconsciously" performed by the person, or performed (neither "consciously" nor "unconsciously") by brain centers or other organs spoken of as if they themselves were persons. The use of such phrases

---

longer think of inference as a uniquely human activity involving consciousness. (*The Intelligent Eye* [New York, 1970], p. 30.)

I think it misleading to say that the little man leads to "intolerable philosophical difficulties," because I do not see that little machines are less "conscious" than little men. To adopt what Dennett calls the "intentional stance" toward batches of transistors or neurons is to speak of them as we speak of conscious beings, and to add "but of course they are not *really* conscious" seems merely to say that we have no moral responsibilities to them. We can neither inquire which such batches are, in Quine's phrase, "tinged with awareness" nor *discover* that inferences can be performed by beings not so tinged. Familiarity with computers does not bring about such a discovery; it only makes attribution of the intentional stance more common and casual.

[23] See Wilfrid Sellars, *Science, Perception and Reality* (London and New York, 1963), p. 182 on "commentaries" and pp. 192ff. on red sense-impressions.

does not commit us to attributing intellect and character to brain centers any more than speaking of a "red sense-impression" as the common factor in various illusions commits us to the existence of something both "inner" and red. But once we get off the "subroutine" level and onto the hardware level, anthropomorphism is no longer in place.

To see the force of this commentary, suppose that some special sort of neural current came down the optic nerve when and only when psychological theory predicted the occurrence of a red sense-impression (and so for all other perceptual situations). If we knew this fact, we should simply skip the "subroutine" explanation and go straight to hardware. The notion of "sense-impression" would no longer have a role (unless there were other theoretical entities postulated by psychological theory which required this notion for their explication). If things did turn out to be as simple as this, then the "computer" analogy would no longer seem particularly relevant—any more than it does for one-celled animals, where the step from behavior to physiology is too short to make the notion of "levels" seem in point.

This is to say that if physiology were simpler and more obvious than it is, nobody would have felt the need for psychology. This conclusion may seem odd, particularly in the light of Dodwell's remark (quoted above) that "the principle of the subroutine operation is not itself to be understood and explained just by examining the hardware, in just the same way that the point of multiplication tables could not be grasped by examining the brain."[24] But this

---

[24] Fodor also has suggested that the distinction between "functional" (or "program") analysis and "mechanical" (or "hardware") analysis in psychology is irreducible and not just a matter of convenience. See his "Explanations in Psychology," in *Philosophy in America*, ed. M. Black (Ithaca, 1965), p. 177. I have argued against this suggestion in "Functionalism, Machines, and Incorrigibility," *Journal of Philosophy* 69 (1972), 203-220.

remark is seriously misleading. It embodies a confusion between the evident:

> If we did not know what multiplication was, looking into the brain would never tell us

and the dubious:

> If we did know what multiplication was, we could not tell that someone was doing a certain bit of multiplication by looking at his brain.

The latter is dubious because we just do not know whether or not there are quite simple neurophysiological parameters associated with certain mental operations. It is immensely unlikely that there are, but there is no a priori reason why some suitable brain-probe-cum-microscope might not show something which the trained observer would report as "Ah, you're multiplying forty-seven by twenty-five" (and be right every time). More generally, the question of what is best explained in hardware terms and what in program terms depends entirely on how ad hoc the hardware happens to be, and on how perspicuously it is laid out. Ad hocness and perspicuousness are, obviously, relative to choice of vocabulary and level of abstraction—but then so is the hardware-software distinction itself.[25] Given the right sort of hardware and the right parameters, it certainly *is* possible to "understand and explain the principle of the subroutine just by examining the hardware." Indeed, we can imagine machines in which it would be easier to find out what the machine was up to by opening it up and looking than by reading the program.

Since the brain is almost certainly *not* such a machine, the point here is one of principle, but the principle has

[25] On this sort of relativity, see William Kalke, "What Is Wrong with Fodor and Putnam's Functionalism," *Nous* 3 (1969), 83-94. For criticism of Kalke's paper and of my own parallel paper (cited in note 24), see B. J. Nelson, "Functionalism and the Identity Theory," *Journal of Philosophy* 73 (1976), 379ff.

philosophical importance. For it shows that the distinction between psychology and physiology is not a distinction between two distinct subject matters in any stronger a sense than is, say, the distinction between chemistry and physics. It might have turned out that chemical phenomena such as the formation of compounds never had anything to do with the submicroscopic makeup of the elements in question. But in fact they do, and so now whether we use physicists' or chemists' terms to explain a reaction is a matter of convenience or pedagogy. If it turns out that physiology has as much to do with multiplying as electrons have to do with explosions, then the psychology-physiology distinction will be equally pragmatic. So the paradoxical conclusion offered earlier—that had physiology been more obvious psychology would never have arisen—can be reaffirmed. Indeed, we can strengthen it and say that if the body had been easier to understand, nobody would have thought that we had a mind.[26]

It is time now to sum up this way of dealing with the infinite-regress argument. The central point is just that explanatory entities postulated by psychologists reduplicate problems in the explananda only when these problems are bad problems anyway—for example, "How is recognition possible?" Philosophers like Malcolm and Ryle are accustomed to bad philosophical answers to bad philosophical questions: "How is motion possible?—as the actualization of the potential qua potential"; "Why does nature follow laws?—because of God's benevolence and omnipotence." Consequently they tend to see such questions lurking behind even quite specific and limited research programs. They are not always wrong, since psychologists still some-

[26] As I trust chapter two has made clear, I do not mean by this that we should not have thought of ourselves as having beliefs and desires, and as seeing, inferring, and so on. But we would not have saddled ourselves with the notions of a "separable active intellect," a Cartesian "immaterial substance," or Lockean ideas. Our concept of mind would have been much closer to Ryle's or Aristotle's than to the Cartesian concept we presently have.

times offer their latest "model" as resolving ancient philosophical problems.[27] But suppose such models as those Dodwell has in mind—proposals about subroutines which are neither introspectable (like the "executive process") nor physiologically decipherable (like the "hardware")—are viewed neither as contributions to resolving Cartesian pseudo-problems nor as discoveries about some nonphysical sort of entity. Then the infinite-regress argument has no force. For whether or not hardware-correlates for these subroutines ever turn up, the success in prediction and control of behavior made possible by the experimental discovery of such subroutines would be enough to show the reality of the objects of psychological inquiry.[28] Dodwell's

[27] See, for example, Seymour Papert's "Introduction" to Warren S. McCulloch, *Embodiments of Mind* (Cambridge, Mass., 1965). Papert, in explaining the importance of McCulloch's work, tells us that "we need no longer be trapped by the dilemma" of

a split . . . between psychology, which was based on mechanism but which was unable to reach the complex properties of thought, and philosophy, which took the properties of thought seriously but could be satisfied with no conceivable mechanism. (p. xiv)

The insight which is to resolve this dilemma has as its "principal conceptual step"

the recognition that a host of physically different situations involving the teleonomic regulation of behavior in mechanical, electrical, and even social systems should be understood as manifestations of one basic phenomenon: the return of information to form a closed central loop. (p. xvi)

Papert here supposes that the "properties of thought" which bothered philosophers were those relevant to purposiveness. But neither the distinction between justification and causal explanation nor that between consciousness and its lack—which are the two great ways of dividing epistemology from psychology—is clarified by clarifying purposiveness. Nor would Bergsonians, who *are* worried by purposiveness, feel soothed by contemplating automatic record-changers.

[28] It is tempting to think of "intervening variables" postulated by psychologists (with "subroutines" written in terms of them) as *mere* place-holders for undiscovered neurological processes. We usually do, indeed, assume that when neurophysiology reaches a certain point it will serve as a touchstone for choice among competing psychological

suggestion is that nothing succeeds like such success when it is a matter of establishing the nonmythical and "scientific" character of one's subject, and this may pretty well be the last word on the matter.

Applying this point to the Rylean dilemma about acquired and unacquired abilities I sketched, we can cheerfully admit that any such model-building must grant that nature has wired in some unacquired abilities to perform higher-order mental operations. At least some of those little men performing subroutines in various brain-centers will have to have been there since birth. But why not? If one gives up the notion that empirical psychology is going to do what the British Empiricists failed to do—show how a *tabula rasa* gets changed into a complicated information-processing device by impacts upon peripheral sense-organs —then one will not be surprised that half of the adult's subroutines were wired into the infant's brain on instructions from the chromosomes. Further, it will not strike one as important to our understanding of the nature of man or his mind to discover just *which* were wired in then and which came along later.[29] Finally, it will not seem odd that

---

"models of the mind." But it is important to see that even if we somehow discovered that neurophysiology will never reach the stage we had hoped for, this disappointment would not make the psychologists' work any more dubious, either "methodologically" or "metaphysically."

[29] The notion that it is important to discover what is "innate" comes out in such questions as "Does all knowledge (information is the contemporary term) come through the sense organs or is some knowledge contributed by the mind itself?" (J. J. and E. J. Gibson, "Perceptual Learning: Differentiation or Enrichment?" *Psychological Review* 62 [1955], 32.) Gibson and Gibson take this Kantian question with entire seriousness, and urge that, *pace* Hume and Helmholtz, perceptual learning is not unconscious inference from memory-traces, but simply "increased sensitivity to the variables of the stimulus array" (p. 40). Yet it is very difficult to imagine how experiment could help decide between this view and, say, Gregory's neo-Helmholtzian interpretation of standard experiments in perceptual learning. Cf. R. L. Gregory, *Eye and Brain* (New York and Toronto, 1966), especially such passages

something "abstract" (like a capacity for recognizing similarity in difference) is as unacquired as such "concrete" capacities as making a differential response to C-sharp. For we can simply remind ourselves that the latter is itself as "abstract" as an ability could well be, and no more abstract than any ability must be. The whole notion of concrete-versus-abstract abilities, which is accepted as uncritically by Fodor as by Kant, is of a piece with the notion of the "irreducibly physical" versus the "irreducibly psychical." Nobody can say how to draw these lines except in relation to the temporary purposes of inquiry. But the Cartesian attempt to draw them once and for all and the "empiricist" and "behaviorist" attempts to "reduce" the one to the other have created the view that certain deep mysteries which had confounded the philosophers may yet be penetrated by psychological research. The incautious use of the infinite-regress argument by Malcolm and Ryle should be seen, I believe, as an understandable reaction against this notion that psychology can succeed in solving problems which philosophers have posed.

I can now tie together the result of examining the "infinite regress" argument with that of the last section by saying that the notion of psychological states as inner representations is unobjectionable but fairly uninteresting. To say that psychological states are states postulated to explain behavior, ones which we do not yet know how to identify with physiological states, is not to discover the true nature of the mind; it is only to reemphasize that there is no "nature" to be known. The analogy between minds and computers drawn by Dodwell and Fodor is better than Plato's analogy between minds and aviaries simply because the

---

as at p. 11: "The senses do not give us a picture of the world directly; rather they provide evidence for checking hypotheses about what lies before us." See Fodor's discussion of Gibson, which I cite and briefly discuss in section 4.

former avoids the *epistemologically* (not metaphysically) misleading picture of introspection as observation of our interior. Illumination from such analogies is a matter of responding to what philosophers are worried about, and they are worried about unified science on the one hand and "subjectivity" on the other. If we agree that mentalistic explanations would not have arisen if our hardware had been more perspicuous, that will be enough to make the mind-body distinction pragmatic rather than ontological. That, in turn, is enough to reconcile us to the fact that we may *never* get a neurophysiological account of what is going on inside us which is as perspicuously related to psychological states as the engineer's account of how the hardware "realizes" the computer's program. Once, for Quinean reasons, we stop thinking that the possibility or impossibility of such an account can be determined by "philosophical analysis," we can see that the unity of science is only endangered by ghosts, not by the unknown or the irreducible. Just as the suggestion that the atoms of Democritus and Newton's shining lights are merely geometrodynamical bumps does not bother anybody's "physicalistic" instincts, neither does Putnam's point that we shall never have a micro-particulate explanation of why square pegs will not fit in round holes. The permanent need for mentalistic talk only seems dangerous to philosophers who think of "the mental" as involving reference to ghosts, and Sellars's treatment of the givenness of the mental takes care of them. Sellars shows that when we introspect, no nonphysical item is present to a nonphysical observer. He thus wards off the threatened loss of "scientific objectivity." Once again, the seeds of metaphysical problems are found in epistemological difficulties, and specifically in the notion that to understand how we have a right to be so sure that we are nostalgic we must erect an ontological divide between nostalgia and neurons.

243

4. PSYCHOLOGICAL STATES AS REPRESENTATIONS

We must, however, beware of attempts to erect a new sort of mental-physical barrier on the line which divides the abstract from the concrete, representations from non-representations, rather than along lines of greater and less certainty. To see what such an attempt looks like, consider Fodor's rehabilitation of traditional empiricist accounts of perception:

> It is, I take it, an empirical question whether psychological processes are computational processes. But if they are, then what must go on in perception is that a description of the environment that is *not* couched in a vocabulary whose terms designate values of physical variables is somehow computed on the basis of a description that is couched in such a vocabulary.[30]

Fodor rightly says that if we are to have anything like a "psychological problem of perception" we must have some such model in mind. He criticizes Gibson's suggestion that we could avoid "the problem of how the (presumed) stimulus invariants are detected" by "distinguishing between the stimulus for the *sensory transducers* (viz., physical energies) and the stimulus for the *perceptual organs* (viz., abstract invariants)" by saying:

> ... this way trivialization lies. If one is allowed to use the notion of a stimulus so as to distinguish the input to the retina (light energy) from the input to the optic system (patterns of light energy which exhibit invariances relevant, e.g., to the explanation of perceptual constancies), why not also talk about the stimulus for the *whole organism* (viz., perceptibles)? Thus, the answer to "How do we perceive bottles?" would go: "It is necessary and sufficient for the perception of a bottle that one detect the presence of the stimulus invariant *bottle*."

[30] Jerry Fodor, *The Language of Thought* (New York, 1975), p. 47.

244

... What this shows, I think, is not that the psychological problem of perception is a muddle, but that *stating*
the problem requires choosing (and motivating) a proprietary vocabulary for the representation of inputs. I
have argued that the vocabulary of values of physical
parameters *is* appropriate on the plausible assumption
that sensory transducers detect values of physical parameters and that all perceptual knowledge is mediated by
the activity of sensory transducers. (p. 49n.)

Here Fodor confronts the question I raised in discussing
Quine's attempt to view psychology as naturalized epistemology: If the choice of what is datal is a matter of something deeper than consensus among observers, expressible
in ordinary language, then what criterion can the psychologist use in isolating the "input to our cognitive mechanism"?
Quine wobbles on the point, but Fodor firmly and sensibly
tells us that, unless we take something which our subject
need not know about as his input, we shall trivialize the
notion of "processing in the cognitive mechanism." To my
earlier rhetorical question "Could psychology discover that
the input to the cognitive mechanism is not at the retina,
but rather halfway down the optic nerve?" Fodor would
presumably answer: Yes, for doing it one way rather than
another depends upon which way of drawing lines around
black boxes best splits the organism into the sort of transducers and processors whose descriptions make up a general
and fruitful theory of cognitive processing.

Notice that this answer takes away any connection between the question "How do we recognize bottles?" and the
question "What is indubitably given to the mind, such as
to serve as an infallible touchstone for inference?" For the
question "What does the subject have a right to believe
without conscious inference?" or, more precisely, "What
sort of thing can he justify merely by such remarks as 'I
saw it clear as I see you now' or 'I know English'?" has
nothing whatever to do with the question "What bit of the

245

organism shall we pick as interface with the world?" or more precisely, "What choice shall we make of 'a proprietary vocabulary for the representation of inputs'?" Fodor is admirably explicit on this point:

> But whatever relevance the distinction between states of the organism and states of its nervous system may have for *some* purposes, there is no particular reason to suppose that it is relevant to the purposes of cognitive psychology. (p. 52)

> . . . the states of the organism postulated in theories of cognition would not count as states of the organism for purposes of, say, a theory of legal or moral responsibility. But so what? What matters is that they should count as states of the organism for *some* useful purpose. In particular, what matters is that they should count as states of the organism for purposes of constructing psychological theories that are true. (p. 53)

We need only add that what goes for moral or legal responsibility goes also for epistemic responsibility—the organism's being justified in believing this or that. No roads lead from the discovery of the organism's various interfaces with the world to criticisms of the organism's views about the world, or, more generally, from psychology to epistemology. What the empiricists got right about perception was that the sense-organs must be thought of as having a vocabulary that is impoverished compared to the "vocabulary in which the hypotheses are couched"—couched by either the processing unit(s) or the subject itself. They were doubtless also right in commending Galileo for preferring his eyes to his Aristotle, but this epistemological judgment has no particular connection with their theory of perception.

We can now see that Fodor's picture of the mind as a system of inner representations has nothing to do with the image of the Mirror of Nature I have been criticizing. The crucial point is that there is no way to raise the skeptical question "How well do the subject's internal representations represent reality?" about Fodor's "language of thought." In particular there is no way to ask where, or how well, the products of spontaneity's theories represent the source of receptivity's evidence, and thus no way to be skeptical about the relation between appearance and reality. Nor is there anything general to say about the gap between the evidence contributed by receptivity and the theories contrived by spontaneity. A different sort of gap is crossed by the requirement that the vocabulary of a sensory mechanism be composed of "natural kind terms in some (ideally completed) physical science" (p. 45). This vocabulary will be "more impoverished" than that of the "processors" in the sense that there will be a many-one relation between sets of values of physical parameters and the terms which the processors use in their hypotheses. The relation will thus be like that between science and common sense. The Quinean "underdetermination of theory by evidence" is thus built into the model, in that many common-sensical ways of speaking will be compatible with the one true (ideally completed) description of the world by physical science, and many possible "processor" languages can mediate between these. To find out something epistemological by learning features of "the language of thought" would only be possible if, in between the scientific vocabulary used by sensory mechanisms and the various vocabularies consciously used by the subject, there were a vocabulary used by the processors, knowledge of which would help the subject discover the truth about things in general. Only this sort of "psychological reality" could take the place of "what is given to the mind without interpretation" as an epistemological touchstone of justification. But it is hard to see why the psychological reality of certain colors, grammars, or moral principles will correspond to their use in explaining or judging nonpsychological realities. We should expect such correspondence only if we view the processing units which psychological theory isolates as in some way "our better part," the successor of reason as the natural ruler over

247

the rest of the soul, or as our true self. Fodor and cognitive psychology have no interest in any such honorific status for the internal code; that code, like FORTRAN, or the binary representation of numbers, is *just* a code, not an aid in telling the true from the false.

To see this point against the background of the previous chapters, recall the claim that the epistemological tradition confused causal explanations of the acquisition of belief with justifications of belief. When causal explanations are given in the internal code, the assumption that this code can be used to detect the acquisition of *true* belief would amount to the assumption that "truth-generating mental processes" were natural kinds within psychological theory. But Fodor would presumably agree that there is no reason whatever to think that such evaluative terms mark out such natural kinds. As he says about creativity:

> It may be that the processes we think of as creative don't form a natural kind for purposes of psychological explanation, but that, nevertheless, every *instance* of such a process is an instance of rule-guided, computational activity of one sort or another. . . . The categories *creative/boring* may simply cross-classify the taxonomy that psychology employs.
>
> My main point, however, is that the mere fact that creative mental processes are *mental* processes does not ensure that they have explanations in the language of psychology under *any* of their descriptions. It may be that good ideas . . . are species of mental states which don't have mental causes. (pp. 201-202)

The rise of the notion of knowledge as a matter of rightly ordered inner representations—an unclouded and undistorting Mirror of Nature—was due to the notion that the difference between the man whose beliefs were true and the man whose beliefs were false was a matter of "how their minds worked." If this phrase is taken in the sense of "what they would say in a conversation," it is true but shallow and unphilosophical. To make it deep and philosophical, one must believe, with Descartes and Locke, that a taxonomy of mental entities and processes will lead to discoveries which will provide one with a method of discovering truth, and not just truth about the mind.[31] But Fodor's envisaged psychological taxonomy is not an epistemological taxonomy. It leaves both the method and the substance of the various other disciplines which make up culture to sink or swim on their own. Only the assumption that one day the various taxonomies put together by, for example, Chomsky, Piaget, Lévi-Strauss, Marx, and Freud will all flow together and spell out one great Universal Language of Nature—an assumption sometimes attributed to structuralism —would suggest that cognitive psychology had epistemological import. But that suggestion would still be as misguided as the suggestion that, since we may predict everything by knowing enough about matter in motion, a completed neurophysiology will help us demonstrate Galileo's superiority to his contemporaries. The gap between explaining ourselves and justifying ourselves is just as great whether a programming language or a hardware language is used in the explanations.

It might be thought, however, that if we construe epistemology not as certifying success in discovering *truth* but rather as developing canons of *rationality*, then a knowledge of the internal code *will* give us something to go on. Fodor, perhaps unintentionally, suggests such a view when

31 Cf. Hiram Caton, *The Origins of Subjectivity: An Essay on Descartes* (New Haven, 1973), p. 53: "The great difference between the Aristotelian and Cartesian methodology is that, for Descartes, mind is a principle of science." Contrast the lack of connection between the *De Anima* and the *Posterior Analytics* with Locke's assumption that an inquiry into "the grounds and degrees of belief, opinion and assent" can be carried out by a "historical, plain method" which begins with "the original of those ideas, notions, or whatever else you please to call them, which a man observes, and is conscious to himself he has in his mind, and the ways whereby the understanding comes to be furnished with them" (*Essay* I, 1, ii-iii).

249

he speaks of the discovery of this code as showing "how rationality is structured." But the only content he gives to this notion of "rationality" is provided by the following passage:

> If the main line of this book is right, then the language of thought provides the medium for internally representing the psychologically salient aspects of the organism's environment; to the extent that it is specifiable in this language—and only to this extent—does such information fall under the computational routines that constitute the organism's cognitive repertoire. . . . But now I want to add that some organisms, at least, appear to have considerable freedom in determining how this representational system shall be employed and that that freedom is typically rationally exploited. . . . If subjects really do *calculate* how internal representations are to be deployed, then these calculations, too, must be defined over representations; i.e., over representations of representations. Some properties of the language of thought must, in short, be represented in the language of thought since the ability to represent representations is, presumably, a precondition of the ability to manipulate representations rationally.[32]

Here "rationality" means the adjustment of means to ends, and the ability of organisms to do this with their representations differs from their ability to do it with their hormones only in that a metalinguistic vocabulary is required to describe the former ability. But to grasp the metalinguistic vocabulary which the organism uses for this purpose is not to grasp anything as general as the phrase "the structure of rationality" might suggest, but rather something as particular as the tricks the programmer employs to insure that the computer will switch from one subroutine to another as needed to optimize efficiency. We do not understand more

[32] Fodor, *The Language of Thought*, p. 172.

about what it is to be a rational inquirer or agent from understanding such tricks than we do from understanding what makes the pituitary gland release this hormone rather than that. Nor would it make sense to criticize the subject's *conscious* representation of his environment—that is, the vocabulary in which he states his views—on the ground that it did not represent these aspects as well as do "the computational routines that constitute the organism's cognitive repertoire." "Rational" is no better than "true" (or "honest" or "chaste" or "good") as a candidate for an evaluative notion which we might understand better by knowing how our mind works. For our judgment as to how rationally evolution has designed us, or how rational evolution has managed to make us, must be made by reference to our views on the ends we are to serve. Knowledge of how our mind works is not more relevant than knowledge of how our glands or our molecules work to the development or correction of such views.

If we are to find epistemological relevance in the doctrine of internal representations, then, it will have to be in the rationalist overtones of the "innatist" views common to Chomsky and Fodor rather than their explicit antireductionist intent. An inference from the Chomsky-Fodor notion of a wired-in language (and metalanguage) of thought to a rationalist epistemology is offered by Vendler. Consider the following provocatively anti-Wittgensteinian passage:

> . . . the most reasonable explanation is that a child must learn his native tongue in a way similar to the way one learns a second language. He must have, in other words, a native equipment that codes the fundamental illocutionary, syntactic, and semantic features of any possible human language. . . . Such a system of native "ideas" provides the framework which is then filled up progressively through the influence of a more specific code representing the features of the mother tongue. . . . As for the content of this native stock of concepts, we can at the present time

251

do no more than make educated guesses. Yet, I think, the task of spelling it out in detail is not an impossible one: Aristotle, Descartes, Kant, and recently Chomsky have succeeded in marking out domains that must belong to this framework. . . . These are, then, the "clear and distinct" ideas which lend intelligibility to the rest. They are "a priori" in origin and self-contained in their development: experience cannot change their content. No experience is relevant to one's idea of what it is to assert or to request something; what it is to believe or to decide; what is truth or necessity; what is a person, an object, a process, or a state; what are change, purpose, causation, time, extension, and number. If these ideas need clarification, the way to obtain it is to reflect on what we all implicitly know and show forth in the correct use of language. . . .[33]

This inference from a wired-in vocabulary to a set of beliefs which can only be "clarified" and not changed runs up against Quine's criticism of the distinctions between fact and language, science and philosophy, clarifying meanings and changing beliefs. But a more fundamental objection is that Vendler requires not just the premise that there is a fixed language of thought but the premise that our knowledge of the nature of that language is itself immune to correction on the basis of experience. This is the same premise which Kant used when explaining that we could understand our possession of synthetic a priori truths if and only if our mind contributed those truths.[34] But Fodor's claim that the discovery of the language of thought will be a long-drawn-out empirical process has as a corollary that we may always be quite wrong about what this language is, and thus wrong about what is a priori. Kant's claim that if we know what goes on inside we can legitimize our certainties before the tribunal of pure reason harks back to Descartes's

[33] Zeno Vendler, *Res Cogitans* (Ithaca, N.Y., 1972), pp. 140-141.
[34] K.d.r.V., Bxvii.

claim that "nothing is easier for the mind to know than it-self." But though epistemology is an armchair discipline, psychology is not; this is one reason why psychology cannot serve epistemological ends.[35]

I can sum up this discussion of inner representations by recurring once more to the confusion between explanation and justification. The notion of "representation," as it is employed by psychologists, is ambiguous as between, roughly, pictures and propositions—between, for example, retinal images (or their counterparts somewhere deep in the visual cortex) and beliefs such as "That's red and rectangular." Only the latter serve as premises, but only the former are "unmediated," and the tradition of British empiricism ran them together, with familiar results. Fodor's representations-in-the-processors are propositions rather than pictures, so they are not subject to Green's and Sellars's criticisms of the empiricist notion of "givenness." On the other hand, they are not necessarily propositions toward which the subject has attitudes. Indeed, the subject's attitudes toward those propositions of which he is cognizant float free of the views of the processors. As Dennett remarks in criticism of Fodor,

[35] An interesting non-Chomskyan attempt to link up epistemology with psychology is offered by Gilbert Harman in *Thought* (Princeton, 1973). He finds the connection between the two in the topic of "Gettier examples"—examples in which true justified belief is not knowledge because, roughly, a person is assumed to have used a false premise in the inference which led him to the belief in question. Harman needs a theory of "real reasons" for believing, and this leads him to what he describes as "psychologism" (pp. 15ff.). However, it is not clear whether Harman can find a link between empirical psychological inquiry and the armchair postulation of specific unconscious inferences (involving "real reasons") as demanded by our intuitions about Gettier examples. See Michael Williams, "Inference, Justification and the Analysis of Knowledge," *Journal of Philosophy* 75 (1978), 249-263, and Harman's "Using Intuitions about Reasoning to Study Reasoning: A Reply to Williams," ibid., 433-438. If Harman is able to establish such a link he will have isolated something right in Locke's attempt to treat knowl-edge in terms of the mechanics of inner space. But a link between *justification* and psychological processes would still be missing.

two subjects can hold the same belief even if their respective processors don't even speak the same language.[36] So there need be no *inference* from the propositions held by the processors to those held by the subject, even though attributing various propositional attitudes to processors may be the best possible way of *explaining* how the subject came to hold the belief that he did. Unlike the empiricist's "ideas," the causal process which runs from the retinal images through various propositional attitudes held by various processors to the output of the subject's speech center need not correspond to any train of inference which justifies the subject's views. Explanation may be private, in the sense that, for all we know or care, physiological quirks might make yellow men or red-haired men process information in quite different languages and by quite different methods than do white men, web-footed men, or whatever. But justification is public, in the sense that dispute between these various people about what to believe will probably make no reference to how their quirky minds work, nor should it. So the claim that we possess a system of internal representations embodies, at worst, not only the confusion between pictures and propositions but a more general confusion between causation and inference.

In fact, however, this confusion is present only in philosophical interpretations of cognitive psychology, not in actual psychological explanation. When Wittgensteinians criticize psychology it is not really psychology but the confusion of epistemology with psychology which is their target. Psychologists, out of a misguided urge to be "philosophical," sometimes make this confusion. Contemporary psychologists, in revolt against behaviorism, sometimes like to think

[36] Daniel Dennett, "Critical Notice" of *The Language of Thought*, *Mind* 86 (1977), 278: "If one agrees with Fodor that it is the job of cognitive psychology to map the psychologically real processes in people, then since the ascription of belief and desire is only indirectly tied to such processes, one might well say that beliefs and desires are not the proper objects of study of cognitive psychology."

of themselves as doing "scientifically" what Locke and Kant did in their armchairs. But there is all the difference in the world between saying:

> We must isolate those nonpropositional items of awareness which are the foundation for belief in propositions

and saying:

> We can treat items such as patterns of neural excitation as if they were beliefs in order to use the metaphor of "inference from data" in constructing models of mental processes.[37]

Psychologists need say only the latter. If they confine themselves to this, they can follow Putnam in treating the distinction between "brain process" and "mental process" as of no greater philosophical interest than that between "hardware description" and "description of the program."[38] The temptation to say the former—the epistemologically motivated temptation to "discover the link between the mind and the body"—can be treated on a par with the temptation to raise the question "How can the computer tell that the pattern of electrical charges coming down the wire is the total of the day's cash receipts?" The whole seventeenth-century notion that we learn more about what we should believe by understanding better how we work can be seen to be as misguided as the notion that we shall learn whether to grant civil rights to robots by understanding better how they work. The man-machine analogy will be seen as helping us not only as a source for useful models of organisms,

---

[37] On this difference, see the strictures of J. O. Urmson, "Recognition," *Proceedings of the Aristotelian Society* 56 (1955-56), 259-280.

[38] See Putnam's 1960 article "Minds and Machines," reprinted in *Mind, Language and Reality* (Cambridge, 1975), pp. 362-385 (especially the concluding paragraphs). Putnam was the first philosopher to point out clearly that the moral of the analogies between computers and people was not "Computers help us understand the relation between mind and body" but rather "There cannot be any problem about the relation between mind and body."

but as helping us bear in mind the difference between men as objects of explanation and men as moral agents, concerned to justify their beliefs and their actions. It may also help us, as I shall be claiming in chapters seven and eight, to give up the notion that these two ways of viewing ourselves need to be "synthesized."

CHAPTER VI

Epistemology and Philosophy of Language

1. Pure and Impure Philosophy of Language

There are two sources for the discipline presently called "philosophy of language." One is the cluster of problems pointed out by Frege and discussed, for example, by Wittgenstein in the *Tractatus* and by Carnap in *Meaning and Necessity*. These are problems about how to systematize our notions of meaning and reference in such a way as to take advantage of quantificational logic, preserve our intuitions about modality, and generally produce a clear and intuitively satisfying picture of the way in which notions like "truth," "meaning," "necessity," and "name" fit together. I shall call this set of problems the subject matter of "pure" philosophy of language—a discipline which has no epistemological *parti pris*, nor, indeed, any relevance to most of the traditional concerns of modern philosophy. An ancestry can be traced for some of Frege's problems in Parmenides, Plato's *Sophist*, and some other ancient and medieval writings, but they are issues which rarely intersect with other textbook "problems of philosophy."[1]

The second source for contemporary philosophy of language is explicitly epistemological. The source of this "impure" philosophy of language is the attempt to retain Kant's picture of philosophy as providing a permanent ahistorical framework for inquiry in the form of a theory of knowledge. The "linguistic turn," as I have said in chapter four, started as the attempt to produce a nonpsychologistic empiricism by rephrasing philosophical questions as questions of "logic."

---

[1] Consider the difficulty of tying in the *Sophist* with the *Republic*, or *Meaning and Necessity* with the *Logical Structure of the World*.

Empiricist and phenomenalist doctrines could now, it was thought, be put as the results of "the logical analysis of language" rather than as empirical psychological generalizations. More generally, philosophical points about the nature and extent of human knowledge (e.g., those which Kant made about knowledge-claims concerning God, freedom, and immortality) could be stated as remarks about language.

Treating philosophy as the analysis of language seemed to unite the merits of Hume with those of Kant. Hume's empiricism seemed substantively true, but methodologically shaky because it reposed on nothing more than an empirical theory of the acquisition of knowledge. Kant's criticisms of "bad" philosophy (e.g., natural theology) seemed both more systematic and more forceful than Hume's, but seemed to presuppose the possibility of a nonempirical methodology. Language, unlike transcendental synthesis, seemed a suitably "natural" field of inquiry—but, unlike introspective psychology, linguistic analysis seemed to offer the promise of a priori truth. To say that a material substance was constituted by the synthesis of a manifold of intuition under an a priori concept seemed "metaphysical" whereas to say that any meaningful remark about such a substance could be put in terms of phenomenalistic hypothetical statements seemed both necessarily true and methodologically unmysterious.[2] Kant had taught that the only way in which a priori knowledge could be possible was if it were knowledge of our contribution—the contribution of our faculty of spontaneity—to the constitution of the object of knowledge. Rephrased by Bertrand Russell and C. I. Lewis, this became the view that every true statement contained our contribution (in the form of the meanings of the component terms)

[2] Cf. Hilary Putnam's discussion of idealism and phenomenalism in *Mind, Language and Reality* (Cambridge, 1975), pp. 14-19. Putnam there presents the traditional view, which I have been denying, that the "linguistic turn" enabled philosophers to provide substantive solutions to traditional problems.

as well as the world's (in the form of the facts of sense-perception). The attack on this latter notion which I described in chapter four has produced two strikingly different movements in recent philosophy of language. One of these is best represented by Davidson, and the other by Putnam. The first reaction is in the direction of a purified and de-epistemologized conception of the philosophy of language. One outcome of so recasting the subject is to discard what Davidson calls "the third dogma" of empiricism, namely, the "dualism of scheme and content, of organizing system and something waiting to be organized"—a dogma which I have argued in chapter four is central to epistemology generally as well as to empiricism in particular.[3] Davidson distinguishes between philosophical projects which form part of "the theory of meaning properly so-called" and those motivated by "some adventitious philosophical puritanism."[4] Roughly, Frege and Tarski pursued the first sort of project, whereas Russell and Carnap and Quine mingled pure theory of meaning with impure epistemological considerations—those which led them, at various times and in various ways, to various forms of operationalism, verificationism, behaviorism, conventionalism, and reductionism.[5] Each of these was an expression of an underlying "philosophical puritanism" which held that anything incapable of being "logically constructed" out of certainties (the data of sense, or the rules of language) was suspicious.

In Davidson's view, the question of "how language works" has no special connection with the question of "how knowledge works." The fact that truth is discussed in con-

[3] See Donald Davidson, "On the Very Idea of a Conceptual Scheme," *Proceedings of the American Philosophical Association* 47 (1973-74), 11.
[4] Donald Davidson, "Truth and Meaning," *Synthese* 7 (1967), 316.
[5] Putnam trenchantly criticizes Quine on this point. Cf. Putnam, *Mind, Language and Reality*, pp. 153-191 ("The Refutation of Conventionalism"). However, as I shall be arguing, Putnam himself becomes involved in the same confusion.

nection with both questions should not mislead us into thinking that we can infer

> A theory of meaning will analyze the meaning of all referring expressions other than those for sensory qualia in terms of those which do refer to sensory qualia

from

> Our only evidence for empirical truths is the patterns of qualia in our sensory fields.

A theory of meaning, for Davidson, is not an assemblage of "analyses" of the meanings of individual terms, but rather an understanding of the inferential relations between sentences.[6] To understand these relations is to understand the truth-conditions for the sentences of English, but for lots of simple sentences ("An oak is a tree," "Russia is our fatherland," "Death is inevitable") there are no more enlightening truth-conditions to be given than for "Snow is white."

The case is different with sentences ascribing beliefs or actions, however, or those containing adverbial modifiers— or any other sentence such that the inferential relationships obtaining between it and neighboring sentences are not revealed by the ordinary apparatus of quantificational logic without reparsing. In these cases, we get truth-conditions which are not trivial, are hard to construct, and are testable only by their susceptibility to integration within a theory of truth-conditions for other sentences. "The desired effect," Davidson says, "is standard in theory building: to extract a rich concept (here something reasonably close to translation) from thin little bits of evidence (here the truth values of sentences) by imposing a formal structure on enough bits."[7] Not only has this program nothing to do with epis-

---

[6] See Davidson, "Truth and Meaning," pp. 316-318.

[7] Donald Davidson, "In Defense of Convention T" in *Truth, Syntax and Modality*, ed. H. Leblanc (Amsterdam, 1973), p. 84. For the bland metaphysical upshot of the theory, see Davidson's "The Method of

temology, but its "ontological" results are bound to be bland. It does not, for example, serve any of the usual sentimental purposes of metaphysical system-building to learn from Davidson that we probably just have to go ahead and quantify over persons, rather than "reducing" them to things, in order to have a truth-theory for action-sentences. The philosophical interest of the program is, indeed, largely negative: by showing what philosophy of language comes to when purified of attempts to imitate either Kant or Hume, it throws the "adventitious puritanisms" of earlier programs into bold relief. The actual results of the hard work on adverbial modification and the like which would result from concerted efforts to carry out Davidson's suggestions would do little to help or hinder any solution of any of the textbook problems of philosophy.

Davidson's work can best be seen as carrying through Quine's dissolution of the distinction between questions of meaning and questions of fact—his attack on the linguistic reinterpretation of Kant's distinction between the receptivity of sense and the a priori concepts given by spontaneity. Davidson is saying that if we are serious in renouncing an a priori knowledge of meaning, then the theory of meaning is going to be an empirical theory. Thus there can be no special province for such a theory save, roughly, the traditional province of the grammarian—the attempt to find ways of describing sentences which help to explain how those sentences are used. From this perspective, Quine's "canonical notation" should not be conceived of as an attempt "to limn the true and ultimate structure of reality,"[8] but rather as an attempt to find the most perspicuous ways of describing a fairly small portion of reality—the use of language. The point of constructing a "truth theory of English" is not to enable philosophical problems to be put

Truth in Metaphysics," *Midwest Studies in Philosophy* 2 (1977), pp. 244-254, especially the concluding paragraphs.
[8] W.V.O. Quine, *Word and Object* (Cambridge, Mass., 1960), p. 221.

in a formal mode of speech, nor to explain the relationship between words and the world, but simply to lay out perspicuously the relation between parts of a social practice (the use of certain sentences) and other parts (the use of other sentences).

The opposite approach to Davidson's in recent philosophy of language is found in Dummett and in Putnam. Dummett still holds to the slogan common to Vienna and Oxford—the claim that "philosophy has, as its first if not its only task, the analysis of meanings." Davidson, as far as I can see, has no such attachment to the notion of "analyzing meanings." Dummett goes on to say something which Davidson does not, and which he would, as far as I can see, have no reason to say: "the theory of meaning, which is the search for such a model, is the foundation of all philosophy, and not epistemology, as Descartes misled us into believing."[9] In the view which I am urging in this book, this claim is multiply misleading. For it is misleading to say that Descartes misled us into believing that epistemology was the foundation of all philosophy. Rather, what he did was to make it possible for Locke and Kant to develop an epistemological problematic which replaced the scholastic problematic. He made possible a discipline in which metaphysics was a matter of making the world safe for clear and distinct ideas and for moral obligation, and in which the problems of moral philosophy became problems of meta-ethics, problems of the justification of moral judgment. This is not to make epistemology the foundation of philosophy so much as to invent something new—epistemology—to bear the

[9] Michael Dummett, *Frege's Philosophy of Language* (London, 1973), p. 559. In his polemics against Davidson's holism, Dummett insists that one cannot have an adequate philosophy of language without the two Kantian distinctions (given-versus-interpreted and necessary-versus-contingent) attacked by Quine and Sellars. See especially "What Is a Theory of Meaning? (I)" in Samuel Guttenplan, ed., *Mind and Language* (Oxford, 1975), pp. 97-138. The defense of the former distinction is most explicit at p. 137 and of the latter at pp. 117ff.

name "philosophy." The picture of ancient and medieval philosophy as concerned with *things*, the philosophy of the seventeenth through the nineteenth centuries with *ideas*, and the enlightened contemporary philosophical scene with *words* has considerable plausibility. But this sequence should not be thought of as offering three contrasting views about what is primary, or what is foundational. It is not that Aristotle thought that one could best explain ideas and words in terms of things, whereas Descartes and Russell rearranged the order of explanation. It would be more correct to say that Aristotle did not have—did not feel the need of—a theory of knowledge, and that Descartes and Locke did not have a theory of meaning.[10] Aristotle's remarks about knowing do not offer answers, good or bad, to Locke's questions, any more than Locke's remarks about language offer answers to Frege's.

Dummett sees philosophy of language as foundational because he sees epistemological issues now, at last, being formulated correctly as issues within the theory of meaning. He agrees with Descartes about the importance of the issues which emerged out of the "way of ideas," but he thinks that we have only recently been able to state them properly. Just as Spinoza and Leibniz thought that they were doing well what the scholastic metaphysicians had done awkwardly (e.g., investigating the nature of substance), so Dummett and Putnam think that they are doing well what epistemologists have done awkwardly (investigating the issue between realism and idealism). But Descartes, we can see by hindsight, was self-deceived; by the time of Kant it became clear that if we start from Cartesian concerns we are not going to be able to raise the good old metaphysical questions. Davidson stands to Russell, Putnam, and Dummett, in this respect, as Kant stood to Descartes, Spinoza, and Leibniz. Davidson's distinction between giving a theory of meaning

[10] See Ian Hacking, *Why Does Language Matter to Philosophy?* (Cambridge, 1975), p. 43.

263

and "adventitious philosophical puritanism" is a contemporary parallel to Kant's distinction between the legitimate and the illegitimate uses of reason.

If we adopt this view of new philosophical paradigms nudging old problems aside, rather than providing new ways of stating or solving them, then we will see the second ("impure") type of philosophy of language as a last nostalgic attempt to hook up a new kind of philosophical activity with an old problematic. We will see Dummett's notion of philosophy of language as "first philosophy" as mistaken not because some other area is "first" but because the notion of philosophy as having foundations is as mistaken as that of knowledge having foundations. In this conception, "philosophy" is not a name for a discipline which confronts permanent issues, and unfortunately keeps misstating them, or attacking them with clumsy dialectical instruments. Rather, it is a cultural genre, a "voice in the conversation of mankind" (to use Michael Oakeshott's phrase), which centers on one topic rather than another at some given time not by dialectical necessity but as a result of various things happening elsewhere in the conversation (the New Science, the French Revolution, the modern novel) or of individual men of genius who think of something new (Hegel, Marx, Frege, Freud, Wittgenstein, Heidegger), or perhaps of the resultant of several such forces. Interesting philosophical change (we might say "philosophical progress," but this would be question-begging) occurs not when a new way is found to deal with an old problem but when a new set of problems emerges and the old ones begin to fade away. The temptation (both in Descartes's time and in ours) is to think that the new problematic is the old one rightly seen. But, for all the reasons Kuhn and Feyerabend have offered in their criticism of the "textbook" approach to the history of inquiry, this temptation should be resisted.

In this chapter, I shall be largely engaged in urging this "Kuhnian" conception of the relation between philosophy of language and traditional philosophical problems, in opposition to Dummett's more familiar (and, I think, generally accepted) view of their relation. I shall do so by criticizing "impure" philosophy of language and its illicit transfers of problems from epistemology into philosophy of language. Evidently, I cannot survey the whole field, so I shall stick to a topic that provides the greatest temptation to think that explanations of how language works will also help us see how "language hooks onto the world" and thus how truth and knowledge are possible. This is the so-called issue of conceptual change, around which most recent polemics about "realism," "pragmatism," "verificationism," "idealism," and "conventionalism" have centered. I think that Davidson is right in saying that the notion of "conceptual change" is itself incoherent, and that we need to see through it in order to recognize why debates about it seem both so important and so unlikely to be resolved.

So I shall, in the next section, discuss the issues purportedly raised by theory-change for epistemology on the one hand and for philosophy of language on the other. Then, in succeeding sections, I shall discuss Putnam's "realistic" response to these issues in some detail, since Putnam's work seems to me the clearest statement of an "impure" program. I shall be contrasting it with a "pure" or "pragmatist" or "language-game" approach to language, which I think is illustrated by Sellars and by Wittgenstein as well as by Davidson (despite the differences which may seem to set these three in opposition to one another). I hope thereby to show that the issue between the two approaches is not a replay of the issues which separated realists from idealists and pragmatists in the days of philosophy-as-epistemology, and indeed is not really an issue about language at all. I shall be claiming that if we press Quine's and Davidson's criticisms of the language-fact and scheme-content distinctions far enough, we no longer have dialectical room to state an issue concerning "how language hooks onto the world" between the "realist" and the "idealist" (or the "pragmatist"). The need to construct such an issue seems to me one more manifestation of the Kantian need for an over-arching permanent neutral matrix within which to "place" and criticize past and future inquiry. This nostalgia for philosophy as an architectonic and encompassing discipline survives in contemporary philosophy of language only because of the vague association of "language" with "the a priori" and of the latter with "philosophy." Insofar as there is a real issue between "realists" and "pragmatists" in contemporary philosophy of language it seems to me a metaphilosophical one—the issue about whether philosophy can retain its Kantian self-image once the notion of language as the source of a priori knowledge is dropped. On *this* point, to be sure, I shall be siding with the "pragmatists." But I hope that my discussion may help to frame this metaphilosophical issue in less Aesopian language than that in which it is usually stated.

2. What Were Our Ancestors Talking About?

Was Aristotle wrong about motion being divided into natural and forced? Or was he talking about something different from what we talk about when we talk about motion? Did Newton give right answers to questions to which Aristotle had given wrong answers? Or were they asking different questions? This sort of conundrum has inspired a great deal of the best work in philosophy of science and philosophy of language in recent years. Yet, like most philosophical puzzles, its motives and presuppositions are of more interest than the various solutions which have been offered. Why, after all, should we think that there is a more interesting answer to these questions than to the question of whether the ship of Theseus endured the change of each of its planks? Why should we think that the question "What did they mean?" or "What were they referring to?" is going to have a determinate answer? Why should it not be answerable in either way, depending on what heuristic considerations are relevant to some particular historiographical purpose?

The reason we think that there should be determinate answers here is, at a first approximation, that we think that the history of the pursuit of truth should be different from the history of poetry or politics or clothes. We may well feel that questions like "Did the Greeks mean 'temperance' by σωφροσύνη?" and "Do the Nuer refer to the soul as *kwoth*?" can be dismissed by saying that there is no special reason to think that any given one-word expression in one culture can be matched with a one-word expression in a very different culture. Indeed, we may feel that even lengthy paraphrases will be of little help, and that we must just get into the swing of the exotic language-game.[11] But in the case of science, such an attitude seems perverse. Here, we are inclined to say, there jolly well is something out there—motion and its laws, for example—which people either meant to refer to, or at least *were* referring to without realizing it. Scientific inquiry is supposed to discover what sorts of objects there are in the world and what properties they have. Anybody who conducted serious inquiry could only have been asking which predicates were to be pinned on which things. When we find it hard to say which thing Aristotle was talking about, we feel that there must be a right answer somewhere, because he must have been talking about *some* of the things *we* talk about. Even if he imagined unreal objects and uninstantiated properties, he must have given sense to his talk about them by some intertwined talk about, or other interaction with, what was *really* there. This feeling is the root of instrumentalist remarks like "All this talk about kinds and laws of motion is just a complicated way of classifying sensory experiences." This need to say that talk about something we don't recognize is "really"

11 See Clifford Geertz, "Thick Description: Toward an Interpretive Theory of Culture" in his *The Interpretation of Cultures* (New York, 1973).

talk about something we do recognize used to be gratified by simply assuming (in "Whiggish" fashion) that our misguided ancestors had "really" been talking about whatever our best-approved contemporary inquirers claimed that they were talking about. Thus we were told that Aristotle had really been talking about gravitation when he spoke of natural downward motion, that ignorant sailors really referred to the horns of narwhals when they talked of those of unicorns, that "caloric fluid" was a misleading way of describing the transmission of energy between bouncing molecules, and that Kierkegaard was describing our relations to our fathers in the flesh when he talked of Abraham's relation to God.

Two developments have made philosophers nervous in recent years about this "what they were really talking about" strategy. These developments are, roughly, breakdowns of each of the two "dogmas of empiricism" identified by Quine. The first dogma enshrined what Quine called "essentialism"—the notion that one could distinguish between what people were talking about and what they were saying about it by discovering the essence of the object being discussed. In its linguistic form, this was the doctrine that one could discover which term in our language translated a term in that of the ancient scientists, and then discover the essence of the referent of both terms by distinguishing between the analytic statements which told one the terms' meaning and the synthetic statements which expressed possibly false beliefs about this referent. The second dogma held that such a translation *could* always be found, and that such analytic statements *could* always be formulated, because to determine the meaning of any referring expression one need only discover which reports in a "neutral observation language" would confirm, and which would disconfirm, a statement asserting the existence of the referent in question.

The conviction that science differed from softer discourse in having "objective reference" to things "out there" was

268

bolstered in pre-Quinean days by the thought that even if there were no such things as Aristotelian essences that could become immaterially present in the intellect, there certainly were points of contact with the world in the presentations of sense. This contact, plus the ability of an operationalist "meaning-analysis" to characterize the essence of the referent in terms of the presentations to be expected from it, seemed to give science what was lacking in religion and politics—the ability to use contact with the real as the touchstone of truth. The horror which greeted Quine's overthrow of the dogmas, and Kuhn's and Feyerabend's examples of the "theory-ladenness" of observation, was a result of the fear that there might be no such touchstone. For if we once admitted that Newton was better than Aristotle not because his words better corresponded to reality but simply because Newton made us better able to cope, there would be nothing to distinguish science from religion or politics. It was as if the ability to tell the analytic from the synthetic, and the observational from the theoretical, was all that stood between us and "irrationalism."

I have suggested in previous chapters that this identification of rationality with the philosophical dogmas of the day reflects the fact that, since Kant, philosophy has made it its business to present a permanent neutral framework for culture. This framework is built around a distinction between inquiry into the real—the disciplines which are on "the secure path of a science"—and the rest of culture. This is the sort of distinction which we find in the last paragraph of Hume's *Enquiry*, in the first paragraph of the preface to the second edition of the *Critique of Pure Reason*, and in the manifestoes by Russell and Husserl cited in chapter four. If philosophy is essentially the formulation of the distinction between science and nonscience, then endangering current formulations seems to endanger philosophy itself, and with it rationality (of which philosophy is seen as the vigilant guardian, constantly fending off the forces of darkness). Given this conception of the dogmas which

269

Quine overthrew, the response of many philosophers was to find some way of formulating the desired distinction which would (a) keep the philosophy of language as much in the center of the picture as it had been since the days of the Vienna Circle, (b) not involve any recourse to the notion of language as the realm of the a priori, (c) provide an answer to questions about whether Newton and Aristotle had a common referent (and if so, what it was). This desire was the root of what has come to be called "the theory of reference," a term now roughly coextensive with what I have been calling "impure philosophy of language."

Before this desire became explicit, however, there was a preliminary stage of disarray which found philosophers asking for a theory of "meaning-change." This demand arose primarily from a reaction to Feyerabend's claim that the traditional empiricist view had presupposed a "condition of meaning invariance"—presupposed, that is, that "all future theories will have to be phrased in such a manner that their use in explanations does not affect what is said by the [other] theories, or factual reports to be explained."[12] Feyerabend, like Kuhn, was concerned to show that the meaning of lots of statements in the language, including lots of "observation" statements, got changed when a new theory came along; or, at least, that granting that such change took place made more sense of the facts of the history of science than the standard textbook view which kept meanings constant and let only beliefs change. The response of many philosophers to such historical examples was to grant that meanings *could* shift as a result of new discoveries—that the permanent neutral framework of meanings within which rational inquiry could be conducted was not so permanent as had been thought. But, they said, there must be such a thing as a "rational" and principled change of meaning, and it is now our task, as the guardians and explicators of

[12] Paul Feyerabend, "How To Be a Good Empiricist" in *Challenges to Empiricism*, ed. Harold Morick (Belmont, Calif., 1972), p. 169.

the rationality natural to natural scientists, to explain what principles are involved. Feyerabend himself had been content to suggest that meanings changed every time any feature of use changed, but cooler heads thought there must be some middle view between "meanings remain and beliefs change" and "meanings change whenever beliefs do." This led to the feeling that there ought to be a way to mark off a change of beliefs within Kuhn's "normal science" from the shift in norms which occurred in a "scientific revolution." Granted, philosophers said, that the textbook account of theory-change is misleading, still, anything the historiographer of science needs philosophy can provide. We shall set about to discover those conditions in which successive changes in belief produce something that is not merely a change in belief but a change in "conceptual scheme."[13]

The notion that it would be all right to relativize sameness of meaning, objectivity, and truth to a conceptual scheme, as long as there were some criteria for knowing when and why it was rational to adopt a new conceptual scheme, was briefly tempting. For now the philosopher, the

[13] Fred Suppe, in his "The Search for Philosophic Understanding of Scientific Theories" (in *The Structure of Scientific Theories*, ed. Suppe [Urbana, 1974], pp. 3-241) classifies this project as the attempt to construct a "*Weltanschauungen* analysis" of scientific theory-change (cf. esp. pp. 127ff.). Many of the authors whom Suppe discusses would, I think, quarrel with the implications of the term, and with some of the details of Suppe's presentation. But the general lines of Suppe's treatment of this period in the development of recent philosophy of science seem to me accurate and illuminating. Another document useful for understanding this period is *Conceptual Change*, ed. Glenn Pearce and Patrick Maynard (Dordrecht, 1973), which has some very useful papers on the question of "meaning-change," especially those by Binkley, Sellars, Putnam, Barrett, and Wilson. The line I am taking in this chapter is in harmony with Binkley's and Sellar's papers, but I think that both men take too seriously the question which Binkley formulates as "How is our system of epistemic appraisal to be applied in contexts of changing meanings?" (p. 71). In my view, there is no such system—no overarching structure of rationality. Barrett's criticisms of Putnam chime with those offered by Fine and by me in the articles cited below in note 26.

guardian of rationality, became the man who told you when you could start meaning something different, rather than just the man who told you what you meant. But this attempt to retain the philosopher's traditional role was doomed. All the Quinean reasons why he could not do the one were also reasons why he could not do the other. The philosopher had been portrayed, since the beginnings of "the linguistic turn," as a man who knew about concepts by knowing about the meanings of words, and whose work therefore transcended the empirical. But as soon as it was admitted that "empirical considerations" (e.g., the discovery that there were spots on the moon, the discovery that the États-Généraux would not go home) incited but did not require "conceptual change" (e.g., a different concept of the heavens or of the state), the division of labor between the philosopher and the historian no longer made sense. Once one said that it was rational to abandon the Aristotelian conceptual scheme as a result of this or that discovery, then "change of meaning" or "shift in conceptual scheme" meant nothing more than "shift in especially central beliefs." The historian can make the shift from the old scheme to the new intelligible, and make one see why one would have been led from the one to the other if one had been an intellectual of that day. There is nothing the philosopher can add to what the historian has already done to show that this intelligible and plausible course is a "rational" one. Without what Feyerabend called "meaning invariance," there is no special method (meaning-analysis) which the philosopher can apply. For "meaning invariance" was simply the "linguistic" way of stating the Kantian claim that inquiry, to be rational, had to be conducted within a permanent framework knowable a priori, a scheme which both restricted possible empirical content and explained what it was rational to do with any empirical content which came along. Once schemes became temporary, the scheme-content distinction itself was in danger, and with it the Kantian notion of philosophy as made possible by our a priori knowledge

272

of our own contribution to inquiry (the schematic, formal element—e.g., "language").

3. IDEALISM

Philosophers came to realize fairly quickly that the search for a criterion of meaning-change was as disastrous to the notion of philosophy qua analysis of meanings as the notion of the right to revolt had been to political philosophy qua study of sovereignty. So they realized that Feyerabend had misstated his own point when he spoke of "meaning-change." This criticism was most effectively made by Putnam:

Feyerabend cannot escape the same difficulties that have bedeviled the Positivists. . . . To see that this is the case, it suffices to recall that for Feyerabend the meaning of a term depends upon a whole *theory* containing the term. . . . One might, of course, take the radical line that *any* change in theory is a change in the meaning of terms. . . . But I expect Feyerabend would not take this line. For to say that any change in our empirical beliefs about Xs is a change in the meaning of the term X would be to abandon the distinction between questions of meaning and questions of fact. To say that the semantical rules of English cannot at all be distinguished from the empirical beliefs of English speakers would just be to throw the notion of a semantical rule of English overboard. . . . All appearance of sensation would have vanished if Feyerabend had taken this course. For the "sensation" here depends on sliding back and forth between a noncustomary conception of meaning and the customary conception.[14]

Appreciation of this point led philosophers into a second stage of the debate over our relation to ancestral theories and exotic cultures. It was recognized that if one was whole-

[14] Putnam, *Mind, Language and Reality*, pp. 124-125.

heartedly Quinean in one's attitude toward the notion of "meaning" one would not even *want* to ask "Did they mean the same thing by '——'?" What, then, had all the fuss been about? Presumably about how we could assign truth-values to various statements. We want to know whether to say, "Aristotle said mostly false things about motion" or rather to say, "Aristotle said mostly true things about what *he* called 'motion,' but we don't believe there is any such thing." Further, we want to say in some cases, "Here Aristotle goofed, even in his own terms" and in other cases, "Here we have a statement which would be true if *anything* in Aristotelian physics were, but which, alas, refers to something which does not exist and thus is false." Or, to put it still another way, we want to distinguish between Aristotelian falsehoods which are a result of the nonexistence of what he was talking about, and those which result from his misuse of his own theoretical apparatus—just as we want to distinguish between the falsehood of "Holmes lived on Baker Street" and that of "Holmes was married." To make the distinction between internal questions (where the answers are given within the culture, the theory, the story, the game) and external ones (answered by whether it is a culture we are members of, a theory we accept, a story we believe, a game we play), we can get along with the notion of "reference" and skip that of "meaning." "Meaning" only seemed important because it provided a way to pick out an object in the world, which we could then determine to be the same or not the same as some object countenanced by our own culture, theory, story, or game. Once we give up the notion of meaning, we also give up the notion of reference as determined by meaning—of the "defining attributes" of a term picking out the referent of the term.

The need to pick out objects without the help of definitions, essences, and meanings of terms produced, philosophers thought, a need for a "theory of reference" which would not employ the Fregean machinery which Quine had rendered dubious. This call for a theory of reference became assimilated to the demand for a "realistic" philosophy of science which would reinstate the pre-Kuhnian and pre-Feyerabendian notion that scientific inquiry made progress by finding out more and more about the same objects.[15] It was not that either Kuhn or Feyerabend had denied this, but rather that their views about the incommensurability of alternative theories suggested that the only notions of "truth" and "reference" we really understood were those which were relativized to a "conceptual scheme." If there was no necessity that there be a single observation language common to all alternative theories, as Feyerabend and Kuhn had suggested (and Quine and Sellars had given further reasons for believing), then the empiricist notion that one could always give operational definitions of theoretical terms had to be dropped. Quine's attack on the first dogma had made the notion of "definition" dubious, and his holistic attack on the second, combined with Sellars's claim that "givenness to sense" was a matter of acculturation, made the notion of "operational definition" doubly dubious. The antireductionist implications of all this anti-empiricist polemic were such that something which seemed much like idealism began to become intellectually respectable. It seemed possible to say that the question of what was real or true was not to be settled independently of a given conceptual framework, and this in turn seemed to suggest that perhaps nothing really existed apart from such frameworks.[16] So the notion that we *could* find a common matrix

[15] Cf. ibid., pp. 196ff.

[16] Actually, this suggestion only occurred to *critics* of Quine and Kuhn, who then pounced upon it as a *reductio*. Cf. Suppe, "Search for Philosophical Understanding," p. 151: ". . . if science always views the world through a disciplinary matrix . . . then isn't Kuhn committed to some form of antiempirical idealism?" Israel Scheffler makes the charge of idealism in chapter 1 of his *Science and Subjectivity* (Indianapolis, 1976) but in later chapters he seems to me to show how, even after we have given up C. I. Lewis's notion of the "given" and most of the empiricist mythology discussed in chapter four, we can nevertheless have control of theory by observation (in the form of control by less

of inquiry—something which overspanned all actual and possible "conceptual frameworks"—was very attractive to those who felt that there must be *something* true about the old-fashioned pre-Quinean and pre-Kuhnian notion of increasingly accurate representations of nature being found in its mirror.

Actually, however, this clamor about "idealism" is a red herring. It is one thing to say (absurdly) that we make objects by using words and something quite different to say that we do not know how to find a way of describing an enduring matrix of past and future inquiry into nature except in our own terms—thereby begging the question against "alternative conceptual schemes." Almost no one wishes to say the former. To say the latter is, when disjoined from scary rhetoric about "losing touch with the world," just a way of saying that our present views about nature are our only guide in talking about the relation between nature and our words. To say that we have to assign referents to terms and truth-values to sentences in the light of our best notions of what there is in the world is a platitude. To say that truth and reference are "relative to a conceptual scheme" sounds as if it were saying something more than this, but it is not, as long as "our conceptual scheme" is taken as simply a reference to what we believe now—the collection of views which make up our present-day culture. This is all that any argument offered by Quine, Sellars, Kuhn, or Feyerabend would license one to mean by "conceptual scheme." However, Putnam, having cleared up part of the

---

controversial beliefs over more controversial beliefs). Scheffler's claim (p. 39) that "we simply have a false dichotomy in the notion that observation must be either a pure confrontation with an undifferentiated given, or else so conceptually contaminated that it must render circular any observational test of a hypothesis" seems just what Kuhn himself would want to say about the issue. As Michael Williams has pointed out to me, Kuhn is simply not concerned with skepticism, either pro or con, but is almost always read by philosophers as if he were advancing skeptical arguments.

confusion created by Feyerabend's talk of meaning-change, unfortunately proceeded to treat the difference between Feyerabend and himself not as a difference between taking the notion of "meaning" seriously and abandoning it, but rather as the difference between an "idealistic" and a "realistic" theory of meaning.

To see how this pseudo-issue developed is to understand the final stage in the development of "the theory of reference" out of the so-called problem of conceptual change. Putnam says, for example:

> What is wrong with positivist theory of science is that it is based on an idealist or idealist-tending world view, and that that view does not correspond to reality. However, the idealist element in contemporary positivism enters precisely through the theory of meaning; thus part of any realist critique of positivism has to include at least a sketch of a rival theory.[17]

By an "idealist-tending world view," Putnam means roughly a view which "regards or tends to regard the 'hard facts' as just facts about actual and potential *experiences*, and all other talk as somehow just highly derived talk about actual and potential experiences" (p. 209). He thereby treats positivism's desire for operational definitions as motivated not by a need to guarantee an analytic-synthetic distinction and thus a fixed framework for inquiry (in the way I have treated it above), but by a Berkeleian desire to avoid questions about the relation between experience and an independent reality. This is, I think, wrong-headed as history, but it is not particularly important. What is important is Putnam's insistence that "the positivist today is no more entitled than Berkeley was to accept scientific theory and practice—that is, his own story leads to no reason to think that scientific theory is true or that scientific practice tends to discover truth" (p. 209). Putnam thinks

[17] Putnam, *Mind, Language and Reality*, p. 207.

277

of philosophers as typically having either strongly "anti-realistic or strongly realistic intuitions":

> . . . the antirealist does not see our theory and Archimedes' theory as two approximately correct descriptions of some fixed realm of theory-independent entities, and he tends to be sceptical about the idea of "convergence" in science—he does not think our theory is a *better* description of the *same* entities that Archimedes was describing. But if our theory is *just* our theory, then to use *it* in deciding whether or not X lies in the extension of χρυσός is just as arbitrary as using Neanderthal theory to decide whether or not X lies in the extension of χρυσός. The only theory that it is *not* arbitrary to use is the one the speaker himself subscribes to.
>
> The trouble is that for a strong antirealist *truth* makes no sense except as an intra-theoretic notion. . . . The antirealist can use truth intra-theoretically in the sense of a "redundancy theory"; but he does not have the notions of truth and reference available *extra-theoretically.* But *extension is tied to the notion of truth.* The extension of a term is just what the term is *true of.* Rather than try to retain the notion of extension via an awkward operationalism, the antirealist should reject the notion of extension as he does the notion of truth (in any extra-theoretic sense). Like Dewey, for example, he can fall back on a notion of "warranted assertibility" instead of truth. . . . Then he can say that "X is gold (χρυσός)" was warrantedly assertible in Archimedes' time and is not warrantedly assertible today . . . but the assertion that X was in the extension of χρυσός will be rejected as meaningless, like the assertion that "X is gold (χρυσός)" was true. (p. 236)

It is difficult to find a philosopher who meets Putnam's criteria for being an "antirealist." Kuhn occasionally hints that he finds the notion of "a better description of the same entities" objectionable, but most philosophers who have been influenced by his criticisms of positivistic philosophy of science have seen no need to go this far. Again, philosophers who are dubious about the notion of a theory of connections between words and the world, and who, like Sellars, are inclined to relativize "true" to conceptual frameworks, nevertheless would never call meaningless either of the assertions which Putnam thinks they ought to call meaningless. Sellars would interpret "warranted assertible in our conceptual framework but not true" as an implicit reference to another, perhaps not yet invented, conceptual framework in which the statement in question would not be warranted assertible. Philosophers who, like James and Dewey and Strawson, are dubious about the "correspondence theory of truth," nevertheless have no sympathy with the notion of nature as malleable to thought, or with the inference from "one cannot give a theory-independent description of a thing" to "there are no theory-independent things." As usual in debates between "idealists" and "realists," both sides wish the other to assume the burden of proof. The so-called idealist claims to be able to give a satisfactory sense to everything which common sense, and even the philosophy of language, wants to say, and asks what the realist can possibly add. The realist insists that the idealist view has counter-intuitive consequences which only a theory of a relation called "correspondence between thought (or words) and the world" can safeguard us against.

Putnam has three lines of argument, each designed to show that there is a significant issue between the realist and his opponent and that the realist is right. The first is an argument against construing "true" as meaning "warrantedly assertible" or any other "soft" notion having to do with relations of justification. This is supposed to show that only a theory about relations between words and the world can offer a satisfactory construal. The second is an argument to the effect that a certain kind of sociological fact which needs explanation—the reliability of standard methods of scientific inquiry, or the utility of our language

279

as an instrument for coping with the world—can only be explained on realist grounds. The third is an argument that only the realist can avoid inferring from "many terms used in the sciences of the past did not refer" to "it is overwhelmingly likely that no term used by our scientists refers," a conclusion he finds objectionable.[18] I think that only the third of these arguments really joins issue with a real-life opponent. My examination of this argument will consist of the discussions of reference, truth, and relativism in the next three sections. In the remainder of this section, however, I shall try to say enough in criticism of Putnam's first two arguments to show why only the third need be taken seriously.

Putnam's claim that no notion like "warranted assertible" will have the same syntactic features as "true" is perfectly justified. But it is not clear that it is relevant to any philosopher's claim. Philosophers who suggest that "true" means "warranted assertible" usually either (a) relativize the notion of truth to a language, theory, stage of inquiry, or conceptual scheme, or (b) explain that we do not need a notion of "true" once we have the notion of "warranted assertible." In other words, they either suggest a revision in our normal use of "true," or suggest abandoning the term altogether. As Putnam himself notes, arguments against such notions as *analyses* of "true" are as easy as Moore's arguments against attempts to define "good," and for pretty much the same reason. "True but not warranted assertible" makes as good sense as, for example, "good but not conducive to the greatest happiness" or "good but disapproved of by all cultures so far." Philosophers who are concerned (as Tarski and Davidson are *not*) to tell us something about truth which will explain or underwrite the success of our *search* for truth are like philosophers who

[18] Putnam, "What Is 'Realism'?" *Proceedings of the Aristotelian Society*, 1976, p. 194. (Reprinted with changes as Lectures II-III in his *Meaning and the Moral Sciences* [London, 1978], a book which appeared after this chapter was written.)

want to tell us more about "good" than that it is used to commend, something which will explain or underwrite moral progress. But there may be little of this sort to be said. To use the analogy with moral philosophy once again, it is no help in understanding either why "good" is indefinable, or how it is used, to explain that a good action is one which corresponds to the Form of the Good, or to the Moral Law. It is equally pointless to be told that true statements correspond to the way the world is.[19]

The appropriate position for the "antirealist" is just to admit that nothing will explicate "theory-independent truth," just as nothing will explicate "noninstrumental goodness" or "nonfunctional beauty," and to move the burden of proof back to Putnam. The way in which it should be shoved back is, roughly, to ask, "What would we lose if we had no ahistorical theory-independent notion of truth?" This question seems as reasonable as the question "What did we gain when Socrates taught us to use 'good' in such a way that 'bad for me, but nevertheless good,' 'bad for Athens, but nevertheless good' and even 'abhorrent to the gods, but nevertheless good' made sense?" That we have such notions of truth and of goodness—notions which float free of all questions of justification—is unquestionable. It is equally unquestionable that this notion of truth has certain properties which no notion of assertibility or justification is going to have (e.g., to cite some of those which Putnam notes: if a statement is true, so are its logical consequences; if two statements are true, so is their conjunction; if a statement is true now it always is). This notion may not be much older than the time of Socrates and Aris-

19 See Nelson Goodman, "The Way the World Is" in his *Problems and Projects* (Indianapolis, 1972), pp. 24-32, esp. p. 31: "There are many ways the world is, and every true description captures one of them." Goodman's point seems to me to have been developed best by Davidson, in "On the Very Idea of a Conceptual Scheme" (discussed below) and in "Mental Events" (discussed in chapter four, section 5 above).

totle, before which "logical consequence" would not have been intelligible. But, whatever the provenance, the fact that we possess such a notion is in itself no guarantee that there will be an interesting philosophical theory about it. Most of what passes for discussion of "truth" in philosophy books is, in fact, about justification, just as most of what passes for discussion of "goodness" is about pleasure and pain. The price of sharply distinguishing the *transcendentalia* from their common-sense counterparts may be to leave one without material for theory-construction, and without problems to resolve.

Putnam, however, is very explicit that there are problems to be resolved which have nothing to do with justification, and the second of the arguments to which I have referred is a direct reply to the question "What do we need the notion of truth, as opposed to justification, *for?*" Putnam's answer is that we need it to explain the reliability of our procedures of inquiry. More specifically, we need it to explain the fact of "convergence" in science—the fact that the old bad theories nonetheless present, as they approach our own time, better and better approximations of our present theories.[20] The obvious objection to this starting point is that this "convergence" is an inevitable artifact of historiography. It seems clear that there will always be a natural way of telling the story of theory-succession (or of the succession of religions or forms of government) which shows our predecessors gradually, if jerkily, progressing to where we are now. There is no reason to think that the antirealist will lack a story to tell about the causal effects upon our ancestors of the objects spoken of by our present theory. He too can describe how these objects helped to bring about justified but false descriptions of themselves, followed by equally justified, incompatible, and slightly better descriptions, and so on down to our own day. If, however, "convergence" is seen not as a

[20] See Putnam, "Reference and Understanding," in *Meaning and the Moral Sciences*, pp. 97-119. I owe my knowledge of this paper to a preprint kindly supplied by Professor Putnam.

fact about the history of the various disciplines but as a fact about the results of tests of new theories, then the realist may seem in a better position to make use of this fact. Boyd, who has collaborated with Putnam in developing this line of argument, interprets "convergence" as the "reliability" of such a principle as

> it should be inquired, in the light of available theoretical knowledge, under what circumstances the causal claims made by the theory might plausibly go wrong, either because alternative causal mechanisms plausible in the light of existing knowledge might be operating instead of those indicated by the theory, or because causal mechanisms of sorts already known might plausibly be expected to interfere with those required by the theory in ways which the theory does not anticipate.[21]

It is hard to imagine anyone taking exception to such a principle, so the issue is not joined until Boyd claims that we can only account for this principle's leading to useful results "on a realistic understanding of the relevant collateral theories":

> Suppose you always "guess" where theories are most likely to go wrong experimentally by asking where they are most likely to be false as accounts of causal relations, given the assumption that currently accepted laws represent probable causal knowledge. And suppose your guessing procedure works—that theories really are most likely to go wrong—to yield false experimental predictions— just where a realist would expect them to. . . . What explanation beside scientific realism is possible? Certainly *not* the mere effect of conventionally or arbitrarily adopted scientific traditions. . . . Unless, as no empiricist would suggest, the world is molded by our *conventions*, there is no way that the reliability of this principle could merely be a matter of convention. (p. 12)

[21] Richard N. Boyd, "Realism, Underdetermination and a Causal Theory of Evidence," *Nous* 7 (1973), 11.

Boyd here confuses the sense in which a procedure is reliable in respect of an independent test (as thermometers are reliable indicators of how uncomfortable it is outside) with the sense in which a procedure is reliable because we cannot imagine an alternative. To check new theories by old ones is not an optional procedure. How else would we check them? The fact that new theories often go wrong just where old ones say they might is not something which requires explanation. It would require explanation if they went wrong somewhere else. We could only make it appear that the "nonrealist" is at a loss to explain the relevance of old theories to testing new ones if we took this straw man to be claiming that new theories arrive completely equipped with equally new observational languages, testing procedures, and regulative principles of their own. But a "new theory" is simply a rather minor change in a vast network of beliefs. Its truth, as James said, is largely a matter of its ability to perform "a marriage function" between the deposit of old truth and the "anomaly" which suggested it in the first place. Only some of Feyerabend's more strained conceits suggest that we should grant a new theory immunity from any test based on the results of an old one. Such suggestions have nothing to do with the question of whether we need a notion of "truth" in addition to one of "warranted assertibility."

4. REFERENCE

To show that we *do* need such a notion we must turn to Putnam's third argument, which has the virtue of presenting us with a more plausible "antirealist" than those who have been discussed so far. This argument centers around what Putnam calls the need to block "the disastrous meta-induction that concludes 'no theoretical term ever refers.' "[22]

[22] Putnam, "What Is Realism?" p. 194.

What if we accept a theory from the standpoint of which electrons are like *phlogiston?*
Then we will have to say electrons don't really exist. What if this keeps happening? What if all the theoretical entities postulated by one generation (molecules, genes, etc., as well as electrons) invariably "don't exist" from the standpoint of later science?—this is, of course, one form of the old skeptical "argument from error"—how do you know you aren't in error *now?* But it is the form in which the argument from error is a *serious* worry for many people today, and not just a "philosophical doubt."
One reason this is a serious worry is that eventually the following meta-induction becomes overwhelmingly compelling: *just as no term used in the science of more than 50* (or whatever) *years ago referred, so it will turn out that no term used now* (except maybe observation terms, if there are such) *refers.* (pp. 183-184)

Putnam says that blocking this meta-induction is "obviously a desideratum for the Theory of Reference." This is puzzling, for two reasons. First, it is not clear what philosophical standpoint could show that revolutionary change in science had come to an end—that we will *not* stand to our descendants as our primitive animist ancestors stand to us. How are we supposed to step outside our own culture and evaluate its place relative to the end of inquiry? Second, even if there were such a philosophical standpoint, it is not clear how the theory of reference could possibly supply it. Suppose we have decisive intuitions about the answer to such questions as "If Jones did not do the mighty deeds attributed to him, but Smith (previously unknown to history) did most of them, does 'Jones' refer to Jones or to Smith?" Suppose, less plausibly, that our intuitions about such puzzle cases as this are firm enough to lead us to a general theory which informs us, without appeal to intuition, that we and Dalton refer to the same things by "molecule" whereas "caloric fluid" was never used to refer to the mo-

285

tion of molecules.[23] Such a theory might push the premises of the suggested meta-induction farther into the past—since now we might have to look back five thousand years rather than fifty years for a science none of whose theoretical terms referred. But this could hardly satisfy a skeptic who had developed a serious worry about the status of our science relative to that of, say, the Galactic civilization of the future. Such a skeptic would presumably only be satisfied by a theory of reference which showed that at all ages and places scientists had mostly been referring to the same things, thus depriving the meta-induction in question of *any* interesting premises.

Now in one obvious sense we know perfectly well—prior to any theory—that they have been referring to the same things. They were all trying to cope with the same universe, and they referred to *it*, although doubtless often under unfruitful and foolish descriptions. To discover, as a result of the next scientific revolution, that there are no genes, molecules, electrons, etc., but only space-time bumps, or hypnotic suggestions from the Galactic hypnotists who have manipulated our scientists since the time of Galileo, or whatever, would still not put us out of touch with either the world or our ancestors. For we would proceed to tell the same sort of story of the emergence of better descriptions of the world out of false, confused, unfruitful, descriptions of the world which we tell about, say, the rise of Milesian science —in both cases, it would be the story of a triumph of reason, and in both cases it would be the application of reason to the same world. In general, there is no intelligible suggestion one can make about what the world might really turn out to be like which seems a basis for "serious worry." (The suggestion that there might be some *un*intelligible description of the world—one which was expounded within an untranslatable conceptual scheme—is another worry al-

[23] I owe the example to Rom Harré's *The Principles of Scientific Thinking* (Chicago, 1970), p. 55.

together, which has no need for, and no possibility of getting, inductive support. I discuss this other worry in connection with Davidson's attack on the notion of "conceptual scheme" in the following section.)

Still, this notion of "bad description of the same thing" may seem to fudge an issue. "Reference" seems an all-or-nothing affair. It may seem better to say that "caloric fluid" either does or does not refer to the motion of molecules than to say that "caloric fluid" and "motion of molecules" are two abbreviations for (better and worse) descriptions of the same phenomenon, whatever it may eventually turn out to be. We may feel that referring to the motion of molecules should be like referring to individual people or middle-sized physical objects—we either pick out *them* or we don't. This feeling is enhanced if we have recently been reading Tarski, and further enhanced if we are disinclined to view theoretical statements in the quasi-instrumentalist way Sellars does—as material principles of inference licensing the utterance of other statements. We will then want sentences like "Heat is the motion of molecules" to be true in the straightforward "corresponding" way that "White is the typical color of snow" is true. So it may seem important, for purposes of understanding "how language works," to think in terms of expressions' "picking out entities" rather than simply being used "to describe reality." Let it be so. Still, it is hard to see why we need do more to assuage the skeptic than to be "Whiggish" in our historiography. We can just write things up so as to make even the most primitive of animists talk about, for example, the motion of molecules, radium, genes, or whatever. We do *not* thereby assuage his fear that molecules may not exist, but then *no* discovery about how words relate to the world will do that. For "the world," as known by that theory, is just the world as known to the science of the day.

So far, then, we have the following dilemma: either the theory of reference is called upon to underwrite the success of contemporary science, or else it is simply a decision about

287

how to write the history of science (rather than the provision of a "philosophical foundation" for such historiography). The one task seems too much to ask, and the other
too slight to merit the title of "theory." At this point it
would be well to ask where the notion of "theory of reference" came from in the first place. What sort of thing is it
that it should be burdened with the task of blocking skepticism, thus doing the job we had always hoped epistemology would do? In my view, the notion that there is such a
theory results from running together two quite different
considerations, namely:

> the fact, noted by Kripke, Donnellan, and others, that
> there are counter-examples to the Searle-Strawson cri-
> terion for reference—that is, that S refers, in his use of
> "X," to whatever entity would make most of his central
> beliefs about X true[24]

> the fact that the usual (Frege, Searle, Strawson) assump-
> tion that meaning, in the sense of beliefs or intentions (or,
> more generally, entities in the heads of users of words),
> determines reference suggests that the more false beliefs
> we have the less "in touch with the world" we are.

The two considerations taken together suggest that the
usual "intentionalist" notion of how words hook onto the
world is both wrong in particular cases and philosophically
disastrous. So in recent "impure" philosophy of language, it
has become almost a dogma that the "idealist"-sounding
doctrines of Quine, Wittgenstein, Sellars, Kuhn, Feyerabend (and other heroes of this book) are to be refuted by

[24] Most recent discussion of these counter-examples stems from Keith
Donnellan, "Proper Names and Identifying Descriptions" and Saul
Kripke, "Naming and Necessity," both of which appear in *Semantics
of Natural Language*, ed. Davidson and Harman (Dordrecht, 1972). See
Stephen P. Schwartz, ed., *Naming, Necessity and Natural Kinds* (Ithaca,
1976) for further articles attempting to construct a general theory to
deal with such counter-examples, and a useful review of the literature
in the editor's "Introduction."

going back to the first principles of semantics, overturning Frege's "intentionalist" theory of reference, and substituting something better.[25] The idea is that if the world reaches up and hooks language in factual (e.g., causal) relationships, then we shall always be "in touch with the world," whereas in the old Fregean view we are in danger of losing the world, or may never have hooked onto it in the first place.

We should, however, be suspicious of the notion of a clash between an old—intentionalist—and a new, "causal" (or, more generally, nonintentionalist and therefore "realist") theory of reference. The clash is produced by the equivocity of "refer." The term can mean either (a) a factual relation which holds between an expression and some other portion of reality whether anybody knows it holds or not, or (b) a purely "intentional" relation which can hold between an expression and a nonexistent object. Call the one "reference" and the other "talking about." We cannot *refer* to Sherlock Holmes but we can *talk about* him, and similarly for phlogiston. "Talking about" is a commonsensical notion; "reference" is a term of philosophical art. "Talking about" ranges over fictions as well as realities, and is useleʌs for realist purposes. The assumption that people's beliefs determine what they are talking about works as well or as badly for things which exist as for things which do not, as long as questions about what exists do not arise. In a community where there are no conflicting theories (physical, historical, "ontological," or whatever), but in which it is well known that some of the people and things truly spoken of do exist while others are fictions, we could indeed use the Searle-Strawson criteria. We *are* talking about whatever most of our beliefs are true of. The puzzle cases (the cases in which intuition tells us that people are *not* talking about whatever entity makes most of their beliefs true) arise only when we know something they don't.

25 Putnam's "The Meaning of 'Meaning' " and his "The Refutation of Conventionalism" (both included in his *Mind, Language and Reality*) are the fullest expressions of this attitude.

Thus if we discover that there was a hitherto unknown man named Smith who did 99 percent of the deeds attributed to a mythical Jones, but that the tales about Jones actually accreted around a man named Robinson, we may want to say that when we speak of Jones we are *really* talking about Robinson and not about Smith.

If this notion of "really talking about" is confused with *reference*, it becomes easy to think (as do Putnam and Kripke) that we have "intuitions" about reference, intuitions which might be the basis for a nonintentional and "theory-independent" "theory of reference." But this is to think that the question

    a. What is the best way to express the falsehood of the usual beliefs about Jones—by saying that they were about nothing at all, truths about a fiction, or falsehoods about a reality?

should be answered on the basis of an answer to

    b. Is there an entity in the world connected to our use of "Jones" by the relation of "reference"?

In the view Putnam and Kripke adopt, (b) is a sensible question, and is antecedent to (a). Answering (a) is not a matter of expository or historiographical convenience, in this view, but a matter of hard fact—a fact determined by the answer to (b). In the view I am recommending, (b) does not arise. The only factual issue in the neighborhood concerns the existence or nonexistence of various entities which are talked about. Once we have decided on the latter factual question, we can adopt one of four attitudes toward beliefs in which (by the common-sensical Searle-Strawson criterion) the person in question is talking about nonexistent entities: We can

    1. declare all of them false (Russell) or truth-valueless (Strawson)

or

2. divide them into the ones which are false or truth-valueless because they are about nothing and those which are "really about" some real thing and which thus may be true

or

3. divide them into the ones which are false or truth-valueless because they are about nothing and those which are "really about" fictional entities, and which thus may perhaps be true

or

4. combine strategies (2) and (3).

The "really" in "really about" marks our departure from the Searle-Strawson criterion for aboutness, but it does not mark an invocation of our intuitions concerning a matter of fact. It is like the notion of "really a good thing to have done" used when, although somebody has acted in a prima facie shameful way, a more extended and informed view of the matter suggests that common-sensical criteria of moral worth should be set aside. In the moral case, we are not having an intuition about the factual connection between the deed and the Form of the Good; we are simply recasting our description of the situation in a way which avoids paradox and maximizes coherence. Similarly in the case of decisions about who was really talking about what.

It may seem that the issue between the view I am suggesting and the Putnam-Kripke view turns on the question of "Meinongianism"—of whether one can refer to fictions. But it does not. In the sense in which the use of the term *refer* is governed by the inference from

"N" refers and N is ∅

to

N exists (is not a fiction),

then of course one cannot refer to fictions. This is the usual way in which the term *refer* is used, and I have no wish to use it differently. But the moral I draw from the fact that this condition defines the notion of "reference" is that "reference" has nothing in particular to do with either "talking about" or "really talking about." "Reference" only arises when one has made one's decision about the various strategies used to express the error that one finds in the world—the decision among (1)-(4) above—and then wishes to cast the result of one's decision into "canonical" form, that is, into a language which uses standard quantificational logic as a matrix. This is what I meant by saying that "reference" is a term of art. It is also the reason it is not something we have intuitions about. So I conclude that the "intuition" with which the Searle-Strawson criterion conflicts is merely the intuition that when there is dispute about what exists there may be dispute as to what is "really being talked about," and that the criterion for "really about" is not the Searle-Strawson one.

What, then, is it? There is no answer to this question, no such "criterion." The considerations which dictate choice between strategies (1)-(4) above are so diverse that the request for a criterion is out of place. We might be tempted to say that "really talking about" is a relation that can hold between an expression and what *we* think exists, as opposed to "talking about," which holds between an expression and what its user thinks exists, and to "refers," which can hold only between an expression and what really and truly does exist. But this would be wrong, since, once again, not only can we talk about nonexistent entities, but we can be discovered to have *really* been talking about nonexistent entities. Really talking about X is not the same as talking about a real X. "Really" here is just a matter of "placing" the relative ignorance of the person being discussed in the context of the relatively greater knowledge claimed by the speaker. There are as many ways of doing that as there are

292

contexts of discourse. Consider, for example, "You think you are talking about Thales, but you are really talking about a tale told by Herodotus"; "You think you are talking about your analyst, but you are really talking about yourself"; "You think you are talking about a fictional deity named Artemis, but you are actually talking about a flesh-and-blood woman who lived in Thebes in the ninth century B.C."; "You think you are talking about lithium, but you are really talking about kryptonite."[26]

I think, then, that the quest for a theory of reference represents a confusion between the hopeless "semantic" quest for a general theory of what people are "really talking about," and the equally hopeless "epistemological" quest for a way of refuting the skeptic and underwriting our claim to be talking about nonfictions. Neither the one nor the other demand need be satisfied for the purposes of a Davidsonian "pure" philosophy of language. The first demand is, roughly, a demand for a decision-procedure for solving difficult cases in historiography, anthropological description, and the like—cases where nothing save tact and imagination will serve. The latter demand is for some transcendental standpoint outside our present set of representations from which we can inspect the relations between those representations and their object. (This is the demand which Berkeley told us we could not meet, which Kant met only by calling the world "appearance," and which the image of the Mirror of Nature makes us think we ought to be able to meet.) The question "What determines reference?" is ambiguous between a question about the best procedure for comparing large coherent sets of false beliefs (other epochs, cultures, etc.) with ours and a question about how to refute the skeptic. Debates about theories of reference get their

26 I have developed this view about reference at greater length in "Realism and Reference," *The Monist* 59 (1976), 321-340. For a parallel criticism of Putnam on this topic, see Arthur Fine, "How to Compare Theories: Reference and Change," *Nous* 9 (1975), 17-32.

concreteness from attempts to answer the first part of the question, and their philosophical interest from hints that they might somehow answer the second. But nothing can refute the skeptic—nothing can do what epistemology hoped to do. For we discover how language works only within the present theory of the rest of the world, and one cannot use a part of one's present theory to underwrite the rest of it. Theory of reference is as hopeless as a "theory of transcendental constitution of the object" for this purpose.

Putnam (in an address delivered after the bulk of this chapter was written) has largely recanted his "metaphysical realism"—the project of explaining successful reference by some means which does not presuppose that success. In this address, he makes the point I have just been making about "causal theories." He says that what the metaphysical realist wanted, but could not have, is a view of "truth as radically nonepistemic"—that is, one in which "the theory that is 'ideal' from the point of view of operational utility, inner beauty and elegance, 'plausibility,' simplicity, 'conservatism,' etc., *might be false*."[27] The metaphysical realist *thought* he needed to say this because it seemed the only way of clearly separating "true" from "warranted assertible." But, as Putnam says, even if one defines "true" *à la* Tarski in terms of the relation of satisfaction, we shall be able to map *any* set of beliefs onto the world in terms of this relation. Further, there will be lots of *different* ways in which this can be done, and *there are no constraints on ways of doing it other than constraints on theories generally*. Our best theory about what we are referring to is merely noncontroversial fallout from our best theory about things in general. As Putnam says: ". . . a 'causal' theory of reference is not (would not be) of any help here: for how 'causes' can uniquely refer is as much of a puzzle as how 'cat' can, on the

27 Putnam, "Realism and Reason," *Proceedings of the American Philosophical Association*, vol. 50 (1977), p. 485. (This paper has now been reprinted in *Meaning and the Moral Sciences*. The passage appears there at p. 125).

metaphysical realist picture."[28] Similarly, no matter what nonintentional relation is substituted for "cause" in our account of how the things in the content reach up and determine the reference of the representations making up the scheme, our theory about what the world is made of will produce, trivially, a self-justifying theory about that relation.

5. TRUTH WITHOUT MIRRORS

Putnam's recantation comes down to saying that there is no way to make some empirical discipline do what transcendental philosophy could not do—that is, say something about the scheme of representations we are employing which will make clear its tie to the content we wish to represent. But if there is no such way, then we can fall in with Davidson's claim that we need to drop the scheme-content distinction altogether. We can admit that there is no way to make the notion of "scheme" do what philosophers traditionally wanted to do with it—that is, make clear certain special constraints which "rationality" exerts and which explain why our ideal theories must "correspond to reality." Putnam now agrees with Goodman and Wittgenstein: to think of language as a picture of the world—a set of representations which philosophy needs to exhibit as standing in some sort of nonintentional relation to what they represent—is *not* useful in explaining how language is learned or understood. But, at least in his writings prior to his recantation, he thought that we could still make use of this picture of language for purposes of a naturalized epistemology; language-as-picture was not a useful image for understanding how one used language, but it was useful for explaining the success of inquiry, just as "a map is successful if it corresponds in an appropriate way to a particular part of the earth." Putnam is here making the same move as that made

28 Putnam, "Realism and Reason," p. 486 (p. 126 in *Meaning and the Moral Sciences*).

295

by Sellars and Rosenberg. These men *do* identify "true" with "warranted assertible by us" (thereby allowing truth about nonexistent objects) but they then proceed to describe "picturing" as a nonintentional relation which supplies an Archimedean point by reference to which we may say that our present theory of the world, though to be sure *true*, may not picture the world as adequately as some successor theory. The difference in terminology is unimportant, since what all three philosophers want is simply to make it possible to answer the question "What guarantees that our changing theories of the world are getting better rather than worse?" All three want a Wittgensteinian meaning-as-use theory to handle what I have called the problems of "pure" philosophy of language, and a Tractarian picturing relation to handle epistemological problems.

Putnam's criticism of his own previous attempts to make sense of such a transcendental guarantee applies equally to Sellars and Rosenberg. He says:

> Metaphysical realism collapses just at the point at which it claims to be distinguishable from Peircean realism—i.e., from the claim that there is an ideal theory. . . . Since Peirce himself (and the verificationists) always *said* metaphysical realism collapses into incoherence at *just* that point, and realists like myself thought they were *wrong*, there is no avoiding the unpleasant admission that "they were right and we were wrong" on at least one substantive issue.[29]

Compare this passage with Sellars's discussion of Peirce:

> . . . although the concepts of "ideal truth" and "what really exists" are defined in terms of a Peircian conceptual structure they do not require that there ever be a Peirceish community. Peirce himself fell into difficulty because, by not taking into account the dimension of "picturing," he

[29] Putnam, "Realism and Reason," p. 489 (p. 130 in *Meaning and the Moral Sciences*).

296

had no Archimedean point outside the series of actual and possible beliefs in terms of which to define the ideal or limit to which members of this series might approximate.[30]

Sellars's point here is that Peirce's identification of "the truth" with "the opinion fated to be ultimately agreed to by all" makes it seem that the very existence of truth and reality depends upon such hazardous matters as the continuation of the race and of the Enlightenment's notions of rational inquiry. So Sellars wants to substitute a way of looking at human inquiry which views "fated to be agreed upon" as a description of a causal process which leads to the creation of self-representings by the universe. Thus we find Rosenberg echoing the later Peirce's idealistic metaphysics of evolutionary love:

> We can understand our representational activities . . . only by redescribing them in terms of the concepts of a *total* theory of the universe as a physical system which, of natural necessity, evolves subsystems which in turn necessarily project increasingly adequate representations of the whole. To put it crudely, we must come to see the physical universe as an integrated physical system which necessarily "grows knowers" and which thereby comes to mirror itself within itself.[31]

Both Sellars and Rosenberg rightly view the coming-into-being of the Mirror of Nature as made possible by the existence of minds, but they urge (as does Putnam) that mentality and intentionality are irrelevant to understanding how the Mirror mirrors. The crucial sort of representing—the one which helps us say how and why we are superior to our ancestors—is one which takes place not relative to a scheme of conventions, not relative to intentions: "Picturing

[30] Wilfrid Sellars, *Science and Metaphysics* (London and New York, 1968), p. 142.

[31] Jay Rosenberg, *Linguistic Representation* (Dordrecht, 1974), p. 144.

is a complex matter-of-factual relation and, as such, belongs in quite a different box from the concepts of denotation and of truth."[32]

So if Putnam's recantation is right, it bears directly on the point that Sellars and Rosenberg thought crucial. Putnam is saying that the attempt to get a set of nonintentional relationships (such as those offered by a causal theory of reference or by a Sellarsian notion of "more adequate picturing") is always vitiated by the fact that those relationships are simply further parts of the theory of the world of the present day. This criticism of any possible naturalization of epistemology leaves us, Putnam thinks, with what he calls "internal realism"—the view that we can explain the "mundane fact that language-using contributes to getting our goals, achieving satisfaction, or what have you" by saying "not that language mirrors the world but that *speakers* mirror the world—i.e., their environment—in the sense of *constructing a symbolic representation of that environment.*"[33] Internal realism, in this sense, is just the view that, according to our own representational conventions, we are representing the universe better than ever. But that, in turn, is just complimenting ourselves for, say, having invented the term *lithium* to represent lithium, which hasn't been represented for all these years. The difference between the recanted "metaphysical" realism and the uncontroversial internal realism is the difference between saying that we are successfully representing according to Nature's own conventions of representation and saying that we are successfully representing according to our own. It is the difference between, roughly, science as a Mirror of Nature, and as a set of working diagrams for coping with nature. To say that we are coping, by our lights, pretty well is true but trivial. To say that we are mirroring correctly is "only a picture," and one which we have never been able to make

---

[32] Sellars, *Science and Metaphysics*, p. 136.

[33] Putnam, "Realism and Reason," p. 483 (p. 123 in *Meaning and the Moral Sciences*).

sense of. Nature may, for all we know, necessarily grow knowers which represent her, but we do not know what it would mean for Nature to feel that our conventions of representations are becoming more like her own, and thus that she is nowadays being represented more adequately than in the past. Or, rather, we can make sense of this only if we go all the way with the Absolute Idealists, and grant that epistemological realism must be based on personalistic pantheism.

I have been trying in this section to present Putnam's simple but devastating point that nonintentional relations are as theory-relative as intentional relations as a general criticism of the whole attempt to naturalize epistemology by first transforming it into the philosophy of language and then getting a naturalistic account of meaning and reference. The common motive of Quine's "Epistemology Naturalized," Daniel Dennett's hints at an "evolutionary epistemology," the revivification by Kripke and Fisk of the Aristotelian notions of essence and natural necessity, various causal theories of reference, and Sellarsian theories of picturing has been to de-transcendentalize epistemology while nevertheless making it do what we had always hoped it might: tell us why our criteria of successful inquiry are not just *our* criteria but also the *right* criteria, nature's criteria, the criteria which will lead us to *the truth*. If this motive is finally given up, then philosophy of language is simply "pure" Davidsonian semantics, a semantics which does not depend upon mirror-imagery, but which, on the contrary, makes it as difficult as possible to raise philosophically interesting questions about meaning and reference.

Let me now proceed, therefore, to describe how Davidson ties in his discussion of truth with his attack on the "scheme-content" distinction and mirror-imagery generally. In the first place, he wants to say that the notion of statements' being true because they correspond to ("picture," "adequately represent") reality is just fine for all the cases in which it is philosophically uncontroversial—cases like "Snow is white." It is even fine for such cases as "Perseverence keeps honor bright," "Our theory of the world corresponds to physical reality," and for "Our moral philosophy conforms to the Idea of the Good." These too are true if and only if the world contains the right sorts of things, and is laid out in the way the statements suggest. There is no occasion, in Davidson's view, for "philosophical puritanism" which would depopulate the world of honor, or physical reality, or the Idea of the Good. If one wants to say that there are no such things, then one can give an alternative theory of the world which does not contain them, but this will not be a *semantical* theory. Discussions of the way in which truth is correspondence to reality float free of discussions of what there is in heaven and earth. No roads lead from the project of giving truth-conditions for the sentences of English (English as it is spoken, containing all sorts of theories about all sorts of things) to criteria for theory-choice or to the construction of a canonical notation which "limns the true and ultimate structure of reality." Correspondence, for Davidson, is a relation which has no ontological preferences—it can tie any sort of word to any sort of thing. This neutrality is an expression of the fact that, in a Davidsonian view, nature has no preferred way of being represented, and thus no interest in a canonical notation. Nor can nature be corresponded to better or worse, save in the simple sense that we can have more or fewer true beliefs.[34]

[34] I am not sure where Davidson stands on the question of truth about fictions, and whether he would allow that a relation of "satisfaction" can hold between "Sherlock Holmes" and Sherlock Holmes. I would hope that he would, since this would underline the separation between Tarskian semantics and "realistic" epistemology which I am emphasizing. In the view I am putting forward, "Sherlock Holmes roomed with Dr. Watson" is as true, and as little in need of "philosophical analysis" as "Snow is white." This means that there can be true statements which do not contain referring expressions. This consequence will not be disturbing if one remembers the distinction between "referring" and "talking about," and thus the distinction between "not

In the second place, Davidson thinks that the notion of "representational scheme" or "conceptual framework" or "intended correspondence" attempts to disjoin the notion of "truth" from that of "meaning," and thus must fail. His most effective way of putting this comes in his claim that the notion of an "alternative conceptual scheme"—for example, one which would contain none of the referring expressions used in ours—is the notion of a language which is "true but not translatable." After a sustained criticism of several

---

referring" and "talking about nothing." But I do not feel clear enough about the issues surrounding the interpretation of Tarski's notion of "satisfaction" to feel confident about the relation between this notion and either of the two others. The general line I want to take is that there are true statements about fictions, values, and numbers, as well as about cats on mats, and that the attempt to find something like "correspondence" in terms of which to "analyze" the former truths on the model of the latter is pointless. Sellars puts this point by saying that not all true statements "picture" the world—only the "basic empirical" ones. I would prefer to say that no true statements picture the world—that picturing is "only a picture," one which has served only to produce ever more convoluted *Sprachstreit*.

On the interpretation of Tarski, see Sellars's claim that "semantical statements of the Tarski-Carnap variety do not assert relations between linguistic and extra-linguistic items" (*Science and Metaphysics*, p. 82) and the contrast between "the 'picture' sense of 'correspond' and the Tarski-Carnap sense of 'correspond' " (p. 143). Sellars's view is that all semantic statements are about intensions, and that "picturing" has nothing to do with semantics. For contrasting views, see John Wallace, "On the Frame of Reference," in *Semantics of Natural Language*, ed. Davidson and Harman, and Hartry Field, "Tarski's Theory of Truth," *Journal of Philosophy* 69 (1972).

For an attempt to work out a view of "true" which distinguishes it from "assertible" *without* attempting to construe it as "standing in a correspondence relation to the extra-linguistic," see Robert Brandom, "Truth and Assertibility," *Journal of Philosophy* 73 (1976), 137-149. Brandom gives an account of why we need "true" in addition to "assertible" for the purpose of what I am calling "pure" philosophy of language—understanding how language works, as opposed to how it hooks onto the world. He thereby diagnoses, I believe, the fundamental confusion between the need for this concept in semantics and the need for it in epistemology, a confusion which motivates "impure" philosophy of language.

301

variations on the traditional mirror-imagery (conceptual schemes as "fitting" reality better or worse, or "classifying" reality differently from one another), Davidson concludes:

> The trouble is that the notion of fitting the totality of experience, like the notions of fitting the facts, or being true to the facts, adds nothing intelligible to the simple concept of being true. To speak of sensory experience rather than the evidence, or just the facts, expresses a view about the source or nature of evidence, but it does not add a new entity to the universe against which to test conceptual schemes.

So, he says:

> Our attempt to characterize languages or conceptual schemes in terms of the notion of fitting some entity has come down, then, to the simple thought that something is an acceptable conceptual scheme or theory if it is true. Perhaps we better say *largely* true in order to allow sharers of a scheme to differ on details. And the criterion of a conceptual scheme different from our own now becomes: largely true but not translatable. The question whether this is a useful criterion is just the question how well we understand the notion of truth, as applied to language, independent of the notion of translation. The answer is, I think, that we do not understand it independently at all.[35]

Davidson's reason for saying that we do not understand this derives from what he calls a "certain holistic view of meaning":

> If sentences depend for their meaning on their structure, and we understand the meaning of each item in the struc-

[35] Davidson, "On the Very Idea of a Conceptual Scheme," p. 16. Unfortunately Davidson in that paper misinterprets Kuhn as meaning "untranslatable" by "incommensurable" (p. 12). It is important for my argument in this book to separate sharply these two notions. See chapter seven, section 1.

ture only as an abstraction from the totality of sentences in which it features, then we can give the meaning of any sentence (or word) only by giving the meaning of every sentence (and word) in the language.[36]

This holistic view of meaning amounts to the view that a theory of meaning for a language must do *no more than* "give an account of how the meanings of sentences depend upon the meanings of words" (p. 304). The crucial move is to say that we need not think that "individual words must have meanings at all, in any sense that transcends the fact that they have a systematic effect on the meanings of the sentences in which they occur" (p. 305). The traditional view is that we anchor language to the world by giving meaning by ostension (or some other nonintentional mechanism— one which presupposes no "stage-setting in the language") to certain individual words, and then going on holistically from there. Davidson's neo-Wittgensteinian point is that even "red" and "mama" have uses—can help make possible the statement of truths—only in the context of sentences and thus of a whole language (cf. p. 308). Whatever role ostension (or neural pathways, or any other nonintentional setup) plays in learning a language, one need not know anything about these mechanisms to know the language, nor to know how to translate that language. The same goes, Davidson points out, for Tarskian truth-conditions for the sentences of English, and this is why it turns out that "a theory of meaning for the language L shows 'how the meanings of sentences depend upon the meanings of words' if it contains a (recursive) definition of truth-in-L"; for

> what we require for a theory of meaning for a language L is that without appeal to any (further) semantical notions it place enough restrictions on the predicate 'is T' [in the schema: s is T if and only if p] to entail all sentences got from schema T when 's' is replaced by a structural

[36] Davidson, "Truth and Meaning," p. 308.

description of a sentence of L and 'p' by that sentence,
... [and so] the condition we have placed on satisfactory
theories of meaning is in essence Tarski's Convention T.
(p. 309)

So, Davidson invites us to conclude:

Since Convention T embodies our best intuition as to how
the concept of truth is used, there does not seem to be
much hope for a test that a conceptual scheme is radically
different from ours if that test depends on the assumption
that we can divorce the notion of truth from that of translation.[37]

Let me try to restate the gist of this argument by pointing
out the connection between Davidson's holism about meaning and his disdain for the notion of "scheme." Someone
who is not a holist in this sense will think that understanding a language is a matter of two distinct processes—tying
some individual words on the world via ostension, and then
letting other words build up meanings around this central
core in the course of being used. He will also think that
understanding what "truth" means involves "analyzing"
every true sentence until ostensions which would make it
true become apparent. This picture of holism ceasing to
apply at the point at which reference is least problematic—
at the interface between language and the world where
demonstratives do their work—is one way to get the scheme-
content distinction going. If we think of language in this
way, we will be struck by the thought that somebody else
(the Galactics, say) will have "cut up" the world differently
in their original acts of ostension and thus given different
meanings to the individual words in the "core" of their language. The rest of their language will thus be infected by
this divergence from our way of giving meaning to the
"core" of English, and so there will be no way for us to com-

[37] Davidson, "On the Very Idea of a Conceptual Scheme," p. 17.

municate—no common points of reference, no possibility of translation. Davidson's attack on these metaphors parallels Max Black's Wittgensteinian criticism of the so-called inverted-spectrum problem—the possibility that some people may (for colors and presumably all other perceptual "quality spaces") start off on the wrong foot. Black points out that we can "divide through" by the difference for all purposes of communication—language will, of course, go through equally well no matter what we were ostending.[38] Similarly, Davidson can say that if a difference in the original ostension does not show up at the holistic level—in the use of the sentences that contain the word—then the theory of meaning for the language can divide through by that difference.

Still, we might want to insist that Davidson's argument concerns only what it is to give a *theory of* meaning and a *theory of* truth. We might claim that all he could possibly do is show that we cannot *verify* the existence of a language which gives a true description of the world unless it is translatable into our own, and that this would not show that there cannot *be* one. This line of argument would be analogous to the criticism of Black's way of dealing with the "inverted spectrum" problem, and similar Wittgensteinian antiskeptical strategies, as "verificationist."[39] I shall close this chapter by replying to this objection.

[38] See Max Black, "Linguistic Method in Philosophy" in *Language and Philosophy* (Ithaca, 1949), esp. pp. 3-8. Black treats the "inverted spectrum" as a paradigm of the sort of skeptical argument which the approach to language he is recommending helps debunk. He is, I think, right in this. Indeed, there is a perspective from which all of what I called "epistemological behaviorism" in chapter four can be derived from the sort of argument which Black offers here.

[39] For this sort of objection, see Barry Stroud, "Transcendental Arguments," *Journal of Philosophy* 65 (1968), 241-256. I have attempted to deal with this objection in "Verificationism and Transcendental Arguments," *Nous* 5 (1971), 3-14, and with some related objections in "Transcendental Arguments, Self-Reference and Pragmatism" in *Transcendental Arguments and Science*, ed. Peter Bieri, Rolf Horstmann and Lorenz Krüger (Dordrecht, 1979), 77-103.

6. Truth, Goodness, and Relativism

In order to get a somewhat broader view of the issue about verificationism, consider the following suggestions:

None of our terms refer

None of our beliefs are true

No translation is possible between English and the language which represents the way the world is

None of our moral intuitions are right (participate in the Idea of the Good, reflect the Moral Law, or whatever)

I take the least plausible of these to be the last. The reason is that what we take to be moral—to be even a *candidate* for participation in the Idea of the Good—is something which roughly satisfies, or is at least not too repugnant to, our present moral intuitions. Are we being rash in thinking of "morally right" as meaning "rather like our own ideal of behavior, only more so"? Is this to neglect a real possibility simply because of the verificationist intuition that we cannot recognize anybody who does *not* appeal to our intuitions as having anything to say about morality?

I think that we can answer these questions best by distinguishing between a philosophical sense of "good" in respect to which "the naturalistic fallacy" arises and an ordinary sense in respect to which it does not. If we ask, "What are the necessary and sufficient conditions for something's being good?" we may say, with G. E. Moore, that it is always an open question whether good has anything to do with any conditions which might be mentioned. Words like "good," *once they have been handled in the way that the philosophical tradition has handled them*, acquire a sense in respect to which this is so. They become the name of a *focus imaginarius*, an Idea of Pure Reason whose whole point is not to be identifiable with the fulfillment of any set of conditions. This is not to say that ἀγαθός served pre-Platonic Greeks as the name of such an unconditioned, nor that *any* word served this purpose before the Pythagoreans and the Orphics and Plato invented idealism (in both its senses). But now there is a specifically philosophical use of "good," a use which would not be what it is unless Plato, Plotinus, Augustine, and others had helped construct a specifically Platonic theory of the absolute difference between the eternal and the spatio-temporal. When Moore appealed to our sense for the meaning of "good" he was appealing to nothing less than this sense, a sense which it is rather hard to get hold of without the knowledge of the history of Western thought commoner in Bloomsbury than in Birmingham. *Principia Ethica* should be read, as should the *Euthyphro*, as a work of edifying pedagogy and quiet moral revolution, rather than as an effort to describe current linguistic or intellectual practice.

There is also, however, an ordinary sense of "good," the sense the word has when used to commend—to remark that something answers to some interest. In this sense, too, one is not going to find a set of necessary and sufficient conditions for goodness which will enable one to find the Good Life, resolve moral dilemmas, grade apples, or whatever. There are too many different sorts of interests to answer to, too many kinds of things to commend and too many different reasons for commending them, for such a set of necessary and sufficient conditions to be found. But this is a quite different reason for the indefinability of "good" than the one I just gave for the indefinability of the philosophical sense of "good." In its homely and shopworn sense, the reason why "good" is indefinable is not that we might be altogether wrong about what good men or good apples are, but simply that *no* interesting descriptive term has any interesting necessary and sufficient conditions. In the first, philosophical sense of "good," the term is indefinable because anything we say about what is good may "logically" be quite irrelevant to what goodness is. The only way to get a homely and shopworn mind to grasp this first sense is to start it off with Plato or Moore and hope that it gets the Idea.

My point in suggesting that there are two senses of "good" is, of course, to make plausible the suggestion that there are also two senses apiece of "true" and "real" and "correct representation of reality," and that most of the perplexities of epistemology come from vacillation between them (just as most of the perplexities of meta-ethics come from vacillating between senses of "good"). To begin by pursuing the analogy between goodness and truth, consider the homely use of "true" to mean roughly "what you can defend against all comers." Here the line between a belief's being justified and its being true is very thin. That is why Socrates had trouble explaining the difference between these two notions to his interlocutors, the same trouble we philosophy professors still have in explaining it to our freshmen. When the pragmatists identified truth with "what we will believe if we keep inquiring by our present lights" or "what it is better for us to believe" or with "warranted assertibility," they thought of themselves as following in the footsteps of Mill, and doing for science what the utilitarians had done for morality—making it something you could use instead of something you could merely respect, something continuous with common sense instead of something which might be as remote from common sense as the Mind of God.

It is the homely and shopworn sense of "true" which Tarski and Davidson are attending to, and the special philosophical sense to which Putnam applies his "naturalistic fallacy" argument.[40] The two concerns pass each other by. Davidson's is the "pure" project of finding a way of diagramming the relations among the sentences of English so as to make perspicuous why people call some longer sentences "true" by seeing this as a function of their calling shorter sentences "true." Putnam's is the "impure" project of show-

[40] See "Reference and Understanding" (*Meaning and the Moral Sciences*, p. 108), where Putnam makes explicit the analogy between his strategy with "true" and Moore's with "good."

ing you that the most complete possible understanding of this matter will leave you as open as ever to the possibility that you have no true beliefs at all. So it will, but, once again, there is an ambiguity at hand which makes the irrelevance look like an opposition. Davidson can say, without any attempt at anticipating the end of inquiry and blocking Putnam's skeptical "meta-induction," that most of our beliefs are true. This claim follows from his claim that we cannot understand the suggestion that most of them are false—a suggestion which has sense only when backed up with the phony notion of an "alternative, untranslatable, conceptual scheme." But it is of no force against the skeptic except insofar as it challenges him to make concrete his suggestion that we have got it all wrong —a project as difficult as it would be to make concrete the more limited claim that all our sentences which end ". . . is morally right" are false. Davidson, like Kant, is saying that we cannot project from the fact that this or that central belief turns out to be false, or this or that moral intuition to be perverse and prejudiced, to the possibility that *all* of them will turn out so. Only in the context of general agreement does doubt about either truth or goodness have sense. The skeptic and Putnam avoid this point by switching to the specifically "philosophical" sense of "good" and "true" which, like the Ideas of Pure Reason, are designed precisely to stand for the Unconditioned—that which escapes the context within which discourse is conducted and inquiry pursued, and purports to establish a new context.

Davidson seems verificationist and conventionalist and relativist if one interprets his claim that "most beliefs are true" as the claim that we are getting close to the end of inquiry, to a grasp of the way the world is, to an utterly unclouded Mirror of Nature. But this is like interpreting him as claiming that we are close to the top of Plato's divided line, to a clear vision of the Idea of the Good. Such an interpretation takes both "true" and "good" as names for the accurate fitting of a scheme of representations to something which supplies a content for that scheme. But as Davidson says:

> It would be wrong to summarize by saying we have shown how communication is possible between people who have different schemes, a way that works without need of what there cannot be, namely a neutral ground, or a common coordinate system. For we have found no intelligible basis on which it can be said that schemes are different. It would be equally wrong to announce the glorious news that all mankind—all speakers of language, at least—share a common scheme and ontology. For if we cannot intelligibly say that schemes are different, neither can we intelligibly say that they are one.
>
> In giving up dependence on the concept of an uninterpreted reality, something outside all schemes and science, we do not relinquish the notion of objective truth—quite the contrary. Given the dogma of a dualism of scheme and reality, we get conceptual relativity, and truth relative to a scheme. Without the dogma, this kind of relativity goes by the board. Of course truth of sentences remains relative to language, but that is as objective as can be. In giving up the dualism of scheme and world, we do not give up the world, but reestablish unmediated touch with the familiar objects whose antics make our sentences and opinions true or false.[41]

To suggest that Davidson is verificationist and relativist in saying that most of our beliefs are true or that any language can be translated into English is just to say that he is not using the "Platonic" notions of Truth and Goodness and Reality which "realists" need to make their realism

[41] Davidson, "On the Very Idea of a Conceptual Scheme," p. 20. I have tried to develop the contrast between giving up the world (as common sense takes it to be) and giving up the World (as the Thing-in-Itself, the World which we might never get right) in "The World Well Lost," *Journal of Philosophy* 69 (1972), 649-666, esp. 662-663.

dramatic and controversial ("metaphysical" rather than "internal," in Putnam's sense). But neither is Davidson "refuting" these Platonic notions by exhibiting their "inconsistency." All he can do with them is do what Kant did with the Ideas of Pure Reason—show how they function, what they can and cannot do.. The trouble with Platonic notions is not that they are "wrong" but that there is not a great deal to be said about them—specifically, there is no way to "naturalize" them or otherwise connect them to the rest of inquiry, or culture, or life. If you ask Dewey why he thinks Western culture has the slightest notion of what goodness is, or Davidson why he thinks that we ever talk about what really exists or say anything true about it, they are likely to ask you what makes you have doubts on the subject. If you reply that the burden is on them, and that they are forbidden to argue from the fact that we would never know it if the skeptic were right to the impossibility of his being right, Dewey and Davidson might both reply that they will *not* argue in that way. They need not invoke verificationist arguments; they need simply ask why they should worry about the skeptical alternative until they are given some concrete ground of doubt. To call this attempt to shift the burden back to the skeptic "verificationism," or a confusion of the order of knowledge with the order of being, is like calling "verificationist" the man who says that he will not worry about whether the things he has called "red" are really red until some concrete alternative is provided. The decision about whether to have higher than usual standards for the application of words like "true" or "good" or "red" is, as far as I can see, not a debatable issue. But I suspect it is the only remaining issue between realists and pragmatists, and I am fairly sure that the philosophy of language has not given us any interesting new debating points.

PART THREE

Philosophy

CHAPTER VII

From Epistemology to Hermeneutics

1. COMMENSURATION AND CONVERSATION

I have argued (in chapter three) that the desire for a theory of knowledge is a desire for constraint—a desire to find "foundations" to which one might cling, frameworks beyond which one must not stray, objects which impose themselves, representations which cannot be gainsaid. When I described the recent reaction against the quest for foundations as "epistemological behaviorism" (in chapter four) I was not suggesting that Quine and Sellars enable us to have a new, better, "behavioristic" sort of epistemology. Rather, they show us how things look when we give up the desire for confrontation and constraint. The demise of foundational epistemology, however, is often felt to leave a vacuum which needs to be filled. In chapters five and six I criticized various attempts to fill it. In this chapter I shall be talking about hermeneutics, so I want to make clear at the outset that I am *not* putting hermeneutics forward as a "successor subject" to epistemology, as an activity which fills the cultural vacancy once filled by epistemologically centered philosophy. In the interpretation I shall be offering, "hermeneutics" is not the name for a discipline, nor for a method of achieving the sort of results which epistemology failed to achieve, nor for a program of research. On the contrary, hermeneutics is an expression of hope that the cultural space left by the demise of epistemology will not be filled—that our culture should become one in which the demand for constraint and confrontation is no longer felt. The notion that there is a permanent neutral framework whose "structure" philosophy can display is the notion that the objects to be confronted by the mind, or the rules

315

which constrain inquiry, are common to all discourse, or at least to every discourse on a given topic. Thus epistemology proceeds on the assumption that all contributions to a given discourse are commensurable. Hermeneutics is largely a struggle against this assumption.

By "commensurable" I mean able to be brought under a set of rules which will tell us how rational agreement can be reached on what would settle the issue on every point where statements seem to conflict.[1] These rules tell us how to construct an ideal situation, in which all residual dis-agreements will be seen to be "noncognitive" or merely verbal, or else merely temporary—capable of being resolved by doing something further. What matters is that there should be agreement about what would have to be done if a resolution *were* to be achieved. In the meantime, the interloc-utors can agree to differ—being satisfied of each other's ra-tionality the while. The dominating notion of epistemology is that to be rational, to be fully human, to do what we ought, we need to be able to find agreement with other hu-man beings. To construct an epistemology is to find the maximum amount of common ground with others. The assumption that an epistemology can be constructed is the assumption that such common ground exists. Sometimes this common ground has been imagined to lie outside us— for example, in the realm of Being as opposed to that of Becoming, in the Forms which both guide inquiry and are its goal. Sometimes it has been imagined to lie within us, as in the seventeenth century's notion that by understanding our own minds we should be able to understand the right method for finding truth. Within analytic philosophy, it

[1] Note that this sense of "commensurable" is not the same as "as-signing the same meaning to terms." This sense—which is the one often used in discussing Kuhn—does not seem to me a useful one, given the fragility of the notion of "sameness of meaning." To say that parties to a controversy "use terms in different ways" seems to me an unen-lightening way of describing the fact that they cannot find a way of agreeing on what would settle the issue. See chapter six, section 3, on this point.

has often been imagined to lie in language, which was supposed to supply the universal scheme for all possible content. To suggest that there is *no* such common ground seems to endanger rationality. To question the need for commensuration seems the first step toward a return to a war of all against all. Thus, for example, a common reaction to Kuhn or Feyerabend is that they are advocating the use of force rather than persuasion.

The holistic, antifoundationalist, pragmatist treatments of knowledge and meaning which we find in Dewey, Wittgenstein, Quine, Sellars, and Davidson are almost equally offensive to many philosophers, precisely because they abandon the quest for commensuration and thus are "relativist." If we deny that there are foundations to serve as common ground for adjudicating knowledge-claims, the notion of the philosopher as guardian of rationality seems endangered. More generally, if we say that there is no such thing as epistemology and that no surrogate can be found for it in, for example, empirical psychology or the philosophy of language, we may be seen as saying that there is no such thing as rational agreement and disagreement. Holistic theories seem to license everyone to construct his own little whole—his own little paradigm, his own little practice, his own little language-game—and then crawl into it.

I think that the view that epistemology, or some suitable successor-discipline, is necessary to culture confuses two roles which the philosopher might play. The first is that of the informed dilettante, the polypragmatic, Socratic intermediary between various discourses. In his salon, so to speak, hermetic thinkers are charmed out of their self-enclosed practices. Disagreements between disciplines and discourses are compromised or transcended in the course of the conversation. The second role is that of the cultural overseer who knows everyone's common ground—the Platonic philosopher-king who knows what everybody else is really doing whether *they* know it or not, because he knows about the ultimate context (the Forms, the Mind, Language) within which they are doing it. The first role is appropriate to hermeneutics, the second to epistemology. Hermeneutics sees the relations between various discourses as those of strands in a possible conversation, a conversation which presupposes no disciplinary matrix which unites the speakers, but where the hope of agreement is never lost so long as the conversation lasts. This hope is not a hope for the discovery of antecedently existing common ground, but *simply* hope for agreement, or, at least, exciting and fruitful disagreement. Epistemology sees the hope of agreement as a token of the existence of common ground which, perhaps unbeknown to the speakers, unites them in a common rationality. For hermeneutics, to be rational is to be willing to refrain from epistemology—from thinking that there is a special set of terms in which all contributions to the conversation should be put—and to be willing to pick up the jargon of the interlocutor rather than translating it into one's own. For epistemology, to be rational is to find the proper set of terms into which all the contributions should be translated if agreement is to become possible. For epistemology, conversation is implicit inquiry. For hermeneutics, inquiry is routine conversation. Epistemology views the participants as united in what Oakeshott calls an *universitas* —a group united by mutual interests in achieving a common end. Hermeneutics views them as united in what he calls a *societas*—persons whose paths through life have fallen together, united by civility rather than by a common goal, much less by a common ground.[2]

My use of the terms *epistemology* and *hermeneutics* to stand for these ideal opposites may seem forced. I shall try to justify it by noting some of the connections between holism and the "hermeneutic circle." The notion of knowledge as accurate representation lends itself naturally to the notion that certain sorts of representations, certain expressions, certain processes are "basic," "privileged," and "foun-

[2] Cf. "On the Character of a Modern European State" in Michael Oakeshott, *On Human Conduct* (Oxford, 1975).

dational." The criticisms of this notion which I have canvassed in previous chapters are backed up with holistic arguments of the form: We will not be able to isolate basic elements except on the basis of a prior knowledge of the whole fabric within which these elements occur. Thus we will not be able to substitute the notion of "accurate representation" (element-by-element) for that of successful accomplishment of a practice. Our choice of elements will be dictated by our understanding of the practice, rather than the practice's being "legitimated" by a "rational reconstruction" out of elements. This holist line of argument says that we shall never be able to avoid the "hermeneutic circle"—the fact that we cannot understand the parts of a strange culture, practice, theory, language, or whatever, unless we know something about how the whole thing works, whereas we cannot get a grasp on how the whole works until we have some understanding of its parts. This notion of interpretation suggests that coming to understand is more like getting acquainted with a person than like following a demonstration. In both cases we play back and forth between guesses about how to characterize particular statements or other events, and guesses about the point of the whole situation, until gradually we feel at ease with what was hitherto strange. The notion of culture as a conversation rather than as a structure erected upon foundations fits well with this hermeneutical notion of knowledge, since getting into a conversation with strangers is, like acquiring a new virtue or skill by imitating models, a matter of φρόνησις rather than ἐπιστήμη.

The usual way of treating the relation between hermeneutics and epistemology is to suggest that they should divide up culture between them—with epistemology taking care of the serious and important "cognitive" part (the part in which we meet our obligations to rationality) and hermeneutics charged with everything else. The idea behind such a division is that knowledge in the strict sense—ἐπιστήμη —must have a λόγος, and that a λόγος can only be given by the discovery of a method of commensuration. The idea of commensurability is built into the notion of "genuine cognition," so that what is "only a matter of taste" or "of opinion" need not fall within epistemology's charge, and conversely, what epistemology cannot render commensurable is stigmatized as merely "subjective."

The pragmatic approach to knowledge suggested by epistemological behaviorism will construe the line between discourses which can be rendered commensurable and those which cannot as merely that between "normal" and "abnormal" discourse—a distinction which generalizes Kuhn's distinction between "normal" and "revolutionary" science. "Normal" science is the practice of solving problems against the background of a consensus about what counts as a good explanation of the phenomena and about what it would take for a problem to be solved. "Revolutionary" science is the introduction of a new "paradigm" of explanation, and thus of a new set of problems. Normal science is as close as real life comes to the epistemologist's notion of what it is to be rational. Everybody agrees on how to evaluate everything everybody else says. More generally, normal discourse is that which is conducted within an agreed-upon set of conventions about what counts as a relevant contribution, what counts as answering a question, what counts as having a good argument for that answer or a good criticism of it. Abnormal discourse is what happens when someone joins in the discourse who is ignorant of these conventions or who sets them aside. Ἐπιστήμη is the product of normal discourse —the sort of statement which can be agreed to be true by all participants whom the other participants count as "rational." The product of abnormal discourse can be anything from nonsense to intellectual revolution, and there is no discipline which describes it, any more than there is a discipline devoted to the study of the unpredictable, or of "creativity." But hermeneutics is the study of an abnormal discourse from the point of view of some normal discourse —the attempt to make some sense of what is going on at a stage where we are still too unsure about it to describe it, and thereby to begin an epistemological account of it. The fact that hermeneutics inevitably takes some norm for granted makes it, so far forth, "Whiggish." But insofar as it proceeds nonreductively and in the hope of picking up a new angle on things, it can transcend its own Whiggishness.

From this point of view, then, the line between the respective domains of epistemology and hermeneutics is not a matter of the difference between the "sciences of nature" and the "sciences of man," nor between fact and value, nor the theoretical and the practical, nor "objective knowledge" and something squishier and more dubious. The difference is purely one of familiarity. We will be epistemological where we understand perfectly well what is happening but want to codify it in order to extend, or strengthen, or teach, or "ground" it. We must be hermeneutical where we do not understand what is happening but are honest enough to admit it, rather than being *blatantly* "Whiggish" about it. This means that we can get epistemological commensuration only where we already have agreed-upon practices of inquiry (or, more generally, of discourse)—as easily in "academic" art, "scholastic" philosophy, or "parliamentary" politics as in "normal" science. We can get it not because we have discovered something about "the nature of human knowledge" but simply because when a practice has continued long enough the conventions which make it possible —and which permit a consensus on how to divide it into parts—are relatively easy to isolate. Nelson Goodman has said of inductive and deductive inference that we discover its rules by discovering what inferences we habitually accept;[3] so it is with epistemology generally. There is no

---

[3] Nelson Goodman's pragmatist attitude toward logic is nicely summed up in a passage which, once again, calls the "hermeneutic circle" to mind: "This looks flagrantly circular. . . . But this circle is a virtuous one. . . . *A rule is amended if it yields an inference we are unwilling to accept; an inference is rejected if it violates a rule we are*

difficulty getting commensuration in theology or morals or literary criticism when these areas of culture are "normal." At certain periods, it has been as easy to determine which critics have a "just perception" of the value of a poem as it is to determine which experimenters are capable of making accurate observations and precise measurements. At other periods—for example, the transitions between the "archaeological strata" which Foucault discerns in the recent intellectual history of Europe—it may be as difficult to know which scientists are actually offering reasonable explanations as it is to know which painters are destined for immortality.

2. KUHN AND INCOMMENSURABILITY

In recent years, debates about the possibility of epistemology as opposed to hermeneutics have gained a new concreteness as a result of the work of T. S. Kuhn. His *Structure of Scientific Revolutions* owed something to Wittgenstein's criticisms of standard epistemology, but it brought those criticisms to bear on received opinion in a fresh way. Since the Enlightenment, and in particular since Kant, the physical sciences had been viewed as a paradigm of knowledge, to which the rest of culture had to measure up. Kuhn's lessons from the history of science suggested that controversy within the physical sciences was rather more like ordinary conversation (on the blameworthiness of an action, the qualifications of an officeseeker, the value of a poem, the desirability of legislation) than the Enlightenment had suggested. In particular, Kuhn questioned whether philosophy of science could construct an algorithm for choice among scientific theories. Doubt on this point made his readers doubly doubtful on the question of whether epistemology could, starting from science, work its way out-

---

unwilling to amend." (*Fact, Fiction and Forecast* [Cambridge, Mass., 1955], p. 67.)

ward to the rest of culture by discovering the common ground of as much of human discourse as could be thought of as "cognitive" or "rational."

Kuhn's examples of "revolutionary" change in science were, as he himself has remarked, cases of the sort which hermeneutics has always taken as its special assignment—cases in which a scientist has said things which sound so silly that it is hard to believe that we have understood him properly. Kuhn says that he offers students the maxim:

When reading the works of an important thinker, look first for the apparent absurdities in the text and ask yourself how a sensible person could have written them. When you find an answer, . . . when these passages make sense, then you may find that more central passages, ones you previously thought you understood, have changed their meaning.[4]

Kuhn goes on to say that this maxim does not need to be told to historians, who, "consciously or not, are all practitioners of the hermeneutic method." But Kuhn's invocation of such a maxim was disturbing to philosophers of science who, working within the epistemological tradition, were bound to think in terms of a neutral scheme ("observation language," "bridge laws," etc.) which would make Aristotle and Newton, for example, commensurable. Such a scheme could, they thought, be used to render hermeneutical guesswork unnecessary. Kuhn's claim that there is no commensurability between groups of scientists who have different paradigms of a successful explanation, or who do not share the same disciplinary matrix, or both,[5] seemed to many such philosophers to endanger the notion of theory-choice in science. For the "philosophy of science"—the name

4 T. S. Kuhn, *The Essential Tension* (Chicago, 1977), p. xii.
5 See "Second Thoughts on Paradigms" (in ibid.) for Kuhn's distinction between two "central" senses of "paradigm," blended in *The Structure of Scientific Revolutions* but now distinguished—"paradigm" as achieved result and paradigm as "disciplinary matrix."

under which "epistemology" went when it hid itself among the logical empiricists—had envisaged itself as providing an algorithm for theory-choice.

Kuhn's claim that no algorithm was possible save a *post factum* and Whiggish one (one which constructed an epistemology on the basis of the vocabulary or assumptions of the winning side in a scientific dispute) was, however, obscured by Kuhn's own "idealistic"-sounding addenda. It is one thing to say that the "neutral observation language" in which proponents of different theories can offer their evidence is of little help in deciding between the theories. It is another thing to say that there can be no such language because the proponents "see different things" or "live in different worlds." Kuhn, unfortunately, made incidental remarks of the latter sort, and philosophers pounced upon them. Kuhn wished to oppose the traditional claim that "what changes with a paradigm is only the scientist's interpretation of observations that themselves are fixed once and for all by the nature of the environment and of the perceptual apparatus."[6] But this claim is innocuous if it means merely that the results of looking can always be phrased in terms acceptable to both sides ("the fluid looked darker," "the needle veered to the right," or, in a pinch, "red here now!"). Kuhn should have been content to show that the availability of such an innocuous language is of no help whatever in bringing decision between theories under an algorithm, any more than in bringing decisions about guilt or innocence in jury trials under an algorithm, and for the same reasons. The problem is that the gap between the neutral language and the only languages useful in deciding the issue at hand is too great to be bridged by "meaning postulates" or any of the other mythological entities that traditional empiricist epistemology invoked.

Kuhn should have simply discarded the epistemological project altogether. But instead he called for "a viable al-

[6] T. S. Kuhn, *The Structure of Scientific Revolutions*, 2d ed. (Chicago, 1970), p. 120.

ternate to the traditional epistemological paradigm"[7] and said that "we must learn to make sense of statements that at least resemble 'the scientist afterward [after the revolution] works in a different world.' " He thought we must also make sense of the claims that "when Aristotle and Galileo looked at swinging stones, the first saw constrained fall, the second a pendulum" and that "pendulums were brought into existence by something very like a paradigm-induced gestalt switch." The unfortunate result of these remarks was to set the pendulum swinging between realism and idealism once again. In order to guard against the confusions of traditional empiricism, we need make no more of the gestalt-switch in question than the fact that people became able to respond to sensory stimulations by remarks about pendulums, without having to make an intervening inference. Kuhn was right in saying that "a philosophical paradigm initiated by Descartes and developed at the same time as Newtonian dynamics" needed to be overthrown, but he let his notion of what counted as a "philosophical paradigm" be set by the Kantian notion that the only substitute for a realistic account of successful mirroring was an idealistic account of the malleability of the mirrored world. We do indeed need to give up the notion of "data and interpretation" with its suggestion that if we could get to the *real* data, unpolluted by our choice of language, we should be "grounding" rational choice. But we can get rid of this notion by being behaviorist in epistemology rather than by being idealist. Hermeneutics does not need a new epistemological paradigm, any more than liberal political thought requires a new paradigm of sovereignty. Hermeneutics, rather, is what we get when we are no longer epistemological.

Putting aside Kuhn's incidental "idealism," then, we may focus simply on Kuhn's claim that no algorithm for theory-choice is available. This led his critics to claim that he was

[7] This and all other quotations from Kuhn in this paragraph are from ibid., pp. 120-121.

licensing every scientist to set up his own paradigm and then define objectivity and rationality in terms of that paradigm—the criticism which, as I said above, has been customarily made of any holistic, nonfoundational theory of knowledge. Thus Kuhn wrote:

> In learning a paradigm the scientist acquires theory, methods and standards together, usually in an inextricable mixture. . . .
>
> That observation . . . provides our first explicit indication of why the choice between competing paradigms regularly raises questions that cannot be resolved by the criteria of normal science. . . . Like the issue of competing standards, [it] can be answered only in terms of criteria that lie outside of normal science altogether, and it is that recourse to external criteria that most obviously makes paradigm debates revolutionary.[8]

And critics such as Scheffler often glossed him as follows:

> . . . the comparative evaluation of rival paradigms is quite plausibly conceived of as a deliberative process occurring at a second level of discourse . . . regulated, to some degree at least, by shared standards appropriate to second-order discussion. The passage just quoted suggests, however, that such sharing of second-order standards is impossible. For to accept a paradigm is to accept not only theory and methods, but also governing standards of criteria which serve to justify the paradigm as against its rivals. . . . Paradigm differences are thus inevitably reflected upward, in criterial differences at the second level. It follows that each paradigm is, in effect, inevitably self-justifying, and that paradigm debates must fail of objectivity: again we appear driven back to non-rational conversions as the final characterization of paradigm shifts within the community of science.[9]

[8] Kuhn, *The Structure of Scientific Revolutions*, 1st ed. (Chicago, 1961), pp. 108-109.

[9] Israel Scheffler, *Science and Subjectivity* (Indianapolis, 1967), p. 84.

It is certainly possible to argue that "paradigm differences are thus inevitably reflected upward," but Kuhn did not in fact argue in this way. He merely said that such reflection into meta-discourse makes it harder to resolve controversies about paradigm shifts than it is to resolve controversies within normal science. So far, critics like Scheffler would not disagree; indeed, as Kuhn has noted, "most philosophers of science would . . . now regard the sort of algorithm which has traditionally been sought as a not quite attainable ideal."[10] The only real question which separates Kuhn from his critics is whether the sort of "deliberative process" which occurs concerning paradigm shifts in the sciences (the sort of process which, as Kuhn shows in *The Copernican Revolution*, can stretch out over a century) is different in kind from the deliberative process which occurs concerning, for example, the shift from the *ancien régime* to bourgeois democracy, or from the Augustans to the Romantics.

Kuhn says that the criteria of choice between theories (even within normal science, where hermeneutic problems may not yet arise) "function not as rules, which determine choice, but as values, which influence it" (p. 331). Most of his critics would agree even to this, but they would insist that the crucial question is whether we can find a range of specifically *scientific* values which should affect such choice, as opposed to "extraneous considerations" (the impact of science on theology, the future of life on earth, and the like) which should not be allowed to enter the "deliberative process." The criteria themselves Kuhn identifies as "accuracy, consistency, scope, simplicity, and fruitfulness" (p. 322)—a more or less standard list—and we might be tempted to say that it would be "unscientific" to permit any values save these to influence our choice. But the trade-offs between satisfaction of these various criteria provide room for endless rational debate. As Kuhn says:

Though the historian can always find men—Priestly, for instance—who were unreasonable to resist [a new theory]

10 Kuhn, *Essential Tension*, p. 326.

for as long as they did, he will not find a point at which resistance becomes illogical or unscientific.[11]

But can we then find a way of saying that the considerations advanced against the Copernican theory by Cardinal Bellarmine—the scriptural descriptions of the fabric of the heavens—*were* "illogical or unscientific?"[12] This, perhaps, is the point at which the battle lines between Kuhn and his critics can be drawn most sharply. Much of the seventeenth century's notion of what it was to be a "philosopher," and much of the Enlightenment's notion of what it was to be "rational," turns on Galileo's being absolutely right and the church absolutely wrong. To suggest that there is room for rational disagreement here—not simply for a black-and-white struggle between reason and superstition—is to endanger the very notion of "philosophy." For it endangers the notion of finding "a method for finding truth" which takes Galilean and Newtonian mechanics as paradigmatic.[13] A whole complex of mutually reinforcing ideas—philosophy as a methodological discipline distinct from the sciences, epistemology as the provision of commensuration, rationality as possible only on the common ground which makes possible commensuration—seems endangered if the question about Bellarmine is answered in the negative.

Kuhn does not give an explicit answer to the question, but his writings provide an arsenal of argument in favor of a negative answer. In any case, a negative answer is implied

[11] Kuhn, *Structure of Scientific Revolutions*, 2d ed., p. 159.

[12] The historical role of Bellarmine's sophisticated objections to Copernican theories is described by Giorgio de Santillana in *The Crime of Galileo* (Chicago, 1955). The significance of Bellarmine's position is discussed by Michael Polanyi in *Personal Knowledge* (Chicago, 1958).

[13] Mechanics was taken as paradigmatic in a double sense by the founders of "modern philosophy." On the one hand, "the method of finding truth" had to be the one which Newton followed, or at least one which would come up with Newtonian results. On the other hand, in such writers as Locke, Newtonian mechanics was a model for the mechanics of "inner space" (the "para-mechanical" mental operations satirized by Reid and Ryle).

by the argument of the present book. The crucial consideration is whether we know how to draw a line between science and theology such that getting the heavens right is a "scientific" value, and preserving the church, and the general cultural structure of Europe, is an "unscientific" value.[14] The argument that we do not centers around the claim that the lines between disciplines, subject matters, parts of culture, are themselves endangered by novel substantive suggestions. This argument can be put in terms of the scope of the criterion of "scope"—one of the standard desiderata for theories listed above. Bellarmine thought the scope of Copernicus's theory was smaller than might be thought. When he suggested that perhaps Copernican theory was really just an ingenious heuristic device for, say, navigational purposes and other sorts of practically oriented celestial reckoning, he was admitting that the theory was, within its proper limits, accurate, consistent, simple, and perhaps even fruitful. When he said that it should not be thought of as having wider scope than this he defended his view by saying that we had excellent independent (scriptural) evidence for believing that the heavens were roughly Ptolemaic. Was his evidence brought in from another sphere, and was his proposed restriction of scope thus "unscientific"? What determines that Scripture is *not* an excellent source of evidence for the way the heavens are set up? Lots of things, notably the Enlightenment's decision that Christianity was mostly just priestcraft. But what were

14 Another example of the same sort is the question raised about "objectivity" by Marxist critics of the traditional distinctions between areas of culture. See, for example, Herbert Marcuse, *One-Dimensional Man* (Boston, 1964), chaps. 6-7. More concretely, we can ask whether there is a clear way of separating out the "scientific" value of getting the heritability of intelligence right from the "political" value of discouraging racism. I think that Marcuse is right in saying that most of the ("bourgeois") intellectual apparatus of the Enlightenment is required to make this distinction. Unlike Marcuse, however, I would hope that we might retain the distinction even after discarding one piece of the apparatus—epistemologically centered "foundational" philosophy.

Bellarmine's contemporaries—who mostly thought Scripture to be indeed the word of God—supposed to say to Bellarmine? What they did say, among other things, was that adherence to Scripture could be disjoined from adherence to various adventitious (e.g., Aristotelian and Ptolemaic) notions which had been used to interpret Scripture. (This was the sort of thing nineteenth-century liberal divines were later to say in connection with Genesis and Darwin.) Were all these arguments about how liberal one's scriptural hermeneutics might legitimately be beside the point? They were attempts to limit, so to speak, the scope of Scripture (and thus of the church)—the opposite reaction to Bellarmine's own attempt to limit the scope of Copernicus. So the question about whether Bellarmine (and, perforce, Galileo's defenders) was bringing in extraneous "unscientific" considerations seems to be a question about whether there is some antecedent way of determining the relevance of one statement to another, some "grid" (to use Foucault's term) which determines what sorts of evidence there *could* be for statements about the movements of planets.

Obviously, the conclusion I wish to draw is that the "grid" which emerged in the later seventeenth and eighteenth centuries was not there to be appealed to in the early seventeenth century, at the time that Galileo was on trial. No conceivable epistemology, no study of the nature of human knowledge, could have "discovered" it before it was hammered out. The notion of what it was to be "scientific" was in the process of being formed. If one endorses the values—or, perhaps, the ranking of competing values—common to Galileo and Kant, then indeed Bellarmine was being "unscientific." But, of course, almost all of us (including Kuhn, though perhaps not including Feyerabend) are happy to endorse them. We are the heirs of three hundred years of rhetoric about the importance of distinguishing sharply between science and religion, science and politics, science and art, science and philosophy, and so on. This rhetoric has formed the culture of Europe. It made us what we are today. We are fortunate that no little perplexity within epistemology, or within the historiography of science, is enough to defeat it. But to proclaim our loyalty to these distinctions is not to say that there are "objective" and "rational" standards for adopting them. Galileo, so to speak, won the argument, and we all stand on the common ground of the "grid" of relevance and irrelevance which "modern philosophy" developed as a consequence of that victory. But what could show that the Bellarmine-Galileo issue "differs in kind" from the issue between, say, Kerensky and Lenin, or that between the Royal Academy (*circa* 1910) and Bloomsbury?

I can explain the notion of "difference in kind" which is in question here by reverting to the notion of commensurability. The desired difference is one which would permit us to say that any reasonable disinterested observer of the Bellarmine-Galileo controversy, taking all the relevant considerations into account, would come down on Galileo's side, whereas reasonable men still differ about the other issues I just mentioned. But this, of course, just brings us back around to the question of whether the values Bellarmine invoked were properly "scientific," whether his attitude counts as "disinterested," and his evidence as "relevant." At this point, it seems to me, we would do well to abandon the notion of certain values ("rationality," "disinterestedness") floating free of the educational and institutional patterns of the day. We can just say that Galileo was *creating* the notion of "scientific values" as he went along, that it was a splendid thing that he did so, and that the question of whether he was "rational" in doing so is out of place.

As Kuhn says in connection with a smaller, though obviously related issue, we cannot differentiate scientific communities by "subject matter," but rather by "examining patterns of education and communication."[15] To know

15 Kuhn, *Essential Tension*, p. xvi.

what counts as relevant to choice between theories about a certain subject is, in periods of normal inquiry, to belong to what Kuhn calls a "disciplinary matrix." In periods when the relevant community of inquirers is in question, in which the lines between "learned men," "mere empirics," and kooks (or, to alter the example, between "serious political thinkers" and "revolutionary pamphleteers") are getting fuzzy, the question of relevance is up for grabs. We cannot determine relevance by focusing on subject matter and saying, for example, "Don't bother with what Scripture said God did, just look at the planets and see what *they* do." *Mere* looking at the planets will be of no help in choosing our model of the heavens, any more than *mere* reading of Scripture. In 1550 a certain set of considerations was relevant to "rational" views on astronomy, and by 1750 a largely different set of considerations was relevant. This change in what was thought relevant can be seen, by hindsight, as drawing proper distinctions among what was really there in the world ("discovering" that astronomy was an autonomous sphere of scientific inquiry), or it can be seen as a shift in cultural climate. It does not greatly matter which way we see it, as long as we are clear that the change was not brought about by "rational argument" in some sense of "rational" in which, for example, the changes lately brought about in regard to society's attitude toward slavery, abstract art, homosexuals, or endangered species, would *not* count as "rational."

To sum up the line I am taking about Kuhn and his critics: the controversy between them is about whether science, as the discovery of what is really out there in the world, differs in its patterns of argumentation from discourses for which the notion of "correspondence to reality" seems less apposite (e.g., politics and literary criticism). Logical-empiricist philosophy of science, and the whole epistemological tradition since Descartes, has wanted to say that the procedure for attaining accurate representations in the Mirror of Nature differs in certain deep ways from the procedure for attaining agreement about "practical" or "aesthetic" matters. Kuhn gives us reason to say that there is no deeper difference than that between what happens in "normal" and in "abnormal" discourse. That distinction cuts across the distinction between science and nonscience. The fierce indignation with which Kuhn's work was greeted[16] was natural, for the ideals of the Enlightenment not only are our most precious cultural heritage but are in danger of disappearance as totalitarian states swallow up more and more of humanity. But the fact that the Enlightenment ran together the ideal of the autonomy of science from theology and politics with the image of scientific theory as Mirror of Nature is not a reason for preserving this confusion. The grid of relevance and irrelevance which we inherit almost intact from the eighteenth century will be more attractive when it is no longer tied to this image. Shopworn mirror-metaphors are of no help in keeping intact the inheritance—both moral and scientific—of Galileo.

3. Objectivity as Correspondence and as Agreement

Kuhn's critics have helped perpetuate the dogma that only where there is correspondence to reality is there the possibility of rational agreement, in a special sense of "rational" of which science is the paradigm. This confusion is aided by our use of "objective" to mean both "characterizing the view which would be agreed upon as a result of

---

16 The ferocity was found, however, mainly among professional philosophers. Kuhn's description of how science works was no shock to the scientists whose rationality the philosophers were concerned to protect. But the philosophers combined a professional attachment to mirror-metaphors with an understanding of the central role these metaphors had played in the Enlightenment, and thus in making possible the institutional basis for modern science. They were right in seeing that Kuhn's criticism of the tradition went deep, and that the ideology which had protected the rise of modern science was in danger. They were wrong in thinking that the institutions still needed the ideology.

argument undeflected by irrelevant considerations" and "representing things as they really are." The two are largely coextensive, and for nonphilosophical purposes no trouble arises from running them together. But if we begin to take seriously questions like "In just what sense is Goodness out there waiting to be represented accurately as a result of rational argument on moral questions?" or "In just what sense were there physical features of reality capable of being represented accurately only by differential equations, or tensors, before people thought of so representing them?" then tension between these two notions begins to arise. We have Plato to thank for the first sort of question and idealism and pragmatism to thank for the second sort. Neither question is answerable. Our natural inclination to return a robust "In no sense" to the first and an equally robust "In the fullest possible and most straightforward sense" to the second will be of no help in getting rid of these questions if we still feel the need to *justify* answers to such questions by constructing epistemological and metaphysical theories.

Since Kant, the principal employment of such theories has been to support intuitions concerning the subjective-objective distinction—either attempts to show that nothing outside of natural science counts as "objective" or attempts to apply this honorific term to morals, or politics, or poems. Metaphysics, as the attempt to find out what one can be objective about, is forced to ask about the similarities and differences among, for example, the discovery (as a result of finally resolving a long-standing moral dilemma) of a new article of the Moral Law, the discovery (by mathematicians) of a new sort of number or of a new set of spaces, the discovery of quantum indeterminacy, and the discovery that the cat is on the mat. The latter discovery—a homely *point d'appui* for the notions of "contact with reality," "truth as correspondence" and "accuracy of representation"—is the standard against which the others are compared in point of objectivity. The metaphysician must thus worry about the respects in which values, numbers, and wave packages resemble cats. The epistemologist must worry about the respects in which more interesting statements share the objectivity possessed by that triumph of mirroring—the appropriate utterance of "The cat is on the mat." In the view which follows from epistemological behaviorism, there is no interesting way to discover whether, for example, there is a Moral Law to be corresponded to. The fact that, for example, "the moral standards entailed by the nature of man" are more at home in Aristotle's hylomorphic universe than in Newton's mechanistic one is not a reason for thinking that there is or is not an "objective" Moral Law. Nor could anything else be. The trouble with metaphysics, just as the positivists said, is that nobody feels clear about what would count as a satisfactory argument within it, although, of course, the same goes for the "impure" philosophy of language which the positivists practiced (e.g., Quine's thesis of the "non-factuality" of the intentional). In the view that I am recommending, we might, in an imaginary age in which consensus in these areas was almost complete, view morality, physics, and psychology as equally "objective." We might then relegate the more debatable areas of literary criticism, chemistry, and sociology to the realm of the "non-cognitive," or "interpret them operationalistically," or "reduce" them to one or another "objective" discipline. The application of such honorifics as "objective" and "cognitive" is never anything more than an expression of the presence of, or the hope for, agreement among inquirers.

Although it will involve some repetition of what has been said above, I think that the debate between Kuhn and his critics is worth taking up yet again in the context of a discussion of the "objective-subjective" distinction, simply because the grip of this distinction is so very powerful, and so charged with moral feeling. Once again, this moral feeling is a consequence of the (entirely justified) notion that the preservation of the values of the Enlightenment is our

335

best hope. So in this section I shall try once again to cut the links which connect these values with the image of the Mirror of Nature.

It is convenient to begin with Kuhn's own way of dealing with the claim that his view opens the floodgates to "subjectivity." He says:

> "Subjective" is a term with several established uses: in one of these it is opposed to "objective," in another to "judgmental." When my critics describe the idiosyncratic features to which I appeal as subjective, they resort, erroneously I think, to the second of these senses. When they complain that I deprive science of objectivity, they conflate that second sense of subjective with the first.[17]

In the sense in which "subjective features" are nonjudgmental, they are, Kuhn continues, "matters of taste"—the sort of thing nobody bothers to discuss, simple reports of one's state of mind. But, of course, the worth of a poem or a person is not, in this sense, a matter of taste. So, Kuhn can say, the worth of a scientific theory is a matter of "judgment, not taste" in the same sense.

This reply to the charge of "subjectivity" is useful as far as it goes, but it does not reach the deeper fear behind the charge. This is the fear that there really is no middle ground between matters of taste and matters capable of being settled by a previously statable algorithm. The philosopher who sees no such middle ground is, I think, reasoning roughly as follows:

> 1. All statements describe either internal states of human beings (their Glassy Essence, the possibly clouded Mirror) or states of external reality (nature).
> 2. We can tell which statements are which by seeing which we know how to get universal agreement on.
> 3. So the possibility of perpetual disagreement is an indication that, no matter how rational debate may seem to

[17] Kuhn, *Essential Tension*, p. 336.

336

be, there is really nothing to debate about—since the subject can only be internal states.

This course of reasoning, shared by Platonists and positivists, produced in the latter the notion that by "analyzing" sentences we can discover whether they are indeed about the "subjective" or the "objective"—where "analysis" means finding out whether there is general agreement among sane and rational men on what would count as confirming their truth. Within traditional epistemology, this latter notion has only rarely been seen for what it is: an admission that our only usable notion of "objectivity" is "agreement" rather than mirroring. Even, for example, in Ayer's refreshingly frank remark that "we define a rational belief as one which is arrived at by the methods which we now consider reliable,"[18] the notion of "reliability" still functions as a hint that we can only be rational by corresponding to the real. Not even his equally frank admission that all the privileged representations in the world will nevertheless permit a man to "sustain his convictions in the face of apparently hostile evidence if he is prepared to make the necessary *ad hoc* assumptions" (p. 95) is enough to defeat Ayer's conviction that in separating the "empirical" from the "emotive" and the "analytic" he is separating "truth about the world" from something else. This is because Ayer, like Plato, adds to the above chain of reasoning the further, foundationalist premise:

4. We are able to eliminate the possibility of perpetual, undecidable rational disagreement only in those areas where unquestioned links to external reality provide a common ground for the disputants.

The claim that where we can find no unquestioned links with (e.g., privileged representations of) the objects to be mirrored there is no possibility of an algorithm, conjoined with the claim that where there is no possibility of an algo-

---

18 A. J. Ayer, *Language, Truth and Logic* (New York, 1970), p. 100.

rithm there can be only the *appearance* of rational agreement, leads to the conclusion that the absence of relevant privileged representations shows that we have only "a matter of taste." Kuhn is right in saying that this is a long way from the ordinary notion of "taste," but, like the equally unordinary notion of truth as something which need have nothing to do with agreement, it has a long history within philosophy.[19] That history has to be understood if one is to see why such bland historiographical suggestions as Kuhn's should trouble the deeper unconscious levels of the trained philosophical mind.

Perhaps the best way to deal with the charge of "subjectivism" brought against Kuhn is to make a distinction between senses of "subjective" other than the one he himself made in the passage I quoted. We can distinguish two senses of "subjective" which will stand roughly opposite each of the two senses of "objective" distinguished earlier. "Objectivity" in the first sense was a property of theories which, having been thoroughly discussed, are chosen by a consensus of rational discussants. By contrast, a "subjective" consideration is one which has been, or would be, or should be, set aside by rational discussants—one which is seen to be, or should be seen to be, irrelevant to the subject matter of the theory. To say that someone is bringing in "subjective" considerations to a discussion where objectivity is wanted is, roughly, to say that he is bringing in considerations

[19] Kant built this notion of truth about reality into German philosophy (and, a fortiori, into philosophy as a professionalized discipline which looked to the German universities for its model). He did so by distinguishing mere coping with phenomena from intellectually intuiting noumena. He also built the distinction between cognitive and aesthetic judgment, and the distinction between the latter and mere taste, into European culture. For purposes of the present dispute, however, his distinction between "aesthetic judgment" which can be right or wrong and "taste" which cannot drops out. Kuhn's critics could more cautiously (but, by their own lights, equally devastatingly) criticize him for making theory-choice in science a matter of aesthetic rather than cognitive judgment.

which the others think beside the point. If he presses these *outré* considerations, he is turning normal inquiry into abnormal discourse—he is being either "kooky" (if he loses his point) or "revolutionary" (if he gains it). For a consideration to be subjective, in this sense, is simply for it to be unfamiliar. So judging subjectivity is as hazardous as judging relevance.

In a more traditional sense of "subjective," on the other hand, "subjective" contrasts with "corresponding to what is out there," and thus means something like "a product only of what is in here" (in the heart, or in the "confused" portion of the mind which does not contain privileged representations and thus does not accurately reflect what is out there). In this sense "subjective" is associated with "emotional" or "fantastical," for our hearts and our imaginations are idiosyncratic, while our intellects are, at their best, identical mirrors of the self-same external objects. Here we get a linkup with "matters of taste," since the state of our emotions at a given moment (of which our unconsidered momentary reaction to a work of art is an example) is indeed undebatable. We have privileged access to what goes on inside us. In this way, the tradition since Plato has run together the "algorithm versus no algorithm" distinction with the "reason versus passion" distinction. The various ambiguities of "objective" and "subjective" illustrate the way in which the confusion can develop. If it were not for the traditional linkage of these distinctions, a historian of inquiry who emphasized similarities between the controversies of scientists and those of literary critics would not have been construed as endangering our minds by upgrading our hearts.

Kuhn himself, however, occasionally makes too large concessions to the tradition, particularly when he suggests that there is a serious and unresolved problem about why the scientific enterprise has been doing so nicely lately. Thus he says:

Even those who have followed me this far will want to know how a value-based enterprise of the sort I have described can develop as a science does, repeatedly producing powerful new techniques for prediction and control. To that question, unfortunately, I have no answer at all, but that is only another way of saying that I make no claim to have solved the problem of induction. If science did progress by virtue of some shared and binding algorithm of choice, I would be equally at a loss to explain its success. The lacuna is one I feel acutely, but its presence does not differentiate my position from the tradition.[20]

As I have argued in connection with Putnam's "metaphysical realism" in the previous chapter, the lacuna should *not* be felt acutely. We should not regret our inability to perform a feat which no one has any idea of how to perform. The notion that we are faced by a challenge to fill this lacuna is one more result of hypostatizing the Platonic *focus imaginarius*—truth as disjoined from agreement—and allowing the gap between oneself and that unconditional ideal to make one feel that one does not yet understand the conditions of one's existence.

In the view I am advocating, the question "Why, if science is merely . . . , does it produce powerful new techniques for prediction and control?" is like the question

[20] Kuhn, *Essential Tension*, pp. 332-333. There are other passages in that book in which, I should argue, Kuhn grants too much to the epistemological tradition. One is at p. xxiii, where he expresses the hope that philosophers' understanding of "reference determination and translation" will help clarify the issues. Another is p. 14, where he suggests that the philosophy of science has a quite distinct mission from the hermeneutic activities of the historian of science: "Philosophy's business is with rational reconstruction, and it need preserve only those elements of its subject essential to science as sound knowledge." This passage seems to me to preserve intact the myth that there is something called "the nature of sound knowledge" for philosophers to describe, an activity quite distinct from description of what counts as justification within the various disciplinary matrices constituting the culture of the day.

"Why, if the change in moral consciousness in the West since 1750 is merely . . . , has it been able to accomplish so much for human freedom?" We can fill the first blank with "adherence to the following binding algorithm . . ." or with "a succession of Kuhnian institutionalized disciplinary matrices." We can fill the second with "the application of secular thought to moral issues" or "the guilty conscience of the bourgeoisie" or "changes in the emotional constitution of those who control the levers of power," or with a lot of other phrases. In no case does anyone know what might count as a good answer. Retrospectively, "Whiggishly," and "realistically" we will always be able to see the achievement desired (prediction and control of nature, emancipation of the oppressed) as the result of getting a clearer view of what is there (the electrons, the galaxies, the Moral Law, human rights). But these are never the sorts of explanations philosophers want. They are, in Putnam's phrase, "internal" explanations—explanations which satisfy our need to tell a coherent causal story about our interactions with the world, but not our transcendental need to underwrite our mirroring by showing how it approximates to truth. To "solve the problem of induction," in the sense Kuhn intends, would be like "solving the problem of fact and value"; both problems survive only as names for a certain inarticulate dissatisfaction. They are the sort of problems which cannot be formulated within "normal philosophy"; all that happens is that this or that technical gimmick is occasionally labeled a "solution" to such a problem, in the vague hope of establishing contact with the past, or with eternity.

What we need, rather than a solution to "the problem of induction," is the ability to think about science in such a way that its being a "value-based enterprise" occasions no surprise. All that hinders us from doing so is the ingrained notion that "values" are "inner" whereas "facts" are "outer" and that it is as much a mystery how, beginning with values, we could produce bombs as how, beginning with private inner episodes, we could avoid bumping into things. Here we come round once again to the bugbear of "idealism" and the notion that the search for an algorithm goes hand in hand with a "realistic" approach to science whereas a relaxation into the merely hermeneutic method of the historian sells the pass to the idealist. Whenever it is suggested that the distinctions between theory and practice, fact and value, method and conversation be relaxed, an attempt to make the world "malleable to human will" is suspected. This produces, yet again, the positivist claim that we must either make a clear distinction between the "noncognitive" and the "cognitive," or else "reduce" the former to the latter. For the third possibility—reducing the latter to the former —seems to "spiritualize" nature by making it like history or literature, something which men have *made* rather than something they *find*. It is the third option that Kuhn seems, to some of his critics, to be suggesting.

This renewed attempt to see Kuhn as verging upon "idealism" is, however, a muddled way of reiterating the claim that something like (4) above is true—that we must see scientists as "in touch with external reality" and therefore able to reach rational agreement by means not available to politicians and poets. The muddle consists in suggesting that Kuhn, by "reducing" the methods of scientists to those of politicians, has "reduced" the "found" world of neutrons to the "made" world of social relationships. Here again we find the notion that whatever cannot be discovered by a machine programmed with the appropriate algorithm cannot exist "objectively," and thus must be somehow a "human creation." In the following section, I shall try to bring together what I have been saying about objectivity with some themes from earlier portions of this book in the hope of showing that the distinction between epistemology and hermeneutics should not be thought of as paralleling a distinction between what is "out there" and what we "make up."

342

4. SPIRIT AND NATURE

It must be confessed that the notion that there is a special set of methods appropriate for the "soft" disciplines—the *Geisteswissenschaften*—does have historical links with idealism. As Apel says, the present opposition between analytic philosophy and "hermeneutics" as philosophical strategies seems natural since

> the metaphysics of the spirit and of the subject in 19th-century Idealism, which should be considered the foundations of the *Geisteswissenschaften* (although the latter certainly put more emphasis upon material research) are taken by the later Wittgenstein as a "disease" of language together with all other concepts of metaphysics in Western philosophy.[21]

The notion that the empirical self could be turned over to the sciences of nature, but that the transcendental self, which constitutes the phenomenal world and (perhaps) functions as a moral agent, could not, has indeed done as much as anything else to make the spirit-nature distinction meaningful. So this metaphysical distinction lurks in the background of every discussion of the relations between the *Geistes-* and the *Naturwissenschaften*. The picture is further complicated by the vague notion that those who like to talk about "hermeneutics" are proposing to substitute a new kind of method (a suspiciously "soft" kind) for some other method (the "scientific method," say, or perhaps "philosophical analysis"). In this section I hope to show that hermeneutics, as discourse about as-yet-incommensurable discourses, has no particular connection with either (a) the "mind" side of Cartesian dualism, or (b) the "constituting" side of the Kantian distinction between the constituting and structuring faculty of spontaneity and the passive faculty of receptivity, or (c) the notion of a method for discovering

21 Karl-Otto Apel, *Analytic Philosophy of Language and the Geisteswissenschaften* (Dordrecht, 1967), p. 35. Cf. also p. 53.

343

the truth of sentences which competes with the normal methods pursued in extra-philosophical disciplines. (Nonetheless, I think that this limited and purified sense of "hermeneutics" I am employing *does* link up with the use of the term by such writers as Gadamer, Apel, and Habermas. I shall try to bring out the connections in the following chapter.)

The dread of "falling into idealism" which afflicts those tempted by Kuhn to reject standard notions of philosophy of science (and more generally of epistemology) is enhanced by the thought that if the study of science's search for truth about the physical universe is viewed hermeneutically it will be viewed as the activity of spirit—the faculty which *makes*—rather than as the application of the mirroring faculties, those which *find* what nature has already made. This latent romantic-classic opposition which lurks in the background of discussion of Kuhn is brought into the open by Kuhn's unhappy use (deprecated in section 2 above) of romantic phrases like "being presented with a new world," instead of the classic "using a new description for the world." In the view I want to recommend, nothing deep turns on the choice between these two phrases—between the imagery of making and of finding. They thus resemble the opposition between "objective" and "nonobjective," or "cognitive" and "noncognitive," which I discussed in the previous section. It is less paradoxical, however, to stick to the classic notion of "better describing what was already there" for physics. This is not because of deep epistemological or metaphysical considerations, but simply because, when we tell our Whiggish stories about how our ancestors gradually crawled up the mountain on whose (possibly false) summit we stand, we need to keep some things constant throughout the story. The forces of nature and the small bits of matter, as conceived by current physical theory, are good choices for this role. Physics is the paradigm of "finding" simply because it is hard (at least in the West) to tell a story of changing physical universes against the background of an unchanging Moral Law or poetic canon, but very easy to tell the reverse sort of story. Our tough-minded "naturalistic" sense that spirit is, if not reducible to nature, at least parasitic upon it, is no more than the insight that physics gives us a good background against which to tell our stories of historical change. It is not as if we had some deep insight into the nature of reality which told us that everything save atoms and the void was "by convention" (or "spiritual" or "made up"). Democritus's insight was that a story about the smallest bits of things forms a good background for stories about changes among things made of these bits. The acceptance of this genre of world-story (fleshed out successively by Lucretius, Newton, and Bohr) may be definatory of the West, but it is not a choice which could obtain, or which requires, epistemological or metaphysical guarantees.

Kuhnians should, I conclude, resist the temptation to dish the Whigs by talking of "different worlds." By giving up such phrases, they would not be conceding anything to the epistemological tradition. To say that the study of the history of science, like the study of the rest of history, must be hermeneutical, and to deny (as I, but not Kuhn, would) that there is something extra called "rational reconstruction" which can *legitimize* current scientific practice, is still not to say that the atoms, wave packages, etc., discovered by the physical scientists are creations of the human spirit. To buy in on the normal science of one's day in constructing the largest possible story to tell about the history of the race is not, unless one also buys the various Platonic dogmas mentioned in the previous section, to say that physics is "objective" in some way in which politics or poetry may not be. For the line between making and finding has nothing to do with the line between incommensurability and commensurability. Or, to put it another way, the sense in which man is a spiritual and not merely a natural being— the sense to which antireductionists like Alasdair MacIntyre, Charles Taylor, and Marjorie Grene have devoted attention —is not a sense in which he is a being who makes worlds. To

345

say, with Sartre, that man makes himself, and that he differs thereby from atoms and inkwells, is quite compatible with repudiating any suggestion that part of his self-creation consists in "constituting" atoms and inkwells. But the confusions among the romantic notion of man as self-creative, the Kantian notion of man as constituting a phenomenal world, and the Cartesian notion of man as containing a special immaterial ingredient need to be examined in some detail. This set of confusions is embodied in much discussion concerning the "nature of spirit," "the irreducibility of the person," the distinction between action and motion, and the distinction between the *Geistes-* and the *Naturwissenschaften*. Since the last distinction is supposedly coextensive with the distinction between hermeneutical and other methods, it is especially important to take it up in order to clarify the notion of hermeneutics which I am offering.

I shall begin unraveling this threefold confusion by taking up the claim that hermeneutics is peculiarly suited to "spirit" or to "the sciences of man," whereas some other method (that of the "objectivizing" and "positive" sciences) is appropriate to "nature." If we draw the line between epistemology and hermeneutics as I have been drawing it—as a contrast between discourse about normal and about abnormal discourse—then it seems clear that the two do not compete, but rather help each other out. Nothing is so valuable for the hermeneutical inquirer into an exotic culture as the discovery of an epistemology written within that culture. Nothing is so valuable for the determination of whether the possessors of that culture uttered any interesting truths (by—what else?—the standards of the normal discourse of our own time and place) than the hermeneutical discovery of how to translate them without making them sound like fools. So I suspect that this notion of competing methods derives from the view that the world comes divided into the areas which can, and those which cannot, be best described in the normal discourse (the "conceptual scheme," to use a pre-Davidsonian phrase) of our own culture. Specifically, this view suggests that people are somehow always going to be so slimy and slippery (Sartre's "viscousness") that they will escape "objective" explanation. But, once again, if one draws the hermeneutics-epistemology distinction as I want to draw it, there is no requirement that people should be more difficult to understand than things; it is merely that hermeneutics is only needed in the case of incommensurable discourses, and that people discourse whereas things do not. What makes the difference is not discourse versus silence, but incommensurable discourses versus commensurable discourses. As physicalists correctly point out, once we can figure out how to translate what is being said, there is no reason to think that the explanation of why it is being said should differ in kind (or proceed by different methods) from an explanation of locomotion or digestion. There is no metaphysical reason why human beings should be capable of saying incommensurable things, nor any guarantee that they will continue to do so. It is just our good fortune (from a hermeneutical point of view) or bad fortune (from an epistemological point of view) that they have done so in the past.

The traditional quarrel about the "philosophy of the social sciences" has proceeded generally as follows. One side has said that "explanation" (subsumption under predictive laws, roughly) presupposes, and cannot replace, "understanding." The other side has said that understanding simply *is* the ability to explain, that what their opponents call "understanding" is merely the primitive stage of groping around for some explanatory hypotheses. Both sides are quite right. Apel rightly notes that

the protagonists of "understanding" (i.e., of the *Geisteswissenschaften*) always attack the supporters of the theory of explanation (i.e., of the objective social or behavioral sciences) from behind—and vice versa. The

347

"objective scientists" point out that the results of "understanding" are only of pre-scientific, subjectively heuristic validity, and that they at least must be tested and supplemented by objective analytic methods. The protagonists of understanding, on the other hand, insist that the obtaining of any data in the social sciences—and therefore any objective testing of hypotheses—presupposes "actual understanding" . . . of meaning.[22]

Those who are suspicious of hermeneutics want to say that the fact that some beings talk is no reason to think they escape the great unified web of predictively powerful laws, for these laws can predict what they will say as well as what they will eat. Those who defend hermeneutics say that the question of what they will say has two parts—what sounds or inscriptions they make (which might become predictable enough, perhaps through neurophysiology), and what these *mean*, which is something quite different. At this point, the natural move for the defenders of "unified science" is to say that it is *not* different, since there are procedures for translating any significant utterance into a single language—the language of unified science itself. Given a single language which contains everything that everybody could ever say (in the way in which Carnap attempted to put together such a language in the *Aufbau*), the question of which sentence of that language is being proffered by the language-user under investigation is no more "special" than the question of what he will have for dinner. Translation into the language of unified science is difficult, but the attempt to translate does not involve different techniques of theory-construction or theory-testing from the attempt to explain dietary habits.

In reply to this, defenders of hermeneutics should just say that, as a matter of brute fact rather than of metaphysical necessity, there is no such thing as the "language of unified science." We have not *got* a language which will serve as a

22 Ibid., p. 30.

permanent neutral matrix for formulating all good explanatory hypotheses, and we have not the foggiest notion of
how to get one. (This is compatible with saying that we *do*
have a neutral, if unhelpful, observation language.) So
epistemology—as the attempt to render all discourses commensurable by translating them into a preferred set of terms
—is unlikely to be a useful strategy. The reason is not that
"unified science" works only for one metaphysical realm
and not for another, but that the Whiggish assumption that
we have got such a language blocks the road of inquiry. We
might always want to change the language in which we do
our explaining. In particular, we might do this because we
have found out how to translate a language spoken by the
subjects of our explanation. But this would be just a special
case of the permanent possibility of someone's having a better idea. Understanding the language spoken by the subjects,
grasping the explanations they give of why they are doing
this and that, may be helpful or may not. In the case of
people who are particularly stupid, or psychotic, we rightly
wave aside their explanations. We attribute intentions and
actions to them in terms they do not accept and may not
even understand. The familiar claim that a speaker's description of himself usually needs to be taken into account
in determining what action he is performing is sound
enough. But that description may perfectly well be set
aside. The privilege attached to it is moral, rather than
epistemic. The difference between his description and ours
may mean, for example, that he should not be tried under
our laws. It does not mean that he cannot be explained by
our science.

To say that we cannot understand a foreign culture if
we insist on Whiggishly interpreting it as holding "too
many" of our own beliefs and desires is just a generalization
of the Kuhnian point that we cannot understand past scientists if we insist on doing the same thing to them. This
can itself be generalized to the claim that we should not
assume that the vocabulary used so far will work on every-

thing else that turns up. The problem is not that spirits are inherently resistant to being predicted, but simply that there is no reason to think (and much reason not to think) that our own spirit has now got hold of the best vocabulary for formulating hypotheses which will explain and predict all the other spirits (or, perhaps, the other bodies). This point is made by Charles Taylor, who puts the question as follows:

> . . . we might be so scandalized by the prospect of such a hermeneutical science that we will want to go back to the verification model. Why can we not take our understanding of meaning as part of the logic of discovery, as the logical empiricists suggest for our unformalizable insights, and still found our science on the exactness of our predictions?[23]

and answers it by listing three reasons why "such exact prediction is radically impossible." He says that

> the third and most fundamental reason for the impossibility of hard prediction is that man is a self-defining animal. With changes in his self-definition go changes in what man is, such that he has to be understood in different terms. But the conceptual mutations in human history can and frequently do produce conceptual webs which are incommensurable, that is, where the terms can't be defined in relation to a common stratum of expressions. (p. 49)

The point that what interferes with predicting the behavior of inhabitants of the unfamiliar culture is simply the incommensurability of their language seems to me exactly right, but I think Taylor proceeds to obscure his own point when he goes on to say:

> The success of prediction in the natural sciences is bound up with the fact that all states of the system, past and

[23] Charles Taylor, "Interpretation and the Sciences of Man," *Review of Metaphysics* 25 (1971), p. 48.

future, can be described in the same range of concepts, as values, say, of the same variables. Hence all future states of the solar system can be characterized, as past ones are, in the language of Newtonian mechanics. . . . Only if past and future are brought under the same conceptual net can one understand the states of the latter as some function of the states of the former, and hence predict.

This conceptual unity is vitiated in the sciences of man by the fact of conceptual innovation which in turn alters human reality. (p. 49)

Here Taylor reinstates the notion of man as a being who changes from the inside by finding better (or, at least, novel) ways of describing, predicting, and explaining himself. Nonhuman beings, as mere *êtres-en-soi*, do not get changed from inside but are simply described, predicted, and explained in a better vocabulary. This way of putting it leads us back into the bad old metaphysical notion that the universe is made up of two kinds of things. The sense in which human beings alter themselves by redescribing themselves is no more metaphysically exciting or mysterious than the sense in which they alter themselves by changing their diet, their sexual partners, or their habitation. It is just the same sense: viz., new and more interesting sentences become true of them. Taylor goes on to say that "the very terms in which the future will have to be characterized if we are to understand it properly are not all available to us at present" (p. 50), and he means this to hold only for human beings. But, for all we know, it may be that human creativity has dried up, and that in the future it will be the *non*human world which squirms out of our conceptual net. It might be the case that all future human societies will be (as a result, perhaps, of ubiquitous technocratic totalitarianism) humdrum variations on our own. But contemporary science (which already seems so hopeless for explaining acupuncture, the migration of butterflies, and so on) may soon come to seem as badly off as Aristotle's hylomorphism.

The line that Taylor is describing is not the line between the human and the nonhuman but between that portion of the field of inquiry where we feel rather uncertain that we have the right vocabulary at hand and that portion where we feel rather certain that we do. This *does*, at the moment, roughly coincide with the distinction between the fields of the *Geistes-* and the *Naturwissenschaften*. But this coincidence may be *mere* coincidence. In a sufficiently long perspective, man may turn out to be less δεινός than Sophocles thought him, and the elementary forces of nature more so than modern physicalists dream.

To see this point, it helps to bear in mind that there are plenty of occasions on which we do well simply to ignore the *pour-soi* of human beings. We do this in the case of particularly dull and conventional people, for example, whose every act and word are so predictable that we "objectivize" them without hesitation. Conversely, when we come up against something nonhuman which wriggles out of the conceptual net presently used, it is natural to start talking about an unknown language—to imagine, for example, the migrating butterflies having a language in which they describe features of the world for which Newtonian mechanics has no name. Or, if we do not go this far, we at least fall naturally into the notion that the Book of Nature has not yet been deciphered—that it no more contains "gravitation," say, than it contains "natural motion." The temptation is to anthropomorphize the nonhuman world, or some part of it, just as soon as it becomes clear that, as with the native of an exotic culture, or the genius whose talk is over our heads, we do not "speak the same language." Nature is whatever is so routine and familiar and manageable that we trust our own language implicitly. Spirit is whatever is so unfamiliar and unmanageable that we begin to wonder whether our "language" is "adequate" to it. Our wonder, stripped of mirror-imagery, is simply about whether somebody or something may not be dealing with the world in terms for which our language contains no ready equivalents. More simply still, it is just wonder about whether we do not need to change our vocabulary, and not just our assertions.

I said at the beginning of this chapter that hermeneutics is, roughly, a description of our study of the unfamiliar and epistemology is, roughly, a description of our study of the familiar. Given the somewhat strained interpretation I have just put upon "spirit" and "nature," I could now agree with the traditional view that hermeneutics describes our inquiry into spirit, whereas epistemology is a description of our inquiry into nature. But it would be better, I think, to drop the spirit-nature distinction altogether. As I have already said, this distinction runs together (a) the distinction between that which does not and that which does fit nicely under our present way of explaining and predicting things with (b) the distinction between something which unites all the various characteristics (enumerated in chapter one, section 3) which have, at one time or another, been taken to be distinctively human, and the rest of the world. It also runs both of these distinctions together with (c) the distinction (criticized in chapter three, section 3) between the faculty of spontaneity (the transcendental activity of constitution) and that of receptivity. (It does this by a conflation of our transcendental receptive faculty of sense with the field of sensory presentations which make up the "empirical self"—a conflation Kant himself was unable to avoid.) The result of running together spirit as romantic self-transcending creativity (always liable to begin talking in a way incommensurable with our present language) with spirit as identical with man's Glassy Essence (with all its metaphysical freedom from physical explanation), and with spirit as the "constitutor" of phenomenal reality, was the metaphysics of nineteenth-century German idealism. It was a fruitful set of assimilations, but one of its less fortunate results was the notion that philosophy had a special sphere of its own, quite apart from science. This assimilation helped keep alive the notion of "philosophy" as a discipline centered in epistemology. As long as the notion of spirit as transcendental constitutor (in the Kantian sense) was reinforced by the appeal of Cartesian dualism on the one hand and by that of romanticism on the other, the notion of a presiding discipline called "epistemology" or "transcendental philosophy"—reducible neither to *Naturwissenschaft* (psychophysiology) nor to *Geisteswissenschaft* (the sociology of knowledge)—could survive unquestioned. A further unfortunate legacy was the confusion of the need for nonmechanical translation (and more generally for imaginative concept-formation) with the "irreducibility of the constituting transcendental ego." This confusion kept the idealism-realism issue alive long after it should have been closed down, since the friends of hermeneutics thought (as the quotation from Apel at the beginning of this section illustrates) that something like idealism was the charter of their activity, whereas its enemies assumed that anyone who overtly practiced hermeneutics must be "antinaturalist," and must lack a proper sense of the brute exteriority of the physical universe.

To sum up what I want to say about the "irreducibility of the *Geisteswissenschaften*," then, let me offer the following theses:

Physicalism is probably right in saying that we shall someday be able, "in principle," to predict every movement of a person's body (including those of his larynx and his writing hand) by reference to microstructures within his body.

The danger to human freedom of such success is minimal, since the "in principle" clause allows for the probability that the determination of the initial conditions (the antecedent states of microstructures) will be too difficult to carry out except as an occasional pedagogical exercise. The torturers and the brainwashers are, in any case, already in as good a position to interfere with human freedom as they could wish; further scientific progress cannot improve their position.

The intuition behind the traditional distinction between nature and spirit, and behind romanticism, is that we can predict what noises will come from someone's mouth without knowing what they mean. Thus even if we could predict the sounds made by the community of scientific inquirers of the year 4000, we should not yet be in a position to join in their conversation. This intuition is quite correct.[24]

The fact that we can predict a noise without knowing what it means is just the fact that the necessary and sufficient microstructural conditions for the production of a noise will rarely be paralleled by a material equivalence between a statement in the language used for describing the microstructure and the statement expressed by the noise. This is not because anything is in principle unpredictable, much less because of an ontological divide between nature and spirit, but simply because of the difference between a language suitable for coping with neurons and one suitable for coping with people.

We can know how to reply to a cryptic remark from a different language-game without knowing or caring what sentence in our ordinary language-game is materially equivalent to that remark.[25] Producing commensurability by

[24] This is the kernel of truth disguised in the Quinean claim that the *Geisteswissenschaften* contain no "matters of fact." It is well expressed in a discussion of Quine by Raymond Geuss: "Even when we have a theory of nature which allows us to predict someone's verbal dispositions for all eternity, we still will not thereby understand what he *means*." ("Quine und die Unbestimmtheit der Ontologie," *Neue Hefte für Philosophie*, Heft 8 [1973], p. 44n.).

[25] That all languages are translatable into one another (for the Davidsonian reasons mentioned in chapter six) does not mean that such equivalences can be found (even "in principle"). It just means that we cannot make sense of the claim that there are more than temporary impediments to our know-how—the claim that something called a "different conceptual scheme" prevents us from learning how to converse with another language-user. Nor does it take away the intuition behind the false romantic claim that great poems are untranslatable. They are, of course, translatable; the problem is that the translations are not themselves great poems.

355

finding material equivalences between sentences drawn from different language-games is only one technique among others for coping with our fellow humans. When it does not work, we fall back on whatever does work—for example, getting the hang of a new language-game, and possibly forgetting our old one. This is the same technique we use when nonhuman nature shows itself recalcitrant to being predicted in the vocabulary of traditional science.

Hermeneutics is not "another way of knowing"—"understanding" as opposed to (predictive) "explanation." It is better seen as another way of coping. It would make for philosophical clarity if we just *gave* the notion of "cognition" to predictive science, and stopped worrying about "alternative cognitive methods." The word *knowledge* would not seem worth fighting over were it not for the Kantian tradition that to be a philosopher is to have a "theory of knowledge," and the Platonic tradition that action not based on knowledge of the truth of propositions is "irrational."

CHAPTER VIII

Philosophy Without Mirrors

1. HERMENEUTICS AND EDIFICATION

Our present notions of what it is to be a philosopher are so tied up with the Kantian attempt to render all knowledge-claims commensurable that it is difficult to imagine what philosophy without epistemology could be. More generally, it is difficult to imagine that any activity would be entitled to bear the name "philosophy" if it had nothing to do with knowledge—if it were not in some sense a theory of knowledge, or a method for getting knowledge, or at least a hint as to where some supremely important kind of knowledge might be found. The difficulty stems from a notion shared by Platonists, Kantians, and positivists: that man has an essence—namely, to discover essences. The notion that our chief task is to mirror accurately, in our own Glassy Essence, the universe around us is the complement of the notion, common to Democritus and Descartes, that the universe is made up of very simple, clearly and distinctly knowable things, knowledge of whose essences provides the master-vocabulary which permits commensuration of all discourses.

This classic picture of human beings must be set aside before epistemologically centered philosophy can be set aside. "Hermeneutics," as a polemical term in contemporary philosophy, is a name for the attempt to do so. The use of the term for this purpose is largely due to one book— Gadamer's *Truth and Method*. Gadamer there makes clear that hermeneutics is not a "method for attaining truth" which fits into the classic picture of man: "The hermeneutic phenomenon is basically not a problem of method at

357

all."[1] Rather, Gadamer is asking, roughly, what conclusions
might be drawn from the fact that we have to practice hermeneutics—from the "hermeneutic phenomenon" as a fact
about people which the epistemological tradition has tried
to shunt aside. "The hermeneutics developed here," he says,
"is not . . . a methodology of the human sciences, but an
attempt to understand what the human sciences truly are,
beyond their methodological self-consciousness, and what
connects them with the totality of our experience of the
world."[2] His book is a redescription of man which tries to
place the classic picture within a larger one, and thus to
"distance" the standard philosophical problematic rather
than offer a set of solutions to it.

For my present purposes, the importance of Gadamer's
book is that he manages to separate off one of the three
strands—the romantic notion of man as self-creative—in the
philosophical notion of "spirit" from the other two strands
with which it became entangled. Gadamer (like Heidegger,
to whom some of his work is indebted) makes no concessions either to Cartesian dualism or to the notion of "transcendental constitution" (in any sense which could be given
an idealistic interpretation).[3] He thus helps reconcile the
"naturalistic" point I tried to make in the previous chapter
—that the "irreducibility of the *Geisteswissenschaften*" is
not a matter of a metaphysical dualism—with our "existentialist" intuition that redescribing ourselves is the most

[1] Hans-Georg Gadamer, *Truth and Method* (New York, 1975), p. xi.
Indeed, it would be reasonable to call Gadamer's book a tract against
the very idea of method, where this is conceived of as an attempt at
commensuration. It is instructive to note the parallels between this
book and Paul Feyerabend's *Against Method*. My treatment of Gadamer is indebted to Alasdair MacIntyre; see his "Contexts of Interpretation," *Boston University Journal* 24 (1976), 41-46.

[2] Gadamer, *Truth and Method*, p. xiii.

[3] Cf. ibid., p. 15. "But we may recognize that *Bildung* is an element
of spirit without being tied to Hegel's philosophy of absolute spirit,
just as the insight into the historicity of consciousness is not tied to
his philosophy of world history."

important thing we can do. He does this by substituting the notion of *Bildung* (education, self-formation) for that of "knowledge" as the goal of thinking. To say that we become different people, that we "remake" ourselves as we read more, talk more, and write more, is simply a dramatic way of saying that the sentences which become true of us by virtue of such activities are often more important to us than the sentences which become true of us when we drink more, earn more, and so on. The events which make us able to say new and interesting things about ourselves are, in this nonmetaphysical sense, more "essential" to us (at least to us relatively leisured intellectuals, inhabiting a stable and prosperous part of the world) than the events which change our shapes or our standards of living ("remaking" us in less "spiritual" ways). Gadamer develops his notion of *wirkungsgeschichtliches Bewusstsein* (the sort of consciousness of the past which changes us) to characterize an attitude interested not so much in what is out there in the world, or in what happened in history, as in what we can get out of nature and history for our own uses. In this attitude, getting the facts right (about atoms and the void, or about the history of Europe) is merely propaedeutic to finding a new and more interesting way of expressing ourselves, and thus of coping with the world. From the educational, as opposed to the epistemological or the technological, point of view, the way things are said is more important than the possession of truths.[4]

---

[4] The contrast here is the same as that involved in the traditional quarrel between "classical" education and "scientific" education, mentioned by Gadamer in his opening section on "The Significance of the Humanist Tradition." More generally, it can be seen as an aspect of the quarrel between poetry (which cannot be omitted from the former sort of education) and philosophy (which, when conceiving of itself as super-science, would like to become foundational to the latter sort of education). Yeats asked the spirits (whom, he believed, were dictating *A Vision* to him through his wife's mediumship) why they had come. The spirits replied, "To bring you metaphors for poetry." A philosopher might have expected some hard facts about what it was like on the other side, but Yeats was not disappointed.

Since "education" sounds a bit too flat, and *Bildung* a bit too foreign, I shall use "edification" to stand for this project of finding new, better, more interesting, more fruitful ways of speaking. The attempt to edify (ourselves or others) may consist in the hermeneutic activity of making connections between our own culture and some exotic culture or historical period, or between our own discipline and another discipline which seems to pursue incommensurable aims in an incommensurable vocabulary. But it may instead consist in the "poetic" activity of thinking up such new aims, new words, or new disciplines, followed by, so to speak, the inverse of hermeneutics: the attempt to reinterpret our familiar surroundings in the unfamiliar terms of our new inventions. In either case, the activity is (despite the etymological relation between the two words) edifying without being constructive—at least if "constructive" means the sort of cooperation in the accomplishment of research programs which takes place in normal discourse. For edifying discourse is *supposed* to be abnormal, to take us out of our old selves by the power of strangeness, to aid us in becoming new beings.

The contrast between the desire for edification and the desire for truth is, for Gadamer, not an expression of a tension which needs to be resolved or compromised. If there is a conflict, it is between the Platonic-Aristotelian view that the *only* way to be edified is to know what is out there (to reflect the facts accurately—to realize our essence by knowing essences) and the view that the quest for truth is just one among many ways in which we might be edified. Gadamer rightly gives Heidegger the credit for working out a way of seeing the search for objective knowledge (first developed by the Greeks, using mathematics as a model) as one human project among others.[5] The point is, however, more vivid

[5] See the section called "The Overcoming of the Epistemological Problem . . ." in *Truth and Method*, pp. 214ff., and compare Martin Heidegger, *Being and Time*, trans. John Macquarrie and Edward Robinson (New York, 1962), sec. 32.

in Sartre, who sees the attempt to gain an objective knowledge of the world, and thus of oneself, as an attempt to avoid the responsibility for choosing one's project.[6] For Sartre, to say this is not to say that the desire for objective knowledge of nature, history, or anything else is bound to be unsuccessful, or even bound to be self-deceptive. It is merely to say that it presents a temptation to self-deception insofar as we think that, by knowing which descriptions within a given set of normal discourses apply to us, we thereby know ourselves. For Heidegger, Sartre, and Gadamer, objective inquiry is perfectly possible and frequently actual—the only thing to be said against it is that it provides only some, among many, ways of describing ourselves, and that some of these can hinder the process of edification.

To sum up this "existentialist" view of objectivity, then: objectivity should be seen as conformity to the norms of justification (for assertions and for actions) we find about us. Such conformity becomes dubious and self-deceptive only when seen as something more than this—namely, as a way of obtaining access to something which "grounds" current practices of justification in something else. Such a "ground" is thought to need no justification, because it has become so clearly and distinctly perceived as to count as a "philosophical foundation." This is self-deceptive not simply because of the general absurdity of ultimate justification's reposing upon the unjustifiable, but because of the more concrete absurdity of thinking that the vocabulary used by present science, morality, or whatever has some privileged attachment to reality which makes it *more* than just a further set of descriptions. Agreeing with the naturalists that redescription is not "change of essence" needs to be followed up by abandoning the notion of "essence" altogether.[7]

---

6 See Jean-Paul Sartre, *Being and Nothingness*, trans. Hazel Barnes (New York, 1956), pt. two, chap. 3, sec. 5, and the "Conclusion" of the book.

7 It would have been fortunate if Sartre had followed up his remark that man is the being whose essence is to have no essence by saying

But the standard philosophical strategy of most naturalisms is to find some way of showing that our own culture has indeed got hold of the essence of man—thus making all new and incommensurable vocabularies merely "noncognitive" ornamentation.[8] The utility of the "existentialist" view is that, by proclaiming that we have no essence, it permits us to see the descriptions of ourselves we find in one of (or in the unity of) the *Naturwissenschaften* as on a par with the various alternative descriptions offered by poets, novelists, depth psychologists, sculptors, anthropologists, and mystics. The former are not privileged representations in virtue of the fact that (at the moment) there is more consensus in the sciences than in the arts. They are simply among the repertoire of self-descriptions at our disposal.

This point can also be put as an extrapolation from the commonplace that one cannot be counted as educated—*gebildet*—if one knows *only* the results of the normal *Naturwissenschaften* of the day. Gadamer begins *Truth and Method* with a discussion of the role of the humanist tradition in giving sense to the notion of *Bildung* as something having "no goals outside itself."[9] To give sense to such a notion we need a sense of the relativity of descriptive vocabularies to periods, traditions, and historical accidents. This is what the humanist tradition in education does, and what training in the results of the natural sciences cannot do. Given that sense of relativity, we cannot take the notion of "essence"

---

that this went for all other beings also. Unless this addition is made, Sartre will appear to be insisting on the good old metaphysical distinction between spirit and nature in other terms, rather than simply making the point that man is always free to choose new descriptions (for, among other things, himself).

[8] Dewey, it seems to me, is the one author usually classified as a "naturalist" who did not have this reductive attitude, despite his incessant talk about "scientific method." Dewey's peculiar achievement was to have remained sufficiently Hegelian not to think of natural science as having an inside track on the essences of things, while becoming sufficiently naturalistic to think of human beings in Darwinian terms.

[9] Gadamer, *Truth and Method*, p. 12.

seriously, nor the notion of man's task as the accurate representation of essences. The natural sciences, by themselves, leave us convinced that we know both what we are and what we can be—not just how to predict and control our behavior, but the limits of that behavior (and, in particular, the limits of our significant speech). Gadamer's attempt to fend off the demand (common to Mill and Carnap) for "objectivity" in the *Geisteswissenschaften* is the attempt to prevent education from being reduced to instruction in the results of normal inquiry. More broadly, it is the attempt to prevent abnormal inquiry from being viewed as suspicious solely because of its abnormality.

This "existentialist" attempt to place objectivity, rationality, and normal inquiry within the larger picture of our need to be educated and edified is often countered by the "positivist" attempt to distinguish learning facts from acquiring values. From the positivist point of view, Gadamer's exposition of *wirkungsgeschichtliche Bewusstsein* may seem little more than reiteration of the commonplace that even when we know all the objectively true descriptions of ourselves, we still may not know what to do with ourselves. From this point of view, *Truth and Method* (and chapters six and seven above) are just overblown dramatizations of the fact that entire complaince with all the demands for justification offered by normal inquiry would still leave us free to draw our own morals from the assertions so justified. But from the viewpoints of Gadamer, Heidegger, and Sartre, the trouble with the fact-value distinction is that it is contrived precisely to blur the fact that alternative descriptions are possible in addition to those offered by the results of normal inquiries.[10] It suggests that once "all the facts are in" nothing remains except "noncognitive" adoption of an attitude—a choice which is not rationally discussable. It disguises the fact that to use

---

[10] See Heidegger's discussion of "values" in *Being and Time*, p. 133, and Sartre's in *Being and Nothingness*, pt. two, chap. 1, sec. 4. Compare Gadamer's remarks on Weber (*Truth and Method*, pp. 461ff.).

one set of true sentences to describe ourselves is already to choose an attitude toward ourselves, whereas to use another set of true sentences is to adopt a contrary attitude. Only if we assume that there is a value-free vocabulary which renders these sets of "factual" statements commensurable can the positivist distinction between facts and values, beliefs and attitudes, look plausible. But the philosophical fiction that such a vocabulary is on the tips of our tongues is, from an educational point of view, disastrous. It forces us to pretend that we can split ourselves up into knowers of true sentences on the one hand and choosers of lives or actions or works of art on the other. These artificial diremptions make it impossible to get the notion of edification into focus. Or, more exactly, they tempt us to think of edification as having nothing to do with the rational faculties which are employed in normal discourse.

So Gadamer's effort to get rid of the classic picture of man-as-essentially-knower-of-essences is, among other things, an effort to get rid of the distinction between fact and value, and thus to let us think of "discovering the facts" as one project of edification among others. This is why Gadamer devotes so much time to breaking down the distinctions which Kant made among cognition, morality, and aesthetic judgment.[11] There is no way, as far as I can see, in which to *argue* the issue of whether to keep the Kantian "grid" in place or set it aside. There is no "normal" philosophical discourse which provides common commensurating ground for those who see science and edification as, respectively, "rational" and "irrational," and those who see the quest for objectivity as one possibility among others to be taken account of in *wirkungsgeschichtliche Bewusstsein*. If there is no such common ground, all we can do is to show how the other side

[11] See Gadamer's polemic against "the subjectivization of the aesthetic" in Kant's Third Critique (*Truth and Method*, p. 87) and compare Heidegger's remarks in "Letter on Humanism" on Aristotle's distinctions among physics, logic, and ethics (Heidegger, *Basic Writings*, ed. Krell [New York, 1976], p. 232).

looks from our own point of view. That is, all we can do is be hermeneutic about the opposition—trying to show how the odd or paradoxical or offensive things they say hang together with the rest of what they want to say, and how what they say looks when put in our own alternative idiom. This sort of hermeneutics with polemical intent is common to Heidegger's and Derrida's attempts to deconstruct the tradition.

2. SYSTEMATIC PHILOSOPHY AND EDIFYING PHILOSOPHY

The hermeneutic point of view, from which the acquisition of truth dwindles in importance, and is seen as a component of education, is possible only if we once stood at another point of view. Education has to start from acculturation. So the search for objectivity and the self-conscious awareness of the social practices in which objectivity consists are necessary first steps in becoming *gebildet*. We must first see ourselves as *en-soi*—as described by those statements which are objectively true in the judgment of our peers—before there is any point in seeing ourselves as *poursoi*. Similarly, we cannot be educated without finding out a lot about the descriptions of the world offered by our culture (e.g., by learning the results of the natural sciences). Later perhaps, we may put less value on "being in touch with reality" but we can afford that only after having passed through stages of implicit, and then explicit and self-conscious, conformity to the norms of the discourses going on around us.

I raise this banal point that education—even the education of the revolutionary or the prophet—needs to begin with acculturation and conformity merely to provide a cautionary complement to the "existentialist" claim that normal participation in normal discourse is merely one project, one way of being in the world. The caution amounts to saying that abnormal and "existential" discourse is always parasitic upon normal discourse, that the

365

possibility of hermeneutics is always parasitic upon the possibility (and perhaps upon the actuality) of epistemology, and that edification always employs materials provided by the culture of the day. To attempt abnormal discourse *de novo*, without being able to recognize our own abnormality, is madness in the most literal and terrible sense. To insist on being hermeneutic where epistemology would do —to make ourselves unable to view normal discourse in terms of its own motives, and able to view it only from within our own abnormal discourse—is not mad, but it does show a lack of education. To adopt the "existentialist" attitude toward objectivity and rationality common to Sartre, Heidegger, and Gadamer makes sense only if we do so in a conscious departure from a well-understood norm. "Existentialism" is an *intrinsically reactive* movement of thought, one which has point only in opposition to the tradition. I want now to generalize this contrast between philosophers whose work is essentially constructive and those whose work is essentially reactive. I shall thereby develop a contrast between philosophy which centers in epistemology and the sort of philosophy which takes its point of departure from suspicion about the pretensions of epistemology. This is the contrast between "systematic" and "edifying" philosophies.

In every sufficiently reflective culture, there are those who single out one area, one set of practices, and see it as the paradigm human activity. They then try to show how the rest of culture can profit from this example. In the mainstream of the Western philosophical tradition, this paradigm has been *knowing*—possessing justified true beliefs, or, better yet, beliefs so intrinsically persuasive as to make justification unnecessary. Successive philosophical revolutions within this mainstream have been produced by philosophers excited by new cognitive feats—e.g., the rediscovery of Aristotle, Galilean mechanics, the development of self-conscious historiography in the nineteenth century, Darwinian biology, mathematical logic. Thomas's use of

Aristotle to conciliate the Fathers, Descartes's and Hobbes's criticisms of scholasticism, the Enlightenment's notion that reading Newton leads naturally to the downfall of tyrants, Spencer's evolutionism, Carnap's attempt to overcome metaphysics through logic, are so many attempts to refashion the rest of culture on the model of the latest cognitive achievements. A "mainstream" Western philosopher typically says: Now that such-and-such a line of inquiry has had such a stunning success, let us reshape all inquiry, and all of culture, on its model, thereby permitting objectivity and rationality to prevail in areas previously obscured by convention, superstition, and the lack of a proper epistemological understanding of man's ability accurately to represent nature.

On the periphery of the history of modern philosophy, one finds figures who, without forming a "tradition," resemble each other in their distrust of the notion that man's essence is to be a knower of essences. Goethe, Kierkegaard, Santayana, William James, Dewey, the later Wittgenstein, the later Heidegger, are figures of this sort. They are often accused of relativism or cynicism. They are often dubious about progress, and especially about the latest claim that such-and-such a discipline has at last made the nature of human knowledge so clear that reason will now spread throughout the rest of human activity. These writers have kept alive the suggestion that, even when we have justified true belief about everything we want to know, we may have no more than conformity to the norms of the day. They have kept alive the historicist sense that this century's "superstition" was the last century's triumph of reason, as well as the relativist sense that the latest vocabulary, borrowed from the latest scientific achievement, may not express privileged representations of essences, but be just another of the potential infinity of vocabularies in which the world can be described.

The mainstream philosophers are the philosophers I shall call "systematic," and the peripheral ones are those I shall call "edifying." These peripheral, pragmatic philosophers are skeptical primarily *about systematic philosophy*, about the whole project of universal commensuration.[12] In our time, Dewey, Wittgenstein, and Heidegger are the great edifying, peripheral, thinkers. All three make it as difficult as possible to take their thought as expressing views on traditional philosophical problems, or as making constructive proposals for philosophy as a cooperative and progressive discipline.[13] They make fun of the classic picture of man, the picture which contains systematic philosophy, the search for universal commensuration in a final vocabulary. They hammer away at the holistic point that words take their meanings from other words rather than by virtue of their representative character, and the corollary that vocabularies acquire their privileges from the men who use them rather than from their transparency to the real.[14]

[12] Consider the passage from Anatole France's "Garden of Epicurus" which Jacques Derrida cites at the beginning of his "La Mythologie Blanche" (in *Marges de la Philosophie* [Paris, 1972], p. 250):

. . . the metaphysicians, when they make up a new language, are like knife-grinders who grind coins and medals against their stone instead of knives and scissors. They rub out the relief, the inscriptions, the portraits, and when one can no longer see on the coins Victoria, or Wilhelm, or the French Republic, they explain: these coins now have nothing specifically English or German or French about them, for we have taken them out of time and space; they now are no longer worth, say, five francs, but rather have an inestimable value, and the area in which they are a medium of exchange has been infinitely extended.

[13] See Karl-Otto Apel's comparison of Wittgenstein and Heidegger as having both "called into question Western metaphysics as a theoretical discipline" (*Transformation der Philosophie* [Frankfurt, 1973], vol. 1, p. 228). I have not offered interpretations of Dewey, Wittgenstein, and Heidegger in support of what I have been saying about them, but I have tried to do so in a piece on Wittgenstein called "Keeping Philosophy Pure" (*Yale Review* [Spring 1976], pp. 336-356), in "Overcoming the Tradition: Heidegger and Dewey" (*Review of Metaphysics* 30 [1976], 280-305), and in "Dewey's Metaphysics" in *New Studies in the Philosophy of John Dewey*, ed. Steven M. Cahn (Hanover, N.H., 1977).

[14] This Heideggerean point about language is spelled out at length

The distinction between systematic and edifying philosophers is not the same as the distinction between normal philosophers and revolutionary philosophers. The latter distinction puts Husserl, Russell, the later Wittgenstein, and the later Heidegger all on the same ("revolutionary") side of a line. For my purposes, what matters is a distinction between two kinds of revolutionary philosophers. On the one hand, there are revolutionary philosophers—those who found new schools within which normal, professionalized philosophy can be practiced—who see the incommensurability of their new vocabulary with the old as a temporary inconvenience, to be blamed on the shortcomings of their predecessors and to be overcome by the institutionalization of their own vocabulary. On the other hand, there are great philosophers who dread the thought that their vocabulary should ever be institutionalized, or that their writing might be seen as commensurable with the tradition. Husserl and Russell (like Descartes and Kant) are of the former sort. The later Wittgenstein and the later Heidegger (like Kierkegaard and Nietzsche) are of the latter sort.[15] Great systematic philosophers are constructive and offer arguments. Great edifying philosophers are reactive and offer satires, parodies, aphorisms. They know their work loses its point when the period they were reacting against is over. They are *intentionally* peripheral. Great systematic philosophers, like great scientists, build for eternity. Great edifying philosophers destroy for the sake of their own generation. Systematic philosophers want to put their subject on the

---

and didactically by Derrida in *La Voix et le Phénomène*, translated as *Speech and Phenomenon* by David Allison (Evanston, 1973). See Newton Garver's comparison of Derrida and Wittgenstein in his "Introduction" to this translation.

15 The permanent fascination of the man who dreamed up the whole idea of Western philosophy—Plato—is that we still do not know which sort of philosopher he was. Even if the *Seventh Letter* is set aside as spurious, the fact that after millenniums of commentary nobody knows which passages in the dialogues are jokes keeps the puzzle fresh.

secure path of a science. Edifying philosophers want to keep space open for the sense of wonder which poets can sometimes cause—wonder that there is something new under the sun, something which is *not* an accurate representation of what was already there, something which (at least for the moment) cannot be explained and can barely be described.

The notion of an edifying philosopher is, however, a paradox. For Plato defined the philosopher by opposition to the poet. The philosopher could give reasons, argue for his views, justify himself. So argumentative systematic philosophers say of Nietzsche and Heidegger that, whatever else they may be, they are not *philosophers*. This "not really a philosopher" ploy is also used, of course, by normal philosophers against revolutionary philosophers. It was used by pragmatists against logical positivists, by positivists against "ordinary language philosophers," and will be used whenever cozy professionalism is in danger. But in that usage it is just a rhetorical gambit which tells one nothing more than that an incommensurable discourse is being proposed. When it is used against edifying philosophers, on the other hand, the accusation has a real bite. The problem for an edifying philosopher is that qua philosopher he is in the business of offering arguments, whereas he would like simply to offer another set of terms, *without* saying that these terms are the new-found accurate representations of essences (e.g., of the essence of "philosophy" itself). He is, so to speak, violating not just the rules of normal philosophy (the philosophy of the schools of his day) but a sort of meta-rule: the rule that one may suggest changing the rules only because one has noticed that the old ones do not fit the subject matter, that they are not adequate to reality, that they impede the solution of the eternal problems. Edifying philosophers, unlike revolutionary systematic philosophers, are those who are abnormal at this meta-level. They refuse to present themselves as having found out any objective truth (about, say, what philosophy is). They present themselves as doing something different from, and more important than, offering accurate representations of how things are. It is more important because, they say, the notion of "accurate representation" itself is not the proper way to think about what philosophy does. But, they then go on to say, this is not because "a search for accurate representations of . . . (e.g., 'the most general traits of reality' or 'the nature of man')" is an *in*accurate representation of philosophy.

Whereas less pretentious revolutionaries can afford to have views on lots of things which their predecessors had views on, edifying philosophers have to decry the very notion of having a view, while avoiding having a view about having views.[16] This is an awkward, but not impossible, position. Wittgenstein and Heidegger manage it fairly well. One reason they manage it as well as they do is that they do not think that when we say something we must necessarily be expressing a view about a subject. We might just be *saying something*—participating in a conversation rather than contributing to an inquiry. Perhaps saying things is not always saying how things are. Perhaps saying *that* is itself not a case of saying how things are. Both men suggest we see people as saying things, better or worse things, without seeing them as externalizing inner representations of reality. But this is only their entering wedge, for then we must cease to see ourselves as *seeing* this, without beginning to see ourselves as seeing something else. We must get the visual, and in particular the mirroring, metaphors out of our speech altogether.[17] To do that we have to understand speech not only as not the externalizing of inner representations, but as not a representation at all. We have to drop the notion of correspondence for sentences as well as for

16 Heidegger's *"Die Zeit des Weltbildes"* (translated as "The Age of the World-View" by Marjorie Grene in *Boundary II* [1976]) is the best discussion of this difficulty I have come across.

17 Derrida's recent writings are meditations on how to avoid these metaphors. Like Heidegger in "Aus einem Gespräch von der Sprache zwischen einem Japaner und einem Fragenden" (in *Unterwegs zur Sprache* [Pfullingen, 1959]), Derrida occasionally toys with the notion of the superiority of Oriental languages and of ideographic writing.

thoughts, and see sentences as connected with other sentences rather than with the world. We have to see the term "corresponds to how things are" as an automatic compliment paid to successful normal discourse rather than as a relation to be studied and aspired to throughout the rest of discourse. To attempt to extend this compliment to feats of *ab*normal discourse is like complimenting a judge on his wise decision by leaving him a fat tip: it shows a lack of tact. To think of Wittgenstein and Heidegger as having views about how things are is not to be wrong about how things are, exactly; it is just poor taste. It puts them in a position which they do not want to be in, and in which they look ridiculous.

But perhaps they *should* look ridiculous. How, then, do we know when to adopt a tactful attitude and when to insist on someone's moral obligation to hold a view? This is like asking how we know when someone's refusal to adopt our norms (of, for example, social organization, sexual practices, or conversational manners) is morally outrageous and when it is something which we must (at least provisionally) respect. We do not know such things by reference to general principles. We do not, for instance, know in advance that if a given sentence is uttered, or a given act performed, we shall break off a conversation or a personal relationship, for everything depends on what leads up to it. To see edifying philosophers as conversational partners is an alternative to seeing them as holding views on subjects of common concern. One way of thinking of wisdom as something of which the love is not the same as that of argument, and of which the achievement does not consist in finding the correct vocabulary for representing essence, is to think of it as the practical wisdom necessary to participate in a conversation. One way to see edifying philosophy *as* the love of wisdom is to see it as the attempt to prevent conversation from degenerating into inquiry, into a research program. Edifying philosophers can never end philosophy, but they can help prevent it from attaining the secure path of a science.

3. EDIFICATION, RELATIVISM, AND OBJECTIVE TRUTH

I want now to enlarge this suggestion that edifying
philosophy aims at continuing a conversation rather than
at discovering truth, by making out of it a reply to the
familiar charge of "relativism" leveled at the subordination
of truth to edification. I shall be claiming that the difference between conversation and inquiry parallels Sartre's
distinction between thinking of oneself as *pour-soi* and as
en-soi, and thus that the cultural role of the edifying
philosopher is to help us avoid the self-deception which
comes from believing that we know ourselves by knowing a
set of objective facts. In the following section, I shall try to
make the converse point. There I shall be saying that the
wholehearted behaviorism, naturalism, and physicalism I
have been commending in earlier chapters help us avoid
the self-deception of thinking that we possess a deep, hid-
den, metaphysically significant nature which makes us "irreducibly" different from inkwells or atoms.

Philosophers who have doubts about traditional epistemology are often thought to be questioning the notion
that at most one of incompatible competing theories can
be true. However, it is hard to find anyone who actually
does question this. When it is said, for example, that coherentist or pragmatic "theories of truth" allow for the possibility that many incompatible theories would satisfy the
conditions set for "the truth," the coherentist or pragmatist
usually replies that this merely shows that we should
have no grounds for choice among these candidates for "the
truth." The moral to draw, they say, is not that they have
offered inadequate analyses of "true," but that there are
some terms—for example, "the true theory," "the right
thing to do"—which are, intuitively and grammatically,
singular, but for which no set of necessary and sufficient
conditions can be given which will pick out a unique referent. This fact, they say, should not be surprising. Nobody thinks that there are necessary and sufficient conditions

which will pick out, for example, the unique referent of "the best thing for her to have done on finding herself in that rather embarrassing situation," though plausible conditions can be given which will shorten a list of competing incompatible candidates. Why should it be different for the referents of "what she should have done in that ghastly moral dilemma" or "the Good Life for man" or "what the world is really made of"?

To see relativism lurking in every attempt to formulate conditions for truth or reality or goodness which does not attempt to provide uniquely individuating conditions we must adopt the "Platonic" notion of the transcendental terms which I discussed above (chapter six, section 6). We must think of the true referents of these terms (the Truth, the Real, Goodness) as conceivably having no connection whatever with the practices of justification which obtain among us. The dilemma created by this Platonic hypostatization is that, on the one hand, the philosopher must attempt to find criteria for picking out these unique referents, whereas, on the other hand, the only hints he has about what these criteria could be are provided by current practice (by, e.g., the best moral and scientific thought of the day). Philosophers thus condemn themselves to a Sisyphean task, for no sooner has an account of a transcendental term been perfected than it is labeled a "naturalistic fallacy," a confusion between essence and accident.[18] I think we get a clue to the cause of this self-defeating obsession from the fact that even philosophers who take the intuitive impossibility of finding conditions for "the one right thing to do" as a reason for repudiating "objective values" are loath to take the impossibility of finding individuating conditions for the one true theory of the world as a reason for denying "objective physical reality." Yet they should, for formally the two notions are on a par. The reasons for and against adopting a "correspondence" approach to moral

[18] On this point, see William Frankena's classic "The Naturalistic Fallacy," *Mind* 68 (1939).

truth are the same as those regarding truth about the physical world. The giveaway comes, I think, when we find that the usual excuse for invidious treatment is that we are shoved around by physical reality but not by values.[19] Yet what does being shoved around have to do with objectivity, accurate representation, or correspondence? Nothing, I think, unless we confuse *contact* with reality (a causal, nonintentional, non-description-relative relation) with *dealing with* reality (describing, explaining, predicting, and modifying it—all of which are things we do under descriptions). The sense in which physical reality is Peircean "Secondness" —unmediated pressure—has nothing to do with the sense in which one among all our ways of describing, or of coping with, physical reality is "the one right" way. Lack of mediation is here being confused with accuracy of mediation. The absence of description is confused with a privilege attaching to a certain description. Only by such a confusion can the inability to offer individuating conditions for the one true description of material things be confused with insensitivity to the things' obduracy.

Sartre helps us explain why this confusion is so frequent and why its results are purveyed with so much moral earnestness. The notion of "one right way of describing and explaining reality" supposedly contained in our "intuition" about the meaning of "true" is, for Sartre, just the notion of having a way of describing and explaining *imposed* on us in that brute way in which stones impinge on our feet. Or, to shift to visual metaphors, it is the notion of having reality unveiled to us, not as in a glass darkly, but with some unimaginable sort of immediacy which would make discourse and description superfluous. If we could convert knowledge from something discursive, something attained by continual adjustments of ideas or words, into something as

[19] What seems to be a sense of being shoved around by values, they reductively say, is just physical reality in disguise (e.g., neural arrangements or glandular secretions programmed by parental conditioning).

ineluctable as being shoved about, or being transfixed by a sight which leaves us speechless, then we should no longer have the responsibility for choice among competing ideas and words, theories and vocabularies. This attempt to slough off responsibility is what Sartre describes as the attempt to turn oneself into a thing—into an *être-en-soi*. In the visions of the epistemologist, this incoherent notion takes the form of seeing the attainment of truth as a matter of *necessity*, either the "logical" necessity of the transcendentalist or the "physical" necessity of the evolutionary "naturalizing" epistemologist. From Sartre's point of view, the urge to find such necessities is the urge to be rid of one's freedom to erect yet another alternative theory or vocabulary. Thus the edifying philosopher who points out the incoherence of the urge is treated as a "relativist," one who lacks moral seriousness, because he does not join in the common human hope that the burden of choice will pass away. Just as the moral philosopher who sees virtue as Aristotelian self-development is thought to lack concern for his fellow man, so the epistemologist who is merely behaviorist is treated as one who does not share the universal human aspiration toward objective truth.

Sartre adds to our understanding of the visual imagery which has set the problems of Western philosophy by helping us see why this imagery is always trying to transcend itself. The notion of an unclouded Mirror of Nature is the notion of a mirror which would be indistinguishable from what was mirrored, and thus would not be a mirror at all. The notion of a human being whose mind is such an unclouded mirror, and who *knows* this, is the image, as Sartre says, of God. Such a being does *not* confront something alien which makes it necessary for him to choose an attitude toward, or a description of, it. He would have no need and no ability to choose actions or descriptions. He can be called "God" if we think of the advantages of this situation, or a "mere machine" if we think of the disadvantages. From this point of view, to look for commensura-

tion rather than simply continued conversation—to look
for a way of making further redescription unnecessary by
finding a way of reducing all *possible* descriptions to one—
is to attempt escape from humanity. To abandon the notion
that philosophy must show all possible discourse naturally
converging to a consensus, just as normal inquiry does,
would be to abandon the hope of being anything more than
merely human. It would thus be to abandon the Platonic
notions of Truth and Reality and Goodness as entities
which may not be even dimly mirrored by present practices
and beliefs, and to settle back into the "relativism" which
assumes that our only useful notions of "true" and "real"
and "good" are extrapolations from those practices and
beliefs.

Here, finally, I come around to the suggestion with which
I ended the last section—that the point of edifying philosophy is to keep the conversation going rather than to find
objective truth. Such truth, in the view I am advocating, is
the normal result of normal discourse. Edifying philosophy
is not only abnormal but reactive, having sense only as a
protest against attempts to close off conversation by proposals for universal commensuration through the hypostatization of some privileged set of descriptions. The danger
which edifying discourse tries to avert is that some given
vocabulary, some way in which people might come to think
of themselves, will deceive them into thinking that from
now on all discourse could be, or should be, normal discourse. The resulting freezing-over of culture would be, in
the eyes of edifying philosophers, the dehumanization of
human beings. The edifying philosophers are thus agreeing
with Lessing's choice of the infinite *striving for* truth over
"all of Truth."[20] For the edifying philosopher the very idea
of being presented with "all of Truth" is absurd, because
the Platonic notion of Truth itself is absurd. It is absurd

[20] Kierkegaard made this choice the prototype of his own choice of
"subjectivity" over "system." Cf. *Concluding Unscientific Postscript*,
trans. David Swenson and Walter Lowrie (Princeton, 1941), p. 97.

either as the notion of truth about reality which is not about reality-under-a-certain-description, or as the notion of truth about reality under some privileged description which makes all other descriptions unnecessary because it is commensurable with each of them.

To see keeping a conversation going as a sufficient aim of philosophy, to see wisdom as consisting in the ability to sustain a conversation, is to see human beings as generators of new descriptions rather than beings one hopes to be able to describe accurately. To see the aim of philosophy as truth—namely, the truth about the terms which provide ultimate commensuration for all human inquiries and activities—is to see human beings as objects rather than subjects, as existing *en-soi* rather than as both *pour-soi* and *en-soi*, as both described objects and describing subjects. To think that philosophy will permit us to see the describing subject as itself one sort of described object is to think that all possible descriptions can be rendered commensurable with the aid of a single descriptive vocabulary—that of philosophy itself. For only if we had such a notion of a universal description could we identify human-beings-under-a-given-description with man's "essence." Only with such a notion would that of a man's *having* an essence make sense, whether or not that essence is conceived of as the knowing of essences. So not even by saying that man is subject as well as object, *pour-soi* as well as *en-soi*, are we grasping our essence. We do not escape from Platonism by saying that "our essence is to have no essence" if we then try to use this insight as the basis for a constructive and systematic attempt to find out further truths about human beings.

That is why "existentialism"—and, more generally, edifying philosophy—can be *only* reactive, why it falls into self-deception whenever it tries to do more than send the conversation off in new directions. Such new directions may, perhaps, engender new normal discourses, new sciences, new philosophical research programs, and thus new objective

378

truths. But they are not the point of edifying philosophy, only accidental byproducts. The point is always the same—to perform the social function which Dewey called "breaking the crust of convention," preventing man from deluding himself with the notion that he knows himself, or anything else, except under optional descriptions.

4. EDIFICATION AND NATURALISM

I argued in chapter seven that it would be a good idea to get rid of the spirit-nature distinction, conceived as a division between human beings and other things, or between two parts of human beings, corresponding to the distinction between hermeneutics and epistemology. I want now to take up this topic again, in order to underline the point that the "existentialist" doctrines I have been discussing are compatible with the behaviorism and materialism I advocated in earlier chapters. Philosophers who would like to be simultaneously systematic and edifying have often seen them as incompatible, and have therefore suggested how our sense of ourselves as *pour-soi*, as capable of reflection, as choosers of alternative vocabularies, might itself be turned into a philosophical subject matter.

Much recent philosophy—under the aegis of ."phenomenology" or of "hermeneutics," or both—has toyed with this unfortunate idea. For example, Habermas and Apel have suggested ways in which we might create a new sort of transcendental standpoint, enabling us to do something like what Kant tried to do, but without falling into either scientism or historicism. Again, most philosophers who see Marx, Freud, or both as figures who need to be drawn into "mainstream" philosophy have tried to develop quasi-epistemological systems which center around the phenomenon which both Marx and Freud throw into relief—the change in behavior which results from change in self-description. Such philosophers see traditional epistemology as committed to "objectivizing" human beings, and they hope for a successor subject to epistemology which will do for "reflection" what the tradition did for "objectivizing knowledge."

I have been insisting that we should not try to have a successor subject to epistemology, but rather try to free ourselves from the notion that philosophy must center around the discovery of a permanent framework for inquiry. In particular, we should free ourselves from the notion that philosophy can explain what science leaves unexplained. From my point of view, the attempt to develop a "universal pragmatics" or a "transcendental hermeneutics" is very suspicious. For it seems to promise just what Sartre tells us we are not going to have—a way of seeing freedom as nature (or, less cryptically, a way of seeing our creation of, and choice between, vocabularies in the same "normal" way as we see ourselves *within* one of those vocabularies). Such attempts start out by viewing the search for objective knowledge through normal discourse in the way I have suggested it should be viewed—as one element in edification. But they then often go on to more ambitious claims. The following passage from Habermas is an example:

> . . . the functions knowledge has in universal contexts of practical life can only be successfully analyzed in the framework of a reformulated transcendental philosophy. This, incidentally, does not entail an empiricist critique of the claim to absolute truth. As long as cognitive interests can be identified and analyzed through reflection upon the logic of inquiry in the natural and cultural sciences, they can legitimately claim a "transcendental" status. They assume an "empirical" status as soon as they are analyzed as the result of natural history—analyzed, as it were, in terms of cultural anthropology.[21]

[21] Jürgen Habermas, "Nachwort" to the second edition of *Erkenntnis und Interesse* (Frankfurt: Surkamp, 1973), p. 410; translated as "A Postscript to *Knowledge and Human Interests*," by Christian Lenhardt in *Philosophy of the Social Sciences* 3 (1973), 181. For a criticism of the line Habermas takes here—a criticism paralleling my own—see

I want to claim, on the contrary, that there is no point in trying to find a general synoptic way of "analyzing" the "functions knowledge has in universal contexts of practical life," and that cultural anthropology (in a large sense which includes intellectual history) is all we need.

Habermas and other authors who are impelled by the same motives see the suggestion that empirical inquiry suffices as incorporating an "objectivistic illusion." They tend to see Deweyan pragmatism, and the "scientific realism" of Sellars and Feyerabend, as the products of an inadequate epistemology. In my view, the great virtue of Dewey, Sellars, and Feyerabend is that they point the way toward, and partially exemplify, a nonepistemological sort of philosophy, and thus one which gives up any hope of the "transcendental." Habermas says that for a theory to "ground itself transcendentally" is for it to

> become familiar with the range of inevitable subjective conditions which both make the theory possible *and* place limits on it, for this kind of transcendental corroboration tends always to criticize an overly self-confident self-understanding of itself.[22]

Specifically, this overconfidence consists in thinking that

> there can be such a thing as truthfulness to reality in the sense postulated by philosophical realism. Correspondence-theories of truth tend to hypostatize facts as entities in the world. It is the intention and inner logic of an epistemology reflecting upon the conditions of possible experience as such to uncover the objectivistic illusions of such a view. Every form of transcendental philosophy claims to identify the conditions of the objectivity of ex-

---

Michael Theunissen, *Gesellschaft und Geschichte: Zur Kritik der Kritischen Theorie* (Berlin, 1969), pp. 20ff. (I owe the reference to Theunissen to Raymond Geuss.)

22 Habermas, "Nachwort," p. 411; English translation, p. 182.

perience by analyzing the categorical structure of objects of possible experience.[23]

But Dewey, Wittgenstein, Sellars, Kuhn, and the other heroes of this book all have their own ways of debunking "truthfulness to reality in the sense postulated by philosophical realism," and none of them think that this is to be done by "analyzing the categorical structure of objects of possible experience."

The notion that we can get around overconfident philosophical realism and positivistic reductions only by adopting something like Kant's transcendental standpoint seems to me the basic mistake in programs like that of Habermas (as well as in Husserl's notion of a "phenomenology of the life-world" which will describe people in some way "prior" to that offered by science). What is required to accomplish these laudable purposes is not Kant's "epistemological" distinction between the transcendental and the empirical standpoints, but rather his "existentialist" distinction between people as empirical selves and as moral agents.[24] Normal scientific discourse can always be seen in two different ways—as the successful search for objective truth, or as one discourse among others, one among many projects we engage in. The former point of view falls in with the normal practice of normal science. There questions of moral choice or of edification do not arise, since they have already been preempted by the tacit and "self-confident" commitment to the search for objective truth on the subject in question. The latter point of view is one from which we

[23] Ibid., pp. 408-409; English translation, p. 180.

[24] Wilfrid Sellars uses this latter Kantian distinction to good effect in his insistence that personhood is a matter of "being one of us," of falling within the scope of practical imperatives of the form "Would that we all . . . ," rather than a feature of certain organisms to be isolated by empirical means. I have invoked this claim several times in this book, particularly in chapter four, section 4. For Sellars's own use of it, see *Science and Metaphysics* (London and New York, 1968), chap. 7, and the essay "Science and Ethics" in his *Philosophical Perspectives* (Springfield, Ill., 1967).

382

ask such questions as "What is the point?" "What moral is to be drawn from our knowledge of how we, and the rest of nature, work?" or "What are we to do with ourselves now that we know the laws of our own behavior?"

The primal error of systematic philosophy has always been the notion that such questions are to be answered by some new ("metaphysical" or "transcendental") descriptive or explanatory discourse (dealing with, e.g., "man," "spirit," or "language"). This attempt to answer questions of justification by discovering new objective truths, to answer the moral agent's request for justifications with descriptions of a privileged domain, is the philosopher's special form of bad faith—his special way of substituting pseudo-cognition for moral choice. Kant's greatness was to have seen through the "metaphysical" form of this attempt, and to have destroyed the traditional conception of reason to make room for moral faith. Kant gave us a way of seeing scientific truth as something which could never supply an answer to our demand for a point, a justification, a way of claiming that our moral decision about what to do is based on *knowledge* of the nature of the world. Unfortunately, Kant put his diagnosis of science in terms of the discovery of "inevitable subjective conditions," to be revealed by reflection upon scientific inquiry. Equally unfortunately, he thought that there really was a decision procedure for moral dilemmas (though not based on *knowledge*, since our grasp of the categorical imperative is not a *cognition*).[25] So he created new forms of philosophical bad faith—substituting "transcendental" attempts to find one's true self for "metaphysical" attempts to find a world elsewhere. By tacitly identifying the moral agent with the constituting transcendental self, he left the road

25 See Kant's distinction between knowledge and necessary belief at *K.d.r.V.*, A824–B852ff., and especially his use of *Unternehmung* as a synonym for the latter. This section of the First Critique seems to me the one which gives most sense to the famous passage about denying reason to make room for faith at Bxxx. At many other points, however, Kant inconsistently speaks of practical reason as supplying an enlargement of our *knowledge*.

open to ever more complicated post-Kantian attempts to reduce freedom to nature, choice to knowledge, the *pour-soi* to the *en-soi*. This is the road I have been trying to block by recasting ahistorical and permanent distinctions between nature and spirit, "objectivizing science" and reflection, epistemology and hermeneutics, in terms of historical and temporary distinctions between the familiar and the unfamiliar, the normal and the abnormal. For this way of treating these distinctions lets us see them not as dividing two areas of inquiry but as the distinction between inquiry and something which is *not* inquiry, but is rather the inchoate questioning out of which inquiries—new normal discourses—may (or may not) emerge.

To put this claim in another way, which may help bring out its connections with naturalism, I am saying that the positivists were absolutely right in thinking it imperative to extirpate metaphysics, when "metaphysics" means the attempt to give knowledge of what science cannot know. For this is the attempt to find a discourse which combines the advantages of normality with those of abnormality—the intersubjective security of objective truth combined with the edifying character of an unjustifiable but unconditional moral claim. The urge to set philosophy on the secure path of a science is the urge to combine Plato's project of moral choice as ticking off the objective truths about a special sort of object (the Idea of the Good) with the sort of intersubjective and democratic agreement about objects found in normal science.[26] Philosophy which was utterly unedifying, utterly irrelevant to such moral choices as whether or not to believe in God would count not as *philosophy*, but only as some special sort of science. So as soon as a program to put philosophy on the secure path of science succeeds, it simply

[26] The positivists themselves quickly succumbed to this urge. Even while insisting that moral questions were noncognitive they thought to give quasi-scientific status to their moralistic attacks on traditional philosophy—thus making themselves subject to self-referential criticisms concerning their "emotive" use of "noncognitive."

384

converts philosophy into a boring academic specialty. Systematic philosophy exists by perpetually straddling the gap between description and justification, cognition and choice, getting the facts right and telling us how to live.

Once this point is seen, we can see more clearly why epistemology emerged as the essence of systematic philosophy. For epistemology is the attempt to see the patterns of justification within normal discourse as *more* than just such patterns. It is the attempt to see them as hooked on to something which demands moral commitment—Reality, Truth, Objectivity, Reason. To be behaviorist in epistemology, on the contrary, is to look at the normal scientific discourse of our day bifocally, both as patterns adopted for various historical reasons and as the achievement of objective truth, where "objective truth" is no more and no less than the best idea we currently have about how to explain what is going on. From the point of view of epistemological behaviorism, the only truth in Habermas's claim that scientific inquiry is made possible, and limited, by "inevitable subjective conditions" is that such inquiry is made possible by the adoption of practices of justification, and that such practices have possible alternatives. But these "subjective conditions" are in no sense "inevitable" ones discoverable by "reflection upon the logic of inquiry." They are just the facts about what a given society, or profession, or other group, takes to be good ground for assertions of a certain sort. Such disciplinary matrices are studied by the usual empirical-cum-hermeneutic methods of "cultural anthropology." From the point of view of the group in question these subjective conditions are a combination of common-sensical practical imperatives (e.g., tribal taboos, Mill's Methods) with the standard current theory about the subject. From the point of view of the historian of ideas or the anthropologist they are the empirical facts about the beliefs, desires, and practices of a certain group of human beings. These are incompatible points of view, in the sense that we cannot be at both viewpoints simultaneously. But there is no reason and no need to subsume the two in a higher synthesis. The group in question may itself shift from the one point of view to the other (thus "objectivizing" their past selves through a process of "reflection" and making new sentences true of their present selves). But this is not a mysterious process which demands a new understanding of human knowledge. It is the commonplace fact that people may develop doubts about what they are doing, and thereupon begin to discourse in ways incommensurable with those they used previously.

This goes also for the most spectacular and disturbing new discourses. When such edifying philosophers as Marx, Freud, and Sartre offer new explanations of our usual patterns of justifying our actions and assertions, and when these explanations are taken up and integrated into our lives, we have striking examples of the phenomenon of reflection's changing vocabulary and behavior. But as I argued in chapter seven, this phenomenon does not require any new understanding of theory-construction or theory-confirmation. To say that we have changed ourselves by internalizing a new self-description (using terms like "bourgeois intellectual" or "self-destructive" or "self-deceiving") is true enough. But this is no more startling than the fact that men changed the data of botany by hybridization, which was in turn made possible by botanical theory, or that they changed their own lives by inventing bombs and vaccines. Meditation on the possibility of such changes, like reading science fiction, does help us overcome the self-confidence of "philosophical realism." But such meditation does not need to be supplemented by a transcendental account of the nature of reflection. All that is necessary is the edifying invocation of the fact or possibility of abnormal discourses, undermining our reliance upon the knowledge we have gained through normal discourses. The objectionable self-confidence in question is simply the tendency of normal discourse to block the flow of conversation by presenting itself as offering the canonical vocabulary for discussion of a given topic—and, more particularly, the tendency of normal epistemologically centered philosophy to block the road by putting itself forward as the final commensurating vocabulary for all *possible* rational discourse. Self-confidence of the former, limited sort is overthrown by edifying philosophers who put the very idea of universal commensuration, and of systematic philosophy, in doubt.

Risking intolerable repetitiveness, I want to insist again that the distinction between normal and abnormal discourse does not coincide with any distinction of subject matter (e.g., nature versus history, or facts versus values), method (e.g., objectivation versus reflection), faculty (e.g., reason versus imagination), or any of the other distinctions which systematic philosophy has used to make the sense of the world consist in the objective truth about some previously unnoticed portion or feature of the world. *Anything* can be discoursed of abnormally, just as anything can become edifying and anything can be systematized. I have been discussing the relation between natural science and other disciplines simply because, since the period of Descartes and Hobbes, the assumption that scientific discourse was normal discourse and that all other discourse needed to be modeled upon it has been the standard motive for philosophizing. Once we set this assumption aside, however, we can also set aside the various anti-naturalisms about which I have been complaining. More specifically, we can assert all of the following:

Every speech, thought, theory, poem, composition, and philosophy will turn out to be completely predictable in purely naturalistic terms. Some atoms-and-the-void account of micro-processes within individual human beings will permit the prediction of every sound or inscription which will ever be uttered. There are no ghosts.

Nobody will be able to predict his own actions, thoughts, theories, poems, etc., before deciding upon them or inventing them. (This is not an interesting remark about the

387

odd nature of human beings, but rather a trivial consequence of what it means to "decide" or "invent.") So no
hope (or danger) exists that cognition of oneself as *en-soi*
will cause one to cease to exist *pour-soi*.

The complete set of laws which enable these predictions
to be made, plus complete descriptions (in atoms-and-the-
void terms) of all human beings, would not yet be the
whole "objective truth" about human beings, nor the
whole set of true predictions about them. There would remain as many other distinct sets of such objective truths
(some useful for prediction, some not) as there were incommensurable vocabularies within which normal inquiry
about human beings could be conducted (e.g., all those vocabularies within which we attribute beliefs and desires,
virtues and beauty).

Incommensurability entails irreducibility but not incom-
patibility, so the failure to "reduce" these various vocabularies to that of "bottom-level" atoms-and-the-void science
casts no doubt upon their cognitive status or upon the
metaphysical status of their objects. (This goes as much
for the aesthetic worth of poems as for the beliefs of persons, as much for virtues as for volitions.)

The assemblage, *per impossible*, of all these objective
truths would still not necessarily be edifying. It might be
the picture of a world without a sense, without a moral.
Whether it seemed to point a moral to an individual would
depend upon that individual. It would be true or false that
it so seemed, or did not seem, to him. But it would not be
objectively true or false that it "really did," or did not, have
a sense or a moral. Whether his knowledge of the world
leaves him with a sense of what to do with or in the world
is itself predictable, but whether it *should* is not.

The fear of science, of "scientism," of "naturalism," of
self-objectivation, of being turned by too much knowledge
into a thing rather than a person, is the fear that all discourse
will become normal discourse. That is, it is the fear that
there will be objectively true or false answers to every ques-

tion we ask, so that human worth will consist in knowing truths, and human virtue will be merely justified true belief. This is frightening because it cuts off the possibility of something new under the sun, of human life as poetic rather than merely contemplative.

But the dangers to abnormal discourse do not come from science or naturalistic philosophy. They come from the scarcity of food and from the secret police. Given leisure and libraries, the conversation which Plato began will not end in self-objectivation—not because aspects of the world, or of human beings, escape being objects of scientific inquiry, but simply because free and leisured conversation generates abnormal discourse as the sparks fly upward.

5. PHILOSOPHY IN THE CONVERSATION OF MANKIND

I end this book with an allusion to Oakeshott's famous title,[27] because it catches the tone in which, I think, philosophy should be discussed. Much of what I have said about epistemology and its possible successors is an attempt to draw some corollaries from Sellars's doctrine that

> in characterizing an episode or a state as that of *knowing*, we are not giving an empirical description of that episode or state; we are placing it in the logical space of reasons, of justifying and being able to justify what one says.[28]

If we see knowing not as having an essence, to be described by scientists or philosophers, but rather as a right, by current standards, to believe, then we are well on the way to seeing *conversation* as the ultimate context within which knowledge is to be understood. Our focus shifts from the relation between human beings and the objects of their inquiry to the relation between alternative standards of

---

27 Cf. Michael Oakeshott, "The Voice of Poetry in the Conversation of Mankind," in his *Rationalism and Politics* (New York, 1975).

28 Wilfrid Sellars, *Science, Perception and Reality* (London and New York, 1963), p. 169.

justification, and from there to the actual changes in those standards which make up intellectual history. This brings us to appreciate Sellars's own description of his mythical hero Jones, the man who invented the Mirror of Nature and thereby made modern philosophy possible:

> Does the reader not recognize Jones as Man himself in the middle of his journey from the grunts and groans of the cave to the subtle and polydimensional discourse of the drawing room, the laboratory, and the study, the language of Henry and William James, of Einstein and of the philosophers who, in their efforts to break out of discourse to an ἀρχή beyond discourse, have provided the most curious dimension of all? (p. 196)

In this book I have offered a sort of prolegomenon to a history of epistemology-centered philosophy as an episode in the history of European culture. Such philosophy goes back to the Greeks, and goes sideways into all sorts of non-philosophical disciplines which have, at one time or another, proposed themselves as substitutes for epistemology, and thus for philosophy. So the episode in question cannot simply be identified with "modern philosophy," in the sense of the standard textbook sequence of great philosophers from Descartes to Russell and Husserl. But that sequence is, nevertheless, where the search for foundations for knowledge is most explicit. So most of my attempts to deconstruct the image of the Mirror of Nature have concerned these philosophers. I have tried to show how their urge to break out into an ἀρχή beyond discourse is rooted in the urge to see social practices of justification as more than just such practices. I have, however, focused mainly on the expressions of this urge in the recent literature of analytical philosophy. The result is thus no more than a prolegomenon. A proper historical treatment would require both learning and skills which I do not possess. But I would hope that the prolegomenon has been sufficient to let one see contemporary issues in philosophy as events in a

390

certain stage of a conversation—a conversation which once knew nothing of these issues and may know nothing of them again.

The fact that we can continue the conversation Plato began without discussing the topics Plato wanted discussed, illustrates the difference between treating philosophy as a voice in a conversation and treating it as a subject, a *Fach*, a field of professional inquiry. The conversation Plato began has been enlarged by more voices than Plato would have dreamed possible, and thus by topics he knew nothing of. A "subject"—astrology, physics, classical philosophy, furniture design—may undergo revolutions, but it gets its self-image from its present state, and its history is necessarily written "Whiggishly" as an account of its gradual maturation. This is the most frequent way of writing the history of philosophy, and I cannot claim to have avoided such Whiggery entirely in sketching the sort of history which needs to be written. But I hope that I have shown how we can see the issues with which philosophers are presently concerned, and with which they Whiggishly see philosophy as having always (perhaps unwittingly) been concerned, as results of historical accident, as turns the conversation has taken.[29] It has taken this turn for a long time, but it might

[29] Two recent writers—Michel Foucault and Harold Bloom—make this sense of the brute factuality of historical origins central to their work. Cf. Bloom, *A Map of Misreading* (New York, 1975), p. 33: "All continuities possess the paradox of being absolutely arbitrary in their origins and absolutely inescapable in their teleologies. We know this so vividly from what we all of us oxymoronically call our love lives that its literary counterparts need little demonstration." Foucault says that his way of looking at the history of ideas "permits the introduction, into the very roots of thought, of notions of *chance, discontinuity* and *materiality*." ("The Discourse on Language," included in the *Archaeology of Knowledge* [New York, 1972], p. 231) It is hardest of all to see brute contingency in the history of *philosophy*, if only because since Hegel the historiography of philosophy has been "progressive," or (as in Heidegger's inversion of Hegel's account of progress) "retrogressive," but never without a sense of inevitability. If we could once see the desire for a permanent, neutral, ahistorical, commensurating vocabulary as

turn in another direction without human beings thereby losing their reason, or losing touch with "the real problems."

The conversational interest of philosophy as a subject, or of some individual philosopher of genius, has varied and will continue to vary in unpredictable ways depending upon contingencies. These contingencies will range from what happens in physics to what happens in politics. The lines between disciplines will blur and shift, and new disciplines will arise, in the ways illustrated by Galileo's successful attempt to create "purely scientific questions" in the seventeenth century. The notions of "philosophical significance" and of "purely philosophical question," as they are currently used, gained sense only around the time of Kant. Our post-Kantian sense that epistemology or some successor subject is at the center of philosophy (and that moral philosophy, aesthetics, and social philosophy, for example, are somehow derivative) is a reflection of the fact that the professional philosopher's self-image depends upon his professional preoccupation with the image of the Mirror of Nature. Without the Kantian assumption that the philosopher can decide *quaestiones juris* concerning the claims of the rest of culture, this self-image collapses. That assumption depends on the notion that there is such a thing as understanding the essence of knowledge—doing what Sellars tells us we cannot do.

To drop the notion of the philosopher as knowing something about knowing which nobody else knows so well would be to drop the notion that his voice always has an overriding claim on the attention of the other participants in the conversation. It would also be to drop the notion that there is something called "philosophical method" or "philosophical technique" or "the philosophical point of view"

---

itself a historical phenomenon, then perhaps we could write the history of philosophy less dialectically and less sentimentally than has been possible hitherto.

which enables the professional philosopher, *ex officio*, to have interesting views about, say, the respectability of psychoanalysis, the legitimacy of certain dubious laws, the resolution of moral dilemmas, the "soundness" of schools of historiography or literary criticism, and the like. Philosophers often do have interesting views upon such questions, and their professional training as philosophers is often a necessary condition for their having the views they do. But this is not to say that philosophers have a special kind of knowledge about knowledge (or anything else) from which they draw relevant corollaries. The useful kibitzing they can provide on the various topics I just mentioned is made possible by their familiarity with the historical background of arguments on similar topics, and, most importantly, by the fact that arguments on such topics are punctuated by stale philosophical clichés which the other participants have stumbled across in their reading, but about which professional philosophers know the pros and cons by heart.

The neo-Kantian image of philosophy as a profession, then, is involved with the image of the "mind" or "language" as mirroring nature. So it might seem that epistemological behaviorism and the consequent rejection of mirror-imagery entail the claim that there can or should be no such profession. But this does not follow. Professions can survive the paradigms which gave them birth. In any case, the need for teachers who have read the great dead philosophers is quite enough to insure that there will be philosophy departments as long as there are universities. The actual result of a widespread loss of faith in mirror-imagery would be merely an "encapsulation" of the problems created by this imagery within a historical period. I do not know whether we are in fact at the end of an era. This will depend, I suspect, on whether Dewey, Wittgenstein, and Heidegger are taken to heart. It may be that mirror-imagery and "mainstream," systematic philosophy will be revitalized once again by some revolutionary of genius. Or it may be that the image of the philosopher which Kant offered is

393

about to go the way of the medieval image of the priest. If that happens, even the philosophers themselves will no longer take seriously the notion of philosophy as providing "foundations" or "justifications" for the rest of culture, or as adjudicating *quaestiones juris* about the proper domains of other disciplines.

Whichever happens, however, there is no danger of philosophy's "coming to an end." Religion did not come to an end in the Enlightenment, nor painting in Impressionism. Even if the period from Plato to Nietzsche is encapsulated and "distanced" in the way Heidegger suggests, and even if twentieth-century philosophy comes to seem a stage of awkward transitional backing and filling (as sixteenth-century philosophy now seems to us), there will be something called "philosophy" on the other side of the transition. For even if problems about representation look as obsolete to our descendants as problems about hylomorphism look to us, people will still read Plato, Aristotle, Descartes, Kant, Hegel, Wittgenstein, and Heidegger. What roles these men will play in our descendants' conversation, no one knows. Whether the distinction between systematic and edifying philosophy will carry over, no one knows either. Perhaps philosophy will become purely edifying, so that one's self-identification as a philosopher will be purely in terms of the books one reads and discusses, rather than in terms of the problems one wishes to solve. Perhaps a new form of systematic philosophy will be found which has nothing whatever to do with epistemology but which nevertheless makes normal philosophical inquiry possible. These speculations are idle, and nothing I have been saying makes one more plausible than another. The only point on which I would insist is that philosophers' moral concern should be with continuing the conversation of the West, rather than with insisting upon a place for the traditional problems of modern philosophy within that conversation.

Index

Abelard, Peter, 149
abnormal and normal discourse,
11, 320-322, 333, 339, 346, 360,
363, 365-366, 372, 377, 382,
384, 386-389
Adler, Mortimer, 40 n.8, 50 n.21
Aldrich, Virgil, 189 n.20
analytic philosophy, 7-8, 12, 168,
170-173, 192, 316-317, 343, 390
Anaxagoras, 43 n.12, 44
Anscombe, G.E.M., 167 n.3
Anselm, Saint, 149
Apel, Karl-Otto, 343-344, 347-348,
354, 368 n.13, 379
Aquinas, St. Thomas, 6, 44-45,
50 n.21, 52n, 54n, 55, 63, 125,
366-367
Aristotle, 35, 40-41, 44-47, 52, 53n,
55, 63-64, 67, 142, 144-146, 149,
152, 154, 159-160, 163, 210-211,
222, 239n, 249n, 252, 263, 269,
351, 360, 364, 366-367, 394
Armstrong, David, 22-23, 85n,
102n, 115, 117
Arnauld, Antoine, 60 n.32
Augustine, Saint, 45, 50 n.21, 53n,
307
Austin, J. L., 52n, 60 n.32, 62n,
142, 169, 213
awareness, prelinguistic, 181-192
Ayer, A. J., 66n, 112, 337

Bacon, Francis, 42, 43 n.12, 133n
Bain, Alexander, 165
Balz, A.G.A., 57 n.27
Barrett, Robert, 271n
Beck, L. J., 64 n.38

behaviorism, epistemological, 99,
170, 173-182, 193, 209-213, 305
n.38, 315, 320, 325, 373, 376,
379, 385, 393; psychological,
17-18, 66, 94-96, 98-107, 109n,
115, 176, 190, 209-212, 228n, 259
Bellarmine, Cardinal, 211, 328-
331
Bennett, Jonathan, 48 n.18, 142
Bergmann, Gustav, 175-177
Bergson, Henri, 166, 240 n.27
Berkeley, George, 49 n.18, 64, 277,
293
Bernstein, Richard, xiv, 119n
Binkley, Robert, 271n
Black, Max, 305
Blanshard, Brand, 185 n.18
Bloom, Harold, 168 n.6, 391
Boorse, Christopher, 195n
Bouwsma, O. K., 100, 228
Boyd, Richard, 283-284
Boyle, Robert, 133n
Bradley, M. C., 116 n.20, 165
Brandom, Robert, 179n, 301n
Brandt, Richard, 83-84, 86, 93, 118
Braun, Lucien, 133n
Brentano, Franz, 18, 61 n.32, 193,
199, 207-208
Broad, C. D., 7, 39 n.6
Brucker, Jakob, 133n
Brumbaugh, Robert, xiii
Burtt, E. A., 65 n.39
Busch, Eric, 119

Campbell, Keith, 44 n.13, 83-84,
86, 93, 118
Carnap, Rudolph, xiii-xiv, 7, 169,

395